Reality

Through the new looking glass

Intel/Windcrest®/McGraw-Hill, Inc.

New York St. Louis San Francisco Blue Ridge Summit, Pa. Auckland Bogotá
Caracas Hamburg Lisbon London Madrid Mexico City Milan Montreal
New Delhi Paris San Juan São Paulo Singapore Sydney Tokyo Toronto

FIRST EDITION
FOURTH PRINTING

Library of Congress Cataloging-in-Publication Data
Pimentel, Ken.
   Virtual Reality: through the new looking glass / by Ken Pimentel
and Kevin Teixeira
      p. cm.
  Includes index.
  ISBN 0-8306-4064-9 (pbk.) ISBN 0-8306-4065-7
   1. Human-computer interaction.   2. Virtual reality.   I. Teixeira,
Kevin.   II. Title.
QA76.9.H85P56   1992
006--dc20   92-26808
                                     CIP

Acquisitions editor: Ron Powers
Book editor: Kellie Hagan
Production: Katherine G. Brown, Director of Production
         Olive Harmon, Typesetting
         Susan E. Hansford, Typesetting
         Tina Sourbier, Typesetting
         Jana Fisher, Layout
         Brenda M. Plasterer, Layout
         Kelly Christman, Proofreading
         Nancy Mickley, Proofreading
Index: Jodi L. Tyler
Design: Jaclyn J. Boone, Designer
         Brian Allison, Associate Designer
Cover design: Teresa Twigg
Cover art: "The Lawnmower Man" image courtesy of Allied Vision Lane Pringle
         Productions, ©1992. Animation by Angel Studios, Carlsbad, Calif.

Virtual

Ken Pimentel & Kevin Teixeira

This book would never have been possible without the love and support of our best friends—our wives, Patty and Terri. They not only believed in the book when it was still an idea in our heads, but they provided encouragement and ideas through all the long weekends and nights.

Dedication

"Let's pretend the glass has got all soft like gauze, so that we can get through. Why, it's turning into a sort of mist now, I declare! It'll be easy enough to get through—"

She was up on the chimney-piece while she said this, though she hardly knew how she had got there. And certainly the glass *was* beginning to melt away, just like a bright silvery mist.

In another moment Alice was through the glass, and had jumped lightly down into the looking-glass room. The very first thing she did was to look whether there was a fire in the fireplace, and she was quite pleased to find that there was a real one, blazing away as brightly as the one she had left behind.

— Lewis Carroll, *Through the Looking Glass*

Contents

Appendices

Acknowledgments

A special thanks to the members of the VR community who opened their doors and provided valuable input and support to this project. People such as Brenda Laurel formerly of Telepresence Research, Steve Ellis, and Michael McGreevy of NASA-Ames, Randy Walser of Autodesk, Walter Greenleaf of Greenleaf Medical Systems, Mark Bolas of Fake Space Labs, Bruce Bassett from Virtual Research, Brian Blau from IST, George Zachary from VPL Research, Dr. Nomura from Matsushita, Pete Tinker from Rockwell, Suzanne Weghorst from the HIT Lab, and dozens of others.

Thanks also to the entire cast at Sense8, especially Tom Coull, Pat Gelband, Eric Gullichsen, and Ben Discoe. Lisa Johnson deserves a special mention for her persistence in obtaining all the pictures used in this book.

There's no way this book could have been made without the enthusiastic support of Vince Thomas, Janet Brownstone, Pauline Albert, Pam Pollace, Anna Laurita, Andy Howard, and Chip Krauskopf. We hope the final results vindicate their faith in the project. A special thanks to Dennis Carter and Jim Jarrett for their support of the ongoing Intel VR program.

The Computer Museum in Boston, the Jack Tilton Gallery in New York, the Banff Center for the Arts, and Jenny Holzer were instrumental in providing background information and access to new communities hungry to learn about VR. We look forward to working with all of them in the future.

Thanks to the staff of Windcrest/McGraw-Hill—Ron Powers, Brad Schepp, Carol Noster, Kim Martin, and Kellie Hagan—for the great job in producing and promoting this book.

Finally, thanks to our family and friends who endured our single-minded determination to finish this book.

Foreword

The human being is an intensely visual animal. Most of our information comes from visual images that are interpreted by an extremely efficient image-processing computer—the human brain. On the other hand, computers have typically responded only to implements such as keyboards and mice.

Now with virtual reality, computers and the human mind are entering a realm where communication between the two can proceed at a much more intimate level. This qualitatively new capability holds the promise of extending the range of computer-assisted human experience in completely new directions. Certainly, we are only at the beginning of a major new extension of the use of computer technology.

Simulation has been an important use for computers from the beginning. Originally, just being able to calculate in more detail allowed better prediction of physical phenomena—starting with artillery ballistics. As computer capability and availability has grown, however, simulations have become more complex. Flight simulators are used to train pilots, contributing both increased safety and economy to the process. Increasingly, graphical data presentations are replacing tables of numbers as the output of computations. The result is a greatly enhanced ability to interpret results.

VR is the next major step in making the results of computer manipulation easy for the human brain to interpret. *Virtual Reality: Through the New Looking Glass* outlines the current thinking and future directions of this fascinating technology that sits at the foundation of "humanized" computing.

   — Gordon E. Moore, Chairman, Intel Corp.

Introduction

"Cyberspace. Reality isn't enough anymore!"
 — **John Walker, Autodesk**

Virtual reality is a breakthrough technology that allows you to step through the computer screen into a 3-D artificial world. You can look around, move around, and interact within computer worlds every bit as fantastic as the wonderland Alice found down the rabbit hole. All you have to do is put on the special video goggles, and then almost anything is possible—you can fly, visit exotic lands, play with molecules, swim through the stock market, or paint with 3-D sound and color.

In the past two years, virtual reality (VR) has gone from being an obscure scientific toy to being touted as the future of computing. Dozens of VR conferences and hundreds of articles have seemingly appeared overnight in England, Germany, France, the U.S. and Japan. The word on the street is that VR is something special, just maybe one of those rare concepts that come along and change everything else.

While VR has generated a lot of excitement, however, few people have actually put on a pair of VR goggles, worn a wired glove, and visited a virtual world. Despite all the attention, detailed information has been hard to locate. Where did VR come from? Who first thought it up and how is it accomplished? What are people really doing with it today? And where can I get one? We've written this book to answer these questions, and hopefully justify why virtual reality deserves all of the excitement.

For many people, the first time they heard about entering a computer world and flying through data was in William Gibson's science-fiction novel, *Neuromancer*. Published in 1984, it became an inspiration to young VR builders. It describes life in the next century when the world's telephone system has been superseded by the Matrix, the interconnected sum total of all the world's computer networks.

Cyberspace is Gibson's term for this alternative computer universe in which data exists like cities of light. Information workers (and corporate data bandits) use a special virtual reality system, called a deck, to jump into the Matrix and travel its data highways. The deck gives them the experience of being physically free to go anywhere in cyberspace.

"Cyberspace. A consensual hallucination experienced daily by billions of legitimate operators, in every nation, by children being taught mathematical concepts . . . A graphic representation of data abstracted from the banks of every computer in the human system. Unthinkable complexity. Lines of light ranged in the nonspace of the mind, clusters and constellations of data. Like city lights, receding . . ."

No longer science-fiction, virtual reality products exist. In Europe, the U.S., and Japan, there are programs going on at places like NASA, Tokyo University, and the Human-Interface Lab in Seattle, Washington. It's being pursued inside companies like Boeing, IBM, NEC, DEC, Intel, Fujitsu, Sun Microsystems, and Autodesk.

But the real innovation is happening at the grass-roots level. The Silicon Valley myth of starting a business out of a garage and growing it into successful company is still alive and well at VPL Research, Sense8, Fake Space Labs, Greenleaf Medical Systems, Virtual Research, and more.

VR is still a very young technology, so most of the solid information on it is scattered about in research papers, reports, magazine articles, and inside the heads of the young entrepreneurs who are charting its territory. Trying to follow VR through the mass media is confusing at best. It's made up of snapshots, highlights, brief encounters, and reported sightings.

At one extreme is the Hollywood techno-horror movie, *Lawnmower Man*, which portrays VR as some exciting but dangerously mind-altering technology. On the other hand, a recent issue of *Forbes* magazine (June 22nd 1992) writes that it's a revolutionary invention that will change the way business uses computers. Could they both be right? We decided to write this book to try and end the confusion and shed some light on what's possible and what isn't possible with virtual reality.

We've based the book on our combined years of experience developing, designing, and teaching about virtual reality and computer technology. We've written articles, built worlds, and given speeches as well as hundreds of public VR demonstrations—including a live, on-air experience for the "CBS Morning News" show. Instead of flying the hosts through a psychedelic landscape or a shoot'em-up game, we had them design, build, and remodel a house in real time, on their own, with goggles and wands, to show what could really be done with virtual reality (see Fig. I-1). In June of 1992, in conjunction with the Jack Tilton Gallery, we coproduced the first virtual reality art exhibit in New York, just down the street from the Museum of Modern Art.

I-1
Picture of KT and KP on "CBS Morning News" set with anchors.

This book is designed to serve as your tour guide to virtual reality. Think of it like a guidebook to Bali, a gateway to adventure. We're going to give you the local history, describe transportation requirements, and tell you what to bring with you and what to do when you get there. We'll even suggest side trips to some exotic islands no one has visited yet.

Each section is filled with photographs and illustrations. And there are interviews and reports from the adventurous virtual explorers who have gone ahead of you— the people who are trying to turn virtual dreams into real products and applications.

This book is organized into three parts. Actually, it's three books in one, so you can find the information you want and skip what you don't want. Our objective is to provide you with the kind of book we wish we had when we first stepped through the new looking glass.

What is virtual reality and where did it come from? The name has become a media buzzword, cut loose from its original intentions and caught up in a cultural excitement over potential and imagined uses of the technology.

The term *virtual reality* was coined by Jaron Lanier, founder of VPL Research, to distinguish between the immersive digital worlds he was trying to create and traditional computer simulations. The history of virtual reality and what makes virtual worlds different from other simulations is what the first part of this book, *Stepping through the new looking glass*, is all about.

There are several different methods for providing virtual realities and variations of them. VR is more than a computer technology that places the user inside a 3-D world; it's the artificial world itself and a new kind of experience. It's also a method of communicating ideas. Inside a virtual world, everything is potentially alive because the laws of reality are up to the designer. The computer can just as easily bring to life the world of atoms as it can let you fly through space.

The first chapter gives an overview of what's happening in the field and describes the varieties of virtual experience, while explaining what kind of methods are being used. With this overview it's possible to journey into the land of VR with some sense of what's going on.

Given the suddenness with which virtual reality has burst on the public scene, it would seem to have been born overnight. But the desire for immersive experiences, the ticket to enter another world, is an age-old desire. From Renaissance artists to the creation of motion pictures, modern civilization has been moving steadily towards more participation in imaginative worlds.

Today's movie industry is a worldwide phenomenon. For an industry so large it's amazing that there is almost no research and development effort. The basic technology has remained stuck at the level of color that was introduced in the 1940s. There have been dreamers, however, who saw the potential of providing richer, more realistic experiences. They attempted to create them with innovations such as Cinerama and Sensorama. Their efforts foreshadowed what would finally be possible with the new technology of computers.

Chapters 2, 3, and 4 track the development of virtual realities. While artists and the movies understood realism, the computer industry understood interaction. It was left to computer pioneers to finally step through the looking glass into dynamic, responsive, artificial worlds.

The early pioneers in this area were looking for the ultimate display technology, one in which the computer would disappear and allow users to navigate naturally with their eyes, ears, feet, and hands. Over the last 30 years, developments at NASA and elsewhere finally led to the emergence of a commercial virtual reality industry.

How this book is organized

Stepping through the new looking glass

21st century tools The history of virtual reality is made up of false starts, inventive dead ends, and a lot of hard work. Today, it's a fledgling industry based on computers and a wide range of exotic technology. What makes it all work? What is a wired-glove and how do VR goggles create a virtual world?

Part two: 21st century tools is a layman's guide to VR technology. It steps behind the magician's curtain to explain how the tricks are accomplished. It takes you inside the structure and components of reality engines, wands, and worlds.

Chapter 5 provides an overview of the technology behind virtual reality. It explains the science and language for creating virtual worlds, which is a new form of communications that encompasses not only the visual, but the auditory and tactile. For each sensory effect there are a range of technologies for supplying the information.

The technology for providing VR is no longer limited to scientific research centers. Chapter 7, *Desktop VR,* presents the basic building blocks for designing a virtual reality system using a desktop personal computer. The most common image people have of virtual reality is somebody sitting in a chair with what looks like a scuba mask strapped to his face, with a metal box over his eyes. VR technology, however, has already gone a long way beyond this.

Chapter 8, *Gloves, goggles, & wands,* goes into detail about the input and navigation tools for working in a virtual environment. It explains what goes into a set of goggles and how the two tiny LCD screens inside them create a sense of 3-D space.

Beyond a basic description of the hardware, this section explores the way a virtual world is built. A virtual world is part animation, part computer-aided design, and lots of imagination. There are special software tricks that give a virtual world greater levels of realism without bogging down the computer. The goal of this section is to remove the mystery of how virtual reality works and explain what's involved in building a VR system of your own.

Brave new worlds After learning about what VR is, where it came from, and how it works, you're bound to be wondering "What can I do with it?'' *Part three: Brave new worlds* is a tour through all the wonderlands and practical applications being developed using virtual reality.

Our brains do some pretty sophisticated image processing to present us with the 3-D view of the world we call reality. Chapter 9, *Designing virtual worlds,* looks at the psychological, philosophical, and artistic reasons for creating virtual experiences. It includes ideas and suggestions from designers who have been building worlds and suggests that they can find inspiration from theatrical and artistic practices.

Chapter 10, *Business enters the cyberage*, explores the design, manufacturing, and business uses of VR. Developers at Boeing, Lockheed, Matsushita, and NASA have shared some of the ways in which they're using VR technology with us. Virtual reality is more than a new design tool, however; it's also a method of managing information so money mangers and business executives can make faster, more effective decisions. VR is already being used in sales and marketing situations in Japan where customers design and tour their own custom kitchens before buying.

The American medical industry is already a very high-tech realm, and one for which VR tools are being developed. The chapter on VR medical technology looks into how doctors will combine these VR tools with CAT scans, MRI, X-rays, and a host of other equipment to explore and heal our bodies.

There are already surgical procedures where surgeons work via tiny remote-controlled TV cameras inside the patient while they manipulate devices on the outside. The various gloves and goggles developed for virtual reality also offer many useful medical applications, from measurement to rehabilitation procedures.

Chapter 12, *Entertainment*, might be the most fun to read. The technology of VR has already reached the level where the quality is good enough for arcades and theater systems. W-industries in England, BattleTech in Chicago, and the creative minds at LucasArts in Marin, California already have VR entertainment systems in development or on the market. These simulation theaters move you past the discussion of how-to technology and into the content of your experiences. What does it mean when you can enter strange new worlds, ride a bike around Paris, or battle monsters over lunch—and then return to the everyday world?

The uses of virtual reality in the Arts brings us to the edge of where VR might take us. The role of the artist is not only to express ideas and emotions through various media, but also to provide insight into the nature of perception and consciousness. As a culture, we look to artists not only to champion new ideas but also to challenge them. Virtual reality is a field in need of such examination.

Beyond debating its merits, virtual reality might create a completely new category of art—a nonmaterial, interactive art form of the mind. One where there's no longer a separation between art object and art viewer. Through the computer's ability to control and manipulate our senses, the visual experience can now be given the same properties as music. Will this become a new kind of drug as some people fear, or a means for new and insightful experiences?

The final chapter, *The next generation*, pulls the curtain aside to reveal technology advances both just over the horizon and imagined for the future. What is the potential for hyper-realistic virtual worlds? When will cyberspace be possible and what will be the social impact when VR becomes widely available? What kind of world will tomorrow be?

Television has already warned us that there's a need for a new kind a literacy, a visual literacy of experience. What is real and what is truth when what we know is no longer played out on a screen, but acted out inside of a favorite world? The future is no longer approaching, it's here.

Are you ready? Turn the page to begin your travels into virtual reality country. We've included a resource appendix at the end so you can find companies, people, universities, and other institutions to keep you going after you've finished reading. One thing we should warn you of, however—this trip doesn't include a return ticket. Like the steam engine, the telephone, and the television, virtual reality is a technology that will keep moving ahead, causing other changes around it. This book is one trip you won't be coming back from.

Part one

Stepping through the new looking glass

The disappearing computer

"I like John's one-sentence definition of cyberspace: 'The place you are when you're on the phone.'"

—Mitch Kapor, Founder of Lotus, quoting John Perry Barlow, Technology reporter and lyricist for the Grateful Dead

This morning, at the NASA Ames Research Center in Mountain View, California, Dr. Lew Hitchner explores the surface of Mars. He's wearing virtual reality (VR) goggles with two tiny liquid crystal display (LCD) screens inside. They give him a 3-D view of the rocky Martian landscape, Utopia Planitia (see Figs. 1-2 and 1-3), that was reconstructed from satellite data sent back by a Viking spacecraft stationed on Mars. With a change of software, he'll be flying across the sprawling canyons of Valles Marineris later this afternoon.

Just down the hallway in the "view lab," Dr. Stephen Ellis is remotely controlling robots, wearing VR goggles and a wired glove. The glove senses the movements of his hand and fingers, and a computer interprets and transmits them as commands for a robot arm. Ellis sees what the robot sees and the robot mimics his movements, even though he and the robot are in different rooms and can't see each other. Someday, using VR, robots will act as human eyes, arms, and ears on other planets.

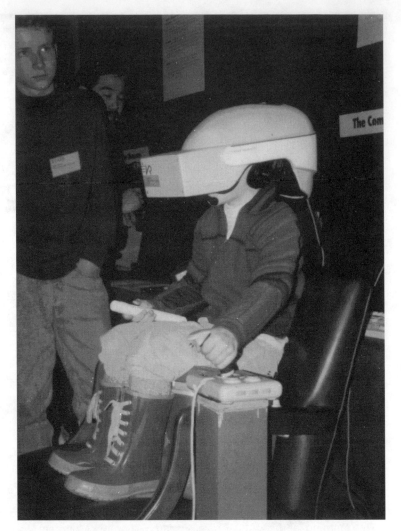

1-1
Child using the IntelSense8 Artroom demo at The Computer Museum in Boston.

Hitchner and Ellis are part of a NASA VR program. The goal of the program is to explore planets without physically sending people there. Instead, in the future robots will let many people visit as virtual astronauts.

In Seattle, Washington, Chris Esposito runs the Computer Interface Group at Boeing Corporation. The company has committed to completely developing its next generation of commercial aircraft using computers. "We've already identified three dozen applications for virtual reality, spanning the entire range of a product's life-cycle. From concept development to manufacturing and maintenance operations, even in-flight uses. And the list is getting longer."

Dr. Nomura of Matsushita, Japan is working on a commercial VR kitchen designer, using VPL Research equipment. A Shinjuku department store is already using one of his systems to help Japanese consumers redesign their kitchens. A customer provides a drawing of his kitchen layout, which is loaded into the computer. He can

1-2
Virtual visit to the Martian surface. Photographs collected by NASA's Viking 2 Lander are instantly reassembled by computer to generate appropriate views, depending on where the participant is looking.

then select the appliances, colors, and features he wants in his kitchen using the system. After he's arranged everything, he puts on VR goggles and a wired glove to take a tour of his design. He can open drawers, turn on the water in the sink, turn the appliances on and off, and even listen to birds through the window. If everything looks, feels, and sounds the way he wants it to, the computer places the customer's order based on the layout and items selected.

Sitting in an office in Marin, California, Eric Gullichsen and Patrice Gelband talk about being the first to create a networked PC virtual-reality demo for The Computer Museum in Boston—the world's first VR museum exhibit. The show, based on their WorldToolKit software, ran on Intel486™ microprocessor-based PCs, and included an application designed specifically to introduce people to virtual reality.

"You find yourself in one of two worlds," Gelband explains. "One world is the Workroom, where two people working together can assemble a house of predesigned building blocks: walls, windows, and pillars. The other world is the Artroom, where they can sketch brilliantly colored drawings together in the air.

1-3
340-degree panoramic view of Utopia Planitia region of Mars, captured by the Viking 2 Lander. Outlined box shows view depicted in Fig. 1-2.

[You] . . . control a wand in these virtual worlds. The wand grabs building blocks with a touch and moves them wherever you want. In the Artroom, the wand leaves a trail of tiny colored triangles, which light up and gradually fade away, just like waving a soap bubble wand that leaves a trail of bubbles in the air. As they light up, the triangles weave a trail of musical tones. Wave the wand around your head and the sound moves around you. You can even compose with it to make a kind of musical sculpture."

"Virtual reality is about discovery, about doing things that couldn't be done before, expressing ideas that couldn't be expressed before," Gullichsen adds.

At a grand old cathedral in San Francisco that has been converted into a theater, on Saturday night a full-house audience puts on 3-D glasses to visit *Invisible Site*, a George Coates Performance Works (GCPW) multimedia play that uses actors, 3-D projections, film, real-time animated computer graphics, and some sophisticated theater tricks to give people "*virtual* virtual reality" experience.

"It's a way of evoking the sense of awe that immersing yourself in virtual reality produces," George Coates says, and adds with a chuckle, "Someday we'll be handing out VR goggles instead of 3-D glasses."

On stage, characters enter a store of the future, called Invisible Site, that sells virtual reality experiences. Once inside, as customers, they dress in goggles and gloves. Then they enter "cyberspace" through a computer network, where they visit new worlds and assume completely new identities.

After the show, the audience heads towards San Francisco's nightclub dance district, where Toon Town is getting ready to open its doors. The clubs really come alive after 2 A.M., when the "ravers" appear: engineers, accountants, artists, clerks, and data information workers dressed in wild clothes with even wilder hairstyles. They come for the music, the dancing till dawn, and the "virtual scene."

The owners of the club run the shows, and each night is different from the last. They use Amiga computers, PCs, video editing equipment, film, lasers, and light shows, and invite unusual musicians to entertain, such as bands with handmade electronic instruments. Like rap music artists who build new music by sampling other recordings, they create and project their graphics, animation, and sampled video in a constant improvisation on people, screens, mirrored globes, and all interior surfaces of the building. It lasts until morning, a light show that evokes the sense of a constantly evolving environment.

Like George Coates, Toon Town has found an audience hungry for new media concepts—using computers to visit, simulate, create, and control new worlds. In a corner of the club, dozens of people line up to pay for a chance to sit down, put on goggles, and fly around in a virtual world. "They all expect to be using one at home in a couple of years," says Vince Thomas, one of the club's owners.

A second group of people in the club is gathered to use the Mandala Machine, where a Toon Town patron is dancing and playing imaginary musical instruments. His image is captured by a video camera and fed into a computer, where it's combined with interactive video and animation, and projected onto the wall in front of him. He controls the animation through his movements as he watches himself on the wall in the scene—with synthesized notes erupting as he slaps the virtual drums (see Fig. 1- 4).

1-4
Using real-time image-processing techniques, a video camera captures a person's outline and combines it with a 2-D graphic of musical instruments. Hand movements, detected by the computer, can activate each instrument in turn.

This is a very small sample of what's going on in the exploding realm of virtual reality. Don't worry if at first you feel a bit confused. VR is both a new technology and a set of ideas—concepts that are spreading faster than the hardware and software that produce them. There are several different approaches that fall under the label of *virtual reality*, though they don't all use the same effects to achieve the same results.

Worldwide, VR is happening in protected pockets of technology; inside giant corporations, universities, and small entrepreneurial start-ups; in Berlin and North Carolina; covering Japan; and especially in the San Francisco Bay Area. Although Silicon Valley has a lot to do with this new industry, there's more to VR than "high tech." VR has spawned a new interaction between musicians, artists, entrepreneurs, and electronic tinkerers. A rare excitement is in the air, an excitement that comes from breaking through to something new. Computers are about to take the next big step—out of the lab and into the street—and the street can't wait.

"As long as you can see the screen, you're not in virtual reality. When the screen disappears, and you see an imaginary scene . . . then you are in virtual reality."

> **—Gabriel D. Ofeisch, Emeritus Professor of Educational Technology at Howard University**

Experiential computing

Virtual reality is all about illusion. It's about computer graphics in the theater of the mind. It's about the use of high technology to convince yourself that you're in another reality, experiencing some event that doesn't physically exist in the world in front of you. Virtual reality is also a new media for getting your hands on information, getting inside information, and representing ideas in ways not previously possible.

Virtual reality is where the computer disappears and you become "the ghost in the machine." There's no little screen of symbols you must manipulate or type commands into to get the computer to do something. Instead, the computer retreats behind the scenes and becomes invisible, leaving you free to concentrate on tasks, ideas, problems, and communications.

For four generations, people have experienced a type of virtual reality using the telephone. It has now been over 100 years since the introduction of the telephone, and today it's so deeply embedded in our cultural consciousness that we give it as much thought as a doorknob. As a society, we've forgotten what a shock the telephone was when it was first introduced—the strangeness of listening to a ghostly, disembodied voice.

Today we rely on the telephone not only to communicate, but to give us the sense of someone else's presence, even though in reality we're listening to an electromechanical re-creation of a human voice. We've learned to ignore the telephone and concentrate on the conversation—the interactivity makes the difference. While the quality of sound reproduction influences our willingness to believe the illusion, so too does our cultural acceptance of the illusion.

Alan Kay, computer pioneer and Apple Computer fellow, has thought a long time about the way humans and computers could work together. Part of his concept of a "dynabook" (a mobile, networked, multimedia, clipboard-sized computer), conceived more than 20 years ago, is coming to fruition today in small notebook computers.

What's still missing is the point-of-view simulations he included in his dynabook vision, the kind of simulations VR now makes possible. His product vision was people-oriented, not hardware-oriented. He was interested in the way technologies could be used by people, and the way they disappeared when their ease of use and functionality crossed a certain threshold.

"I read McLuhan's *Understanding Media* and understood that the most important thing about any communications medium is that message receipt is really message recovery; anyone who wishes to receive a message embedded in a medium must first have internalized the medium so it can be subtracted out to leave the message behind." [Kay, 1990]

Media is the plural form of *medium*. *Webster's Ninth New Collegiate Dictionary* describes *medium* as ". . . a means of effecting or conveying something . . . a channel or system of communication, information, or entertainment." Computers are a medium, a means or agency for doing something. What Kay suggests is that for the computer to really work, the way we use it has to become so comfortable, familiar, and effortless (like the television, telephone, and light-switch) that we can unconsciously subtract it out and focus only on its function—the communication, information, and entertainment it provides.

Like the telephone, computers are a communications medium. Like the telescope and microscope, virtual reality is also a tool for revealing new ways of looking at information. VR gives users an efficient and effortless flow of data, details, and information in the most natural format possible—vision, sound, and sensations presented as an environment, part of the natural media of human experience and thought.

"The primary defining characteristic of VR is inclusion; being surrounded by an environment. VR places the participant inside information."
    —**Dr. William Bricken, Human Interface Technologies Lab**

New inventions are rarely appreciated for what they are when they first arise. Around the turn of the century, when the automobile first appeared on city streets, it was called a *horseless carriage*. It was built like a buggy and moved about as fast as a horse. Nobody could imagine then that in just a few years it would change our pace of life, the face of the land, the economy, and the quality of the air we breathe.

"Build it and see what happens" is the maxim inventors have lived by for millennia. Often, inventors can't foresee what their discoveries will actually be used for, or the side effects they might cause. Alexander Graham Bell thought the telephone would be useful as a way to pipe music to people. The developers of radio (and later television) imagined that their devices would launch a world of two-way communications to replace the telephone.

Where does this new development, virtual reality, fit in? Is it new, or just another form of television? What makes it special? Can it take you inside the new digital world of the computer and let you see things you've never seen before? If so, how?

The first great wave of the computer revolution was hardware based; mainframes, mini computers, and personal computers automated the workplace. Computers became office rolodexes, electronic filing cabinets, typewriters, accounting ledgers, drafting tables, and the company mail. They've changed the way individuals work, providing them with access to more information, but people have had to struggle with the computer to get at the information—and often struggle alone.

Now, as an increasing amount of media is converted into the digital language of computers, computers are beginning to adapt to people. Digitizing analog signals translates the media of sound, video, text, and graphic images into machine language, a mixture of ones and zeros (bits) that can be decoded and shared by other computers. With digitization, all media and information can be intertwined and blended together—sometimes even transformed into each other. Computers are now beginning to speak to us, listen to us, and completely customize the information we use to suit our needs and learning styles.

In the 1980s, we began to experience the start of a second computer revolution with the success of the compact disk (CD). The analog signals we had all been listening to were now digital on CD. The early 1990's phase of this second revolution is "digital video." For example, Sony now has a product called the Mavica Instant Video System. This "smart" video camera provides autoflash, auto-exposure, and automatic shutter speeds. It uses a two-inch magnetic floppy disk to record up to 50 still images in digital bits. The disk can be viewed, saved, or erased for reuse. The camera is available for under $200.

Digital technology has also been the major springboard for VR, and it's getting ready to take some leaps, as the examples at the beginning of this chapter suggest. There are many different formats and a variety of systems that are calling themselves *virtual reality*. Throughout this book, we'll try to carefully categorize what we mean by virtual reality, and use more specific labels to separate the various forms. One such distinction is between VR and multimedia.

Within the next few years, the controls for almost all the analog machines we know will be controlled by digital circuits. The computer's ability to manipulate and communicate makes it a "meta-medium," a medium in which all previous media are combined and regenerated. This has led to both multimedia computers and virtual reality, each with its own unique potential.

"Being able to mix together existing [media] forms, such as photos, images, sound, and books, and then come up with something new is what multimedia is all about," says Sandra Morris, multimedia developer and author of the book *Multimedia Applications Development Using DVI Technology*. "The difference between virtual reality and multimedia is that VR is about creation, while multimedia is about bringing the old media forms together into the computer. They don't change so much as they get combined in new ways. VR is about creating something completely new."

Multimedia and virtual reality both benefit from digital technology developments. However, as Morris points out, a large distinction between virtual reality and multimedia is the creation of environments versus the juxtaposition of existing media. Multimedia allows a person using a computer to read the script of a play on half of the computer screen while watching it be acted out on the other side of the screen, complete with narrative sound. It also allows people to send electronic mail that contains both an audible voice and video images from PC to PC.

Comparatively, virtual reality capabilities allow a person using a computer to assemble complex three-dimensional star fields of the galaxy and fly around in the data to understand how the universe is structured. This research is being performed by astronomers at the National Supercomputing Center in Ohio, using Cray supercomputers. As a result, the astronomers are now seeing things in the data they couldn't experience before, and were surprised to see, such as the way vast numbers of galaxies are clumped together in threads, ribbons, and clusters, leaving tremendous, empty voids between them.

Projected reality

Although many believe that full immersion, as in the previous section, is the only true approach to virtual reality, even partial immersion into virtual reality can have a similar effect on its audience.

VIDEOPLACE by Myron Krueger is an example of a projected environment that Krueger calls "artificial reality." VIDEOPLACE, first developed in the 1970's, uses two rooms, each with wall-sized video screens, a computer, and a video camera. Unlike a videophone, which displays only the other person on the screen, VIDEOPLACE displays colorized silhouettes of users onto the screen. In essence, users watch themselves as they're projected into a virtual world, as opposed to seeing the world through the eyes of a computer in place of their own eyes.

VIDEOPLACE is both a form of telecommunications and a new, more human, computer interface. Using silhouettes, Krueger allows people using VIDEOPLACE to focus entirely on their interactions and experiences, not the equipment itself. Krueger can also enhance the experiences of people using VIDEOPLACE by adding effects not ordinarily found in day-to-day reality; for example, users can "fingerpaint" colored designs and messages to each other in the air.

Another example of projected reality is the Mandala Machine, created by the Vivid Group (mentioned earlier in the chapter). This system overlays the real video images of users onto an artificial world of computer-graphic images (see Fig. 1-5). The system perceives users' images in motion, analyzes them, makes sense of what it sees, and responds instantly with graphics, video effects, and synthesized sound.

1-5
Video cameras capture the motion of performers in front of a specially colored screen. The computer then combines the performer's image with that of any computer-generated world.

Augmented reality is the use of transparent glasses onto which data, diagrams, animation, or video can be projected to aid people who need to be simultaneously in the real world and also be able to access additional data to do their jobs.

Augmented reality

Boeing is exploring the possibilities of such a system for use by aircraft engine mechanics. In this case, the mechanic's glasses could display schematic diagrams, parts lists, and text without blocking out the image of a real-world engine. Someday, a structural layout of a jet engine assembly, positioned accurately over an actual engine, could provide a simulated form of x-ray vision for a mechanic actively performing repairs. Even those parts of the engine reachable only with hands out of view could become visible.

In general, then, the term *virtual reality* refers to an immersive, interactive experience generated by a computer. Although the press is already playing up future scenarios of high-resolution systems that might fully replace reality, currently only primitive methods of providing object movement and tactile feedback are beginning to be explored.

Virtual reality

In its most common use today, VR immersion means the use of a head-mounted display (HMD) and headphones for sound. However, sensory immersion could someday become so deep that every sensory channel would be simulated by the computer to convince the mind that it's really in another world. Total sensory immersion would theoretically include temperature, tactile sensations, bodily movement, sounds, images, and even odors.

The power of immersion is its ability to focus someone's perceptual powers on a specific problem or experience. Virtual reality immersion can act as a powerful lens for extracting knowledge from data by turning it into experience, as shown by the person wearing VPL EyePhones in Fig. 1-6.

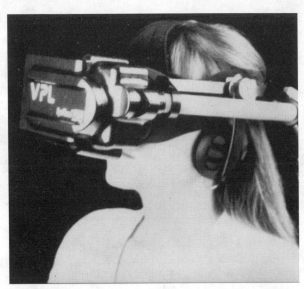

1-6
One method of immersion is based on using a head-mounted display device, such as VPL Research EyePhones, to view a virtual world. Sensors track the participant's head movements, allowing the computer to generate the appropriate image.

Telepresence *Telepresence*, another form of virtual reality, uses video cameras and remote microphones to immerse the user so deeply as to project him into a different place, as shown in Fig. 1-7. Robotic control, such as the planetary exploration work at NASA Ames, is the most immediate example under research, but there are also potential medical uses for telepresence. In surgical procedures, doctors already use video cameras and fiber-optic cables to view patients' bodies. With VR, they could actually "go inside of" patients to direct their work or inspect the work of others.

Meet me in the interface Like any tool, the hardware to create virtual realities isn't the experience itself. The methods for creating virtual realities are all ways of matching the user up with the interface.

"An interface is a 'contact surface.' It reflects the physical properties of the interactors, functions to be performed, and the balance of power and control . . .

We naturally visualize an interface as the place where contact between two entities occurs. The less alike those two entities are, the more obvious the need for a well-designed interface becomes."

—**Brenda Laurel,** *The Art of the Human-Computer Interface*

1-7
A remotely controlled vehicle (seen in the background near the van) uses stereoptic cameras to transmit real-time images back to a stereoptic display. When viewed through electronic flicker glasses, the operator sees a 3-D, or stereo view of the remote scene.

Virtual reality is the place where humans and computers make contact. Just as the steering wheel, brake, clutch, stick-shift, and dashboard instruments are the interface between a driver and a car, virtual reality is an interface between humans and computers. In both cases, these interfaces act as contact points where human movements are translated into commands that direct the machine's operation, and also where the machine's condition is communicated to the user.

The shape and function of each interactive contact point is designed to meet the needs of both the machine and the user. In the case of a car, although we think of ourselves as controlling the machine, when the gas meter gauge nears empty or red lights on the car's dashboard flash, it would appear that the car is actually commanding us. Similar reactions could be expected from virtual reality interactive contact points.

The car, like the telephone, has been with us for so long that we tend to ignore it when we use it. It functions as a bodily extension, allowing us to expand our physical capabilities. Similarly, computers allow us to extend the capabilities of our minds. Like car engines, computers are useless by themselves; they require an operator and an interface to transfer their power into useful functions. In the case of virtual reality, the interface hides the computer engine from the operator. It both extends and limits what we can do with a computer.

The evolution of human-computer interfaces has been an ongoing trade-off between the limits of the equipment, the creativity of the programmers, and users' willingness to put up with the results. Historically, the interface has been designed to leverage human capabilities to the advantage of computers, not humans. All too often, it would seem that the interface has been as much a way for the programmer to control the behavior of the user as a way for the user to control the behavior of the computer. In turn, this often places great limitations on a human's ability to use a computer.

In the 1940s, the first computers were built using vacuum tubes, and required plug boards, dials, and switches to operate. Controlling the computer required dozens of trained technicians to service the machine; setting up the unit to solve a problem could take days. And the results were a cryptic series of printed mathematical codes.

During the Eisenhower years, computer interfacing evolved slightly, with the use of punch-card stacks to run software programs. The results, however, were still cryptic printouts of mathematical codes. Access to the information was restricted to an elite group of people who typically wore white jackets and met in restricted rooms to emerge after several days with answers to problems.

As the 1960s and 1970s progressed, users began to have direct access to computers through individual workstations, instead of working through intermediaries in corporate computing centers. Sometimes people appeared to look into screens, as if they were crystal balls, to discern knowledge from computers. Gradually, computers became more efficient; tubes were replaced by transistors, which were replaced by integrated circuits.

Fast, alphanumeric terminals made it possible to present large amounts of information to the user electronically. This allowed the computer to interface with a user through a "menu" of choices. The user could make selections from the menu by simply pressing one or two keys. Menus and data entry, modeled on filling in forms, became the standard for applications intended to be used by nonspecialists (almost everyone).

The microprocessor, introduced in 1971, made the personal computer possible and provided a hardware interface platform for modern graphical software interfaces. These graphical interfaces (GUIs), which were developed at Xerox PARC and later gained public notice when used for the Apple Macintosh, have transformed our conversational interactions with computers.

In the past, you typed commands into the computer to receive alphanumeric key responses. But now you can graphically select the objects displayed on a screen and receive graphic output representations of information, sometimes in full color. It's no longer necessary to read lists of filenames that scroll down the entire length of a screen; computer software and application files are symbolized by icons that act as representations for the ways we organize our offices. Icons can appear as books, folders, and trashcans. Using a cursor, you can manipulate symbols on a computer screen to accomplish various tasks, without even touching a computer keyboard.

Now, with virtual reality, the window of the GUI that has kept us outside the screen looking in has dissolved, and we can step through the glass—replacing the desktop metaphor with a complete environment. How is this unique? Virtual reality is a human-computer interface in which the computer creates a sensory-immersing environment that interactively responds to and is controlled by the behavior of the user.

The two key words here are *sensory-immersing* and *interactively*. The creation of an environment requires the immersion of your senses in a computer-generated world to create the experience of "being there." The question isn't whether the created virtual world is as real as the physical world, but whether the created world is real enough for you to suspend your disbelief for a period of time. This is the same mental shift that happens when you get wrapped up in a good novel or become absorbed in playing a computer game. You stop considering the quality of the interface media and accept the computer-generated world as a viable one (just as you might accept the voice on a phone as real, even with a bad connection).

What is the value of immersion? One powerful effect of immersion is its ability to focus your attention. It's common to say that people immerse themselves in their work. Immersion means to block out distractions and focus selectively on just the information with which you want to work. The power to concentrate on work seems to be a prerequisite for highly creative and intelligent people.

Immersion

While Picasso's creativity was as much a mystery to him as to everyone else, one easily verifiable behavior was the intense way he did everything—even signing his name. He would bend over, place his face very close to the page, and nothing else existed for him for the moment but that act.

Howard Rheingold suggests that the use of immersion can be traced as far back as the ceremonial caves of prehistoric humans. Youngsters were brought into the darkness of painted caves, where stories were told, images and songs were revealed in precise sequence, and the youths became immersed in their coming-of-age ceremonies.

Only by shutting out the rest of the world and immersing themselves in this separate space could the learning occur that changed a child into an adult. Brenda Laurel draws parallels between the immersive qualities of virtual reality and theater, itself a descendant of religious ceremony.

In the theater, your attention is focused on the actors' performances. Through lights, setting, drama, and music you're invited to lose yourself in their story. When it works, the theater has the power to engage you, focus you, and hold your attention. This immersive, ritualized experience can convince, teach, and inspire you. It might even provide you with a kind of emotional catharsis.

Interactivity, like immersion, is a crucial aspect of VR. There are two unique aspects of interactivity in a virtual world: navigation within the world and the dynamics of the environment. Navigation is simply a user's ability to move around independently, as if inside an environment (see Fig. 1-8). Constraints can be set by the software developer for access into certain virtual areas, allowing various degrees of freedom—you can fly, move through walls, walk around, or swim.

Interactivity

Another aspect of navigation is the positioning of a user's point of view. Controlling point of view might mean watching yourself from a distance, viewing a scene through someone else's eyes, or moving through the design of a new building as if in a wheelchair, to test if it really will be wheelchair accessible.

1-8
Users of Fujitsu's VR system navigate through a fanciful aquarium world full of interesting creatures. Virtual worlds can be either abstract or realistic in nature.

The dynamics of an environment are the rules for how its contents (people, rocks, doors, everything) interact in order to exchange energy or information. A simple example of dynamic rules are the Newtonian laws used to describe the behavior of billiard balls reacting to the impact of a cueball. A medical simulation would be based on the dynamics of the human body. Alice's looking-glass wonderland would follow the wacky laws that Lewis Carroll created, based partially on the game of chess (he was a Cambridge mathematician as well as a writer).

Because the computer, fitted with the right equipment, can control and manipulate the complete human range of visual, auditory, and even kinesthetic sensations, almost any form of "reality" a developer can think up can be simulated.

Every object and its relationship to every other object (including the user) is a design element at the discretion of the developer. Among these elements are the location, color, shape, and size of the environment; the plasticity of walls; the laws of gravity; and the capabilities and functions of objects and actors in the environment. As a result, virtual reality is the experience of *being in another world*, a world governed by selected laws, and inhabited by objects (and actors) with whatever properties the creator chooses to assign.

It is this flexibility for creating and representing responsive environments that has created the excitement about virtual reality. 3-D movies have come and gone, and Disneyland provides rides like Star Tours, which passively immerse people in other worlds. But to go into a world that responds to you, and uniquely to you—that is virtual reality. It means you can represent problems as complete environments and then bring all of your human senses to bear on finding answers. Ultimately, it means a time will come when there will be nothing you can visualize that can't be shared with someone else.

"Language serves not only to express thoughts, but to make possible thoughts which could not exist without it."
   —Bertrand Russell

Language, writing, and mathematics are symbol systems with vast powers to communicate meaning, allowing people to construct and communicate mental representations. They are tools that have made science possible, thinking tools for making thinking tools. But they're also abstracts, or stand-ins, for the real thing— the inner experience of the imagination. Virtual reality is a new thinking tool, a way of directly representing what we think.

Down through the centuries, great leaders, artists, scientists, and thinkers in every field have struggled with the gap between their inner visions and how little of it they were able to communicate. In a letter to a friend, Einstein revealed that his primary mode of thought was not abstract words or mathematical symbols, but rather a kind of mental "play" he used in order to come up with his great theories:

"The psychic entities which seem to serve as elements in thought are certain signs and more or less clear images which can be 'voluntarily' reproduced and combined . . . The above mentioned elements are, in my case, of visual and some of the muscular type. Conventional words or other signs have to be sought for laboriously only in a secondary stage, when the mentioned associative play is sufficiently established and can be reproduced at will."

While he is usually described as a visual thinker, it's important to note here that Einstein refers to both his visual and muscular thinking modes, and calls them *entities* (which suggests dynamic properties). It was this combination of internal experiences, an internal sensory language of experience, that led to his theories and writings. Virtual reality can be used to translate information (mental or symbolic) into experiences that people can explore in the same kind of purposeful play that Einstein experienced in his thoughts.

Simply, virtual reality, like writing and mathematics, is a way to represent and communicate what you can imagine with your mind. But it can be more powerful because it doesn't require you to convert your ideas into abstract symbols with restrictive semantic and syntactic rules, and it can be shared with other people.

VR can reveal processes that might be invisible to you because they're distant in time and space, occur too fast or too slow, or are too large or too small for human physical senses. Because VR can incorporate events, symbols, and media from other forms of communications in addition to recreating what is in your mind, virtual reality mirrors back to you how your mind works.

Like the inventions of writing, several thousand years ago, and more recently movies, virtual reality will make possible the expression and construction of ideas never before dreamed possible. Virtual reality might not only change the way we communicate, it might also change the way we think.

"When [Marshal McLuhan] said 'the medium is the message,' he meant that you have to become the medium if you use it . . . That's pretty scary. It means that even though humans are the animals that shape tools, it is in the nature of tools and man that learning to use tools reshapes us."

—**Alan Kay, 1990**

More than a "fantasy machine," virtual reality might very well be the lifting of the curtain on one of the real uses of computers—the creation of the first universal meta-language that can allow us to move from living in an information age to participating in a knowledge age.

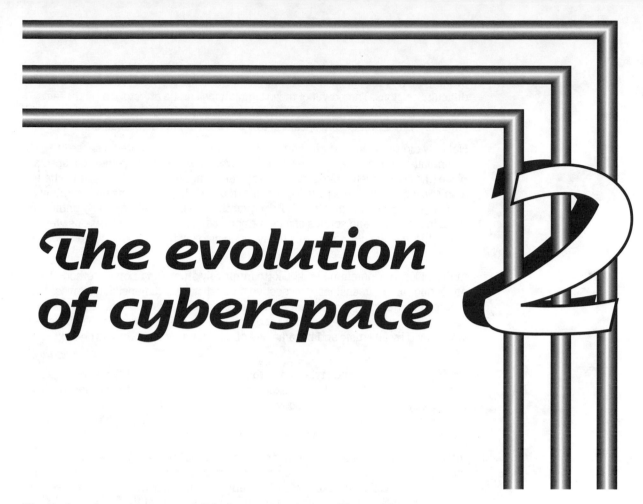

The evolution of cyberspace

"Reality has always been too small for human imagination. The impulse to create an 'interactive fantasy machine' is only the most recent manifestation of the age-old desire to make our fantasies palpable—our insatiable need to exercise our imagination, judgment, and spirits in worlds, situations, and personae that are different from those of our everyday lives."

—Brenda Laurel, *Computers As Theater*

Throughout history, attempts have been made to capture the essence of an experience and distill it in some form to make it available for us to enjoy and analyze. Through the direct experience of theater, music, and paintings, people have been able to perceive both the real and imaginary expressions of other worlds, other times, new ideas, and new perspectives on old ideas. Computers and virtual reality aren't the first tools to change the way people absorb, debate, and relate to knowledge.

The Greeks of the 4th and 5th centuries B.C. used the theater, public debate, and storytellers as tools for thought. They were discovering and inventing a new world order of science, art, and society. The theater was a way to engage and focus the public's attention, to take them to the distant shores of Troy or the halls of Olympus while simultaneously involve them in the great philosophical debates, acted out in the emotions and decisions of dramatized events.

These carefully constructed simulations gave spectators new points of view by putting them in the shoes of people not unlike themselves who were faced with difficult decisions. The power of these simulations can be attested to by the fact that over 2000 years after their creation they're still performed and are still engaging, entertaining, and speaking to audiences about the human condition.

Not only did these simulations entertain and educate, they created a sense of community among the attendees. Men and women had gone together to a special place (the shows were held during the annual spring religious festivals) and shared a unique experience. The plays communicated and shaped the virtual community of thought among ancient Greeks. Engaging the audience's attention by immersing them in the sights and sounds of a performance, these creative simulations weren't unlike the way we use computers today, or envision using them in the not-too-distant future.

In the 1400s, the Florentine artist Giotto intuitively stumbled upon a method of projecting three-dimensional perspective onto a flat, two-dimensional canvas. This method of organizing objects and relationships upon the canvas as if there was a single point of view created a sense of depth. Within a few years Giotto's discovery was copied by all artists and became one of the foundations of art for the next 500 years.

Through all the changing styles of art, the basic assumption of 3-D perspective has been a constant. Like theater, we expect paintings to take us into another world. Even today, the notion of perspective has such a powerful grip on the consciousness of society that modern art that doesn't use perspective (cubist and abstract art, for example) has gone largely unaccepted by the general public.

In 1455, the invention of the printing press and the subsequent development of the mass-produced book changed peoples' sense of community and their relationship to knowledge. Unlike the medieval Christian era, where knowledge, as represented by the church and marketplace politics, was experienced within a group setting, books strengthened the idea of private thought and opinion, of individuality. The right to study ideas and knowledge was no longer limited to special people, places or times, or the accident of birth, but became commodities to be shared. The rise of democracy and the printing press went hand in hand.

Through reading, the experience of being immersed in a special imaginative and contemplative state of mind, similar to the absorbing engagement that good theater evoked, could be experienced alone. Writers developed the skills and techniques for debate and story-telling on the printed page to produce a sense of realism and presence in the virtual simulations they created within peoples' minds.

The printed page became a way of creating a shared community of ideas and experiences, even though the individuals might have never met. The printed book became a magic carpet ride, taking readers on journeys down rabbit holes, stranding them on desert islands, and involving them in the emotional life of fictional characters and the great intellectual debates of their times (Gulliver's Travels is one of the greatest and earliest examples).

Books were the first mass-produced commodity, a means of idea production and distribution that made other ideas and inventions possible. More than painting, music, or theater, the printed page allowed people to develop an idea, an attitude, and a state of mind that could be shared with others. Concepts became something that could be examined repeatedly, shared, and debated by everyone.

The use of perspective in art created a bias in the public for viewing images with a sense of depth. Painting was suppose to be about transporting the viewer into the presence of the scene, the painting acting as a window into another place or time. The success of books also helped fuel this hunger among the public for the experience of being somewhere else, not just in their imagination. As the industrial revolution began to unfold, new inventions and techniques began to appear that fed this hunger and allowed people to immerse themselves in new experiences.

In 1788, the Scottish painter Robert Barker painted a 360-degree view of the city of Edinburgh. He displayed the 10-foot tall canvas in a circular room 60 feet across. Viewers could enter into the center of the specially constructed room and be surrounded by the scene. He called it a *panorama*. He succeeded at providing a new level of realism because the image filled more than 180 degrees of the viewer's horizontal field of view (it would be another 150 years before Hollywood rediscovered this technique and named it Cinerama). These created environments soon became a popular form of entertainment throughout Europe and North America.

Panorama paintings

Sometimes, in order to increase the sense of realism, actual objects would be cleverly blended into the foreground of the picture so that it was difficult to tell where the real object ended and the painting began. Clever use of indirect lighting was also used to suggest light emanating from the painting.

Panoramas were created of London and of various battle scenes (see Fig. 2-1). In 1883, *The Battle of Gettysburg* was exhibited by Paul Philippoteaux in several American cities and can still be seen today at the Gettysburg National Military Park in Pennsylvania. These were the first early experiments at providing a sense of immersion in a virtual experience. Their popularity was based on the reaction of the audience to feeling that it was getting a first-hand experience of another place and time. Their weakness was that scenes were static and devoid of movement.

2-1
Panorama painting in which real objects in the foreground are "blended" into the painting to achieve additional realism.

At the end of the 19th century, the fledgling motion-picture industry quickly distracted audiences away from the static panoramas. Within a few years, they were rolled up, stored away, and mostly forgotten.

Stereoscopic pictures

In the mid 1800s, the new technology of photography became popular. For the first time, people were able to take and reproduce accurate images of real places, people, and events. Almost as soon as photography was introduced, a viewing technique was developed to further enhance the sense of realism. In 1833, Wheatstone invented the stereoscopic display, allowing individuals to use a simple device to view stereo images with a strong sense of depth (see Fig. 2-2). At its height of popularity, Wheatstone's invention could be considered the 1800s' version of a video game. Every home had to have one.

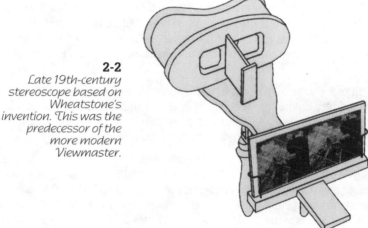

2-2
Late 19th-century stereoscope based on Wheatstone's invention. This was the predecessor of the more modern Viewmaster.

Stereoscopic images were created by either taking a picture of a scene, shifting the camera a couple of inches to the side, and taking another picture, or by using a special camera with two lens and two sets of negatives. This essentially duplicated the pair of images as seen by both eyes. When the two images were viewed so that the left eye received only the left image and the right eye only the right image, a sense of depth and realism was achieved.

This invention was further refined by David Brewster in 1844 and evolved into the mass-produced Viewmaster of the mid-1900s. Unfortunately, the stereoscopic viewers suffered from the same limitation as the panorama painting. They were both incapable of displaying moving images.

The success of the stereoscopic viewer was based on its inexpensive ability to provide an entertaining illusion of reality. It enjoyed a long reign of popularity before the increasing availability of dynamic images on film and TV proved too irresistible for consumers. Yet another entertainment form was swept aside by the growing dominance of the new visual medium of film and TV.

"Film is truth at 24 frames per second."
   —Jean-Luc Godard

Using static scenes or pictures to recreate a previous event or to provide a sense of being somewhere else was only partially successful. Within minutes the participant would have explored the visual information provided and be ready for fresh stimulation. Because visual perception focuses on movement in an image, your attention will wander when movement is missing. Realizing that you're looking at only a picture, no matter how artfully created, you quickly lose your suspension of disbelief.

Another weakness of static images is their limited ability to tell a story. It's the difference between reading a detailed paragraph describing a hilltop scene, and reading a novel about the events and personalities that shaped the scene. A medium that could not only keep your attention using moving images but also tell a complex story would have great potential.

Edison's invention of the Kinetoscope in 1889 and the first public demonstration in 1894 was the birth of that medium, although Edison didn't realize it at the time. He was primarily interested in developing a visual accompaniment for his very successful phonograph. Edison intended the Kinetoscope to become a home-entertainment machine capable of illustrating the sound from the phonograph.

The Kinetoscope was based on a loop of film, guided through a complicated series of rollers, and contained in a chest-high viewing enclosure. After depositing a nickel (initially 25 cents, until the novelty wore off), you could look through a small window on top of the device, turn a handle, and watch a three- to five-minute film (see Fig. 2-3).

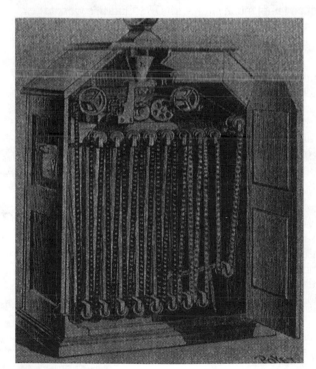

2-3
Inside look at Edison's Kinetoscope. Film is looped through a series of rollers so it can be continuously played, and a hand crank controls the speed of the film.

Almost overnight, parlors sprang up all over the country, catering to the public's demand for this new experience. Edison rejected the notion of using his device to project images for a large audience; instead, he believed that the future belonged to individual experiences.

Hollywood would prove otherwise. In 1895, two brothers, Auguste and Louis Lumiere, projected their first film (*La sortie des ouvriers de l'usine Lumiere*) to a private audience in Paris. Film historians designate this as the world's first moving picture. They called their system Cinematographe, which eventually became the name of the new medium.

The business of synthesizing reality was born. Now life could be captured on film as it occurred, historical events recreated, and fictional stories brought to life. Inexpensive to duplicate, the resulting experience could be widely distributed. Almost immediately, a rapidly expanding industry was formed around the new medium, providing audiences with new visual experiences for a fee.

"Initially the image quality was grainy and poor. The frame rate varied from 14–24 frames per second and the equipment was cumbersome and expensive. In the first few years, technologists and experimenters controlled the medium and created productions with little or no dramatic or narrative content."

—Cook, 1981 (A description of the film industry in 1896)

It's interesting to note that this depiction is equally valid of today's virtual reality industry and indicates the many parallels between these two industries.

Development of narrative

Initially, film was used to simply document the staged plays of the time. Everything was filmed from a static perspective with no camera movement. (The concept of a "camera shot" wasn't introduced until much later, with D.W. Griffith's work in 1908.) It wasn't until 1902 that Melies' film, *A trip to the Moon*, clearly exhibited the changing role of film from a documentary to a narrative role.

"One afternoon in the fall of 1896, while Melies was filming a Parisian street scene, his camera jammed in the process of recording an omnibus as it emerged from a tunnel. When he got the machine working again, a funeral hearse had replaced the omnibus, so that in projection the omnibus seemed to change into a hearse. By this accident, Melies came to recognize the possibilities for the manipulation of real time and real space inherent in the editing of exposed film. He had discovered that film need not obey the laws of empirical reality, as his predecessors had supposed, because film was in some sense a separate reality with structural laws of its own."

—David A. Cook, 1981

From this start, it would take nineteen years before the camera and editing innovations of D.W. Griffith would appear in the monumental film *The Birth of a Nation* (1915). Griffith single-handedly created most of the camera work and editing techniques that are still in use today. He revolutionized the use of film to narrate a story. He introduced the concept of the camera shot, where the camera cuts to a close-up of a scene to provide more dramatic effect or simply to allow the actors to more easily articulate emotion.

In addition, he invented the idea of cutting between different scenes of action to depict parallel events, such as a woman inside a house and the action taking place outside the building by burglars attempting to break in. Griffith rapidly cut between these parallel events and thereby created a sense of tension. These new techniques were at first regarded suspiciously by the executives of Biograph where Griffith worked. His wife, Linda Arvidson Griffith, reported the following encounter:

"When Mr. Griffith suggested a scene showing Annie Lee waiting for her husband's return to be followed by a scene of Enoch cast away on a desert island, it was altogether distracting.

'How can you tell a story jumping about like that? The people won't know what it's about.'

'Well,' said Mr. Griffith, 'doesn't Dickens write that way?'

'Yes, but that's Dickens; that's novel writing; that's different.'

'Oh, not so much, these are picture stories; not so different.' "

—Linda A. Griffith, 1969

Griffith exploited the freedom of the new medium and explored its many possibilities. He's considered perhaps the greatest cinematic genius in history. Today, similar geniuses are among us—those who are conceptualizing how the new medium of virtual reality can be used as a medium of expression. What new techniques will they invent? What revolutions will they lead?

During the early 1900s, technology kept refining the cinematic experience. Sound made its debut in 1923 as the first sound-on-film Phonofilm was shown in New York City. For the first time since the Kinetoscope, sound was synchronized to the film action. The success of Warner Brothers' *The Jazz Singer* (1927), signaled the end of the silent era and ushered in "the talkies."

Within two years almost all American theaters had converted to sound at the staggering cost of $300 million dollars (more than several billion in today's dollars), and audiences began pouring into theaters. Sound's popularity ensured the survival of the major studios during the difficult years of the Depression.

Right on its heel, the three-color Technicolor process was introduced in 1932, but the difficulties and expense of working with it limited its use to major features. By 1946, two-thirds of the entire U.S. population (100 million people) went to the cinema weekly. It became a fixture in every community.

People went there to get news, learn about the world, be entertained, and escape to exotic locations. Viewers imagined themselves through the eyes of their favorite actors and actresses, vicariously experiencing what transpired on the silver screen. For them, film represented more than just photons striking a screen; it became part of their lives. The film industry was never again to enjoy such immense popularity.

From Edison's first flickering images, the desire to improve the cinematic experience led to increasing levels of realism. The introduction of color, multi-channel sound, wider screens, and even stereoscopic images (more commonly known as 3-D), all contributed to enhancing the illusion of reality.

Initially, the film industry treated many of these technological advancements as mere gimmicks designed to lure people into the theater. As the novelty wore off, however, a greater reliance on storytelling occurred and the emphasis shifted from technology to content. Along the way, some of the gimmicks that couldn't contribute to the story were dropped (such as 3-D effects).

Today, most virtual experiences are also based on gimmicks. As the entertainment industry begins to recognize the enormous potential of cyberspace experiences, there will probably be a proliferation of gimmicks until storytellers master the new art. It might take a few years, but it should be worth waiting for.

Television

Technology once again provided a new medium (and the cinema's great rival), as regular broadcasts of television signals began in 1941. It's interesting to compare the introduction of television with the introduction of virtual experiences. Here was a technology fascinating to view, though limited in content and image quality. Crowds formed wherever it was initially demonstrated. Ideas abounded about possible applications, but predictions fell far short of actual uses. Sound familiar?

Television provided a mass distribution system bringing much of the impact of movies into everyone's home. No longer did people have to go to the theater—now the theater was delivered to the home. Much as VCRs later drew viewers away from network broadcasting, television sets drew people away from the movies.

In addition, television could do what movies could never do; it could put viewers on the scene live, or in *real time*. It introduced the concept of *telepresence*, the sense of being there through the eyes of the camera. While the 1991 war in the Persian Gulf dramatizes this effect, it was the Kennedy assassination that first truly drove this point home as the entire nation participated in the disaster and mourning.

Over the years, television's potential for escapism and distortion of the nation's moral fabric has been debated; much as today, similar debates swirl over the role of virtual reality. Few adults are fully comfortable with the role television plays in our lives. Fifty years after its introduction, we're still trying to understand the impact and influence of television on our lives.

Cinerama

Using television and film to create a sense of realism had one important drawback; the audience felt as if they were watching the action through a large window or frame. All the drama was out there beyond the window; nothing ventured inside the theater. The audience was isolated from directly experiencing the events shown on the screen. 3-D movies were marginally successful at breaking through this barrier and bringing the action inside, but they didn't succeed because they were too gimmicky.

To allow a more direct experience, a larger image would have to be captured and displayed so that it would fill the audience's entire field of view. Our eyes can see about 180 degrees horizontally and about 150 degrees vertically. Depending on where someone sits in a theater, a 35mm film screen could be as small as 50 degrees horizontally and 38 degrees vertically. This is about 5 percent of our visual field. Television is much worse. Various approaches were tried to expand the view, and in the early 1950s Fred Waller convinced producer Mike Todd to invest $10 million in a new process called Cinerama (see Fig. 2-4).

Three synchronized 35mm film cameras recorded each scene from slightly different views. In the theater, three projectors displayed the separate images onto a specially built screen that curved around the audience and provided almost an entire 180 degrees of horizontal view. The image was now three times as wide and nearly twice as tall (it used a taller film format). With six times the visual image and six-track stereophonic sound, it dramatically increased the perception of experiencing reality rather than looking through a window.

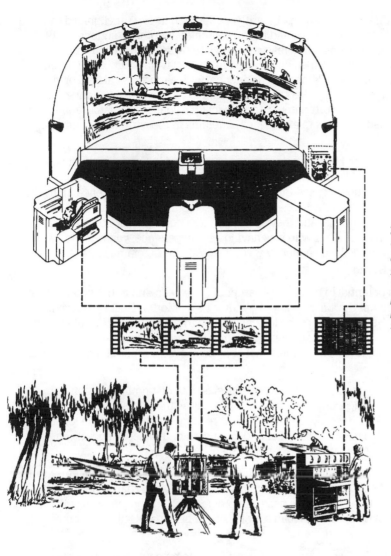

2-4
Cinerama illustration depicting the use of three separate cameras to record the action which is later played back by three film projectors onto a very wide screen.

Narrative movies such as *How the West was Won* (1962), and *The Wonderful World of the Brother's Grimm* (1962) were shot using this process. Though popular, the cost of outfitting theaters and difficulties in synchronizing and producing films using three cameras instead of one proved too formidable. *How the West was Won*, for example, required the services of three directors (John Ford, Henry Hathaway, and George Marshall) and four cinematographers, and cost over $14 million to shoot.

At its height of popularity, only one hundred theaters in the world were equipped to show Cinerama films. After 1963, movies were no longer produced using the Cinerama format, but it's credited with bringing audiences back to cinemas in numbers unseen since 1946. It proved that audiences would respond to experiences that had a greater sense of presence—of "being there."

Hollywood, threatened by the popularity of television in 1950, recognized the value of the wide-screen experience and began searching for other solutions. In 1953, simpler processes such as Cinemascope and later 70mm Panavision were developed for the wide screen and are still in use today (in addition to Omnimax, which is the ultimate wide-screen experience, with almost a total field of view horizontally and vertically). People were willing to pay for the experience of being immersed in a movie. Fortunately, Morton Heilig (a young cinematographer from Hollywood), had a chance to experience Cinerama in the early 1950s prior to its demise.

"I became fascinated by Cinerama after reading about it. I was already involved with cameras and film and the technological influences in film. On a visit back to New York I went down to see Cinerama. This was a pivotal experience in my life. The narrator described the scene, the curtain swept back, revealing a screen four times bigger than normal and they showed a roller coaster ride. You no longer identified with some actor who was having your experience, you had the experience yourself. I subsequently went to see all the Cinerama films."

—**Morton Heilig**

Sensorama

Realizing its potential to reduce the barrier of the screen and to transport the audience through the window into the movie itself, Morton Heilig proposed a radical idea. He decided that the logical future of the film industry would be that of supplying highly realistic experiences to large audiences. His goal was the complete elimination of all barriers that kept people from accepting the cinematic illusion.

Methodically, he studied the sensory signals used to distinguish illusion from reality. He isolated sight, sound, touch, and smell as the primary senses needed for stimulation. Next, he analyzed what current technology could provide for sensory stimulation. This resulted in a clear understanding of the pieces missing to complete his concept of the "experience theater."

Stereophonic sound and stereoscopic images were already commercially available. If Heilig could combine them with a full field of view better than Cinerama, and figure out how to stimulate the nose and provide tactile sensations, his goal would be achieved. With little more than simple faith in his ideas, Heilig attempted to revolutionize Hollywood.

Unfortunately, Hollywood wasn't listening. Despite repeated attempts to communicate his call to revolution, he didn't find any support in the film industry. After moving to Mexico in 1954 and receiving financial backing for some initial research, his backer was killed in an accident, forcing Heilig to return to New York.

By 1960 he and a partner created a personal version of the experience theater as a way to demonstrate his concepts. Similar to an arcade machine, it was called Sensorama (shown in Fig. 2-5). It was outfitted with handlebars, a binocular-like viewing device, a vibrating seat, and small vents that could blow air when commanded. In addition, stereophonic speakers were mounted near the ears, and close to the nose, a device for generating odors specific to the events viewed stereoscopically on film.

One of the recorded "experiences" was a motorcycle ride through Brooklyn. The seat vibrated, you felt the wind against your face, and you even smelled different

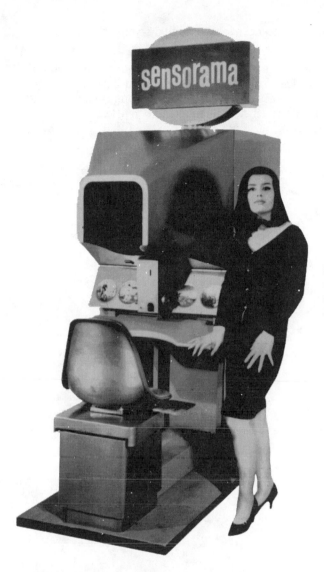

2-5
*Early promotional picture
depicting one of the
Sensorama prototypes.*

odors as you passed along the street—a full sensory experience that hasn't been duplicated since, even with today's $250,000 computerized virtual experiences.

Of course, you couldn't direct the motorcycle to turn down your favorite street (it wasn't interactive), but you received a very direct experience as a passive observer. This was the logical evolution in the search for realistic, immersive experiences, but the film industry didn't realize it.

They also had problems with the economics of Heilig's ideas. Films absorb very high production values that either must be amortized over time or across a mass market to get the necessary return on investment. Movies are very expensive to produce, but relatively easy to reproduce and distribute. And they can be experienced by large groups so that costs can be spread out over repeated viewings by large audiences. Heilig's stand-alone ride would require thousands of "rides" to pay back its cost, or otherwise the cost of each ride would be prohibitively expensive.

Of course, Hollywood would also miss the significance of the video-game craze of the 1980s and the multi-billion dollar revenues it generated. Video games provided personal entertainment through dedicated hardware. The film industry is one of few that is successful despite spending an insignificant amount on research and development on new technologies.

After a few more unsuccessful attempts at marketing Sensorama and the development of another prototype for a different backer, Heilig had to accept the inability of the industry to recognize Sensorama's potential. Finally, the first cyberspace machine was covered up and rolled away to storage. Things could have turned out quite a bit different.

Pioneers in cyberspace

" '. . . Computers are a lot worse than real life. You have to be hit over the head with that before you realize how true it is.'

'Why bother, then?' [Brand] asked. 'Why not stick with real life?' Strassman didn't hesitate: 'Because you can't automate real life. I can't get this shrimp to swim if I draw it on real paper with a real brush.'

Junior deities, we want to be. Reality is mostly given. Virtual reality is creatable."

—Stewart Brand, *The Media Lab*

As Morton Heilig struggled to convince a reluctant entertainment business to back his ideas, the first minicomputer based on transistors rather than tubes became available in 1960. The Digital Equipment Corporation's (DEC) PDP-1 was the harbinger of the technology that would, more than 25 years later, succeed at popularizing virtual experiences where Sensorama failed.

The PDP-1 represented a revolution in computer affordability and performance. Based on the new silicon technology, computers began spreading out to universities and research institutes across America.

Interacting with these early computers was difficult because they weren't designed from a user point of view. Card-punch and batch processing required the user to adapt to the needs of the computer instead of the other way around. Time sharing and interactive video screens didn't exist in 1960 and it would be almost twenty years before the first personal computer would appear. Using one of these early computers was a frustrating experience—there had to be a better way.

In the early 1950s, an engineer in Mountain View, California, Douglas Engelbart, decided to figure out a way to turn computers into a powerful problem-solving tool that anyone could use. With a background in working with radar systems for the Navy, Engelbart realized that video screens could be used instead of paper to display the computer's output.

His next breakthrough was realizing that they could also be used to control the computer, to provide it with input. This was a revolutionary idea, given that both video screens and computers were relatively rare and inaccessible.

Engelbart spent the next several years organizing his thoughts and trying to gain access to the few computers available at the time. While working at SRI in Menlo Park in the mid 1960s, the Advanced Research Projects Agency (ARPA, forerunner to DARPA and sponsored by the US Defense Department) provided funding for Engelbart to pursue his ideas.

He finally had the resources to build the mind augmentation devices he had been dreaming of for the last decade. His lab, the Augmentation Research Center (ARC) was responsible for some of the key computer-human interface developments that we use today.

In 1968, he gave an amazing demonstration at the Fall Joint Computer Conference. Using a crude pointing device (the first mouse), he selected a document to read from an iconic representation on a video display. This opened up and displayed the contents of the document on the screen. Still using the mouse, he cut and pasted a section of text elsewhere in the document. Remember, almost everyone used punched cards to talk to computers at the time. This was a radically new way to use computers. Alan Kay had this to say about the performance:

"We thought of Douglas as Moses opening the Red Sea. You know he was like a biblical prophet . . . they were actually doing the kinds of things that people still dream about today . . . I think of it as the vision of what we today call personal computing or desktop computing."
—Alan Kay (Palfreman and Swade, 1991)

Not only did Engelbart invent word processing, but he also demonstrated the rudiments of a hypertext environment. This was a real breakthrough—now people could interact with computers in a more direct and natural way. While Cinerama and Sensorama struggled to break down barriers in the film experience, Engelbart was breaking down the same barriers with computers.

The ultimate display

Back on the East coast, Ivan Sutherland was also busy changing the way people interacted with computers. He realized the enormous importance of getting computers to conform to the way people worked and thought, instead of the people conforming to computers. Credited with being the "father of computer graphics" by the industry he helped found, he pioneered many of the basic methods of using computers to represent 2-D and 3-D images.

His Sketchpad program in 1962 demonstrated the use of a light pen to draw images on a computer screen, and was the precursor to the multi-billion dollar computer-aided design (CAD) industry of today. In 1965, Sutherland published an article entitled *The Ultimate Display*, in which he described the following:

"We live in a physical world whose properties we have come to know well through long familiarity. We sense an involvement with this physical world which gives us the ability to predict its properties well. For example, we can predict where objects will fall, how well-known shapes look from other angles, and how much force is required to push objects against friction. We lack corresponding familiarity with the forces on charged particles, forces in non-uniform fields, the effects of nonprojective geometric transformations, and high-inertia, low-friction motion. A display connected to a digital computer gives us a chance to gain familiarity with concepts not realizable in the physical world. It is a looking glass into a mathematical wonderland."

—Ivan Sutherland, 1965

Another example of Sutherland's creativity was the development of the first computer-based head-mounted display (HMD) in 1966 at the MIT Lincoln Laboratory and later at the University of Utah. He had to invent from scratch most of the technology that twenty years later NASA would use to assemble the modern virtual environment.

Sutherland's head-mounted display earned the nickname *the sword of Damocles* due to the mass of hardware that was supported from the ceiling above the user's head. The weight of the HMD was too much to bear without some additional support. A mechanical apparatus determined where the viewer was looking and monoscopic wire-frame images were generated using two small cathode ray tubes (CRTs) mounted alongside each ear.

The sword of Damocles

Optics focused the image onto half-silvered mirrors placed directly in front of the eyes. The mirrors allowed the computer-generated images to overlay the view of the world (in contrast, most of today's VR systems obscure the view of the outside world). Users of the system viewed a wire-frame cube floating in space in the middle of the lab. By moving their head around they could see different aspects of the glowing cube and determine its size and placement (see Fig. 3-1).

When Sutherland joined the University of Utah, he continued to refine the hardware and software until, in 1970, the first fully functional HMD was completed. His final system consisted of several hardware accelerators to improve the performance of the graphics system and the generation of stereoscopic images instead of monoscopic.

In general terms, there's no difference between this system and the system that was to emerge from NASA Ames almost twenty years later. The long search for a synthesized reality had finally lead to a system capable of generating virtual objects. Finally, the visions of Sutherland and Engelbart were realized. The barrier between the computer and the user had finally been eliminated; the user was now inside the computer.

During World War II, the military discovered the value of training pilots in flight simulators. A pilot's chances of coming back from a mission jumped up to 95 percent if he had made it through his first five missions. Thus, anything that increased their chances of surviving those first missions was critical to saving his life.

Early reality simulators

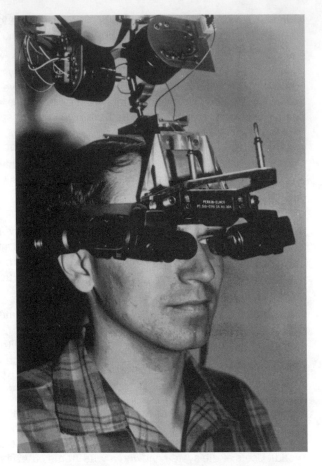

3-1
*Sutherland's head-
mounted display worn by
Donald L. Vickers at the
University of Utah.*

As early as 1929, the Link corporation was building flight simulators. A full-sized mock-up of a fighter cockpit was constructed and mounted on a motion platform. The cockpit physically pitched, rolled, and yawed based on the pilot's actions. Results from the simple Link trainer showed that a pilot's training could be successfully simulated on an earth-bound platform.

Decades later, as aviation became more complex, spending thousands of dollars on a flight simulator that saved millions of dollars in operating a real fighter or replacing one lost made sense. These economics were the driving force behind an entire industry committed to the realistic simulation of airplanes, helicopters, tanks, and even ships.

Early simulators had one major limitation. Real-time visual feedback was impossible. The pilot couldn't view the outside world or watch it change by moving the control stick. Without visual feedback, training was limited to instrument flying.

This all changed in the early 1950s, as commercial video cameras became available. Cameras were mounted on movable platforms suspended over scale models of airports. Motion of the camera platform was controlled by the simulator pilot. If the pilot pulled back on the control stick, the camera tilted back, projecting a new image on the pilot's front window. The camera "flew" over the model, controlled by the pilot.

This improvement in the reality increased the simulation's effectiveness. Soon, multiple cameras were combined to project additional perspectives, allowing left and right views along with forward views. Over the next twenty years, video cameras continued to shrink in size as models grew in complexity. The advent of sophisticated computers capable of generating similar images slowly replaced the cameras and models. However, this technique is still widely used in movies by Hollywood's special-effects wizards.

While working on the first electronic head-mounted display, Ivan Sutherland recognized the potential for computers to generate the images for the flight simulators instead of video cameras and scale models. Sutherland teamed up with David Evans in 1968 to create electronic "scene generators." Later that year, they formed *Evans and Sutherland* to sell these systems.

Scene generators

Instead of constructing scale models from paint, foam, and glue, the computer constructed images using stored data. Any 3-D object could be digitized and entered into the computer. For example, an airport could be represented as a large number of 3-D points with lines connecting each point. After a series of calculations, a view from any vantage point could be constructed.

Custom hardware accelerated the calculations so that each scene was drawn in a fraction of a second, in less time than you can blink. This process of calculating and drawing images is called *rendering*. A rapid sequence of scenes rendered by the computer would appear movie-like to the pilot. Controlling the computer like a movable camera platform created the same sense of flying around the model.

The number of scenes rendered in a fixed amount of time is called the *update rate*, and is measured in frames per second (fps) or hertz (Hz). Early scene generators (circa 1973) achieved around 20 fps with simple 3-D models (200–400 polygons). Studies showed that pilot training performance suffered below this update rate.

Scene complexity is the critical factor controlling update rates. A 3-D image of a cube might be drawn at 60 fps, but a 3-D image of an airport, with buildings, hangars, and other aircraft might bring a computer to its knees—drawing only a single frame every second. With complexity and speed, a balance must be struck. As computers become faster, either model complexity or update rates can increase, but rarely both. This constant tension won't be resolved soon.

One of the first flight simulators to use computers was built by General Electric Company's Electronics Laboratory for the Navy in 1972. Their Advanced Development Model was used as an instrument to measure the effectiveness of computer-generated images for pilot training. Consisting of three independent rendering channels, images were projected onto three screens that surrounded the physical mockup of the cockpit. This provided the pilot with a realistic 180-degree field of view (see Fig. 3-2).

This early simulator revealed many of the demands of simulating reality. The Navy discovered that the complexity of a scene (determined by the number of polygons) and texturing (each polygon is "painted" with an image) was crucial in providing adequate velocity and altitude cues for line ups and landings on both airfields and

3-2
The Advanced Development Model (ADM), one of the first flight simulators using computer generated graphics.

aircraft carriers. The Advanced Development Model also showed that simulation of haze significantly contributed to the realism of the experience. Generally, the more realistic the image, the better the training.

Just to prove that there's an exception to any rule, they also noticed that pilots were having difficulties orienting themselves with respect to the featureless surface of the ocean. Their solution was to draw a checkerboard pattern on it to provide additional perspective cues—a good example of how decreasing realism can sometimes improve training effectiveness.

As early as 1979, the military was experimenting with head-mounted displays. If an effective one could be built, it could significantly reduce the expense and physical size of the simulation system. By projecting the image directly into the pilot's eyes, bulky screens and projection systems could be eliminated.

One of the first of these, McDonnell Douglas's VITAL helmet (see Fig. 3-3), used an electromagnetic head tracker to sense where the pilot was looking. Dual monochromatic cathode ray tubes were mounted next to the pilot's ears, projecting the image onto beam splitters in front of the pilot's eyes.

This allowed the pilot to view and manipulate mechanical controls in the cockpit, while seeing the computer-generated image of the outside world. Problems with bulky headgear and the unnaturalness of viewing through beam-splitters, however, limited the acceptance of these early head-mounted displays.

For over twenty years, America's armed forces have been manufacturing realities in order to improve the effectiveness of their personnel. It has proven conclusively the usefulness and cost-effectiveness of simulation training. In addition, these same simulators have become standard training tools for commercial aircraft. Better qualified pilots mean safer planes.

Without the initial investment by NASA and the Defense Department, many of these technologies would have taken much longer to evolve. It's likely that virtual reality could not exist in its present form without this initial investment. It's one of many valuable spin-offs of military research.

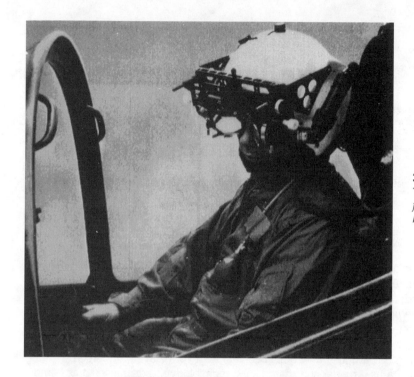

3-3
VITAL helmet, one of the first commercially available head-mounted displays.

At the same time Sutherland was donning his new head-mounted display at the University of Utah, Myron Krueger was experimenting with combining computers and video systems to create *artificial realities* (a term he later coined to describe this new experience) at the University of Wisconsin.

Krueger had the same driving passion as Engelbart and others to use computers to establish natural dialogues with people. The computer would be taught about people instead of people having to learn the computer. Krueger established simple interactive demonstrations that allowed users to walk up and immediately start interacting with computer-generated images.

In his most famous work, *VIDEOPLACE* (1976), the user's body image is captured by a video camera in real time and represented as a silhouette on a large video projection screen in a darkened room. It's like watching your shadow projected on a video screen. Using image processing techniques to detect edges of the silhouette, users can "finger paint" by holding up a finger and then moving it. A trail of colored paint will appear on the video screen following the movements of the finger. Holding up five fingers erases the image.

In addition, an animated creature named CRITTER can be introduced into the image (see Fig. 3-4). This synthesized being appears to chase your image and attempts to climb your silhouette to reach the top of your head. CRITTER can also be directed to dangle from a finger where an abrupt movement will cause it to fall to the bottom of the screen.

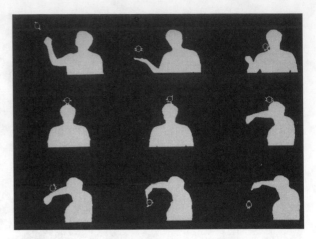

3-4
Sequence of frames showing Myron Krueger's CRITTER intereacting with the outline of the participant.

Krueger was doing something new here. He had changed the definition of what a computer could do and how it interacted with people. The computer had almost disappeared, to be replaced with a friendly and benign sprite. Krueger's mix of video image processing and computer graphics took him into a new realm where the computer allowed a new form of artistic expression in the form of these artificial realities. He pioneered a unique form of nonintrusive virtual environments. It wasn't necessary for the participants to don special clothing or wear a cumbersome viewing apparatus (Krueger considered such technology but dismissed it as being too intrusive).

Artificial reality has come to represent an experience similar to but different than what is commonly called virtual reality. We've coined the term *projected reality* to help differentiate the two approaches. In Krueger's application, you see yourself projected into the action happening on a screen instead of directly experiencing yourself in an environment. This is a crucial difference.

In VIDEOPLACE and Krueger's related efforts, participants are aware that they're in a darkened room and interacting with computers through a "window" in front of them. Virtual reality, on the other hand, like Sensorama and Sutherland's head-mounted display, takes you through this window and into a new experience.

Both intrusive and nonintrusive technologies will continue to develop and hopefully combine to provide us with the best of both worlds. Krueger makes an important point about the influence of computers and our interaction with them in a recent essay about future interfaces:

"When judging user interfaces, our usual standard of goodness is the efficiency with which one can progress from point A to point B using the application. At some point we must recognize that our lives are spent in between. As more of our commercial and personal transactions are accomplished through computers, the quality of the experience provided by the computer interface has bearing on the quality of life itself. Therefore, the aesthetics of interaction will be as important as the efficiency."
—Krueger, 1991

One way to improve the quality of our interaction with computers is to learn Hollywood's techniques of entertainment. Hollywood understands realism and narrative—what it takes to involve the audience and create compelling experiences. Hollywood has had almost 100 years to learn about keeping the audience's attention and providing a pleasant experience. No one ever had to go back to the movies once the novelty wore off; the movies had to create attractive experiences to keep bringing users back. Of course, this need to appeal to the masses can lead to mediocrity, the rule of the lowest common denominator.

If Hollywood understands narrative and realism, computer people understand interactivity. They know how to use computers to create a form of conversation with the user; exchanging data and responding back and forth. Computer people have traditionally not worried much about realism or the attractiveness of screens, and users have been compelled to use computers to get particular tasks done. However, the computer industry can learn from the movie moguls. And in turn, film makers can learn from computer people.

Interaction with computers became a life or death experience for pilots in the 1970s, as the capabilities of advanced jet fighters began to exceed that of the humans to control them. Imagine the cognitive hurdle of learning the F15. It has nine different buttons on the control stick and seven more on the throttle. In the stress and confusion of battle, pilots always had to pick the correct one. Mistakes could be fatal.

Super cockpit

As anyone who has peeked into the cockpit of a modern airplane can attest, the complexity and quantity of dials, gauges, and switches is staggering. Fighter pilots must manage this bewildering barrage of information even as they suffer from brief blackouts during high-G turns. Realizing the need to manage the quantity of information presented to pilots, the United States Air Force started looking for new technologies and research candidates.

With a background in creating visual displays for the military since 1966 and extensive research in the field of visual perception, Thomas Furness III had the experience the Air Force needed. After years of fighting for funding, Furness finally got the go-ahead to prototype a state-of-the-art control system at Wright-Patterson Air Force Base in Ohio. In 1982, he demonstrated a working model of the Visually Coupled Airborne Systems Simulator, or VCASS (see Fig. 3-5). It resembled Darth Vader's helmet in the movie Star Wars. Test pilots wore the oversized helmet and sat in a cockpit mockup.

Instead of a normal view, pilots saw only an abstract or symbolic representation of the world outside (see Fig. 3-6). These synthetic images were projected onto screens in the helmet, masking off the view outside. Seeing only symbolic representations of landmarks, flight paths, and potential hazards reduced the distraction caused by an overload of visual information.

We use the same principle when we pull a map instead of an aerial photograph out of the glove box of a car. Symbolic information on the map is much easier to decipher than detailed aerial pictures. Information is reduced to the minimum that's necessary for achieving a goal, navigation in this case.

The VCASS used a 6D position and orientation tracker, from a company called Polhemus, to monitor where the pilot was looking. Electromagnetic pulses, generated by a source, were picked up by a small sensor mounted on the helmet.

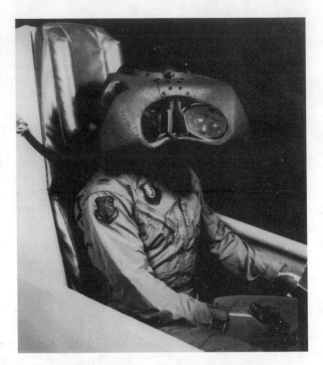

3-5
Pilot wearing "Darth Vader" helmet as part of the Super Cockpit project directed by Tom Furness.

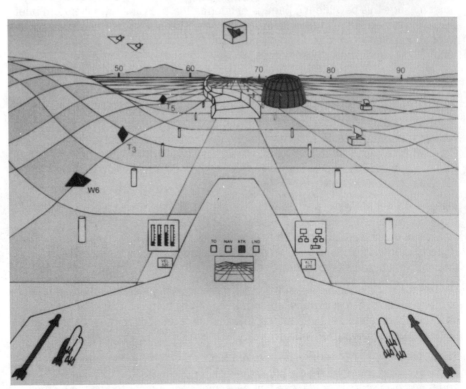

3-6
Super Cockpit view in which an abstract world is generated to reduce and simplify information presented to the pilot.

Processing the signal yielded an accurate reading of the current position and orientation of the helmet. Using this information, the computer rendered the appropriate view. By obscuring images from outside the cockpit, immersion in a symbolic world was achieved.

Technology and funding allowed Furness to render more complex images than Sutherland's simple wire-frame cubes. In addition, custom 1-inch diameter CRTs with 2000 scan lines projected the images, almost four times the resolution of a typical TV set. Virtual environments could be viewed in much more detail than anything commercially available even today.

The Air Force saw enough promise in VCASS that a second phase was funded, known as Super Cockpit. An article in *Air & Space* magazine described how future pilots would use this technology:

"When he climbed into his F-16SC, the young fighter jock of 1998 simply plugged in his helmet and flipped down his visor to activate his Super Cockpit system. The virtual world he saw exactly mimicked the world outside. Salient terrain features were outlined and rendered in three dimensions by the two tiny cathode ray tubes focused at his personal viewing distance. Using voice commands, the pilot told the associate to start the engine and run through the checklist . . .

Once he was airborne, solid clouds obscured everything outside the canopy. But inside the helmet, the pilot 'saw' the horizon and terrain clearly, as if it were a clear day. His compass heading was displayed as a large band of numbers on the horizon line, his projected flight path a shimmering highway leading out toward infinity.

A faint whine above and behind him to the left told the pilot even before the associate announced it that his "enemy" . . . was closing in . . ."
  —Thompson, 1987

By rethinking the entire process of flying a jet fighter, Furness created a powerful yet natural method of interacting and controlling an aircraft's complex machinery His tools were the computer and the head-mounted display. They allowed him to construct a virtual world that gathered the storm of navigation, radar, weapons, and flight-control data into a single manageable form. Symbolic representations of the outside world and sensor data provided a filtered view of reality, thus simplifying the operation of the aircraft.

VCASS, one of the most advanced simulators developed, demonstrated the effectiveness of virtual reality techniques. Furness joined Engelbart, Sutherland, and Krueger in tearing down the barrier separating computers from their users. Removing this barrier allowed pilots to enter a strange new world carved out of the silicon of the computer. Radar became their eyes and ears, servos and electromechanical linkages their muscles, and the plane obeyed their spoken commands. Flying would never be the same.

So far, researchers probing the man-machine interface had focused primarily on the simulation of sights and sounds. From Sutherland's initial experiments with head-mounted-displays, Krueger's playful interaction using video cameras and projection systems, and Furness's integrated HMD and 3-D sound environment, all three researchers explored the visual and audio dimensions of the human perceptual system. Not since Heilig and his Sensorama had anyone focused much attention on recreating tactile or force-feedback cues.

Reach out & touch with UNC

Even without sight, our sense of touch allows us to construct a detailed model of the world around us. The roughness of concrete, the smoothness of glass, and the pliability of rubber communicate detailed cues about our environment. Theoretically, computers could create a virtual world using tactile feedback just as they had with sights and sounds. Frederick Brooks, at the University of North Carolina (UNC) set out to chart this unexplored territory.

Ivan Sutherland's vision, defined in his 1965 paper "The Ultimate Display," became the basis for Brooks' research in the early 1970s. Realizing that little work was being done with force or tactile feedback, he decided to pursue combining computer graphics to force feedback devices. He not only agreed with Sutherland and Engelbart that computers could be mind- or intelligence-amplification devices; he set out to show how it could be done.

One early project by Brooks, called GROPE-II, proposed a unique molecular docking tool for chemists. Detecting allowable and forbidden docking sites between a drug and a protein or nucleic acid is crucial in designing effective drugs. Because both drug and nucleic acid molecules are complex 3-D structures, locating effective docking sites is a daunting task.

Imagine two complex tinker-toy structures two to three feet high. Your job is to manipulate each model, examining how well a knob or groove on one model docks with those on another. There might be hundreds of potential sites to test. Brooks wanted to create a tool capable of simulating the physical feel of docking a molecule. He reasoned that chemists would be much more effective if they could get their hands on a molecule and actually feel the tug and pull of docking forces.

Tinker-toy representations of two molecules could be rendered by the computer. Chemists could then use a special device to grab one of the molecules and attempt to dock it with the other. An Argonne remote manipulator (ARM) was modified for this purpose. Originally used for handling radioactive materials, they were operated by a mechanical hand-grip that controlled a remote robotic arm.

UNC acquired a surplus ARM and modified it for their purposes by adding extra motors to resist the motion of moving the hand-grip. Controlled by a computer, the ARM exerted physical force against the operator's hand.

After assembling a system in 1971, Brooks and his students were disappointed to learn that available computer technology wasn't up to the task. They couldn't simulate anything more complex than simple building blocks, let alone the intricacies of molecular docking. So the GROPE-II system was moved into storage, keeping a lonely vigil until the arrival of more powerful computers.

GROPE-III It wasn't until 1986 that computing power had increased sufficiently to justify dusting off the system and having another go at the problem. A simulation of a drug with over 1500 atoms and a protein of 21 atoms was modeled on the new GROPE-III system.

Wearing polarized eyeglasses, the chemist viewed a stereoscopic image of the molecules. This gave her a sense of depth as she tried to manipulate the molecule using the ARM, (shown in Fig. 3-7). Even with one hundred times the computing power of the original GROPE-II, the simulation was so complex that it took a third of a second to render each image (3 fps). This resulted in jerky, noncontinuous

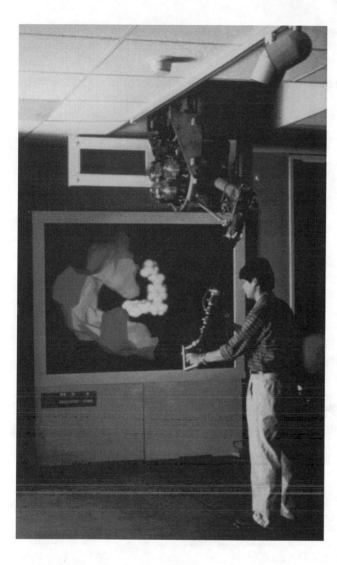

3-7
UNC's Grope III system allows you to "feel" the forces involved in finding the appropriate docking site between two molecules.

motion. For realistic modeling, closer to twenty frames per second would be required.

Despite the limited performance, Brooks' researchers learned that the system could still be effective for studying docking problems. By reducing the complexity of the model, they increased the update rate to ten frames per second.

Now docking the model felt like holding a six-inch bar magnet in your hand and moving it closer to an identical magnet fixed in place. Identically charged surfaces repelled each other, pushing your hand away. Oppositely charged surfaces attracted, pulling your hand closer. You could feel the force field surrounding the molecules.

At UNC, chemists could feel forces impossible to directly experience without the aid of the computer. The researchers also noted an important warning in their 1988 paper: "Unlike a computer system, the manipulator arms, if used improperly, have the physical capability of destroying themselves and their environment. Therefore, follow the instructions carefully and exactly."

Computers can generate incorrect images or sounds without harming the operator. However, incorrect forces in a system like GROPE could have unhealthy consequences.

Chemists weren't the only ones to have their minds amplified at UNC. Architects were also among the chosen few. For centuries, they had struggled with communicating their vision to those around them. Using scale models and perspective drawings helped, but were inflexible. If the customer wanted changes, the model would have to be rebuilt or the drawing redone. This was both expensive and time-consuming. Architects and their clients would benefit tremendously if they had a tool that allowed them to visit the design and walk around it before it was even constructed.

Computer-simulated architecture

In the mid '80s, UNC decided to construct a new multimillion dollar building called Sitterson Hall. This was to be the new home of Brooks' group of researchers. As they would be spending many hours within its walls, the researchers were very interested in the building's design. They decided to create a simulation of the structure using the technology they had spent years developing.

With blueprints as a guide, they modeled the structure in 3-D using the computer instead of building a scale model in foam or wood. Using a powerful graphics computer, they were able to position the viewpoint anywhere in the model and quickly render the scene. By controlling the direction and speed of the viewpoint, they were able to generate a consecutive series of images of the interior or exterior.

It was like watching a film that someone had shot while walking down a hallway of the yet-to-be constructed building. But, unlike a movie, you could interactively decide which hallway or room to explore. No limits were imposed on where you might wander.

Taking this a step further, they hooked up a treadmill and movable handlebars to the computer. This allowed you to physically walk down hallways while steering yourself by turning the handlebars. The image of the hallway was projected on a screen in front of you, although in later demonstrations they used a simple head-mounted device based on LCD screens.

The experience was realistic enough that they determined that a certain partition in the lobby caused a cramped feeling. Once the architects experienced the simulation, they agreed and the partition was moved.

This computer simulation provided valuable knowledge that was then used to improve the environment. Architects could now directly experience their design and improve upon it based on what they learned from their virtual explorations. Clients exposed to the simulation could provide valuable feedback long before the first concrete was poured. Architecture, perhaps more than any other field, is poised to reap the benefits of virtual reality.

UNC's research through the mid-1980s explored the boundaries of force-feedback simulations. They proved the potential for virtual environments to provide useful tools for both chemists and architects. Much of this work took advantage of the growing sophistication and power of computer systems. In fact, without the order-of-magnitude increase in computing power that was occurring every four to five years, UNC researchers couldn't have achieved what they did.

By the mid-1980s, all the important components of today's virtual reality systems existed in one form or another, awaiting an inventive mind to bring all the pieces together and the exploration of virtual worlds to begin in earnest.

In 1981, Michael McGreevy, who was studying for a Ph.D. in cognitive engineering, and Dr. Stephen Ellis, a cognitive scientist, began a program of research in spatial information transfer at NASA Ames, emphasizing the interpretation of 3-D displays. Aware of the pioneering work by Sutherland and Furness in using head-mounted displays, McGreevy put forth a proposal in 1984 to craft a similar system for NASA called a *virtual workstation*.

Putting it all together at NASA

Based on the ideas and applications mentioned in the report, McGreevy obtained a small amount of seed money ($10,000) from division management to build a prototype display system. He had followed with interest the work done at Wright-Patterson Air Force Base by Thomas Furness III on the state-of-the-art VCASS for pilots.

VCASS had the necessary qualities of high resolution and the ability to quickly render complex images that McGreevy needed to pursue his research in the simulation of virtual environments. But VCASS had one problem: it would cost a million dollars just for the helmet. This was a limitation that overshadowed the system's qualities. McGreevy would simply have to build his own.

The most expensive part of the VCASS helmet was the use of custom CRTs that generated the high-resolution images seen by the pilot. If these could be replaced with a less expensive display and combined with special lenses that allowed a much wider field of view, McGreevy would have his helmet. He sought the help of contractors Jim Humphries, Saim Eriskin, and Joe Deardon to develop his low-cost alternative to VCASS.

Fortunately, a consumer product had recently appeared on the scene that solved their most important problem—the need for a small inexpensive display that could be worn on the head. Black-and-white hand-held TVs, based on LCD technology (Sony called theirs a "Watchman") had recently become available. A quick trip to Radio Shack netted two such devices. The early LCD displays had limited resolution of 100×100 pixels (contrasted to the millions of pixels in the VCASS displays), but they were a start and the price was right.

Next, the LCD displays were mounted on a frame similar to a scuba mask that was then strapped onto your face. Special optics in front of the displays focused and expanded the image so it could be viewed without effort. McGreevy dubbed the odd-looking device the Virtual Visual Environment Display (VIVED, pronounced *vivid*). It was the only $2000 head-mounted display on the planet.

To test their novel display, they needed to create independent left and right eye images, or stereo pairs. Without a computer to do this, they turned to a different source. Two video cameras, mounted side by side, were wheeled up and down the hallway to create stereo videotapes. Their first production was a walking tour from NASA's human factors lab, through the offices of the division, and on to the hanger where the XV-15 Tilt-Rotor aircraft was being developed. When users watched the videos through the VIVED system, they had a sense of "being there."

McGreevy and Amy Wu, his support programmer, proceeded to develop the hardware and software necessary to create the rest of the virtual workstation. They patched together a Picture System 2 graphics computer from Evans and Sutherland, two 19" display monitors, a DEC PDP-11/40 host computer, and the same Polhemus head-tracker used by Furness.

The Evans and Sutherland graphics system generated separate (stereo), wide-angle perspective images on each of the two display monitors. To convert the video signal into the proper format for the head-mounted display, two video cameras were mounted so that each pointed directly at one of the 19" displays.

Next, the Polhemus head-tracking sensor was mounted on top of the VIVED display, communicating the position and orientation of the wearer's head movements to the PDP-11/40. Users who strapped the odd contraption onto their face suddenly found themselves immersed in a computer-generated world (see Fig. 3-8).

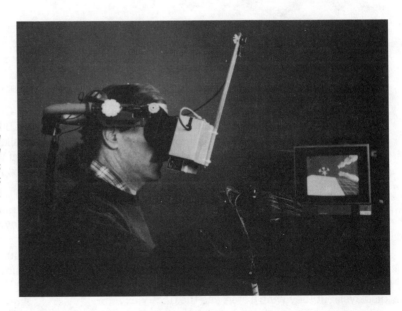

3-8
Original head-mounted display built by Michael McGreevy and James Humphries for NASA Ames VIVED project.

Data from one of McGreevy's earlier projects to study air-traffic-control issues was used for this first virtual environment. Users felt as if they were standing on a horizontal computer-generated grid that stretched out to the horizon. Turning their head, they saw a featureless grid extending to infinity in all directions. Simple 3-D wireframe models of tiny aircraft hung suspended in mid-air.

Users could walk around and inspect each aircraft in turn. The aircraft were fixed in space but, with a little programming, you might find yourself at the center of a swirling confusion of planes busily landing and taking off again.

As word got out of McGreevy's achievements, a steady stream of visitors from industry, academia, and the military made their way to the small cluttered lab where a revolution was taking place. By 1985, McGreevy and crew had created history's first example of a practical head-mounted stereoscopic display system. Unlike previous examples, this one would eventually capture the attention of the public and trigger a small industry.

Scott Fisher joined NASA's VIVED project the same year, 1985, that Michael McGreevy headed East for a two-year training stint in Washington D.C. Fisher's background from the Architecture Machine Group at MIT and his more recent tenure at Atari's Research Center (ARC) gave him valuable insight in directing the research at NASA.

Fisher was interested in extending the initial system by including a wired glove, voice recognition, 3-D sound synthesis, and tactile feedback devices. His objective was to develop a system that could be the foundation for many different forms of research into virtual environments. While Fisher conceptualized, McGreevy fought the necessary funding battles to keep the program alive at NASA.

While at ARC, Fisher had met Thomas Zimmerman, the developer of a new kind of glove that could be used to measure the degree of bend or flex in each finger joint. Zimmerman had originally developed the glove with the intent of using it as an instrument to create music. By hooking it up to a computer that controlled a music synthesizer, wearers could play invisible instruments simply by moving their fingers. It was designed to be the ultimate "air guitar."

Wired gloves

Because it accurately tracked finger movements, Fisher realized that it could be used as an input device to create a virtual hand that would appear in the computer-generated worlds being developed at NASA. If you were wearing the glove and the NASA helmet, and looked at your hand, you would see a caricature of it generated by the computer. If you wiggled your fingers, the image would wiggle its fingers. For the first time, a representation of a person's physical body would become part of the simulation.

In 1983, Zimmerman teamed up with Jaron Lanier (who had also recently left Atari) to wed the glove technology to Lanier's ideas of a virtual programming interface for nonprogrammers. This collaboration evolved into a company, VPL Research, which was officially founded in 1985. They called their first product a *DataGlove*. That same year, Fisher ordered one of the unique gloves for his work at NASA.

By the time the glove arrived in 1986, NASA's VIVED group had grown to include Warren Robinett (an Atari video-game programmer and creator of *Rocky's Boots* and the popular Atari *Adventure* game) and later Douglas Kerr, another programmer. Robinett used his programming skills to create dramatic demonstrations of the versatility of this new visualization tool.

He was, however, somewhat constrained by the less than state-of-the-art equipment McGreevy had assembled on his shoe-string budget. Just as Ivan Sutherland was limited to rendering worlds in glowing green vectors back in 1968, Robinett was limited to stick-figure and wire-frame representations of real-world objects. Making the most of the available tools, Robinett created simulations of architectural structures, hemoglobin molecules, the space shuttle, and turbulent flow patterns.

By the end of 1986, the NASA team had assembled a virtual environment that allowed users to issue voice commands, hear synthesized speech and 3-D sound sources, and manipulate virtual objects directly by grasping them with their hand. No longer was the computer this separate thing you sat in front of and stared at; you were now completely inside. You communicated with it by talking and gesturing instead of typing and swearing.

Probably the most important thing NASA achieved was demonstrating that all this was possible by assembling an assortment of commercially available technologies that weren't a fortune to acquire or develop. Pandora's box had been sitting around for awhile—others had peeked into it, but NASA threw it wide open.

Cybernauts venturing into NASA's virtual worlds had to outfit themselves with a collection of gear that a scuba diver might recognize, particularly because the original design used a scuba-mask frame to mount the LCD displays. Instead of a glass window into the undersea world, the displays were glass windows into the virtual world.

The goal of the NASA design was to completely isolate the user from the outside world. Furness had pioneered this same approach with his Darth Vader helmet. NASA also added headphones that further contributed to the isolation. Reality no longer intruded. The virtual world commanded all the user's attention.

The cybernaut's lifeline was a series of cables that led from the head gear and DataGlove to an array of computers and control boxes. Just as early divers used compressor pumps and air hoses to provide access to their new world, virtual explorers were similarly connected to their reality-generating machines. In their exploration of these new virtual environments, cybernauts were like divers descending alone into the undersea realm.

Sticking your head into one of these early NASA HMDs, you would first notice the grainy or low-resolution image. It was like looking through a magnifying glass at a TV screen; you could see how the image was composed of individual points or picture elements. Because of this, the image quality was a great deal worse than anything usually seen on a computer monitor.

Normally, you don't notice that images on your TV or computer screen are composed of tiny dots. With the NASA display, it was glaringly obvious. As Myron Krueger has so aptly pointed out, the image quality was so poor that you would be declared legally blind in most states if you had similar vision.

After adjusting to the low resolution, the next thing you would notice was that, by moving your head, the stick-figure representation of the world would also move. A sensor attached to the top of the HMD registered the position and orientation of your head. As you moved, the computer would query the sensor (every 60th of a second) and redraw the image.

You would also notice that the image noticeably lagged behind your head movements. If you quickly moved your head it would take about one-fifth of a second or 200 milliseconds for the computer to catch up. You soon learned to make slower head movements. It's not fun being out of sync with reality.

Holding up your gloved hand in front of you, you would see a simple, blocky, wire-frame representation of a hand. You could turn it and move your fingers, and the disembodied hand would mimic the motion. Using fiber-optic sensors to measure the flex of each finger joint and an additional position and orientation sensor, the computer knew exactly where your hand was and what movements your fingers made.

Seeing the representation of your hand suddenly changed your perspective. You now had a perceptual anchor in the virtual world. You were actually inside the computer because you could see your hand in there.

Imagine sitting a foot away from your television screen while watching a commercial for detergents. Now imagine that you're wearing a special glove, like the one in Fig. 3-9, that allows your hand to pass unimpeded through the glass screen. Your hand is now part of the commercial and you can see it just as if you had recorded it with a video camera. Move your hand and the video image of your hand moves. Finally, imagine using your gloved hand to grasp the box of detergent in the commercial and change its position. NASA had achieved something similar to this. Of course, you couldn't feel your hand touching the box; that would come later.

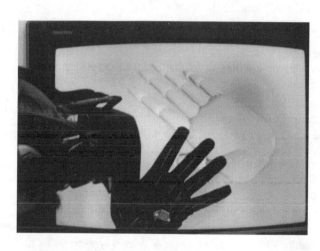

3-9
Close-up of VPL's DataGlove. Fiber-optic sensors, running across the knuckles, detect bent fingers. The participant sees the computer generated image of his hand in the display.

To move about the tinker-toy world, you simply pointed with one gloved finger in the appropriate direction, and the angle of your thumb controlled the speed of your flight. The computer had been taught to recognize that gesture as representing the desire for movement. Other gestures were possible; for example, closing your fist grabbed any object that your hand intersected. As long as you kept your hand closed, the object stayed stuck to it. This allowed you to move objects around. Opening your hand released the object.

Attached to the HMD was a small mike that allowed you to give simple voice commands to the computer. Fisher had simply purchased a commercially available voice recognition package and had it connected to the system. Voice input was important because, once you put the HMD on, you could no longer use the keyboard or find any buttons to control your environment. A voice synthesis package had also been connected into the system. If you spoke a command, after a slight pause, a robotic voice echoed it back to you.

3-D sound Fisher was also familiar with another new technology, 3-D or *binaural* sound. Just as stereoscopic images produce a strong sense of depth when viewed correctly, binaural recordings generate the same sense of depth when using headphones. This shouldn't be confused with either *stereo* or *quadraphonic* sound, which are lesser attempts to achieve a binaural effect.

In a perfect 3-D sound system, you wouldn't be able to distinguish between reality and the simulation if you closed your eyes and just listened to the sounds. When you listen to a stereo recording, the musical sources appear somewhere in a flat plane facing you. Listening to a 3-D recording allows the musical sources to appear anywhere in a sphere surrounding your head. In other words, sounds appear above your head, behind it, or in front of your nose.

Based on Elizabeth Wenzel's work in the perceptual psychology of sound and the engineering talents of Scott Foster, president of Crystal River Engineering, Fisher contracted for the development of a system capable of creating 3-D sounds in the virtual world. Fisher wanted to attach sounds to virtual objects and have the sound follow the object if it moved.

Imagine you've just entered a virtual room. In the middle of the room you can see a small radio that appears to be playing music. You go over and pick up the virtual radio with your gloved hand. Moving the radio around, you notice that the sound follows the location of the wire-frame radio, just as you would expect from a real radio. If this is done correctly, you should be able to close your eyes and pinpoint where the sound is coming from.

Wenzel and Foster were able to create such an effect. When the hardware was completed, it was capable of manipulating up to four sound sources at once—they called it a *convolvotron*. You could now have four different radios, each playing a different tune all at once. More importantly, instead of hearing all four tunes hopelessly fused together, you could distinguish each sound source if you focused your attention on each one. This is the same ability that allows us to distinguish different voices in a crowded room where everyone appears to be talking at once.

NASA's efforts resulted in the first computer-synthesized reality that combined computer-generated stereoscopic images, 3-D sound, voice recognition, voice synthesis, and a device for manipulating virtual objects, as seen by the scientist in Fig. 3-10, who holds an object only he can see. They had mounted a major expedition into the virtual world on a shoestring budget.

3-10
A NASA scientist holds a virtual object in his hands that only he can see. Special gloves allow him to reach into the virtual world and grab or manipulate objects.

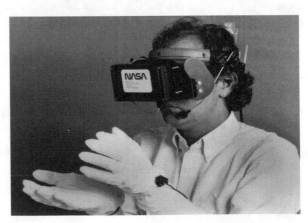

Scientific American published James Foley's article entitled "Interfaces for Advanced Computing" in October 1987. VPL's DataGlove made the front cover. The public finally became aware of NASA's work. The realization that NASA's achievements were based on commercially available equipment and that devices like the HMD could be built for around $2000 triggered new research programs throughout the world.

The same year, McGreevy returned from his two-year stint on the East Coast and resumed control of the project. By 1988, the VIVED project had become the VIEW project (Virtual Interface Environment Workstation). Robinett had left the project to set sail for foreign shores. Douglas Kerr had ported the original software to a new Hewlett-Packard 9000 that had sufficient computing power to draw virtual worlds with shaded surfaces instead of wire-frame outlines (see Fig. 3-11).

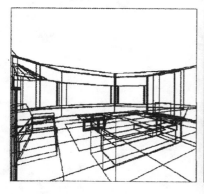 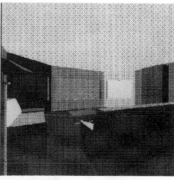

3-11
The virtual world on the left is rendered as a wire-frame model. The one on the right is rendered using flat-shaded surfaces.

You no longer viewed stick-figure representations, and walls finally had surfaces instead of just outlines. Additional improvements were also made to the display resolution of the HMD and to other aspects of the simulation.

By the time Scott Fisher left NASA in 1990 to form Telepresence Research in Palo Alto, California with Brenda Laurel, the research had spread into other departments at NASA. There were ongoing projects to research telepresence and telerobotics, a virtual wind-tunnel project, and a virtual planetary exploration group. The initial seed planted by McGreevy, Fisher, and the pioneers before them had taken root and was beginning to spread. The commercialization of virtual reality would not be far behind.

4 Cyberspace for sale

VPL Research   VPL Research, founded in 1985 in Redwood City, California, became the first company to focus on the manufacture and development of products for virtual environments. Any discussion of VPL Research always starts with a profile of its 31-year-old founder and chief scientist, Jaron Lanier. His distinctive physical presence—John Barlow's *Mondo 2000* article succinctly describes him as "amiable, round, and dread-locked . . . a Rastafarian hobbit"—and provocative visions of virtual reality created a magnet for the media. Lanier has since become the *de facto* spokesperson for virtual reality (to the chagrin of several earlier pioneers).

At the height of the video-game craze in 1983, Lanier created a popular game called Moondust for Atari. The success of the game and the royalties it generated gave Lanier the freedom to pursue the Silicon Valley ethos of entrepreneur.

Lanier wasn't satisfied with using just words to program and control computers. He imagined a computer that could be programmed visually through the use of images. Pursuit of this goal led to him teaming up with Thomas Zimmerman in 1984. Zimmerman's wired glove interested Lanier as a new method of communicating with the computer.

A year later, VPL Research was officially founded and Scott Fisher from NASA came knocking. At the same time, Jean-Jacques Grimaud joined VPL as president and Lanier became Chief Executive Officer. Grimaud's management background and conservative business approach was an important counterpoint to Lanier's eclectic style. Conservative companies had difficulty accepting Lanier's unorthodox appearance and radical image—a big problem if you're trying to sell a $250,000 system.

A team comprised of Zimmerman, Lanier, and Young Harvill reengineered the glove to improve its accuracy and usefulness. Fiber optics for sensing finger flex and a Polhemus sensor for measuring position and orientation of the hand were added. The glove and its supporting software and control electronics slowly evolved.

After delivering a glove to NASA in 1986, VPL continued work on creating software tools for producing virtual worlds much like the ones developed at NASA. Up to this point, VPL was only a supplier of the wired glove. It would be several years after NASA's unveiling of the VIVED system that VPL would begin marketing virtual reality tools of their own.

Because NASA's work was in the public domain, VPL was well positioned to adopt many of the ideas from NASA, improve their design, and begin marketing them. For example, the facemask with LCD screens that McGreevy prototyped was used as the basis for EyePhones, VPL's head-mounted display system.

VPL entered the business of selling complete solutions for virtual reality in 1988. In fact, Lanier is credited with coining the popular term for these synthetic experiences (*virtual reality*). To sell a system for immersive experiences, you need display devices (sight and sound), graphics hardware, interaction devices, and software to make everything run.

VR vendor

For display devices, VPL developed an HMD similar to NASA's for visual display, and then integrated Scott Foster's Convolvotron 3-D sound processor for an aural display. VPL's DataGlove served as a general-purpose interaction device. By combining all this with Apple's Macintosh computer and two Silicon Graphic's workstations, VPL created RB2, or Reality Built for Two, the first commercial VR system. This new form of reality wasn't cheap; it cost $225,000 for a single user or $430,000 for two. In a 1989 product handout, VPL poetically defined the quarter-million-dollar experience:

"VR is shared and objectively present like the physical world, composable like a work of art and as unlimited and harmless as a dream. When VR becomes widely available, it will not be seen as a medium used within physical reality, but rather as an additional reality. VR opens up a new continent of ideas and possibilities."
  —VPL product brochure

VPL began a booming business in selling DataGloves and EyePhones to researchers cobbling together their own systems. Within several years, hundreds of both devices were spread all over the world in garages and labs. By 1990, VPL claimed 500 customers worldwide. Customers for VPL's RB2 system included premier labs in Japan, Europe, and the U.S. that were tackling problems in human-factor simulation and visualization. Examples of some of these applications are reviewed in part 3 of this book, *Brave new worlds*.

Interesting software tools were also evolved to support creating virtual environments. Young Harvill came up with Swivel 3-D as a tool for creating or modeling 3-D worlds and objects. It has since become one of the most popular 3-D modeling packages for the Macintosh, and generates a continuous stream of revenue for VPL.

In addition to Swivel 3-D, Chuck Blanchard designed Body Electric to control the dynamics of the virtual environment. Information from Swivel and Body Electric passed to a rendering program called Isaac, which drew the final images. Swivel and Body Electric ran on a Macintosh while Isaac ran on the Silicon Graphics workstations.

To understand how it all works, follow the process of creating a simple world with a spinning banana. First, sitting in front of a Macintosh, you use a mouse and Swivel 3-D to create a 3-D model of a yellow banana. With Body Electric, you describe how fast the banana should spin, the direction it spins, and what happens if a DataGlove touches it. Finally, the information is passed to the Silicon Graphics workstation and Isaac renders the image.

Body Electric, running on the Macintosh, controls the simulation and the Silicon Graphics machine. If EyePhones and a DataGlove were connected, the banana's stereoscopic image would appear to float in front of your face as it slowly spun about. With the glove on, you could reach out and grab the banana. With a lot more work, you could peel it.

Shared worlds One of the more important concepts demonstrated by VPL was the ability of two people to enter into the same virtual environment and interact. One of the early demonstrations of this involved two people represented as lobsters in the virtual world.

Climbing into a full-body version of the DataGlove called a DataSuit brought their entire body into the simulation instead of just their hand. They could choose how their bodies were represented from a collection of stored parts—lobsters were one of the choices on the menu.

The two systems were networked together, each running the same simulation. Any change in the state of one simulation would be communicated to the other system. If one participant moved his clawed hand, the other person would see the movement.

VPL proved that virtual reality didn't have to be an individual experience, that it could be shared. This represents the most provocative concept that has evolved in this new field. Shared VR opens new worlds of research and entertainment possibilities. As a medium of communication, it might represent what the telephone was to the telegraph.

Communications has improved because the nuances of spoken language are transmitted instead of the impersonality of Morse code. Shared virtual reality can make the world a smaller place and at the same time provide an unlimited world to explore. An intriguing paradox.

As VPL enters its seventh year of operation, it has grown to about 25 people and is still enjoying a comfortable lead over the rest of the nascent VR industry. However, after years of being sole supplier of virtual-reality hardware and systems, it has had to adjust to new competition from start-ups offering similar wares.

As a world-wide recession limits funds for $50,000 HMDs and $225,000 systems, VPL is undergoing change. Recognizing the demand for less expensive solutions, VPL now offers a less expensive system based on a Macintosh Quadra and two Division i860 microprocessor-based graphics boards. Shown at the 1992 MacWorld convention in San Francisco, Microcosm is a low-cost system intended for the architectural market (see Fig. 4-1). Attempting to reestablish a technological edge, VPL also brought forth new gloves and new head-mounted designs.

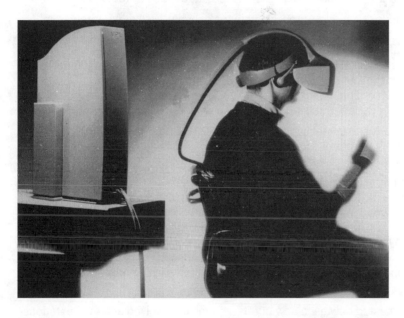

4-1
Microcosm VR sytem.

In mid-1992, Lanier removed himself from day-to-day operations with VPL to pursue his interests in the artistic and technological challenges of VR. A new president was brought in to help manage VPL's transition from small start-up to small company. VPL's success in navigating these turbulent waters will be determined by Lanier's and Grimaud's abilities as steersmen.

Before VPL emerged on the scene, VR was the province of obscure research projects at universities and labs in the US. Sutherland's wire-frame cubes, the military's training simulators, and Furness's Super Cockpit all eventually led to NASA Ames' assembly of commercially available tools to explore virtual environments.

NASA had proven it could be done and VPL set out to prove a market existed. In this, VPL succeeded where Heilig had failed; manufacturing realities became a business. Even though VPL had little to do with inventing VR, their contribution is important because it finally made the technology accessible to the public and industry in general.

Autodesk

John Walker, the reclusive, brilliant programmer and former Chief Executive Officer of Autodesk, read with growing interest of VPL's and NASA's efforts in 1987–1988. An intensely private man and one of the 1982 founders of Autodesk, Walker immediately understood the potential of this new technology to revolutionize computer-aided design (CAD).

Six years after its founding, Autodesk had grown into a large company with over $100 million per year in revenues. Started with a single vision of developing an inexpensive CAD program for the PC, Autodesk had become one of the most successful software companies around. Customers included architects and other designers who previously used expensive analysis and drawing tools running only on mainframes and minicomputers. Autodesk's product, AutoCAD, became a run-away success with over 500,000 users in the U.S. at the end of 1991.

As the demands of running Autodesk grew too onerous, Walker withdrew from day-to-day management to focus on programming and working on his famous internal manifestos. Walker used these eloquent documents to convey his vision to others. In September 1988, "Through the Looking Glass: Beyond User Interfaces" began making the rounds within Autodesk. It documented the progress of computer interfaces from punchcards to virtual worlds, and challenged Autodesk to develop its own Cyberspace tools.

Just as Autodesk had taken mainframe CAD tools and brought them to PCs, Walker realized that VPL's quarter-million-dollar system could be inexpensively recreated on the PC. He defined his vision:

"Now we're at the threshold of the next revolution in user-computer interaction: a technology that will take the user through the screen into the world `inside' the computer—a world in which the user can interact with three-dimensional objects whose fidelity will grow as computing power increases and display technology progresses. This virtual world can be whatever the designer makes it. As designers and users explore entirely new experiences and modes of interaction, they will be jointly defining the next generation of user interaction with computers."

—John Walker, Through the Looking Glass, 1988

Walker documented how each new interface paradigm evolved and the limitations or barriers it created for the user. Table 4-1 lists these "generations."

Table 4-1
User interface generations

Generation	Description	Barrier
First	Plugboards, dedicated set-up	Front panel
Second	Punched card batch, RJE	Countertop
Third	Teletype timesharing	Terminal
Fourth	Menu systems	Menu hierarchy
Fifth	Graphical controls, windows	Screen
Sixth	Cyberspace	?

Source: John Walker. Through the Looking Glass, internal Autodesk memo

Each succeeding generation opened up new applications and markets and made computers easier to use. As they became easier, more people used them to solve more kinds of problems. Markets rapidly expanded to support new demands for hardware and software. We are in the midst of transitioning to the sixth generation and, if previous generations are any guide, we have much to look forward to.

Based on the strength of Walker's vision, the "Autodesk cyberspace initiative" began in the latter part of 1988. Walker chose William Gibson's cyberspace novel *Neuromancer* as the inspiration for naming the project. Initial project members included William Bricken, Eric Gullichsen, Eric Lyons, and Randal Walser. They were later joined by Pat Gelband, Meredith Bricken, Gary Wells, and Christopher Allis.

Desktop cyberspace

Leading the project, William Bricken had an eclectic background in statistics, psychology, Artificial Intelligence programming, and education. Meredith's qualifications were also in education and curriculum design for schools. Eric Gullichsen, a Canadian transplant who epitomizes the tinkerer-hacker, along with Pat Gelband and Randy Walser, became the programmers responsible for crafting the vision. The rest of the crew filled supporting roles.

Posting a sign labeled *Cyberia* on their work area, the team began assembling a Gibsonian "deck." Duplicating NASA's assembly of a head-mounted display from scrounged parts and purchasing VPL's DataGlove gave them the tools of the VR trade—gloves and goggles. Two Matrox graphics boards installed in a Compaq/386 PC provided the rendering horsepower to draw the worlds.

For under $25,000 they replicated VPL's quarter-million-dollar system. Now for virtual reality to fulfill its many promises, a larger pool of researchers, developers, and artists needed access. Autodesk's project demonstrated that day was rapidly approaching.

It arrived in March, 1989 with the demonstration of the first PC-based virtual-reality system. The Autodesk cyberspace team was catapulted into the spotlight as word spread of its achievement. People took notice when a company like Autodesk demonstrated its interest in this new and unproven technology.

Inventing reality

Over the course of the next several months, additional demos were created that explored possible sports-related applications. One of them, a virtual bicycle ride, used a stationary exercise bike as an input device. As you pedaled the bike wearing an HMD, virtual landscapes rolled past you. If you pedaled fast enough, it appeared that you left the ground and flew off into the sky. A boring exercise turned into an exciting trip into a new world.

Pat Gelband used her background in physics to develop the first virtual-reality racquetball game, shown in Fig. 4-2. She knew she was following historical precedent; the first video arcade game, Pong, also involved bouncing a ball off paddles and walls. Holding a modified racquet and wearing a HMD, the player used the racquet to send a computer-generated ball bouncing off the walls and back to her.

All that was missing was the shock of contact between the synthesized ball and the wooden racquet. You simply took swipes at the air, only your eyes discerning the

4-2
While at Autodesk, Pat Gelband developed the first virtual racquetball game as a demonstration of the Autodesk cyberspace system.

impact of ball and racquet. With further refinements, sound and tactile feedback might approximate the actual feel of hitting the ball.

Bending the rules of reality slightly, Gelband programmed the ball to automatically return to the location of the racquet. This lessened the likelihood of someone being hurt in a desperate maneuver to reach the ball. It also lessened the possibility of whacking an innocent onlooker.

Despite the fun and games of cyberspace, the research program began unraveling in August of 1989 as William and Meredith Bricken left Autodesk in a dispute over the future direction of the project. By Thanksgiving, Eric Gullichsen and Pat Gelband departed to form Sense8. Frustrated by the glacial pace of turning their research into real products, they decided to do it themselves.

Randy Walser became project leader and continued demonstrations, but real development ground to a halt. Even John Walker withdrew from Autodesk to pursue his interests from a redoubt in Switzerland.

It wasn't until mid-1990 that Autodesk woke from its slumber and began actively restaffing the project. Rudy Rucker, science-fiction writer and programmer, joined the group along with others. It seemed that Autodesk was again serious about commercializing cyberspace. By the end of the year, Randy Walser provided the first peek at TRIX, an interactive language for cyberspace that John Walker was developing.

Following this were rumors of a Cyberspace Development Toolkit (CDK) in early 1991. CDK would allow AutoCAD owners to bring wire-frame images to life as solid, 3-D objects they could manipulate and view from different angles. By mid-1992, none of these projects had quite made it out the door, though CDK was promised by the end of 1992.

Autodesk's impact on this emerging field shouldn't be underestimated. Whether they revolutionize virtual reality as they did CAD has yet to be decided. But more importantly, they proved that practical systems could be developed for far less money than previously thought.

In the four months after leaving Autodesk's Cyberspace Initiative, Gullichsen and Gelband spent 14-hour days, seven days a week, creating the core of a new object-oriented 3-D simulation language. Starting from scratch, but retaining lessons learned at Autodesk, a tool for rapid prototyping complex 3-D simulations evolved. Driving them was a vision of a development tool that programmers could easily use to create complex virtual environments.

Sense8

Working out of an office in Sausalito, California, they built their first VR system out of two Amigas and two Sony Watchmans. Following in the grand tradition of John Hewlett and David Packard, who started their multi-billion-dollar business from a simple garage in Palo Alto, Gullichsen and Gelband set out to build revolutionary simulation tools.

Gullichsen, an inveterate tinkerer and high-tech wizard, made the Amiga do things it simply wasn't designed to do. Working long nights in an espresso-induced frenzy, Gullichsen became a highly kinetic coding machine. Accompanied by Gelband on her well-worn keyboard, they gave form to the structure of the new product.

Gelband not only developed the advanced rendering technology at the core of the product, her rigorous background in math and physics provided new insights into efficient techniques for representing 3-D objects. In her spare time, she managed the practical details of running the small startup.

With their synergistic talents, they crafted a powerful and flexible tool. In January of 1990, Sense8 was founded. Gelband derived the name from the adjective *sensate*, or perceiving through the senses—appropriate for their new line of work.

Showing the Amiga prototype to contacts at Sun Microsystems led to a contract and loan of workstations to port their software to the Sun system. Recognizing that Gullichsen and Gelband were onto something, Sun hoped to demonstrate technology leadership in this emerging field, and counter Silicon Graphic's lock on the 3-D graphics market.

At this time, Tom Coull joined Sense8 to handle the marketing and sales of the product. Previously a vice president in charge of Software Marketing for a Bechtel subsidiary, Coull brought valuable marketing, business, and legal experience to the new venture.

The three founders survived by obtaining various contracts from the military. One of these involved the development of a low-cost HMD helicopter training simulator. Another contract provided the incentive for developing an IBM PC version of their original system using Texas Instruments TIGA-based graphics boards. Within a single year, their core technology had successfully moved onto three dissimilar platforms.

In the spring of 1990, Gullichsen and Gelband brought one of the few VR systems in the world to Intel for a demonstration. A researcher in Intel's CAD group, Kenneth Pimentel, had arranged for the demonstration as part of a project he was pursuing.

Texturing reality

After setting up the system, everyone in attendance had a chance to explore Sense8's strange new worlds. By carefully lowering a hand-tooled HMD over your face, you suddenly found yourself in a fuzzy checkerboard world. Dual Amiga computers, encased in surplus ammo canisters, generated cartoon-like images of buildings and a large sphere hanging in space.

As you moved your head to look around, more of this strange world was revealed. Grabbing a baseball-sized device mounted on a small platform and pushing it in the appropriate direction sent you flying through the virtual world. After learning to drive with the odd, rubber-coated ball, you could fly into a hanger-like structure that abruptly transported you to yet another intriguing world.

The purpose of the visit was to pick a VR vendor to collaborate on a VR system based on Intel's DVI (Digital Video Interactive) technology. Pimentel had recently received an Intel Applications Fellowship, giving him six months and $100,000 to develop a VR solution based on Intel products.

After meetings with VPL, Autodesk, and the Human-Interface Technology Lab in Seattle, Washington, Pimentel selected Sense8 because they alone appeared capable of delivering a prototype within the six-month deadline. Also important was the hardware independence of their toolkit. Already running on multiple platforms, it spoke volumes for the system's portability.

Working at Intel during the acquisition of DVI Technology from RCA's David Sarnoff Research Center, Pimentel had a unique opportunity to learn about the multiple capabilities of this revolutionary chip set. The engineers at Sarnoff had developed a set of microcode programmable graphics chips unlike any others.

Their capabilities were determined by the microcode they were currently running. In addition, a parallel architecture allowed multiple instructions to be executed in a single clock cycle—advanced features relative to other graphics controllers at the time. Not only could the chip set perform decompression of moving images, allowing 72 minutes of full-screen, full-motion video off a 3½-inch compact disk, it could also be programmed to draw graphics or textures.

Texture mapping is particularly important. A photograph is first scanned into the computer and loaded into the DVI graphic board. Next, the digital image is "mapped" or reshaped to a different position on the screen. Utilizing this in a real-time 3-D rendering turns the normally cartoonish world into a realistic model (see Fig. 4-3).

4-3
The picture on the left shows a computer generated view using only flat-shaped polygons. The picture on the right shows the same view with texture-mapped polygons.

For example, a furniture maker might use this to show a customer a textured 3-D model of a couch. After selecting a scanned swatch of fabric, the swatch would be texture mapped onto the entire surface of the couch. With DVI products, you didn't have to wait minutes to view the result; the new image was drawn instantly. Other controls could allow the customer to walk around or spin the couch to view it from any angle.

Because a lot of scanned images could be stored in the DVI board, a 3-D world could be created rich in detail. Wooden floors, stone fireplaces, pictures on the walls, and rugs on the floor were all possible. Architects could have an interactive rendering tool that represented the world the way it really is, with complex images and textures wherever you look.

Recognizing the potential of DVI products to add a completely new level of realism to virtual worlds, Intel approved funding to pursue developing a PC-based VR system. Working with DVI microcode experts back in Princeton to optimize the rendering algorithms resulted in significant performance gains. Months were spent integrating the new texturing capability with Sense8's core code.

Finally, at the San Francisco Meckler VR conference in late 1990, Sense8 and Intel unveiled the result of their collaboration. Participants were treated to a virtual trip through a garden with realistic trees and a lawn. Passing through a portal, you suddenly dropped into an art museum with scanned images of art hanging on the walls. Another portal gave you a 360-degree, panoramic view of a Mayan temple. Looking in any direction revealed more of the temple surroundings or the sky above.

For two days, attendees waited hours in line for an opportunity to try it. The demonstration represented a breakthrough in PC realism and rendering performance for virtual worlds. Sense8 was clearly onto something.

Based on this initial success, Sense8 developed plans for marketing a product based on the DVI chip set's capabilities. At this point, Gullichsen and Gelband had created an impressive set of core technologies that could be accessed through an elegant and powerful set of programming function calls.

WorldToolKit

Recognizing that it was impossible to predict which industries would represent the largest market for VR, they decided to create a general-purpose development tool. Any industry could then create their own unique tools based on the Sense8 technology.

In June 1991, WorldToolKit became commercially available. Intended for programmers, it contained a C library of over 200 functions and a powerful simulation manager that allowed rapid prototyping of custom applications. 3-D models created with AutoCAD software, or any 3-D modeler that generated DXF files, could be read as objects or stationary backdrops. Device drivers were included for everything from simple mice and joysticks to Polhemus trackers and Spaceballs.

The commercial availability of WorldToolKit represented a dramatic reduction in the cost of VR. Now it was possible to assemble a complete system for less than $25,000, or a third of the cost of competing platforms (by the end of 1991, the cost was down to $20,000 and dropping fast).

It was also well within many research budgets, as evidenced by the amount of sales. Customers ranged from Rockwell, NASA Ames, and Sandia Labs to the Computer Museum in Boston and the Banff Center for the Arts. (Many of these applications are covered elsewhere in this book.) Within a few months, distributors were signed up in England, Italy, Germany, and Japan. WorldToolKit had gone worldwide.

The diversity of the WorldToolKit's customer base portends the widespread use of VR and its significance as an enabling technology. To encourage this, Sense8 adapted WorldToolKit to run on Silicon Graphics and Sun workstations in addition to the PC. In doing so, it became the first VR product to work on more than a single platform. The addition of networking capabilities and 3-D sound allowed worlds to be built that you could share with others and still experience with your eyes closed.

Virtual Reality, Inc.

There are literally dozens of small start-up companies busily attempting to carve a future out of virtual reality. They are so numerous, in fact, that it's impossible to cover all of their efforts and origins. They include suppliers of HMD, gloves, head-trackers, and many other devices. Consider them the outfitters of VR.

In addition, there are research projects at universities in Japan, the U.S., and Europe attempting to provide conceptual frameworks and practical advice in the construction and habitation of virtual worlds. Many of these companies, products, and universities are listed in the resource guide in the back of this book.

Individuals and efforts documented in this chapter are singled out for either their foresight, contributions, or advancement of the new technology. Virtual reality didn't spring forth fully formed. It has emerged slowly, in fits and starts over the last forty years. Only in the last couple years has it been rapidly thrust into the public's eye.

What we've seen so far is just a glimpse of what will be. VR represents a fundamentally revolutionary way of interacting with computers. It also presents us with a powerful new medium of expression that is still evolving and changing. Promises of the technology are rapidly outpacing its capabilities. Understanding how VR works and the technologies driving it are the subject of the next chapter. One of our hopes is that it will help to separate fact from fiction.

Part two

21st century tools

5 *Reality engines*

Picture a virtual environment where gradually rolling hills, covered with grass, lead to a rustic house perched high on a ridge. Below the ridge, a river winds its way through a broad open valley. By controlling your point of view, you can fly across the hills and up to the house's entrance. As you pick up speed, the rush of wind becomes louder.

As you near it, the front door automatically swings open—beckoning you inside. You move through the hallway and into the living room, where low-slung couches and comfortable chairs surround a solid stone fireplace. A lamp glows on a table next to the wall. Hearing the sound of a radio, you turn your head to locate it perched on a tabletop. As you turn, you notice that flames appear to dance and cavort among the logs in the fireplace. Moving over to a large bay window, you see trees dotting the hillsides, and the river far below.

Facing back into the living room, you decide to move the lamp away from the wall. While looking directly at the lamp, you press a trigger button on a joystick, causing a ray to leap out and touch the lamp. A box appears around the lamp signifying its selection, and as you begin to move the joystick the lamp moves also. Moving the lamp around the room, you notice how it causes the shading of furniture and wall surfaces to brighten and darken. You set it down by a chair. Pleased with the result, you fly back out the front door and leave the simulation.

As we near the end of the 20th century, virtual realities like the one described are providing examples of the kinds of tools we'll be working with in the next century. This part of the book describes how to get a jump on these 21st-century tools—today.

The previous description of a virtual environment is just one example of the kinds of realities manufacturable by today's VR systems. At the heart of these systems are *reality engines*, which continuously pump out sensory information, like the fire flickering or the sound of wind in your ears, to keep the illusion alive. VR exists in the interplay or dance of the user and computer responding to each other.

The cycle begins when participants react to what they're seeing and hearing by turning their heads or moving their joysticks. These input signals are processed by the reality engine to create yet another set of sights and sounds.

Referring to the example, the participant reacts to hearing sounds from a radio by turning to look at the radio. As he turns his head, input sensors capture this action and instruct the computer to generate new image and sound signals. This continuous feedback cycle powers the illusion of reality (see Fig. 5-1).

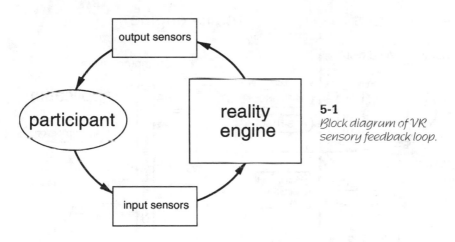

5-1
Block diagram of VR sensory feedback loop.

Feedback is crucial to VR. It represents the interactivity of the medium. If reality engines are the heart of virtual reality, then interactivity is its soul. VR represents the first fully interactive medium.

Movies, for example, are completely noninteractive—you passively watch what's presented. Television, on the other hand, began evolving from noninteractive to interactive when remote controls became available. After all, continuously switching channels or "channel grazing," is a simple form of interactivity (and rumored to be dominated by the male of the species).

In addition to television, other forms of media are becoming interactive. Hypertext, computer games, and multimedia are all part of this trend—fueled by access to inexpensive computing power and the digitization of media. Virtual reality is a logical result of mixing media with interactivity. You finally enter into the media and become part of it.

At its simplest, VR is a tool for enabling the user's immersion into a sensory-rich, interactive experience. Using input and output sensors, a virtual world is fabricated under the control of both the reality engine and the participant.

But how is interactivity and sensory information created, sustained and managed? What's the "magic" behind the technology? This chapter explores the hardware and software tools required for the creation of virtual environments and issues and limitations surrounding their use. Step by step, we will break down a VR system into its basic components and explain each one, revealing the "magic" behind the new looking glass.

Components of a VR system

The term *virtual reality* is widely used and it might mean different things to different people. If anything, its meaning will continue to evolve as the technology and its capabilities change and evolve. Our preferred definition of what VR means today is an immersive experience in which participants wear tracked, head-mounted displays, view stereoscopic images, listen to 3-D sounds, and are free to explore and interact within a 3-D world. Based on this definition, all VR systems can be broken into four separate parts, as shown in the illustration in Fig. 5-2.

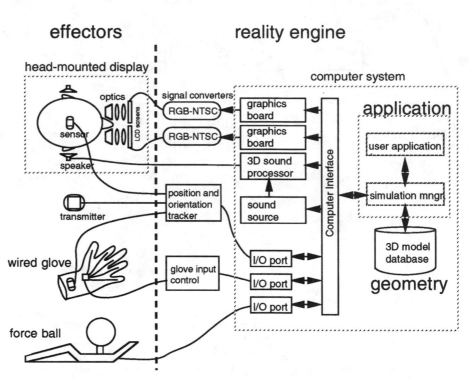

5-2
Diagram of elements that make up a VR system.

Effectors Effectors are a kind of hardware that allows you to experience flying over rolling hills, or moving and rearranging objects in a virtual living room. They include devices that stimulate the senses to create a sense of presence in the virtual world, like HMDs, and control the environment, like a wired glove. Both input and output sensors are considered effectors.

Reality engine   The computer system and external hardware, like sound synthesizing equipment, that supply effectors with the necessary sensory information comprise the reality engine. It's the "heart" of a VR system.

Application   An application is software that describes the context of the simulation, its dynamics, structure, and the laws of interaction between objects and the user. It determines if the virtual world is for designing kitchens or flying B2 bombers. The application determines when doors open, or whether and how lamps are moved.

Geometry   Geometry is the stored information describing the physical attributes of objects (shape, color, placement, etc.). In the example at the beginning of the chapter, geometry would describe the shape of the rolling hills, along with the placement, construction, and color of the house. This information is processed by the application to build the virtual world.

Effectors

Stepping through the barrier of the computer screen, to travel or interact in a virtual world, is the primary goal of a VR system. To do this, sufficient sensory input must be provided for the participants to become immersed in the experience—temporarily suspending their disbelief and becoming engaged with the application. In other words, they accept the synthetic world as a place where they're currently present.

Think of the wrap-around, 360-degree movie at Disneyland. You know you're standing in the middle of a large theater, but as the camera flies through the clouds or across the landscape, you briefly experience a sense of presence. You become the camera as it swoops through mountain passes.

Virtual reality generates a similar sense of presence and requires less sensory input to achieve it than you might think. Our sensory processors (eyes, ears, etc.) have been reliably constructing realities over millions of years of evolution. Just provide a minimum of sensory cues and the brain fills in the rest.

Effectors generate these cues. They're specialized devices, like the HMD, wired glove, or 3-D sound that engage the user in the simulation—just as movie projectors and screen images are effectors in the cinema or headphones on a Sony Walkman.

Currently, most efforts are focused on immersing the visual and aural senses, while research continues with tactile and force feedback. Taste and odors remain unexplored. Though we've made our first faltering steps, we're still a long way from total sensory immersion. The promises (or threats) of Hollywood (as depicted in movies like *Total Recall*) remain to be realized.

Visual cues

Generating the required visual cues is currently the greatest challenge to a VR system. Image rendering is a key component of the overall system expense and forces compromises between cost, performance, complexity, and quality.

However, drawing or rendering is only part of the problem. For someone to believe they're really flying over rolling hills of grass or are inside a house looking around, the movement of their head must be tracked so that the proper image is always in front of them. Imagine a special pair of binoculars; no matter where you look, the correct view of the virtual world is displayed.

While computers generate these images, special sensors track your head orientation, informing the computer of any changes. Several different approaches to head tracking have been developed. Unfortunately, all of them complicate an already complex problem of creating immersive experiences. To understand these problems better, here are the factors controlling visual immersion:

Field of view How much does an image fill your view? Remember the discussion of Cinerama earlier in the book? Using three movie screens instead of one gave audiences a much wider field of view and stronger sense of presence. Special optics can create this same effect in a head-mounted display. While VR displays vary from 80 to 140 degrees, humans have a 180-degree horizontal field of view (see Fig. 5-3). Watching a 19-inch TV from between 4 and 5 inches away will give the same effect, but the special optics in the HMD allow the image to remain in focus.

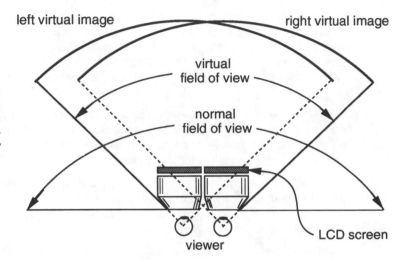

5-3
Special optics are used to create an enhanced field of view of the LCD display screens. It's the same effect as looking at a large projection TV from one to two feet away.

Resolution When you wear the HMD, how grainy does the image look? A byproduct of using the wide field-of-view optics with current low-resolution LCD displays is that the image quality is drastically affected. Typically, LCD displays have between 86,000 and 110,000 colored elements. It takes three elements (1 red, 1 blue, and 1 green) to make a single pixel, or picture element. This means that the eye receives only 30,000 – 40,000 pixels of color information. PCs and workstations commonly have about 1,000,000 pixels of information, or 30 times as many, as shown in Fig. 5-4.

Complexity What is the visual complexity of an image (textures, polygons, etc.)? The world described earlier in the chapter might contain 1000–1500 different 3-D shapes or polygons. For performance reasons, fewer and smaller polygons are better. Rendering or shading styles also determine overall image complexity. The more detail in the scene, the more pleasing and informationally rich it is. However, the additional complexity takes longer for the computer to process, slowing down the frame rate.

Rendering speed How long does it take to render one complete image or frame? Drawing the image of the house on top of the rolling hills must occur within a

5-4
The larger image is a picture of the computer display monitor showing a robotic hand. The smaller, inset image is a picture of the same view taken through wide field-of-view optics.

blink of an eye to be useful for VR. Anything longer will result in the loss of presence. Remember from the discussion of flight simulators that drawing speed is typically measured in frames per second (fps) or Hertz. To achieve a sense of presence, about 10–12 fps is a good target, while greater than 30 fps has diminishing returns.

Perceptual lag   How long does it take to register changes in head orientation or other sensor input? Studies have shown that lags greater than 50 milliseconds affect performance. Lag is primarily composed of sensor lag and the time spent drawing the new image. Sensor lag can vary from three to more than 100 milliseconds, and drawing a 10 fps image adds an additional 100 milliseconds. In a worst-case scenario, this can add up to a noticeable lag of over a quarter second.

Engagement   How interesting is the application? Does it capture your interest? This is one of the most difficult factors to judge, but it can have a tremendous effect on the sense of presence in the virtual world. A simple VR application that allows you to float through a building while looking around is less engaging than a "hands-on" VR application where you struggle to find an appropriate docking site for two molecules.

Different applications place different emphasis on these factors. In the example at the beginning of this chapter, sense of presence is more important than image detail. So resolution can be traded for more field of view. A medical system might do the opposite, choosing resolution over field of view. Until both are available at a reasonable cost, tradeoffs will be required.

Most visual effectors or HMDs work on a simple principle of viewing a small color or monochrome display through a set of wide field-of-view optics (see Fig. 5-5). The optics not only allow you to comfortably focus on the displays placed three inches

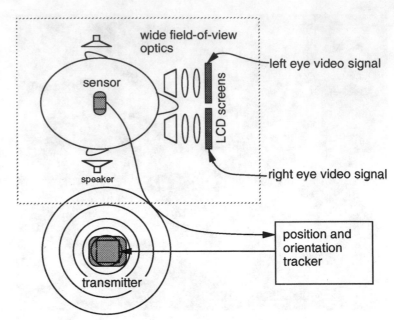

5-5
*Diagram showing
components of a
head-tracked HMD.*

wide field-of-view optics

sensor

speaker

LCD screens

left eye video signal

right eye video signal

transmitter

position and orientation tracker

from your eyes, they also exaggerate the size of the image. Because of this, the image fills your view and creates a sense of immersion.

Stereoscopic views are possible because each eye views a separate display screen. While images are displayed, the outside world is masked off from sight. This allows total immersion in the virtual world and is popular for entertainment, architectural visualization, and applications where the only focus is the virtual world.

This is the kind of immersion used in the example at the beginning of the chapter. The goal is to have the person believe they're in a different place, surrounded by blue sky and rolling hills.

Another approach is to use transparent lenses with half-silvered mirrors to overlay the virtual image over the real world. Known as heads-up display (HUD) or augmented reality because the focus is on enhancing our view of the real world, it could allow surgeons to view virtual diagnostic screens while performing surgery. Vital signs could be displayed where the surgeon might easily glance at them while operating.

Currently, most commercial HMDs provide only the opaque or masked-off view. More expensive HMDs provide HUD displays and are used primarily by the military as targeting displays for helicopter and fighter pilots.

HMDs remain the greatest stumbling block in a VR system. Availability of a low-cost, high-resolution, light-weight design will revolutionize the industry. Several new approaches are covered in Chapter 8, *Gloves, goggles, & wands* that stand a good chance of triggering this revolution.

Because of these new designs, VR might become more practical and affordable sooner than anyone anticipated. However, current technology is marginally effective for anything other than entertainment. Remember Myron Krueger's point that if a person had the kind of vision seen in today's HMDs, they would be declared legally blind!

"After silence, that which comes nearest to expressing the inexpressible is music." **—Aldous Huxley,** *Music at Night, 1931*

Sound cues

After sight, sound is the next most important sensory channel for virtual experiences. It has the advantage of being a channel of communication that can be processed parallel to visual information without being distracting. This same capability allows you to read a book without being distracted by music played at the same time.

In Chapter 8, *Gloves, goggles, & wands*, you'll learn about the *preconscious* power of the visual system that allows you to process information without conscious effort. To a lesser extent, aural processing can be used in much the same way.

Imagine a virtual representation of the stock market, where each stock is represented by a small colored square in an immense grid. The color of the square represents its trading volume while its volatility is represented by the varying pitch of a flute.

As you fly over each square, you hear the stock's volatility while you watch its trading volume. Instead of trying to combine all the variables into a complicated visual image and thereby overloading the visual system, you can use other sensory cues.

Sound can also be used as feedback or as a substitute for tactile sensory cues. If you bump into a virtual object, you might hear a sound informing you of the contact. Or if you move an object, it might make a sound when it comes in contact with other surfaces.

Sound also provides valuable feedback about the nature of the environment. If you drop a brick on a hard surface it makes a different noise than if you drop it on a soft surface.

These cues can teach you about the material properties of the environment and act as limited substitutes for tactile feedback. If you wore a wired glove and moved your hand across a virtual surface, you might hear a modulated sound based on the smoothness or roughness of the surface. After some initial learning, you might even begin to believe that you actually felt something through your fingertips.

Voice synthesis is an additional form of feedback first demonstrated at NASA Ames. It too has many uses: echoing a command, prompting for input, or warning of a dangerous condition.

Because text is nearly impossible to read in a low-resolution HMD, voice synthesis can be used to read textual information out loud in the virtual world. When combined with voice recognition techniques, it allows simple verbal communication with the computer. An important feature if your hands are busy performing other tasks.

In yet another area, sound can contribute to virtual experiences. Studies at MIT's Media Lab demonstrated that simply improving the quality of sound can influence the perception of image quality. When people were shown identical images on two side-by-side TV sets, the one with CD-quality sound was consistently rated as having a better image over the one with standard monaural sound. This same effect can be used to improve the perceived quality of virtual images—especially when current HMD resolution and image quality is so poor to begin with.

NASA Ames pioneered the use of 3-D sounds that can be positioned in the virtual world. 3-D sounds provide important distance and position cues of objects with respect to the participant. In a simulator experiment at NASA Ames, pilots can hear the 3-D sounds of approaching aircraft. Normally, the Traffic Collision Avoidance System (TCAS) alerts pilots to aircraft that have approached too close. By linking the out-the-window position of the approaching aircraft with the virtual sound of the aircraft, pilots were able to more quickly locate the possible threat and take evasive action.

Sound is yet another powerful tool of expression for a world builder. It has the ability to draw you much further into the virtual environment. Can you remember a particularly moving musical piece that gave you chills just listening to it?

Imagine coupling it with compelling virtual images and you get some idea of the potential for expression in this new medium. Of course, few of today's virtual environments generate such strong emotional reactions. Artists are just beginning to use these untapped powers of expression to create powerful new experiences.

Haptic cues Tactile and force feedback are the other senses being actively researched today. Both are part of our *haptic* perceptions. *Tactile feedback* refers to our sense of touch, or pressure applied to the skin. Forces acting on muscles, tendons, and joints are called *force feedback*. When you pick up a baseball, your sense of touch communicates the smoothness of the leather and the roughness of the stitches, and force feedback describes the ball's weight and firmness.

Unfortunately, due to the complexities in accurately simulating and reproducing these forces, a useful device for representing these forces might never exist. Recently, products have emerged that generate a limited sense of force feedback. One of these is a glove with miniature air capillaries that can be pressurized under control of a computer.

First, a special glove is used to record the feel of picking up an object. It measures the amount of pressure at various bend angles of the fingers and hand, thereby creating a force map of the object. After recording the forces, the computer plays them back by controlling the pressure in the glove's capillaries. Though not as solid as the real object, the effect is quite entertaining, but of limited practical use.

Additional work in developing effective tactile sensors using minute finger-tip vibrators is also being researched. These hold the promise of duplicating varying sensations of smoothness, roughness, and simple feedback that something has been touched in the virtual world. This could help counter one of the biggest problems with using a wired glove.

When wearing a glove, you can't easily tell when you've touched an object. Because everything is ghostly and insubstantial, it leads to major difficulties in interaction. You watch your virtual hand pass right through the virtual baseball. Sound feedback could help, but a slight sense of touch in every finger would enhance the experience significantly.

New technologies and materials might revolutionize the development of effective tools for duplicating our haptic senses. But it's more likely to be a few years before you can just "reach out and touch" with a VR system.

Allowing interaction

Because a myriad of devices exist for interacting in a virtual world, choosing the correct one can be difficult. Each one has strengths and weaknesses that need to be considered. For example, grabbing a virtual object with a wired glove might be intuitive, but flying or gesturing requires learning a strange form of sign language that isn't as easy to grasp.

Over the last ten years, the mouse is the only new computer interface device to become widely accepted on desktops. This kind of dominance doesn't exist yet for VR and probably won't for many years. New interaction devices are being researched, developed, and reengineered continuously. Some prove useful, others don't. But lessons are learned as various approaches are tried and tested.

Eventually, a set of tools optimized for virtual explorations will rise from this cauldron of creativity. In fact, ten years from now, current devices will seem practically prehistoric in comparison. This constant flux of ideas and approaches will keep users busy sorting useful techniques from evolutionary dead-ends for some time to come.

Before reviewing various devices, however, it's important to consider types of interactive tasks performed in a virtual environment. These can be broken down into the following categories:

Navigation Navigation means moving your point of view through 3-D space. Examples are moving through a corridor and into another room, flying over a landscape, rotating about, or moving straight up and down. Movement can be constrained or unconstrained.

Selection Selection involves picking a particular element in the 3-D world with the intent of performing an action on it. Examples are selecting a lamp in a living room in order to reorient it, picking a wall to change its color or dimensions, or selecting an object with your hand in order to pick it up.

Interaction After selecting an object, how easy is interaction with it? Some common forms of interaction are moving, deforming, or scaling objects. Once the lamp in the living room has been selected, how you move it to a different location is based on interaction.

Command Some method of controlling or issuing commands to the simulation is required. For example, after selecting an object, you must issue a command to change its color by pressing a button or turning a knob. Remember that wearing HMDs effectively blindfolds you, making the keyboard useless as an input device.

Each device's performance can be evaluated against these four basic tasks. Doing so reveals weaknesses in all current devices. Unfortunately, not one device is successful at all tasks in any kind of simulation. Just as you wouldn't use a hammer to open a window, you need to use the correct tool with VR.

Remember too, that a device's weakness might simply be a function of the software controlling it. Using a mouse can be a good or bad experience depending on how the software controls the interaction. By modifying the interaction, weaknesses can be turned to strengths. Indeed, a rich vein of research is waiting to be mined in the analysis and development of better interaction techniques. It's likely that a whole generation of graduate students will be kept busy researching many of these ideas.

For now, research lags behind the commercialization of many of these devices. We hope that, in coming years, a better balance will be struck to prevent immature technologies from being dropped in the laps of unsuspecting users. Some of the current VR input devices are as follows:

Wired gloves   Wired gloves are composed of fiber-optic, resistive, or mechanical sensors that measure the bend and flex of fingers and the hand (see Fig. 5-6). They usually include a sensor for measuring overall hand orientation and position, known as a six-degree-of-freedom (6 DOF) sensor because it measures a total of six values that define an object's unique position and orientation. Commands are communicated through the use of hand gestures.

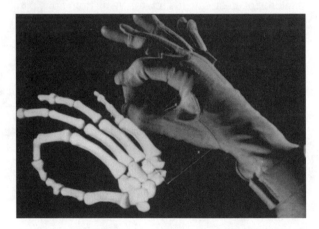

5-6
Another version of the wired glove. As the person bends and flexes his hand, the computer depicts the motion on the display monitor.

The strength of gloves is that they provide intuitive interaction with objects. They also reinforce the sense of presence by allowing you to see your own hand in the virtual world. Their weaknesses are the lack of tactile feedback, difficulty in precisely navigating 3-D space, and the training required to learn an extensive set of gestures.

Force balls   Force balls use mechanical strain gauges to measure the multiple forces or torques applied to a ball-shaped device (see Fig. 5-7). They usually include eight to nine buttons for user-defined commands. Their strength is that they allow for simultaneous input of multiple degrees of freedom, which makes them useful for flight control or object manipulation. Their weakness is that they're nonintuitive, requiring training before use. Object selection hasn't been well addressed, either.

5-7
An example of a force ball. The rubber-coated ball measures forces and torques applied to it.

6 DOF wands and mice   A mouse or wand can be combined with a 6 DOF tracking system. Some of these designs allow the mouse to be used in normal 2-D mode and then automatically switched to 6 DOF once it's lifted off the desk (see Fig. 5-8). Usually one to four switches are available for commands. Its strength is that it provides a simple method of navigating, selecting, and interacting with objects. Its weakness is that performance is very dependent on the type of tracking system used.

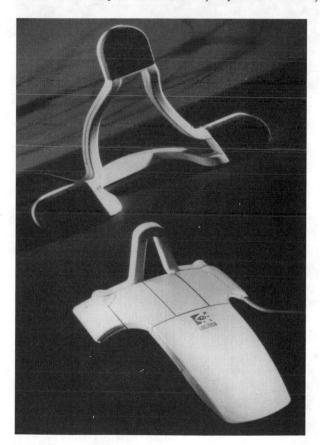

5-8
Ultrasonic tracking allows the Logitech 3-D mouse's position and orientation to be monitored as it moves through space.

Boom A boom is a specialized device for navigation and viewing. It consists of an integrated viewing device and push-buttons for commands, as shown in Fig. 5-9. Its strength is that it's very intuitive for simple navigation tasks, and has a high-resolution image and little sensor lag. Its weaknesses are the lack of support for object selection and limited commands.

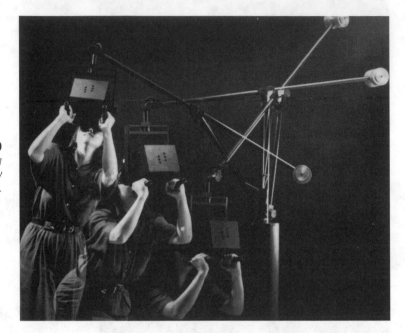

5-9
Time-lapse image of person using a boom device to view a virtual world.

Voice recognition VR systems can effectively use voice recognition techniques based on speaker independence and discrete commands. Each word can control an action. Its strength is in providing a "hands-off" means of controlling the simulation. Its weakness is that it isn't very effective at navigation or directing movement. Due to the computational effort required for recognition, an independent processing system is usually required to operate in parallel with the rest of the VR system.

The next group of devices are either being researched or developed and therefore aren't commonly available; however, they offer other intriguing methods of interaction:

Biosensors These are special glasses or bracelets containing electrodes worn next to the skin. Dermal electrodes are used to monitor muscle electrical activity. They are capable of tracking gross eye movements by measuring muscle movements. There isn't enough data yet to evaluate strengths or weaknesses, but they have the potential to be a natural interface.

Eye tracking Infrared or other optical means are used to track where the eye is currently looking. This technique could be used like biosensors to control view or motion, and could provide a possible interface for those who have lost use of their hands or other motor skills. Again, there isn't yet enough data to evaluate strengths or weaknesses.

The above list is a single snapshot in time of a few current devices and their effectiveness. Because they're all being continually improved, expect many of the weaknesses to be resolved by new materials or interaction modes.

On the far fringe of VR interaction are devices like pivotable surfboards, MIDI (musical-instrument digital interface) devices, and a full-body DataSuit. Though interesting, they haven't been readily adopted.

But just imagine surfing through a 3-D representation of the stock market in search of overlooked market opportunities while playing an electronic flute to select particular industry segments. Brightly colored cubes flash by as you maneuver through a checkerboard landscape of dynamically changing shapes.

Playing a rapid sequence of notes on your flute, you cause the world to suddenly shift as you summon up stocks to replace those previously displayed. Your search continues. Somewhere in that endless digital landscape exists the opportunity you're looking for. As strange as it might seem, the technology exists today to create this.

Whether they're images, 3-D sounds, or tactile vibrations, all aspects of VR must be coordinated and precisely delivered or confusion will result. Think of a symphony and its conductor. The reality engine represents the orchestra, the instruments, the effectors, and the application or simulation manager the conductor.

Reality engines

Working in concert, a virtual experience is constructed from the interplay of the different instruments. Bringing an orchestra to life requires physical power supplied by musicians; bringing a reality engine to life requires significant computing power supplied by hardware.

Only within the last ten years has the required processing power become widely available and affordable. This is an outgrowth of efforts from companies like Intel, Sun, and Motorola to deliver ever more powerful computer chips. Virtual reality is just one of many technologies, like cursive handwriting recognition and speech recognition, that have been waiting in the wings for the right combination of silicon and software.

A peek under the hood of a virtual reality system reveals an engine that an average PC user would quickly recognize. In fact, at the heart of most commercially available VR machines is either an Amiga, Macintosh, or Intel-based personal computer. Special devices and software turn ordinary PCs from word processors into reality generators. If you were to simplify a VR system, focusing only on the reality engine, you'd wind up with the illustration in Fig. 5-10.

To create a virtual-reality system, you'd start with a personal computer or workstation, and add hardware to supplement sound and graphics creation. Because stereoscopic images require separate video images for each eye, two graphics boards need to be added. Alternatively, two separate computers can be used, as long as some method of keeping them synchronized exists (without this, it becomes distracting if your left eye is in one world and your right eye is in a different one).

Before the video output from the graphics boards can be used by the head-mounted display, it usually has to be converted to the same kind of signal your VCR accepts (NTSC), though some HMDs accept the computer's video signal directly.

external hardware · computer system

5-10
Diagram showing major components of a reality engine.

If 3-D sound is used, special boards are required, along with some method of creating synthesized sounds or playing back sampled ones. Communication with other VR devices, like head-trackers, wired gloves, and force balls, is done through standard input/output ports found on the back of every computer.

All these pieces taken together represent quite a number of additions to the original system. This is why many VR vendors provide complete system integration to minimize the confusion of assembling such a Gordian knot of cables, connectors, and boards. Table 5-1 summarizes some of the different hardware approaches major VR vendors are currently offering.

Table 5-1
Hardware platforms used by major VR vendors

Platform	Vendor	Graphics sub-system	Sound
Amiga	W Industries	TI 34020 (custom)	built-in
Intel-PC	Sense8, Division	Intel i750™, i860™ CPU	MIDI, 3D sound
Macintosh	VPL	i860™ CPU	built-in, 3D sound
Sun	Sense8	GX+	
SGi	Sense8,VPL	GL	MIDI
IBM RS6000	Division	i860™ CPU	
Custom	Division	i860™ CPU	built-in

As you can see, quite a mix of hardware is represented. Generating complex 3-D images in a fraction of a second determines, more than anything else, whether certain hardware can be used for a virtual-reality system. If smooth, 3-D images can't be generated in real time, then the computer can't be used for VR.

Our everyday sense of reality isn't experienced in discrete "chunks," nor does it pause before resuming. Virtual environments must be smooth and responsive to be useful. Human perceptual studies show that response times of under 100 milliseconds are generally considered interactive, or real time. Response times slower than this become noticeable and affect performance.

Real-time requirements

Within this tiny slice of time, not much more than a blink of an eye, the reality engine must process the entire cycle of retrieving user input (head or hand movements), performing calculations, and generating a new image for the head-mounted display. Most of the time is spent rendering the new image, or left and right images in the case of stereoscopic views. This is the reason why all commercial VR systems use powerful graphics hardware to accelerate the rendering process.

If it takes 100 milliseconds to make one pass through the event loop, then one frame is rendered every 0.1 second or 10 frames in one second. This doesn't sound very impressive when you consider that movies are shown at 24 fps and TVs display at 30 fps.

However, it's important to understand the difference between playback experiences like movies and interactive experiences like virtual reality. Movies and TV simply play back previously recorded images, while VR systems calculate new images from scratch every frame. Images aren't prestored or prerendered. This is a crucial difference, because it allows interactive movement of your point of view to any location or orientation in the 3-D world.

Imagine generating the images of rolling hills and the house mentioned at the beginning of this chapter. One way would be to use an imaginary camera that could take a spherical picture of a scene from any vantage point. Using this camera and a 3-D rendering program, you could follow a path through the 3-D world, taking a picture every few steps. Replaying the correct images, you would appear to travel along a 3-D path and be able look all about you.

Storing all possible positions and views, however, would require quite a few gigabytes (1000 megabytes) of space, so that isn't a practical solution. Instead, VR systems interactively calculate what you would see depending on where you are in the 3-D world.

And they allow you to wander anywhere off the beaten path and perhaps discover some new sight previously missed, unlike the camera method, which supplies only a single line of action. This level of interactivity sets virtual reality apart from other noninteractive forms of visualization.

6 Virtual-world building blocks

The basic building blocks

What is the virtual world composed of? What are its basic building blocks of matter? Answers to questions like these invariably depend on the implementation.

However, most virtual environments share some fundamental aspects—which you can learn about by disassembling a virtual world into its component parts. The following definitions are loosely based on Sense8's WorldToolKit development tools:

Objects

Objects are discrete 3-D shapes that can be independently interacted with. A movable lamp or sofa, a flying bird, and a swimming fish are all examples. They can be represented by visible, audible, or tactile cues. This can lead to interesting juxtapositions, where you can feel an object but not see it, or hear it but not see or feel it.

Objects are optionally subject to physical laws. If you drop an object, does it fall? Several objects can be assembled hierarchically into a single object—like a hand composed of fingers, which in turn is composed of finger segments. Moving the hand moves all the related pieces.

Objects are typically the movable elements in a virtual world. There are *static* objects, which don't move until interacted with, and *dynamic* objects, which move based on simulation control—like an automatic door that opens as you approach it, or a rotating carousel. Without objects, virtual environments would be static and lifeless—limited to simple walkthroughs.

Only a single stationary backdrop is present at one time. It can't be moved or broken into smaller elements. Typically, it's the underlying structure upon which the virtual environment is built. In the example from the previous chapter, the rolling green hills and structure of the house would be the stationary backdrop. This is a choice made by the world designer to prevent participants from moving the house, the hills, or the walls in the house—these capabilities might distract from the task at hand.

Backdrop

Though the backdrop remains fixed in place, it doesn't mean that it can't be interacted with; often, the colors and other physical properties can be modified. For example, a wall that's part of a backdrop can change color or appearance, but it can't be moved or resized.

The viewpoint is the perspective, or point of view, of the observer in the virtual world. By controlling the viewpoint with a sensor like a joystick, the observer can navigate the virtual world. By attaching a head-tracking sensor to the viewpoint, the motion of the observer's head also controls the viewpoint, allowing him to look around naturally. Multiple viewpoints are possible; they can even be shown on the same display, allowing you to see ahead of and behind you at the same time—a useful trick in some situations.

Viewpoints

Sensors are all the physical devices, like head-tracking sensors, wired gloves, and force balls, that are used in a virtual world. Sensors can be attached to viewpoints or to objects. If attached to viewpoints, then movement of the physical sensor moves the participant's point of view equivalently. If attached to an object, like attaching the 3-D model of a hand to wired-glove sensors, you can see your fingers wiggle on your virtual hand.

Sensors

Multiple light sources can be positioned and oriented anywhere in the world. Different forms exist, such as directed, spot, and ambient. Intensities and colors can be interactively modified. Light is dynamically calculated, so you can move a light around and watch different surfaces light up.

Lights

The universe is the current environment of the simulation. It includes objects and related entities: lights, sensors, viewpoints, and sound channels. The simulation manager is aware only of entities previously "added" to the universe. And only objects in the universe are actually drawn on the display.

Universe

Objects and entities that exist outside the universe are ignored until they're added to the simulation. This allows multiple objects to be loaded into an application, and added or removed as necessary. By keeping them part of the application and not deleting them, you can quickly put them back into the simulation. See Fig. 6-1 for a diagram of this process.

For example, several different models of sofas might be loaded into an application, but only one added to the universe. The user could step through the various sofa models by removing the old sofa and then adding the next model. This kind of flexibility is important in developing complex simulations.

Using this model to conceptualize a virtual world is just one of several possible choices. Because of the malleable nature of VR, other representational models exist

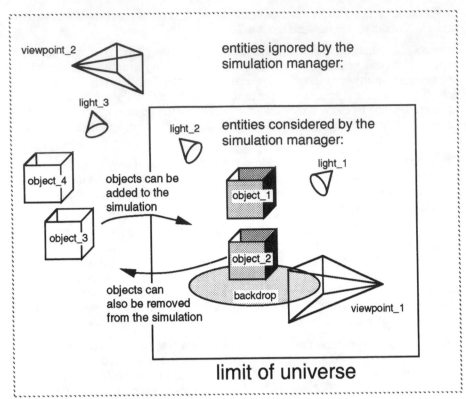

entities ignored by the simulation manager:

viewpoint_2

light_3

entities considered by the simulation manager:

light_2

light_1

object_4

objects can be added to the simulation

object_1

object_3

object_2

backdrop

objects can also be removed from the simulation

viewpoint_1

limit of universe

limit of application

6-1
Logical components of a virtual simulation. Entities can be moved in and out of the simulation manager's consideration.

and are just as relevant. This is just one approach that has already been implemented and is being used to build virtual environments.

Keep in mind that current VR systems have only a vague understanding of real physical properties. Dropping a virtual glass onto a virtual floor of a kitchen doesn't cause it to shatter or make a sound unless the world designer specifically programmed it to do so.

Simple underlying physical principles like these are almost completely missing from current systems. Another magnitude increase in computing power will be required before complex dynamics or kinematics become standard aspects of a virtual environment. Simulating reality is no mean feat.

Simulation management

Orchestrating computational resources, interface devices, and system resources to manufacture a semblance of reality is the responsibility of the *simulation manager* and *application* in a virtual-reality system. Think of the simulation manager as the core of a spreadsheet program (like Lotus 1-2-3, or Microsoft's Excel), and the VR application as the actual spreadsheet that appears on the computer screen.

You use the spreadsheet's graphical interface to harness the power of the simulation engine at the core of the spreadsheet program. Through this interface, you determine the nature of your simulation. It could be a financial, scientific, or even a home diet simulator. The spreadsheet interface is a blank slate waiting for problems to solve.

In the same way, a VR application uses the capabilities of the simulation manager to rapidly construct and model visualization problems. Just as the user's spreadsheet defines what kind of problem is being analyzed, the VR application defines the kind of 3-D simulation that is being presented.

At the beginning of the previous chapter, a simulation of a landscape and house was described. Inside the house, a lamp was selected and moved from one position to another. The application defined how this interaction would occur and gave instructions to the simulation manager, which then directed the hardware to carry out the task.

Depending on your imagination and tools, you can create almost any kind of virtual environment. In fact, the many different VR applications covered in the third part of this book prove the flexibility of this new technology.

Just as there are many issues to consider when looking at different spreadsheet programs, the same is true of the tools necessary for simulation management:

Simulation-management tools

Interface to the simulation manager How are applications created? Do they require programming, or do they use graphical interfaces? This usually determines who can use the tool and its flexibility.

Device support How many different interface devices can be used? It's too early in the development of VR to single out a single interface technology as the best one for all purposes. Support for multiple devices allows you to experiment and pick the correct one for an application.

Object control What can you do with an object once you've selected it? Can you interact with it or modify its shape, position, and appearance? Objects should have tasks that can be independently executed, like an automatic door that opens as you approach. Collision detection is another key feature. It constrains objects so they don't interpenetrate, or warns you when they do. Additionally, constraints and hierarchical behavior simplify creating links between objects, such as the fingers of a hand. If you move the hand, you want the fingers to automatically follow.

Simulation control Many different attributes control a simulation. Rendering style, lighting, viewing angle, communication with other programs, and databases are just a few. Support for modeling of mass, gravity, momentum, and other physical properties could also be useful. Advanced tools even allow networking of multiple simulations so that more than one participant can interact in the same virtual world.

Modeling support How are 3-D models created? Some tools provide a simple modeling capability or read common file formats. More powerful tools allow interactive creation of objects within the virtual environment itself.

As you can see, someone investigating the development of a VR application must grapple with many issues. Other considerations of price, performance, and platform support are important, but the intent here is to focus on just capabilities. The first consideration and probably the most important, is the interface to the simulation manager. Three possibilities exist:

Interface options

Compiled libraries   Compiled libraries are also known as an API, or application programming interface or toolkit. They typically provide the most flexibility in creating a virtual environment. The cost of this flexibility is that you generally have to be a programmer to use them and you usually need to compile your application every time you make a change. A compiled library is the tool of choice for those interested in developing complex, stand-alone virtual reality applications. Nonprogrammers should avoid using it.

Scripted language   A scripted language simplifies the creation of simulations. Even nonprogrammers can pick up the language in a relatively short amount of time. It typically uses an interpretive environment, where changes are instantly incorporated into the simulation. It's similar to learning a database programming language. Scripting generally trades off some flexibility for a much simpler interface to the simulation manager.

Graphical   This is the tool for the point-and-click crowd. If properly done, it provides a simple intuitive interface to the simulation manager. Basic simulations can quickly be created and modified. It's a very accessible tool for nonprogrammers, but might be more difficult to use for intricate simulations. VPL's *Body Electric* graphic interface is an example of this approach, as shown in Fig. 6-2.

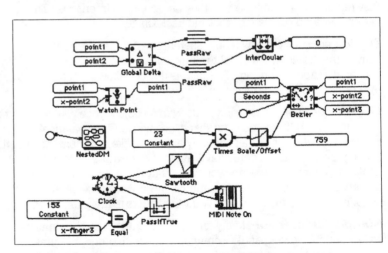

6-2
VPL's Body Electric is an example of a graphical method of describing the dynamics of a virtual environment.

Each of these interfaces allows different kinds of interaction with the simulation manager and its simulation event loop. This loop is the locus of control for a VR system, which means that the entire simulation depends on its consistent, rhythmic timing.

Performing a calculation in 0.1 second or even 10 seconds isn't important in a spreadsheet because the simulation is time-independent. But if the VR system's simulation event loop took 0.2 second instead of 0.1 second, you'd notice it because the world would suddenly become less interactive.

Event loop   When running a VR application, the computer repeatedly loops through a sequence of events until the simulation quits. This is known as the *simulation event loop*. A single pass through the loop is considered a *tick* and often occurs in a fraction of a second.

Unlike a clock where each tick represents a precise amount of time, a simulation manager's tick varies constantly because it depends on the complexity of the scene and how long it takes the computer to render it. The number of frames per second and the number of ticks per second is always identical.

In the example at the beginning of the previous chapter, the participant enters a virtual living room and proceeds to move a lamp that is incorrectly positioned. This interaction can be dissected to better understand how the event loop functions (see Fig. 6-3). Most of the steps in the event loop are performed automatically by the simulation manager without the programmer's help. These steps are identified with a [SM].

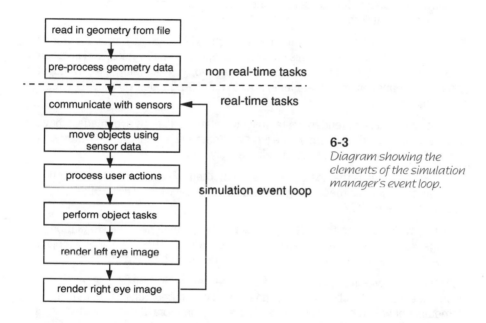

6-3
Diagram showing the elements of the simulation manager's event loop.

Query sensors   [SM] Each input sensor attached to the reality engine has to be polled as to its current state. For example, the head-tracker has to communicate the current position or orientation of the participant's head. The simulation manager looks at its list of currently enabled input sensors, and questions each one in turn. The state of each sensor is stored away for later use.

Update objects   [SM] At this point the stored information from the sensors is used to update the position and orientation of any objects they're attached to. Sensors can be attached to viewpoints, as in the case of head-tracking, or to other objects, as in the case of the lamp. Sometimes more than one sensor is attached to an object. For example, your viewpoint might be controlled by both a head-tracking sensor and a joystick. This would allow you to look around while at the same time flying over the rolling green hills.

User actions   This is the world designer's chance to control and direct the simulation. User actions define the type of interaction that will occur between the participant and the virtual environment. This is the break or pause in the event loop where control is passed to the world designer's unique set of rules or specifications.

For example, based on an event like the lamp being selected, you might connect the lamp to the sensor controlling movement. It could be a joystick, wired glove, or any other device. The next time through the event loop, if the sensor is moved, the lamp will also move.

Object tasks   [SM] Any object can have a task that's automatically executed every tick. This allows autonomous activity by objects in the simulation. In the earlier example, the front door automatically opened for the participant as they neared it. In this case, the distance between the door and the user is tracked and, if the user passes a certain point, it triggers an event causing the door to begin rotating open. Each successive tick the door opens slightly wider.

Render   [SM] Once all activity has been registered for a single frame, the world is ready to be rendered (drawn). This is a complex operation all by itself, and is covered in greater detail in the next chapter. Basically, it involves examining the 3-D model or geometry information and determining how to draw 3-D models on the 2-D screen of the display device.

VR systems capable of rendering stereoscopic views (left/right eye images), have to perform this task independently for each eye. Sometimes, dual graphics hardware allows these images to be drawn simultaneously.

If the reality engine is the heart of a VR system, then the event loop is the portion of the brain that controls the beating of the heart. It endlessly cycles until the simulation is terminated.

Now that we've defined the building blocks and explained how the simulation manager supervises how the blocks are handled, it's time to examine how objects and backdrops are actually represented and understood by the computer.

Geometry

3-D structures, whether a house or a landscape, can be described as a series of 3-D coordinate values. A collection of such values is called *geometry* or *model* data. Remember how in the discussion of early scene generators, Sutherland and others discovered the technique of using computers to interactively draw scenes of airports and landscapes?

Prior to that discovery, video cameras had been mounted on movable platforms over detailed miniature models to generate similar views. Computers were found to be much more effective than video cameras, which eventually became obsolete for this purpose. VR systems use computers in the same way to image or render 3-D worlds.

Any point in space can be described using three coordinate values: X, Y, and Z. With three such points, a flat triangular shape can be defined, and with eight points, a cube. The illustration in Fig. 6-4 shows how a cube would be viewed from a particular point in space.

Simple rules of perspective guide the computer in creating the 2-D image on the video screen using 3-D information defining the size and placement of the cube.

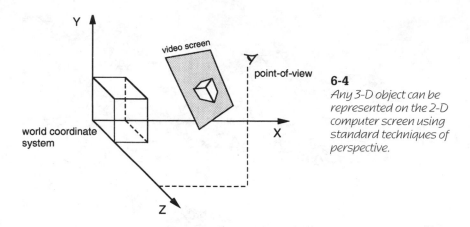

6-4
Any 3-D object can be represented on the 2-D computer screen using standard techniques of perspective.

This is how 3-D graphics are generated—the tricky part is doing it quickly enough for VR.

More complex objects can easily be constructed using simple procedures like the triangular patch. The terrain and house described at the beginning of the previous chapter would require at least 1000 of these basic shapes. To keep track of all this 3-D data, it's organized and stored in special files known as geometry or model files. These files are usually distinct from the actual VR application, and are created using 3-D modeling tools like Autodesk's AutoCAD, Paracomp's Swivel3-D, and Software Systems' Multigen.

To understand the process of modeling a virtual world, imagine trying to construct the earlier described terrain using simple paper shapes. Starting with the hills and valley, triangular shapes can fit together to approximate their surfaces, as shown in Fig. 6-5. By making the triangular pieces smaller, a more natural looking hillside can be created, as illustrated in Fig. 6-6.

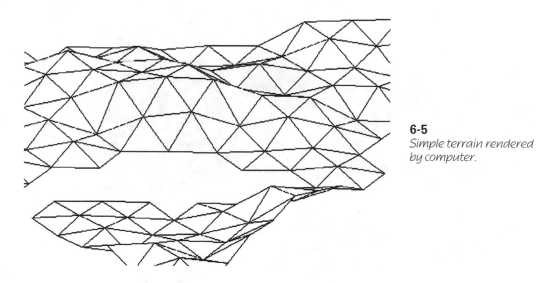

6-5
Simple terrain rendered by computer.

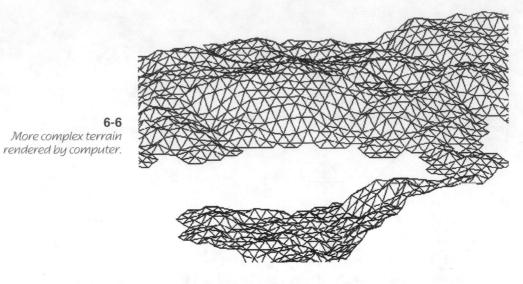

6-6
More complex terrain rendered by computer.

Unfortunately, if you use too many small triangular pieces (or polygons), it will take forever to assemble the world either by hand or by computer. Just to give you some idea, there are around 150 polygons in the first drawing and about 1500 in the second one. The second image, therefore, would require at least ten times the processing power to be drawn as fast as the first image.

For now, let's stick with the first drawing. To make the landscape look more natural, you can simply color each triangle a different shade of green, based on how light strikes its surface, as seen in Fig. 6-7.

This changes the original wire-frame image into one with shaded surfaces. All VR systems render worlds with at least this quality of representation. Shading objects based on a light source helps you recognize outlines and orientations of objects.

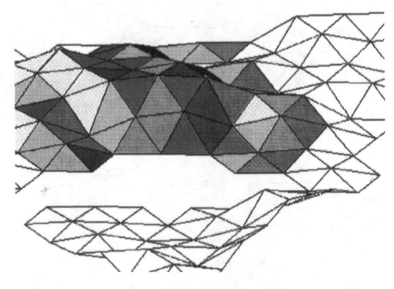

6-7
Simulation of lighting by the computer results in a shaded view of the terrain.

In this case, it helped distinguish the shape of the hills. Even with shading, however, the landscape still appears cartoonish and unnatural. To improve the realism, you can take a picture of a hillside and scan it into a computer (see Fig. 6-8).

6-8
Scanned image of a portion of a hillside.

This rectangular image must then be cut and shaped to fit on the triangular patches. Doing this results in the final image of the terrain, showing real images mapped onto the surface of the triangles, as shown in Fig. 6-9.

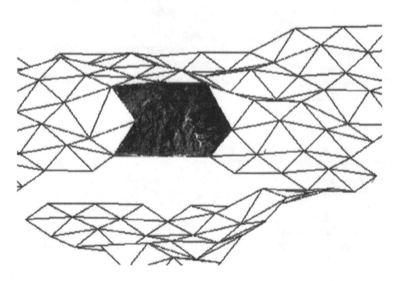

6-9
The hillside image is texture-mapped onto the surface of the terrain, creating a more realistic image.

Applying images in this manner is called *texture mapping*, and requires special hardware to process it quickly enough for a VR system. Texturing can dramatically improve the realism of the finished image, which is why all high-end flight simulators take advantage of this technique.

Satellite photos of terrain, mapped onto 3-D models like the one shown above, allows virtual trips to anywhere on Earth or beyond. You probably saw news clips of a simulated camera ride over the surface of Mars and Venus. It might have appeared to be produced by a real camera, but it was actually a synthetic view created frame by frame on a computer. It clearly demonstrated just how effective this technique can be.

Instead of building worlds out of pieces of cardboard and photographs, VR systems assemble them by calculating how each triangle or polygon (there can be thousands) would look if viewed from a certain distance and direction. Next, all the polygons are sorted so that the ones furthest away from the user's viewpoint are drawn first. In this way, the 3-D scene is built-up from layers of polygons drawn on the screen.

This entire process is repeated every time the viewpoint changes (in a head-tracked VR system, each time the person moves his head slightly). Don't forget, this all has to occur in a blink of an eye to be useful. Which is why real-time 3-D graphics is so computationally intensive, and why the number of polygons in the scene is so important.

The woes of world building

One of the greatest challenges facing a world designer lies in creating the 3-D models needed for building virtual experiences. Because of performance constraints (the update rate decreases as the number of polygons increase), world designers have to carefully construct their world—too many polygons and the world becomes jerky and uninhabitable.

It's like telling a carpenter that he can use only a limited amount of wood to create a house. It forces the carpenter to use each piece of wood wisely and to the greatest effect. So too must the world builder craft his experience. Instead of wood and nails, shaded and textured polygons are cleverly assembled to provide the most effective environment with the fewest number of polygons.

This constraint will always exist, although the threshold or "polygon budget" will increase over time. In 1992 most mid-range VR systems are limited to worlds of roughly 500–1000 polygons in size. When you consider that the average architectural model uses 5000–10,000 polygons, you can see that we're still a few years away from supporting the needs of architects who want to walk through the worlds they've already built without deleting a great deal of detail first.

One method around this restriction is the use of *texture mapping*. It's been said that a picture is worth a thousand words; well, in VR, a texture-mapped polygon is worth at least ten and sometimes even 1000 shaded polygons. Instead of using thousands of polygons to model the complexity of a tree with its branches and leaves, a simple approximation can be made using just two polygons and a realistic image of a tree.

This image is edited with a paint program so that black paint is applied to all parts of the image except the tree. When drawn by the computer, the black paint will become transparent and it will appear that you can look through the branches of the tree. Using a trick developed by the flight-simulation industry, two intersecting polygons and the transparent texture of a tree can be combined to form a very realistic 3-D image of a tree, as illustrated in Fig. 6-10.

6-10
Realistic 3-D trees are created by combining two perpendicular tree images. When viewed transparently, they appear to be fully formed trees.

If you're building a virtual forest with hundreds of trees, tricks like this are critical to creating a sense of realism with only a few polygons to go around. In fact, texture mapping is often the only way a sense of realism can be achieved. Imagine trying to create a 3-D model of a lawn by drawing each blade of grass by hand—it isn't practical nor useful. Instead, a single texture-mapped polygon of a swatch of grass (used repeatedly) would achieve a far better effect.

Very few VR systems have yet to master the complexities of performing real-time texture mapping—primarily because it's a complicated and computationally intensive problem usually requiring specialized hardware. Because of its obvious advantages, however, texture mapping is certain to become a fundamental aspect of all virtual worlds.

This leads to the next problem: though there are dozens of software tools for 3-D modeling, few provide the right combination of features for a virtual-world builder. Ideally you would want a paint program, 3-D modeler, real-time renderer, and interface to a hierarchical database all in a single package. One of these, the Multigen modeling tool is shown in Fig. 6-11.

Few 3-D modeling tools understand the challenges of not only building virtual worlds, but also efficiently managing a complex database of objects and attributes. Except for some notable exceptions from the flight-simulation industry, which cost tens of thousands of dollars, our world-building tools are stuck in the Stone Age. Hopefully, the Bronze Age is right around the corner.

One fundamental problem with all 3-D modeling tools is that they're primarily concerned with only a visual representation of an object. Though these tools might provide powerful capabilities to create photo-realistic scenes, visual information is just one of many different object attributes a virtual world builder must consider.

What are the object's physical properties? How much does it weigh? Where is its center of mass? What is it made of? What sound does it make on contact with another surface? Is its surface spongy or hard, rough or smooth?

6-11
Sophisticated modeling tools and hierarchial databases are needed to create and manage virtual worlds. Powerful tools from the flight simulator industry will eventually become available for desktop systems.

These are just a few of the representational issues. What about the relationship between objects? How do you describe the mechanics of a chain link or all the interconnected parts of a piston engine? How do you define a fluid or a gas? What is its viscosity or color?

This entire book could be filled with all the facets of reality that we can't represent. Imagine a carpenter being asked to build a hundred-story skyscraper using only a stone axe. Today's virtual world builders face a similar task in creating truly realistic experiences.

Of course, most technologically-based media, like film and television, have battled initial limitations only to succeed through the determined efforts of those able to see beyond the limitations. There's much that we can't do with the state of today's technology, but there's also much we *can* do.

At the beginning of chapter 5, *Reality engines*, a virtual experience of flying over green, rolling hills and visiting a house was detailed. This helped set the context for exploring the hardware, software, and perceptual issues involved in a VR system. It also revealed the complexity hidden behind the naturalness of the virtual experience.

Though a correctly designed virtual world can dramatically simplify our interaction with a computer, it's also one of the most complicated systems to build. No one said manufacturing reality would be easy—and it isn't. The next challenge is to take a descriptive virtual experience and figure out how to turn an IBM PC from a word processor into a cyberspace machine.

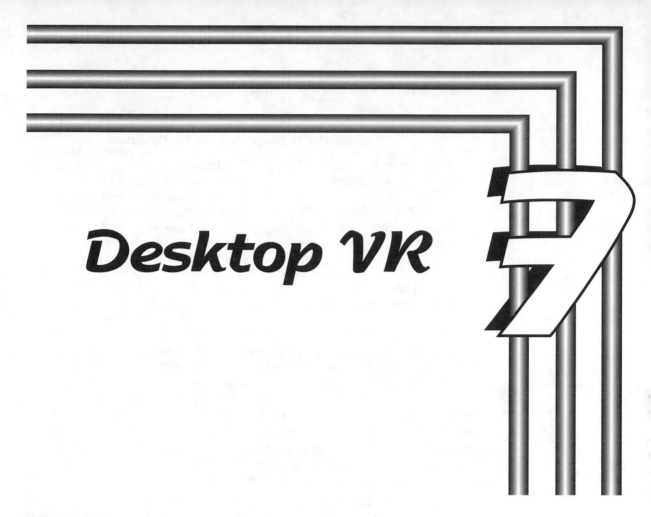

Desktop VR

How is a PC transformed into a magic carpet ride through a virtual world with hills, trees, and wide rivers? How can you use one to create such a world in the first place? The intent of this section is to answer some of the mechanical issues associated with creating a VR system capable of duplicating the virtual experience described at the beginning of chapter 5.

By focusing on a PC solution, we'll demonstrate that VR isn't a technology restricted to those with multimillion dollar budgets—it's well within the reach of average-sized businesses.

Though a PC remains the most inexpensive approach to a VR system, it still isn't inexpensive. Sticking with the definition of virtual reality stated at the very beginning of the previous chapter, a complete PC-based system can be assembled for less than $20,000 in 1992 dollars.

A sample PC-based VR system

However, even a budget this size still limits the configuration. Because several different hardware and software combinations can be assembled to create a virtual experience, there needs to be some method of choosing a particular set of VR tools or devices.

One approach is to first sit down and make a list of the essential elements of the simulation. Next, you need to match each requirement with appropriate hardware or software tools. This configuration is based on the requirements for being able to create the virtual world presented in chapter 5. The results are shown in Table 7-1.

Table 7-1
VR application requirements and configuration

Requirement	Configuration
grass-covered hillsides	texture-mapping hardware
stereoscopic view	two graphics boards or two PCs
sense of "being there"	head-mounted display, head-tracking
locating sound of radio	3D sound hardware
changing pitch of wind sound	sound synthesizer hardware
selecting lamp	interaction device
movement of objects and viewpoint	navigation device
moving lamp	separate objects in simulation
lamp movement changes lighting	dynamic lighting in simulation

Using this information as a guide, your software and hardware decisions will be driven by the requirements of the application. To start with, because texture mapping is required, you'll need to use Sense8's WorldToolKit and two Intel ActionMedia II graphics boards. Next, you'll have to use a powerful Intel 486 microprocessor class PC with a reasonable amount of memory (at least 4Mb) as the computing platform.

To create the sense of immersion, you'll need a head-mounted display like Virtual Research's Flight Helmet. Because these helmets accept only TV-formatted signals (NTSC), you also need a couple of signal converters.

To keep the costs down, a Logitech ultrasonic head-tracker can be used to monitor the helmet orientation. Recreating the sound of the virtual radio so that it's spatially oriented will require a convolving engine like Crystal River Engineering's Beachtron, which also happens to have some sound synthesizing capability (for the wind sound).

Trying to select the lamp while wearing a HMD is a little tricky. A wired glove would be useful, but it's too expensive. Instead, the navigation device will have to do double duty.

To get around the virtual world, a Gravis MouseStick will provide an inexpensive and intuitive solution. Moving objects around and changing lighting dynamically is a feature of Sense8's WorldToolKit, which also supports all the devices listed and described so far.

In addition to all these devices, you also need a 3-D modeler, like Alias Upfront or AutoCAD, to construct the basic objects in the world and an image or paint program that can read in scanned photographs and allow modifications for making custom textures. Each of these pieces plays a role in creating and exploring a virtual environment.

By the time you read this, further developments have probably brought down the cost of such a system to an even lower level. As can be seen in Table 7-2, the HMD

Table 7-2
Relative costs of a PC-based VR system

Product	% of Budget
Virtual Research Flight Helmet	30
(2) Intel ActionMedia II Graphics boards	19
Sense8 WorldToolKit	17
50-MHz i486™ CPU-based PC with 4 Mbytes of RAM and a 100 Mbyte hard drive	12
Beachfron 3D sound	8
Logitech ultrasonic head-tracker	5
(2) NTSC converters	3
3D Modeling program	2
Image or paint program	2
Gravis MouseStick	1

represents the biggest slice of the system. Because each one is hand-tooled, this will remain true until volumes justify mass-production techniques. Table 7-2 reveals the relative expense of various system elements based on a total budget of $20,000.

This is just one way a VR system could be configured. Other devices, software, and hardware could be combined to recreate the necessary experience. This combination is driven primarily by cost. A wired glove could have been used, but at $9000, there's little room for it.

If cost isn't a factor, you could easily spend five times as much money to create a higher-quality experience using higher-resolution displays, more powerful graphics hardware, and more sophisticated interface devices.

We've already described the basic components of a VR system: *effectors, reality engine, application,* and *geometry*. The relationship of these elements to the previously outlined configuration is depicted in Fig. 7-1.

Some assembly required

Additional details on the HMD, head-tracker, and joystick are covered in the next chapter. One of the more interesting features of this system is the use of Intel's ActionMedia II graphics boards. Though typically associated with the compression and decompression of digitized video, these boards have other less-known talents.

Fast 3-D graphics on a PC requires special boards because most Intel-based PCs separate the graphics system from the CPU by a very slow 8Mhz bus. It's like trying to fill a bucket with a small straw. The small diameter of the straw quickly becomes a limiting factor despite additional water pressure. To get around this, a form of compression is used. The CPU sends terse graphics messages to the ActionMedia II board instead of lengthy pixel-by-pixel instructions.

For example, the ActionMedia II board could be instructed with less than 20 bytes to draw an odd-shaped polygon in the center of the display. A typical VGA display, on the other hand, would require a lengthy list of instructions describing the placement of each pixel.

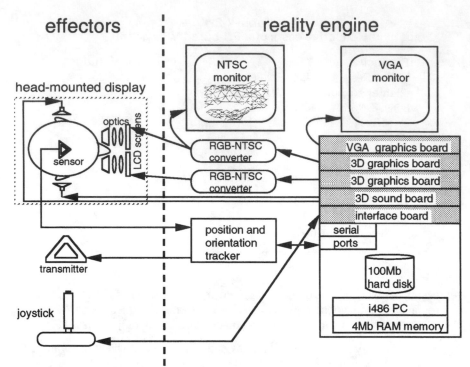

7-1
Components of an IBM PC-based virtual-reality system.

Another advantage is that the DVI board independently draws these images, allowing the CPU to resume calculations after issuing a stream of graphics commands. This combination of parallelism and high-level graphics messaging achieves the necessary performance for real-time graphics. The illustration in Fig. 7-2 provides a quick look inside this unique graphics board.

Arch Luther's book, *Digital Video in the PC Environment*, provides an excellent primer on the DVI technology and its applications. After assembling the system, developing the application is the next step. It's easiest to tackle this in the following order: First, modeling—constructing the physical representation of the rolling hills, house and furniture. Second, application development—defining how the automatic front door works, how the lamp is moved, and how the sound of the radio is located.

Reality on a budget

Every world designer has a "polygon budget" they have to consider when developing a VR application. This is defined as the number of polygons available to build their virtual world at a particular update rate. Designers need to understand how to juggle the conflicting demands of image complexity (measured in polygons) with performance (measured in frames-per-second).

Different combinations of hardware and software yield different polygon budgets. This is also strongly influenced by the expense of the system's graphics hardware. Performance varies from 3000–5000 polygons/sec on a VR system using Intel's ActionMedia II boards, to 300,000 polygons/sec on SGi's reality engine image generators.

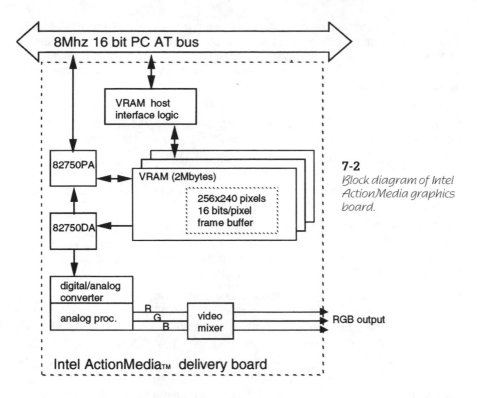

7-2
Block diagram of Intel ActionMedia graphics board.

Determining the polygon budget is as simple as dividing the performance numbers by the required update or frame rate. Because the use of a head-tracking system requires a minimum of 10 frames-per-second in order to minimize lag effects, you have a budget of 300–500 polygons with which to build your world.

Depending on the system configuration, if both left and right eye images are being rendered to create stereo pairs, then this budget will be further reduced by 20–50 percent because of the additional computations for two views. If separate PCs were used to generate the view for each eye, then no degradation in performance would occur.

Because the system mentioned at the beginning of the chapter uses two graphics boards, the impact of stereo is lessened to about 20 percent, or a budget of 250–400 polygons. This then gets divided up between the various objects in the world, such as the landscape, house, and furniture. Knowing how many polygons you can use to build the house determines how much complexity you can put into it.

Now that you know your budget, you can go to work creating the physical models of the landscape, house, and furniture described at the beginning of chapter 5. In order to experience flying into the house perched on the rolling hills, you have to first construct or model the world.

Starting with the terrain, and using a 3-D modeling package like AutoCAD or Swivel 3-D Professional, you must painstakingly assemble dozens of small triangular patches to represent the hills and valleys—a somewhat tedious effort depending on your talents as a 3-D modeler.

Modeling

You can either color each patch green to represent grass, or apply a picture of real grass to each segment of the terrain with texture mapping, described in the final section of chapter 6. When the WorldToolKit software reads the file containing the terrain's geometry information, it can automatically apply a picture of a swatch of grass onto every triangle in the terrain.

Because most 3-D modeling formats don't support texture mapping (specially AutoCAD DXF files) you'll have to use some tricks to save this information in the file. Assembling the terrain, triangle by triangle, is a very slow process.

Other possibilities exist, like using a fractal algorithm (a random method based on Chaos theory, heavily used in computer graphics to generate detailed, imaginary landscapes). The 3-D terrain shown in the section of chapter 6 called *Geometry*, for example, was created using fractal techniques.

Another possibility is using real-world data. There are several government sources of terrain information, like the Department of Defense's Mapping Agency. They have collected elevation data, photographs, and culture data (objects like buildings, factories, etc.) from locations all over the world.

In the flight simulator business, automated tools read in this assortment of data and created a recognizable virtual world of just about any well-traveled location. And if you want to go off-planet, NASA has publicly accessible elevation and image data for Mars and other heavenly bodies.

Continuing on your own world building, you can add trees to the terrain by using the method of two crossed polygons with an image of tree transparently mapped onto each one (discussed at the end of the previous chapter). This allows you to populate the hillside, even on a limited budget.

Constructing a house is done by assembling polygons into walls, floors, windows, sofas, and lamps. Where appropriate, images of stone can be mapped onto surfaces like the fireplace, or wood paneling on the floor or walls. Various companies sell computer disks with hundreds of prescanned and pattern-matched images of wood, stone, and other natural images. These can be a useful starting point, or you can scan any photograph into a computer and modify it.

For example, an animated sequence of flames can be created by taking a scanned picture of a fireplace, modifying the flames with a paint program, and then saving the new image. After doing this four or five times, you create an animation where cycling through the pictures will quickly give the appearance of flickering flames.

For now, however, the first picture in the animation is applied to the opening in the fireplace. Later, using WorldToolKit's texture flipping features, you'll animate this to bring it to life. Figure 7-3 is an illustration of the textures created so far.

7-3
Grass, stone, wood, and fireplace images. These are examples of scanned photographs that can be used as textures and applied to surfaces of 3-D objects.

Virtual Reality

Using the same paint program, you can draw a large bay window so that all the glass is colored pure black. A special WorldToolKit texture mapping mode turns the black color into transparent paint that you can see through. This creates the effect of looking through a framed window at the world outside, as shown in Fig. 7-4.

7-4
Using a special color, transparent windows can be created, allowing you to look through the glass.

You'll have to create the movable lamp and automatic front door separate from the stationary world because there's no standard way to keep objects separate in AutoCAD DXF files (the most popular 3-D file format). The radio will also need to be created separately because you'll want to attach a 3-D sound source to it later in the application. This way, if you move the radio, the sound will move with it. At the end of the world building, the files listed in Table 7-3 have been created.

Table 7-3
Files used to describe the virtual world

File	Type	Description
world.dxf	geometry	contains terrain and house along with furniture
radio.dxf	geometry	single model of the radio
door.dxf	geometry	single model of the front door
lamp.dxf	geometry	single model of the lamp
window.i16	texture	picture of bay window with glass blacked out
fire1-5.i16	texture	5 file animated sequence of flames
grass.i16	texture	scanned image of section of lawn
stone.i16	texture	scanned image of stonework
wood.i16	texture	scanned image of wood paneling
tree.i16	texture	scanned image of tree with outline blacked out

The next task is to create an application that brings the world to life and opens it for exploration. If all you wanted to do was walk around the world just created, no additional work would be needed—this is called a *walkthrough* application. However, if you remember the original description of the virtual experience, it contained several features that require special attention. To bring these features to life will require development of a unique application.

Application development

Starting with the standard walkthrough application, you then must modify it to support the features unique to the particular virtual environment you're creating. Picking apart the description at the beginning of chapter 5, *Reality engines*, you'll find that it has the following unique features:

Object movement   The front door needs to pivot open when the viewer nears it. Additionally, the viewer must be able to select the lamp and move it around the room.

3-D sound   Music must appear to be physically located where the virtual radio object is positioned.

Dynamic sound   Based on how fast the person is moving, the volume and pitch of the wind speed sound must increase or decrease.

Texture animation   In order to make the fire appear to be flickering in the fireplace, the five textured files created earlier need to be sequentially mapped onto the correct place.

Dynamic lighting   When the lamp is moved, it should appear that lights are actually being moved in the simulation.

Sample program outline

To avoid getting bogged down in the particular syntax of a programming language, we're going to document just an outline of the application. The actual WorldToolKit C programming code used to build a walkthrough application can be found in appendix C.

Although some of the following outline is WorldToolKit-specific, most is general enough to cover other VR systems. Indentations are used to give a sense of nesting in the program's flow. Details that the WorldToolKit software handles without any intervention from the user are labeled with a [WTK]. Here is the overall structure:

Load stationary world   Load in the world that was created earlier in this section, including the terrain, house, and most of the furniture.

Load lamp   Load in the lamp and correctly position it in the living room. Also position one of WorldToolKit's light sources so that it's at the correct height and orientation with respect to where the bulb would be in the lamp object.

Load door   Load in the door and correctly position it in the front door opening. Set up the door so that it will pivot around one side. The door object is also assigned a special task to execute once every simulation tick.

Create sensors   [WTK] Initialize sensors used for Logitech head-tracker and Gravis MouseStick devices. This establishes communications and "wakes up" the devices.

Initialize 3-D sound   Initialize Crystal River Engineering's Beachtron convolving engine with appropriate filters for spatializing the sound of the radio.

Initialize sound   Initialize the Beachtron synthesizer to generate the sound of wind when required. Simple random noise generation will be used to duplicate a wind-like sound.

Attach sensors to viewpoint   The viewpoint represents where the participant is in space. By attaching the sensor to the viewpoint, whenever the sensor moves so does the view. This is how people fly in a virtual world.

Initialize viewpoint   Move the viewpoint to a reasonable position and direction so that the participant has a chance to get oriented. In this simulation, it's moved so that it appears to be a few miles from the house on the hill.

Start simulation [WTK] This is where the previously discussed real-time event loop begins. Everything before this has been setting up the simulation. Everything following this is part of the simulation event loop and cycles continuously, executing each step in turn, until some action stops the program from running.

Query sensors [WTK] The Logitech head-tracker is polled about the current orientation of the participant's head. At the same time, the Gravis MouseStick is queried about its current state (whether or not the user has moved it or pressed any buttons).

Update objects [WTK] If the lamp was previously attached to the MouseStick, update its position based on movement of the joystick. If the viewpoint is attached to the sensors, then update the viewpoint with new position and orientation information from the joystick and the Logitech head-tracker.

User actions This is an opportunity for the application or user to influence the simulation. Here is where most of the unique features of this application are implemented:

Animate fire Once every tick, the current fire image is replaced with the next one in the sequence. Just like simple flip book animations, this makes the fire appear to be flickering.

Control wind sound Using measurements of the viewer's speed, adjustments are made to the pitch and volume of the wind sound. The faster the movement, the louder and higher pitched the sound. This reinforces a sense of movement.

Test the MouseStick Test the joystick and see if the trigger button was pressed. Here is one scheme to select the lamp using only the joystick: the user looks directly at the lamp and presses the trigger button; doing so casts a visible ray that intersects with the lamp. A bounding box appears around the lamp to signify selection. Once the trigger is released, the beam disappears and the lamp remains selected. The next time the joystick is moved, the lamp moves instead of the person's viewpoint. This remains in effect until the lamp is deselected.

Move light If the lamp is in the process of being moved, the special light source must also move with it. This gives the effect of moving a lamp with the bulb turned on. The amount of shading on surfaces within the living room is recalculated as the lamp moves, just as it would with a real lamp.

End of user actions Return control back to WorldToolKit's simulation manager.

Object tasks Only the door has been assigned a special task. It checks the distance between the viewer and itself. If this distance is less than a certain amount, the door switches to an open state. If the door is in this state, it gradually rotates about its hinge point a little bit every tick. It might take 10 frames or ticks for the door to swing fully open.

Render [WTK] This is an internal function that simply assembles all the information about the state of the universe and renders the left- and right-eye views appropriately. The video signal is converted to an NTSC format and fed to the head-mounted display.

Loop [WTK] Go back to *Query sensors* and start the loop again.

End simulation The end of the simulation loop, and the simulation.

One way to estimate the complexity of developing an application like this one is to consider the number of lines of code needed to implement it. This example could be constructed with fewer than 500 lines of code, which also means that it could be easily assembled in a week or less.

Within the next couple of years, direct manipulation, or point-and-click tools, will be available to allow nonprogrammers to quickly create similar demonstrations in an hour or two. Unlocking the true potential of using 3-D simulation for visualization awaits the development of such simple but powerful tools.

After starting up the application defined above and then using the joystick to fly the viewpoint into the living room of the house, the image in Fig. 7-5 would appear on the screen.

7-5
Resulting view of a living room created by using the techniques discussed in this chapter.

This application could easily be extended to provide control over the appearance of any object or surface in the scene, such as color or the particular texture applied to a surface. With a little more work, you could begin moving and reshaping walls, or creating brand-new walls in the environment. In the future, buildings will be constructed from inside of a virtual environment instead of as a separate external step. Tools like this have yet to be developed.

Conclusion

The point of this chapter was to remove some of the mystery involved in actually constructing a virtual environment. By applying concepts learned in previous chapters to a concrete example, you can clearly see how this technology works. It's important to experiment with VR tools to understand how they can be effectively applied to solve real problems.

Understanding the capabilities of current VR software tools and devices can help you evaluate future developments. By following the maxim "you need to know where you are to get where you want to be," you can establish a context from the information presented in this chapter. You've glimpsed capabilities of current tools and devices—so you now know where you are. Where we're all headed is still an open question. A few interesting possibilities are explored in part 3, *Brave new worlds*.

Gloves, goggles, & wands

"The empires of the future are the empires of the mind."
   —Sir Winston Churchill, 1874–1965

For Alice to enter her strange, new world, she had to venture down a deep, dark, rabbit hole. Our journey begins a lot more practically. With the assistance of various sensors and tools, you too can enter and interact with new and interesting worlds.

This chapter documents the many peripheral devices of the VR trade and reveals some of the technology and issues with their use. While the previous chapter was a broad brushstroke, covering the hardware and software of VR, this chapter provides fine detail on just how these tools work.

An incredible assortment of sensors already exist for interacting with virtual worlds. All of these various devices serve as tools for either creating sensory input for the user or capturing the user's response for the computer. Head-mounted displays (HMDs) and 3-D sound boards are examples of computer output sensors, while wired gloves and force balls are examples of input or interaction sensors.

Some devices straddle these two categories, like the boom, which has both input and output aspects. Many of these devices represent some of the most interesting developments in the field of VR.

Today, entering a virtual world requires the participant to strap on fairly unwieldy equipment, like some deep-sea diver diving down to lost Atlantis. One intent of this hardware is to isolate the user from the real world and substitute a computer-realized alternative. Currently, most VR experiences are based on isolation from the real world, though other alternatives are also being explored.

As discussed in the previous chapter, sight, sound, and touch are the three senses stimulated by current VR hardware. Most efforts have been directed at providing effective tools for sight and sound, while touch is only beginning to be explored. The information in this chapter will provide a basic understanding of the tools, technologies, and parameters behind the devices that are our portals into virtual environments.

Sight

A large portion of the brain, more so than for any other sense, is dedicated to processing and organizing visual input. In fact, the bandwidth of the visual system far exceeds that of any other sense. Think of the detail present in a single glimpse of your living room. It has been suggested that it would take at least 80 million polygons to represent that same view using a computer-generated image.

Our eyes channel this staggering amount of information into processing centers that filter and reduce the information into something we can use. Much of this processing occurs without conscious effort—it happens continuously without us being directly aware of it. Form, shape, color and depth information is extracted from images without us recognizing the effort.

One of the challenges of virtual environments is to enlist the use of these *preconscious* visualization powers to understand complex issues. By visualizing problems, we can quickly gain new insights or see new patterns revealed that were previously masked in the raw data. And most importantly, this processing occurs without conscious effort.

Many virtual environments are attempting to harness these innate sensory capabilities. In doing so, they become partially dependent on the quality of images presented to the viewer. This is one reason that so many approaches have evolved to view virtual environments. Each approach can be ranked by the degree of *immersion*, or sense of presence, it provides.

Sitting in front of a computer screen and viewing an interactive 3-D simulation of a molecule is less immersive than donning a stereoscopic, head-mounted display and interacting with the molecule directly, but both techniques have their advantages.

The sense of immersion is a product of several parameters related to visual stimulus and other simulation factors, as shown in Fig. 8-1. Because many of these parameters are visual influences, it stresses the crucial role that visual cues play in the creation of an immersive experience.

It's important to realize that we don't yet fully understand the role all these factors play in what is primarily a personal experience—what is immersive to one person might not be to another. Nor can science supply a simple formula for calculating the degree of immersion someone experiences.

It might not even be possible to understand immersion using a purely reductionist approach—where immersion is reduced to its components, which are then immersion threshold

non-interactive		interactivity
slow update rate		fast update rate
low image complexity		high image complexity
non-engaging		engaging
no sound		3D sound
screen display		head-mounted display
low resolution		high resolution
monoscopic		stereoscopic
small field of view		large field of view
no head tracking		head tracking

non-immersive ← → fully immersive

degree of immersion

8-1
Diagram showing factors that govern the degree of visual immersion.

independently studied. Instead, a holistic technique might be necessary because the experience of immersion is more than just the mere sum of its parts.

Notice, too, the many different paths to achieving a sense of presence, or immersion. One path could project a large, stereoscopic, high-resolution image on a wall that you view through LCD flicker glasses, but movement of your head isn't tracked. Another path could be the one most associated with VR, the use of a head-mounted display.

The point is that you can't just focus on one factor while ignoring the others. An effective VR application balances all the issues. Even a simple computer monitor can become a fascinating window into another world if the application is interesting enough to engage the viewer (like many computer video games do).

Virtual displays can be divided into those that are head-mounted and those that aren't. Most people associate virtual reality with either the HMD or the wired glove. HMDs provide the most direct visual experience of virtual worlds. They do this partially by excluding the view of the real world and by enhancing the field of view of the computer-generated world.

Optics In its simplest incarnation, an HMD is composed of optics and a pair of display screens, as shown in Fig. 8-2. The difficult part of HMD design is providing these two elements in a robust, low-weight, ergonomic, and hygienic package. At least ten different HMD manufacturers are striving to create the ultimate display that Ivan Sutherland envisioned over two decades ago.

Using the original NASA Ames HMD design as a guide, we can examine how optics and display screens interrelate. Optics do two things; they allow you to focus on a display screen two to three inches from your face, and they increase the field of view of the displayed image.

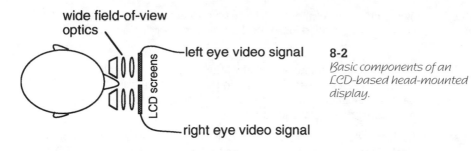

left eye video signal

right eye video signal

wide field-of-view optics

LCD screens

8-2
Basic components of an LCD-based head-mounted display.

The initial optics used by NASA Ames were produced by a small company called LEEP Systems in Waltham, Massachusetts. LEEP had been building special lenses for use with stereoscopic photography when NASA came along and ordered one for their prototype HMD. Because the optics were designed to view the stereoscopic, wide, field-of-view image of a large photographic slide, they were ideal for use with LCD displays salvaged from small portable TVs.

One of the unique characteristics of the LEEP optics is its anamorphic projection for creating a wide field of view. Anamorphic lenses are used by the film industry to squeeze a wide image from a camera on to the dimensions of a standard 35mm film frame. A similar lens on the projector reverses the process and displays the wide image on the screen.

When used with computer-generated images, the computer is supposed to predeform the image before displaying it—though this isn't always done, due to the computational effort of calculating the necessary distortion. This projection is represented by the diagram in Fig. 8-3.

anamorphic projection

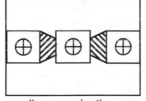

linear projection

8-3
Differences between anamorphic and linear projections.

This projection was designed to provide maximum detail in front of the eye, where it can be resolved, and minimum detail on the periphery, where detail isn't as important. Images viewed through these optics are distorted in a manner known as the "pincushion effect." Normally, straight lines become curved, causing an object in the center of view to bend away from the viewer. If images aren't precorrected for this effect, distortion can become a problem when using these optics.

The degree of distortion varies with the design of the lens. Early LEEP optics had a 90-degree field of view and minimal distortion. The latest versions with 140-degree field of view require some form of correction, which can be done with either cameras and specially modified lenses or through digital or analog image processing.

LEEP optics found their way into almost all of the early HMD designs. VPL used them in their first EyePhones before designing their own optics, and Virtual Research has used them in their helmets. LEEP's optics also addressed a couple of other issues with the designs of HMDs.

Because the distance between a person's pupils varies across the population, the design of an HMD must account for differences in interpupillary distance (IPD). LEEP achieved this by providing a large-exit pupil diameter (see Fig. 8-4). This means that the focal diameter of the image near the eye is quite large, allowing room for a variety of IPDs without making a mechanical adjustment. Optical designs with small-exit pupil diameters require mechanical IPD adjustment.

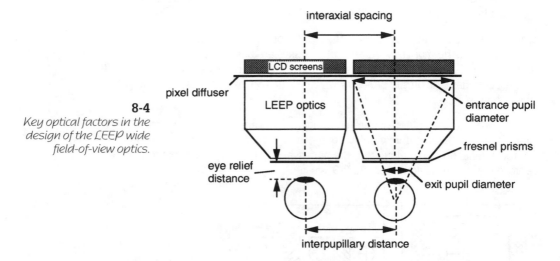

8-4
Key optical factors in the design of the LEEP wide field-of-view optics.

Another important consideration is the interaxial spacing of the optics. A value representing the average IPD likely to be found in the general population (95% of the adult population have IPDs from 50–71 millimeters) is used to ensure that the left- and right-eye visual axes converge instead of diverge when trying to merge two screen images.

While it's easy to cross your eyes inwards (converge), it's painful for each eye to try to look outwards. By using a smaller value for the interaxial spacing, the majority of the population should experience convergence rather than divergence.

Spacing of the optics also places restrictions on the physical size of the LCD screens used in HMDs. If the LCDs are too large, they won't fit side by side in front of the optics, causing additional imaging problems.

One solution that sometimes works is to use a flexible plastic fresnel prism placed over the exit pupil lens. This optically shifts the image either left or right. Normally, if you hook up a VCR to the left and right eye displays of an HMD, you would wind up seeing a double image. With the fresnel prism, the images are shifted closer to each other so that the two images merge into a single one. Some VR systems that produce only monoscopic output use this technique when hooked up to an HMD.

Field of view is one of the more critical optical parameters. Much debate centers around how wide it should be for HMDs. The wider the field of view, the more sense of presence is experienced. Unfortunately, it also worsens the perceived resolution of the LCD displays because the optics magnify the display screens. This is one reason why several HMD manufacturers use field of views as low as 40–50 degrees; they do so in order to increase the perceived resolution of the displays (it also greatly simplifies the optical design).

In some VR applications where detail or text needs to be read, resolution is more important than field of view. However, in other applications, like architectural walkthroughs, this is reversed and field of view becomes more important than resolution. Understanding how this parameter impacts a VR experience is important to a virtual world designer.

Many different optical approaches have evolved with HMD manufacturers. One of the more interesting is an experimental holographic lens that resembles mirrored sunglasses. It's based on the same technology used in supermarket laser scanners. A complex set of optics can be duplicated with an appropriate hologram and recreated on inexpensive, lightweight plastic film.

In this prototype, an LCD display is positioned directly above the eye, pointing down into the lens. A half-silvered mirror reflects the LCD image onto the inner surface of the sunglasses, where the holographic film is applied. After passing through the holographic lens, the image is reflected back into the eye. If the inner surface of the sunglasses is only partially reflective, the viewer will see both the virtual world and the real world through the lens.

It's like wearing a set of dark sunglasses with the virtual world projected on the inside of the lens. Holographic lenses are one of several promising designs well suited for mass production and low cost.

LCDs

HMD builders have struggled to find LCD displays that are acceptable for their needs. Conflicting factors of screen size, housing size, price, availability, image quality, and drive circuitry all have to be carefully considered. One of the more frustrating factors is screen size. A display of 2.5 to 3.5 inches (diagonal measurement) works well with the LEEP optics, but LCD manufacturers are intent on producing sizes larger than this for the portable computer and TV markets.

Housing size is also a consideration because two LCD displays must fit edge to edge in front of the optics, or imaging problems will result. To keep costs down, HMD manufacturers initially used off-the-shelf Sony Watchman 2.7" color LCD displays. They purchased these consumer products wholesale, and then proceeded to dismantle and use them in their high-tech VR goggles. Unfortunately, in late 1991 Sony retired the design that worked best with HMDs, forcing HMD manufacturers to search for other solutions. LEEP's latest HMD is shown in Fig. 8-5.

Several groups have explored the use of custom designed LCDs. NASA Ames worked with Casio to develop a single, wide, monochrome LCD panel that would

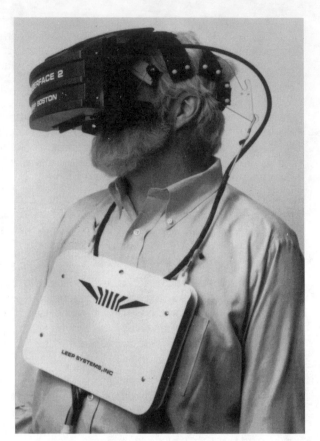

8-5
Cyberface 2, an example of a color, 140-degree field-of-view HMD.

cover both eyes. Unfortunately, out of Casio's initial shipment of prototypes, only two worked, which was one reason the project didn't go any further.

VPL's HRX head-mounted display also utilized a custom-designed LCD with considerably higher resolution than anything else on the market (720×480 elements). Not only was this an expensive solution (it cost $49,000), but VPL began telling customers in mid-1992 that due to reliability problems with the LCDs the HRX had temporarily been pulled from the market.

The biggest problem with most color LCDs is their limited resolution—they have only 360 horizontal and 240 vertical elements. To make matters worse, it takes a combination of three elements (red, green, and blue) to make a single triad, or pixel.

So the entire display represents only 29,000 pixels compared to a standard Apple Macintosh 9-inch display with 175,000 pixels, or a PC VGA display with 307,000 pixels. The limited resolution doesn't matter when you're watching a Sony Watchman from one to two feet away, but viewing it from two to three inches away through a wide field of view optics is far less acceptable.

Another problem with low resolution is that, when you're looking through the optics, each LCD element is clearly visible and becomes distracting. This is partially due to the eye's attraction to edge detail and sharp boundaries. The illustration in

Fig. 8-6 mimics the degradation in image quality due to low-resolution LCD displays.

As you can see, the image on the right is clearly divided into individual elements. It's like looking at the world through a screen door—the pixel boundaries become a barrier between you and the virtual world.

VPL developed a clever method of countering this distraction. They experimented with various filters, like wax paper, to diffuse or blur the image slightly. They found that a soft blur was enough to stop the eye from focusing on the harsh boundaries of the pixels.

In a further refinement, VPL added a small dot pattern on top of the diffuser to counter the fuzziness caused by the diffuser. It was intended to fool the eye into believing that the image was more detailed than it was. Today, almost all LCD HMD manufacturers use some form of diffusion filter to improve the quality of the displayed image.

LCDs have proven to be an inexpensive method of displaying virtual worlds. Because the displays go into consumer products, their costs can be driven quite low. However, the resolution of these displays needs to improve by a factor of ten before they become effective for anything other than entertainment. This kind of dramatic improvement will take a few years to achieve in a low-cost package.

It's likely, however, that other display technologies, such as CRTs, or the approach pioneered by Reflection Technology using a vibrating mirror and LEDs, will fill the need for high-resolution, reasonable-cost displays in the short term.

8-6
Resolution of the left image is typical of what you might see on a 512×480 computer monitor. On the right is the same image as it might appear in a low-resolution LCD display through wide field-of-view optics.

CRTs

One approach to solving the resolution problem is to use commercially available miniature CRTs, with approximately 1000-line resolution. These monochrome displays are typically mounted near the ear and the image is reflected into the viewer's eyes. The military uses this approach because the resolution and brightness of the CRTs allow them to be used as heads-up displays (HUDs), even in bright daylight.

These CRTs are very similar in principle to the inexpensive low-resolution versions found in any video-camera viewfinder. Their biggest limitations are that the displays are mostly monochrome and that you need to take special care because several thousand volts is positioned very close to the user's head. A typical CRT-based design is illustrated in Fig. 8-7.

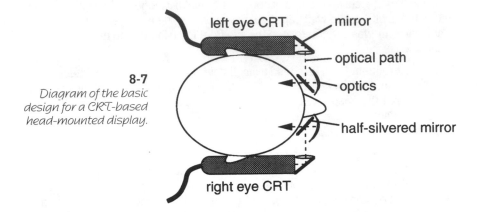

8-7
Diagram of the basic design for a CRT-based head-mounted display.

The CRT image is projected onto a complex set of optics that reflects it into the viewer's eyes (see Fig. 8-8). Sutherland pioneered this technique back in 1968 and it continues to be in use today. One of its key advantages is that the optics in front of the person's eyes can be semi-reflective so that the outside world remains in view. This is crucially important if the person wearing the HMD is also operating an aircraft.

8-8
Prototype of a CRT-based, advanced HUD display helmet designed for helicopter pilots.

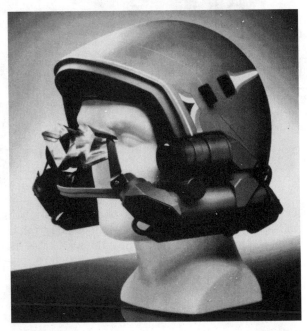

Color is the biggest problem facing CRT displays. Creating a high-resolution miniature color CRT is beyond the capabilities of even today's high-tech wizardry. It simply isn't possible to manufacture a shadowmask (a metal screen placed just behind the glass face) with the required mechanical dimensions.

However, a color display can be created with a single monochrome CRT that has a rapidly switching LCD color filter placed in front of it. By quickly displaying a single scan line or field in first red, then green, and then blue, the eye perceives only the combined color and not the discrete elements.

This technique gives a high-resolution color display without much additional hardware, but it does require a scan frequency of three times the normal rate. A standard workstation monitor with a 1000×1000 pixel display is scanned at least once every 60th of a second, which means that it has about a 60Mhz bandwidth. To avoid flickering, a filtered CRT at the same resolution would have to run three times faster (or at 180Mhz), which requires custom and expensive high-speed electronics.

Even with this limitation, various designs based on this technique are being developed. Tektronix, based in Oregon, has developed a working version of a VGA (640×480) resolution, one-inch color CRT that could eventually be produced for under $1000. This should appear in HMDs sometime in 1993 and could be the breakthrough in display quality that will unleash all sorts of new VR applications.

Using bundled fiber-optic cables, companies like Polhemus Labs and CAE-Link have created a simple, high-resolution head-mounted display (see Fig. 8-9). Doctors have used similar, smaller diameter bundles called *endoscopes* to explore a patient's internal structure without using surgery.

Fiber optics

8-9
Example of using fiber-optic cables in a lightweight head-mounted display.

For HMDs, a color light valve projects a bright, high-resolution image onto one end of a fiber-optic cable about one inch thick that contains at least one million fibers. The image that emerges from the other end is then reflected into the viewer's eyes.

Though the idea is very simple, manufacturing a pair of optically correct cables like this is very expensive and dependent on the number of fibers used. The expense of this approach has restricted its use to only the most advanced HMDs, where cost isn't a significant factor, but resolution and light weight is.

Fiber optics, CRTs, and LCD displays represent the bulk of commercially available techniques for building head-mounted displays. The LCD approach dominates the field, due to its low cost and ease of integration.

An interesting challenge to LCDs is a low-cost monochrome display developed by Reflection Technology. Rapidly vibrating mirrors scan a single column of red LEDs across the user's visual field. As long as everything is carefully synchronized, a full-screen image can be created with just a single column of LEDs. This is all mounted in a small, lightweight package and placed about four inches from the user's face. A mechanical adjustment is provided for focusing the image.

Reflection Technology is currently working with Sun Microsystems to create a 1000×1000 monochrome display for the ultimate portable computer. With its low manufacturing cost, this technology might just succeed if they can also create color displays.

Boom One of the more interesting variations on an HMD design is the boom created by Fake Space Labs in Palo Alto, California. The illustration in Fig. 8-10 shows an example of this special device.

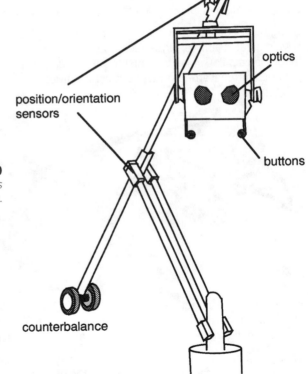

8-10
Diagram showing the key elements of a boom display system.

By using a counterweighted boom design, problems with optic weight, display weight, and display size are eliminated. This also allows much higher-resolution CRT devices to be used instead of the the low-resolution LCD displays. Six shaft encoders measure the position and orientation of the display device, providing complete 6 DOF sensing. The shaft encoders almost eliminate the delay between physically changing your view and seeing it change in the display. Smaller versions that can attach to an engineer's desk are also possible.

The boom provides an easy transition from peeking into the virtual world and interacting with a keyboard and monitor to control the simulation.

Scan conversion

Getting an image from the computer to the HMD is often an overlooked problem. Because most HMDs use LCD displays that were originally intended for use as miniature TVs, they typically require a TV-formatted, or interlaced video signal. This is the same kind of signal produced by a video camera or a VCR.

Unfortunately, most computers don't generate video signals that you can hook up to your TV. Instead, they generate noninterlaced RGB (red, green, and blue) signals. This causes a problem when you're trying to hook a head-mounted display to a computer's video signal.

An interlaced video signal is one where every other line of the display is drawn once every ⅟₆₀ of a second. First the odd horizontal lines are drawn and then the even lines are drawn. Most computer video signals, on the other hand, draw each line of the display in sequential order (noninterlaced).

A noninterlaced signal, however, won't work with a device that requires an interlaced signal. This means that the computer's video signal must be *scan converted* from noninterlaced to interlaced in order to use it with most HMDs.

On some workstation platforms, this can cost as much as the workstation itself. In the PC market, a few graphic boards, like Intel's ActionMedia II, can create an interlaced signal so that only an inexpensive encoder (less than $300) is needed.

One trick for avoiding expensive scan converters is to simply buy two inexpensive video cameras and mount them in a frame pointed at the workstation screen. Then each eye's image is displayed in a separate window and is captured by the camera. As long as the refresh rates of the camera and monitor are correctly synchronized, a flicker-free image from the camera can be run directly into many HMDs.

Several HMD designs are now beginning to use either direct RGB inputs or the interlaced NTSC signal. This will simplify and reduce the cost of interfacing HMDs to computers even further. This is just one of the many small challenges in assembling a VR system.

Depth perception

How a person's visual system converts a 2-D image, mapped on the retina, into the 3-D world we understand is still a subject of much research. The fact that you can still perceive depth with one eye closed implies that a more complicated process than just stereoscopic vision is involved.

Monocular, or pictorial depth perception works by first identifying the nature of an object before determining how far away it is. In other words, you need to know what an object is to know where it should be. Several depth cues contribute to the eye being able to establish the relationship of objects in a scene (Friedhoff, 1989):

Linear perspective This is the same effect that makes parallel railroad tracks converge in the distance. The foreshortening of a building communicates its depth in the same way. In addition, buildings are composed of right angles, which also helps us understand their relationship with other objects.

Occlusion   Objects in the foreground occlude, or obscure, objects in the background.

Shadows   Shadows help establish the interrelationships of objects with each other and with the background.

Detail perspective   Objects become less distinct with distance. You see less and less detail, and objects become smoother.

Aerial perspective   Haze washes out distant objects and makes them appear bluer than they really are.

Motion parallax   As you move your viewpoint, say shifting your head two feet to the left, note how closer objects move more than distant ones.

Combining all these factors helps to precisely position objects within a scene. These are important factors to understand in a virtual environment because the world builder controls the virtual environment's sense of scale, or depth. If a completely abstract world is created where no object is readily identifiable or objects are represented so simply that you can't resolve them, then misunderstandings in depth perception can occur.

Texture mapping can dramatically improve the sensation of depth. By applying a scanned image of wooden paneling to the surface of a virtual bookshelf, you provide the eye with more detail with which to work and resolve relationships. Without it, the brain will start guessing how objects relate, and sometimes make mistakes.

Several other processes are involved in depth perception. One of these, *stereopsis*, involves both eyes cooperating to identify depth. Unlike monocular depth perception, this isn't dependent on form recognition, as demonstrated by Bela Julesz in 1971. While doing perceptual research at Bell Laboratories, he created a series of random dot stereograms such as the one in Fig. 8-11.

8-11
By viewing this from about one foot away, and letting your eyes relax so that you see a single image, a small L-shaped section should appear to float above the page (about 80 percent of the population can see this).

When viewed stereoptically, a small L-shaped section at the center of the pattern appears to float above the plane of the page. Because this floating section becomes apparent only when viewed stereoptically, Julesz proved that differences in horizontal positioning of objects in the left and right eyes is the basis for stereoscopic depth perception. This is also known as *disparity* or *binocular parallax*.

Previous to Julesz's work, it was believed that depth perception was based on first recognizing an object and then determining the angle between the eyes as they're focused on the object. Julesz also discovered that somewhere between 5 and 20 percent of the population has trouble seeing stereoptically, which is believed to be linked to astigmatism.

There are several methods, therefore, of perceiving depth in an image. An important (and expensive) consideration in a VR system is whether or not it should support stereopsis. Generating individual images for the left and right eyes can take as much as twice the computing power as for a single eye.

In a stereoscopic VR system, each eye's image is rendered and scan-converted independently before being seen in the appropriate LCD display of the HMD. In a monoscopic VR system, only a single viewpoint is rendered and scan-converted. This video signal is then fed to both eyes at the same time. The two arrangements are shown in Fig. 8-12.

stereoscopic VR system

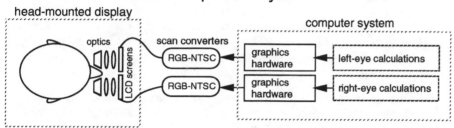

monoscopic VR system

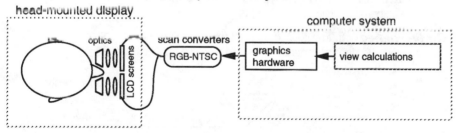

8-12
Diagram showing the difference between a stereoscopic VR system and a monoscopic system.

Different approaches have evolved to support stereoscopic image generation. Some VR systems use two PCs or two workstations linked synchronously together to generate the image pairs. The other approach uses a single PC or workstation with dual graphics hardware in it.

The latter is usually the least expensive and most compact solution, but there might be a performance penalty in using a single PC, depending on the type of 3-D graphics board used. The most performance is gained by having two completely independent systems render each eye image. Of course, this is the most expensive solution, and it complicates programming and using the system. Again, these tradeoffs have to be judged in the context of the application's objectives.

A virtual world designer has to decide how important stereoscopic depth perception is in the design of an application. Stereopsis simplifies the user's selection and interaction with objects in the virtual world.

Try closing one eye and picking a point on an object within two to three feet of you. Now, starting with your finger on the tip of your nose, try to touch the point on the object. Try doing the same thing with both eyes open. In the first case, it's difficult to judge if your finger had traveled far enough or not. In the second case, your finger moves rapidly to the spot without hesitation. The same holds true for similar tasks in the virtual world.

Another benefit of stereopsis is the impact the virtual world has on people. Objects seem to leap out or hang in space. They also seem to be more solid and real, which can be a very compelling aspect of the simulation.

On the other hand, some VR applications work fine on monoscopic systems. These are usually walkthroughs or environments where little direct manipulation of objects occurs. As described earlier, many depth cues exist in even a monoscopic image, so stereopsis isn't crucial. When surveyed after playing a monoscopic VR game, most participants were surprised to find that it wasn't stereoscopic—they became too engrossed in the game to notice.

Remember that stereopsis is just one more factor to consider in a long list of features that control the sense of immersion. A VR system doesn't have to be stereoscopic if other aspects of the simulation provide the sense of immersion. Learning to balance these factors is part of the art of being a virtual world builder.

Viewing parameters   There are several parameters that control how images are displayed or rendered in a VR system. Several of these can be interactively modified for different effects. They are all based on the viewing geometry shown in Fig. 8-13.

Convergence   In a stereoscopic system, you achieve convergence when separate left and right eye images fuse into a single image. Because this will vary

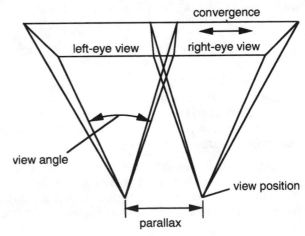

8-13
Viewing parameters under the control of the virtual world designer.

depending on the viewer and optical design of the HMD, an adjustment to the horizontal position of the left and right eye images needs to be provided.

This is sometimes done optically, or by telling the computer to shift the displayed image either to the left or to the right. This shouldn't be confused with parallax (see next section). Convergence simply shifts the entire image within the frame without changing the geometry of either the left- or right-view positions.

Parallax Parallax represents the distance between the viewer's left and right eyes in the virtual world (see Fig. 8-14). It also determines the sense of depth of virtual objects. If you view a mountain from far away, both left and right eyes will see the same image because the two- to three-inch distance between your eyes means nothing when viewing an object miles away. However, if you look at a book from one to two feet away, each eye will see a slightly different perspective.

left   right

8-14
Left and right eye images differ when parallax is considered. Not only is the image shifted over slightly, but you see everything from a different angle.

By alternately opening and closing your left and right eyes, you can see this difference for yourself. The closer an object is to your eyes, the more different it looks from each eye. By controlling this parameter, you can have a building appear as either a tiny toy model or as an immense structure. By switching between a large and small value of parallax, a participant would first feel large and then small relative to other objects in the virtual environment. This is another powerful technique to consider when designing worlds.

View angle Think of the view angle as the size of the camera lens through which the virtual world is viewed. A zoom lens would have a small view angle and a fish-eye lens would have a large view angle. The image in Fig. 8-15 illustrates the effect of changing this parameter.

Resolution Some computer graphics hardware allows you to interactively change the resolution of your image. By lowering the resolution, fewer pixels need to be filled, which speeds up image drawing. Remember that most HMD designs use LCD displays with less than 400×300 pixel resolution.

It's a waste of valuable drawing time to create a 1000×1000 pixel image (eight times as many pixels) that winds up being scan-converted and displayed on such a low-resolution output device. Most workstation-based VR systems have this problem

8-15
Illustration showing the effect of changing the viewing angle of a scene. The left image has a small viewing angle and the right image has a large viewing angle.

because they can't be programmed for lower display resolutions. This will become less of a factor as higher-resolution HMDs become available.

All these parameters provide a virtual world designer with incredible flexibility in presenting virtual experiences. Think of how Hollywood uses camera angles and effects to present a particular view. These same techniques can be borrowed to help dramatize specific aspects of a virtual simulation. A world builder can heighten or reduce the viewer's sense of reality by cleverly shifting these parameters as he experiences a virtual environment.

Back in 1989 there was a single LCD HMD; by the end of 1992 there will be at least six different versions available. This is one of the most high-growth areas of VR investment and development. Hopefully, we'll achieve Sutherland's "ultimate display" sooner than anyone predicted.

Sound

Close your eyes and listen closely to the activity around you. Notice how you can easily identify where sounds are coming from. By measuring the signal delay between your left and right ears, in addition to other factors, your brain can quickly locate the source of a sound. This delay is the *interaural time difference* (ITD) and is part of the study of psycho-acoustics.

Sound reflections off walls and ceilings communicate not only room size, but also whether surfaces are hard or soft. The shift in sound of an approaching vehicle, due to the Doppler effect, helps us to estimate its speed. Listening to sounds when objects interact helps us identify material properties.

The sharp ringing of glass, the knock of wood, and the rustle of paper are all valuable cues about our environment. Including these cues in a virtual reality system will dramatically enhance what can be learned from the simulation.

The uses of sound were covered in chapter 5, *Reality engines*. In this section we'll examine the different methods of sound generation and some of their unique limitations.

Sound generation

By borrowing the same tools musicians use to create sounds, a virtual world designer has almost unlimited flexibility in dealing with sounds. The most popular method of controlling and generating sounds uses the MIDI (musical instrument digital interface) standard. Sounds are first digitally sampled, or converted from analog to digital form (like the data on a CD ROM), then played back using a sequencer.

Any kind of sound can be sampled: voices, musical instruments, and special effects. As they're played back, further modifications can be made, like changes in pitch or the sound envelope, or reverberations (echos). Depending on the complexity of the sequencer, multiple outputs can be generated simultaneously (typically four or more), and each output can usually handle up to 16 notes at a time. Some sequencers can be connected, doubling the number of sound sources.

In the virtual world, the designer simply sends a command, like "play note 14 on channel 1" or "increase pitch by 25 percent on channel 2, note 16." Additional commands control the volume and timing of all notes and channels. One limitation of using an external MIDI sequencer is that it has to be preloaded with all the sounds necessary for the simulation.

By using the MIDI standard, the computer can control hundreds of different kinds of musical devices. Almost all electronic music devices speak the MIDI language. In addition, many different tools exist for the sampling and creation of unique sound effects.

Of course, other nonMIDI sound boards can be used in virtual environments. In fact, computers like the Amiga, Macintosh, and Next have relatively powerful sound-generation capabilities built directly into their systems.

Sound differs from visual information in at least one important regard—it requires a rigidly fixed playback speed. If you start playing back a sound, nothing can interrupt it until it's finished, or the sound will be noticeably distorted.

Sound limitations

The same isn't true for visual signals. You can speed up, slow down, and even pause a movie on your VCR and still easily understand what you're watching. You can't pause a sound recording, however, and if you fast forward or reverse it all you'll hear is something unintelligible.

This difference is important because in virtual environments the frame rate usually varies from instant to instant depending on what the participant is looking at. If sound was synchronized to the frame rate, it would be continuously shifting, like playing back a cassette tape in a badly worn-out tape player. Obviously, sounds used in virtual environments have to be designed to be independent of the frame rate.

This also means that movie-like musical soundtracks, where visual action is synchronized to a prerecorded audio signal, are next to impossible in a virtual environment because there's no easy way to maintain synchronization. Instead, sounds have to be directly keyed to activities or events in the virtual world, like generating the sound of a thud when a door is shut or musical notes when someone presses a particular button.

One other solution is to have virtual environments that run at fixed frame rates. Multimillion dollar scene generators have this capability, but it will be a few years before it's available on lower-cost systems.

3-D sound   So far we've discussed only ambient, or nondirectional, sound channels. To create 3-D sounds, you start with a monaural sound source and pass it to specialized convolving hardware (described in a following section). Any of the techniques previously mentioned can be used to create the initial sound that can then be located at a particular point in the virtual world.

Controlling the placement of the 3-D sound is done through a command such as "locate source1 at the following azimuth, altitude, and distance from the viewpoint." By updating this as the user moves his head, the sound appears to be fixed in space.

The pursuit of 3-D sound has revealed interesting insights in how sounds are received and processed by the brain. Several factors control this ability (Begault, 1987 and Greuel, 1991):

Interaural time difference   The interaural time difference is the time disparity between each ear receiving the same sound. Our ears can distinguish differences as small as 70 microseconds (1-inch resolution).

Interaural amplitude difference   The interaural amplitude difference is the difference in sound pressure (loudness) of the ear closest to the sound.

Frequency difference   As sounds bend around the head, much of the higher frequencies are impaired. High-frequency sounds are less likely to bend than low-frequency sounds because they're more directional. This results in one ear hearing a "brighter" sound than the other.

Head-related transfer functions (HRTFs)   The convolutions of the pinnae, or outer ear not only gather sounds, they also reinforce certain sound frequencies. The HRTFs are a summed measure of the pinnae's response to varying frequencies of sound.

Of all these factors, HRTFs are the most complex to model. Measurements are first gathered by placing small probe microphones inside each ear of a dummy head in an anechoic chamber. A speaker emits a sound at a known frequency while the microphone records the received signal, as shown in Fig. 8-16.

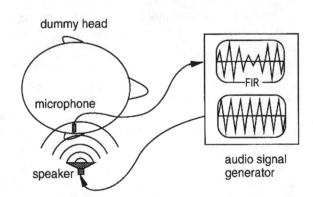

8-16
Diagram that shows the process of collecting finite responses (FIRs) in order to acoustically model the pinnae, or outer ear.

About 150 finite impulse responses (FIRs) are measured while moving the speaker to different locations around each ear. This builds a map of listener-specific "location filters," which are then loaded into a powerful digital signal processor (DSP). Any monaural sound source can then be *convolved* by the DSP to generate separate left and right signals that a listener, wearing headphones, would be able to accurately locate in space.

Because this process occurs in real time, sounds can be interactively moved, or they can appear fixed in space as the listener moves his head. This is how, in the example at the beginning of chapter 5, the person visiting the virtual living room heard a radio playing from a corner of the room. Even as he moved through the living room, the sound of the radio always appeared fixed in the same location.

All the above factors help locate the direction of a sound. To determine its distance, environmental reflections surrounding the sound and the listener become important—especially relationships between the direct sound and the reflected sound.

Though direct sound levels decrease with distance, reflected sounds tend to remain constant. Additionally, high-frequency sounds are attenuated more by distance than low frequencies. Our brains examine these differences along with the delay between reflected and direct sounds to calculate distances.

Because HRTFs are created in an anechoic chamber, they are incapable of mimicking environmental reflections. This means you wouldn't hear any difference between a radio playing in a large virtual room and one playing in a small virtual room. Nor would it matter if the virtual walls were made of a hard or soft surface.

Obviously, this is a poor representation of the way sounds really work. But the same process of convolving sounds can be used to create simple reflective models of rooms and surfaces. Research efforts have already demonstrated the ability to model a cube-shaped room with four different sound sources in each corner. Reflections from each source are modeled by creating a sound source behind each wall that generates the reflected sounds.

To understand how this works, think of yourself standing in the middle of an empty room. Previously, you stationed a friend behind each wall of the same room. When you shout out any word, they have been told to echo the same word back to you. In the same way, sound sources are positioned and programmed to provide echoes of the main source.

Controlling this allows diverse acoustical environments to be recreated. Acoustical parameters such as room size or shape, along with reflective properties such as hard, soft, or metallic walls can be quickly changed.

To do all this, a staggering amount of computing power is required—1200 megaFLOPs (a FLOP is a single floating-point operation; PCs vary from 0.5 to 2 MFLOPs). Continuing improvements in processing power will bring ever more accurate simulations of sounds. You might be surprised to learn that we're far closer to accurately modeling sound than we are to generating realistic images. It might be just a few more years when, closing your eyes, you won't be able to tell the difference between what's real and what isn't.

Haptic

Unlike sight and sound output devices, which deal with easily reproducible forces, tactile or force-feedback devices require complex electromechanical interaction with the human body. It's one thing to slip headphones and a display device on your head, but it's much different to insert your arm and hand into an enclosing structure capable of measuring and reflecting the forces of virtual objects.

It doesn't seem likely that we'll ever be able to achieve the same level of realism with tactile senses that we will with visual and aural senses. The complexity of generating the necessary sensations to clearly recognize the difference between a felt-covered and cloth-covered virtual surface without restricting body movement is far beyond today's technology.

It isn't only a problem of building the mechanical devices to generate the feedback, it's also a problem of understanding and simulating the correct forces. In fact, representational models for describing these forces barely exist.

How do you explain "a felt-covered" surface to a computer? What parameters can help you distinguish between a felt- and a cloth-covered surface? These issues have only recently been addressed, and they're far from being part of today's 3-D CAD systems.

As mentioned earlier, tactile and force feedback are two different forms of haptic perception. Tactile feedback represents the forces acting on your skin, while force feedback is the forces acting on your muscles, joints, and tendons.

Tactile feedback　Wearing a special glove developed in England, you can experience a virtual world in a totally new fashion (see Fig. 8-17). If you visited the house on the hill from chapter 5 wearing one of these gloves, a new dimension of the virtual world would appear.

Reaching out with your gloved hand, you might notice a slight pressure on your fingertips as you touched the surface of a virtual sofa. Nothing would stop you from

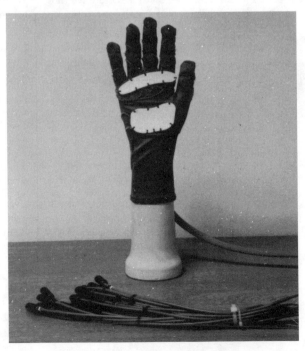

8-17
The Teletact I glove was the first device to provide tactile feedback for a virtual environment.

inserting your hand into the sofa, but the deeper you sank, the more pressure you would feel. Removing your hand, the pressure would disappear.

This is one example of how tactile feedback might be used to help locate virtual surfaces. It's an important contribution because most virtual environments have a ghostly, insubstantial feel to them. Providing even a limited amount of tactile feedback greatly increases the ability to interact with objects. Two different approaches have evolved for tactile stimulation: air pressure and vibratory.

The use of small air bladders was pioneered in 1991 by Airmuscle Limited and the Advanced Robotics Research Center (ARRC) in England. By using a two-glove system, one to measure forces and the other to display them, ARRC created a tool for the simulation of tactile forces.

The input glove possessed 20 force-sensitive resistors (FSRs), distributed across the underside of the hand. The output glove had 20 correspondingly located air pockets that could be proportionally inflated up to 12 pounds-per-square-inch (psi). By using control electronics and a compressor, pressures could be quickly modulated based on real-time input.

Next, working with VPL Research, ARRC combined their glove with VPL's DataGlove. In doing so, they discovered problems with reliability from both a physical and calibration point of view (Stone, 1992). They found that the glove would lose calibration and become highly frustrating to use, and the fingers would exhibit sporadic movements and even bend in physically impossible shapes.

To eliminate these problems, they built a hand-held device called the Teletact Commander, using only three to five air bladders. After attaching a position and orientation sensor to it, they found it to be a successful method of controlling a robotic arm.

The other method of tactile stimulation uses small vibrating transducers. These can be as simple as a voice coil from a disassembled speaker, or as complex as using shape memory alloys. These special alloys change shape and flex when an electrical current is applied to them, as shown in Fig. 8-18. They can be made in just about any size (currently, they're about the size of a paper clip and ⅛ of an inch thick) and can be placed anywhere on the skin's surface.

8-18
These small transducers can create minute vibrations or momentary impulses and can be placed anywhere on the skin.

Unlike air bladders, transducers can respond almost instantly to a control signal. This makes them well suited to generating discrete sensations like moving a finger over a rough surface. However, air bladders generate larger forces than current shape-memory alloys, which makes them more useful for representing the gentle pressure of, say, holding an egg.

Both techniques are starting points in the development and refinement of tactile forces. They serve mostly as experimental tools in learning about the nature of this complicated sense.

Force feedback   In chapter 3 you read about Frederick Brooks' attempts at the University of North Carolina to harness a remote manipulator to explore the use of force feedback in simulating molecular docking. While watching a stereoscopic display, chemists wrestled virtual molecules into appropriate docking sites. They actually "felt" the push and pull of simulated molecular forces transmitted through the robotic arm.

Now imagine feeling the weight of virtual objects, or squeezing a virtual ball to determine if it was a hard golf ball or a soft rubber ball. What if you could reach out with your hand and feel either the unyielding surface of a wall or the thick resistance of water?

At the University of Utah, the same university where Sutherland pioneered his head-mounted display in 1968, a system capable of generating exactly these kinds of forces has been developed. It's based on an exoskeleton that fits closely around the arm and hand. At strategic locations on the upper arm and forearm, a metal collar is snugly attached—like a massive high-tech bracelet. Fingers slip into semi-rigid tubes connected to hydraulic lines or mechanical linkages.

All together, you can move your hand and arm in ten different directions simultaneously (10 degrees of freedom). A computer continuously monitors the precise location and position of all the joints. And despite the fifty-odd pounds strapped to your arm, you don't feel more than a slight tug because the computer constantly adjusts the exoskeleton to appear weightless to you.

When you grasp a virtual object, precise control of hydraulic actuators allows you to actually feel its weight and stiffness. As you move your arm and bump into a virtual wall, the collars around your arm abruptly stop your movements. Suddenly the virtual world has gained mass and substance. Of course, the complexity and expense of using devices like this will restrict them to only the most exclusive VR labs, but it does demonstrate some intriguing possibilities.

VR systems that can simulate and generate tactile and force-feedback signals are still a long way off. This situation will improve as better understanding of these forces becomes incorporated into current VR tools.

Motion platforms   Anyone who saw the movie *Lawnmower Man* might remember a scene where two people were lying face down on a movable bed as they raced through a virtual world. As they maneuvered, their entire bodies pitched and rolled based on their actions.

Although the virtual worlds and movable beds were only special effects (they weren't connected to a real VR system) similar devices do exist. They're known as motion platforms, and are available in many different forms. Their use has been limited to either arcade games or very expensive flight and motion simulators (see Fig. 8-19).

8-19
An example of a sophisticated motion platform built by CAE-Link for use with the Black Hawk flight simulator.

Other than for the movie and high-end simulators, no one has yet combined a simple motion platform with a commercial VR system. Because motion platforms can be easily controlled by a VR system's computer, it's just a matter of time before your sense of balance is just one more perception stimulated by the computer. Expect this to happen in a VR arcade system within the next couple of years.

Taken together, all these various output sensors provide different methods of stepping through the new looking glass into virtual worlds. Through the sensory experience of sight, sound, and touch, we can focus our minds on solving new and complex problems. And by focusing all our powers of perception on a single problem, we can gain new insights and have a more intuitive understanding of the problem.

You gain entry to virtual worlds through sensory portals created by various output sensors. Input sensors, on the other hand, allow for movement and interaction once you enter the virtual world. They are key to unlocking the power of interaction. Without them, you can only experience the virtual world passively.

Input sensors

Most input sensors fall into one of two categories; interaction devices and tracking devices (a few devices fit into either category). Interaction devices provide access (the ability to move and manipulate objects at will), while tracking devices passively monitor various body parts to create a sense of presence, or affordance (the feeling of being physically present in the virtual world). Both types of devices are required for the well-dressed cybernaut, two of whom are shown in Fig. 8-20.

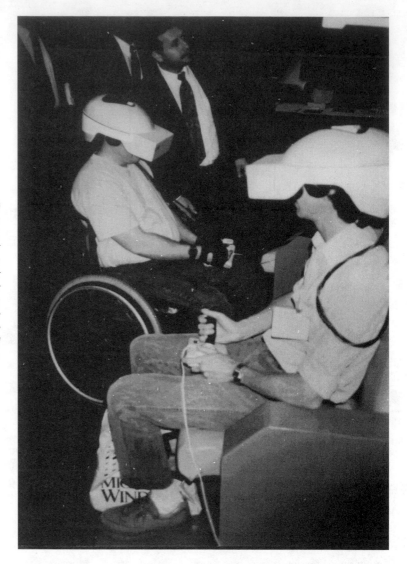

8-20
Two people interacting in the same virtual world, using joysticks for navigation. The person sitting in the chair isn't aware that the other person is using a wheelchair because physical limitations become less obvious in virtual environments.

Interaction devices

Just as you use many different tools for different jobs, the same is true for virtual worlds. You wouldn't use a sledgehammer to open a can of soup, nor should you choose the wrong VR tool for a specific task. Fortunately, a virtual world designer has an increasingly large selection of tools to pick from. The rapid proliferation of devices signals the beginning of a very active VR tool-making business.

In chapter 5, we described four primary VR tasks: *navigation*, *selection*, *interaction*, and *command*. The virtual explorer wants to be able to move, or navigate to a particular point in space, to select objects or other entities, to interact with objects, and to issue commands controlling the simulation or the interaction. In the same chapter we also discussed how different devices offer different levels of support for these different modes of interaction.

The most important thing to remember when using any of the following devices is that their effectiveness is determined by how well the software accesses the device's capabilities. In fact, many times software, more than the physical hardware, determines how these devices are used. This means that by modifying the software you can perform the equivalent of opening a can of soup with a sledgehammer.

Interaction devices can be grouped into several loose categories. There are wired-clothing devices that are worn like a glove or a suit. There are wand devices that you hold in your hand, much like a baton or hand grip. Devices that measure six degrees of freedom (6 DOF) simultaneously are used for navigation and object control. Even a 2-D mouse or a common joystick have their uses in VR. Finally, there's a small class of devices that rely on biologic input like voice recognition, or muscle electrical signals.

Wired clothing

While VPL's DataGlove is one of the most recognized wired-clothing devices, several other approaches exist as well. The basic premise is to wear some external form of tracking device to monitor the position and orientation of key hand or body parts. While this would normally be considered solely a tracking function, wired clothing is usually intended for interaction.

In chapter 3 we described how NASA Ames used VPL's DataGlove device to naturally interact with virtual objects through various techniques. Users could communicate with the computer through simple gestures made with their hands while wearing the wired glove. They could grab virtual objects by sticking a gloved hand into the graphic representation of the object and making a fist.

The computer recognizes the gesture, and the graphic image of the object is attached to the graphic image of the user's hand. When he moves his hand, the object moves with it until he drops it by opening his hand. This is a simple and natural method for interacting with objects.

Wired clothing works by measuring bend angles of various body joints, like fingers, wrists, and elbows. Either mechanical, fiber-optic, or rosistive sensors are used. Each approach offers different advantages and limitations.

Fiber-optic sensors are used in the two most popular versions of the wired glove and wired suit. These work by looping a single strand of fiber-optic cable across a joint, like a knuckle (see Fig. 8-21). As the knuckle moves, the cable bends, which causes a reduction in the amount of light passing through it.

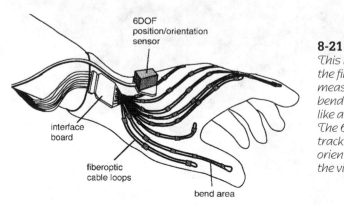

6DOF position/orientation sensor

interface board

fiberoptic cable loops

bend area

8-21
This illustration shows the fiber-optic loops that measure the amount of bend or flex of a body joint like a knuckle or a wrist. The 6 DOF sensor keeps track of the position and orientation of the hand in the virtual space.

This effect is enhanced even more if minute scratches are placed where the cable passes over the knuckle. The varying light output is measured by a photodetector and then communicated to a controller, which summarizes the current state of all the sensors and sends it on to the computer.

For each joint, a separate fiber-optic cable loop is needed, which means as many as 22 sensors might be used in a single glove. The simplicity of the design and its intriguing uses have made it a very popular device, but early versions suffered from a variety of problems that are still being addressed.

Glove users discovered that constant recalibration was necessary because the sensor output was very sensitive to knuckle position. Initial gloves were also very dependent on hand size and tended to be overly fragile. Most of these problems have either been fixed or will be soon. The same technology is used in complete body suits that measure all the major body joint angles.

Electromechanical sensors can also be used to measure bend angles, as shown Fig. 8-22. These bulky devices are designed so that a direct linear relationship exists between the finger joint angle and the sensor angle. This makes them less sensitive to different hand sizes and placement on the fingers.

8-22
This wired glove uses mechanical sensors instead of fiber optics to precisely measure the amount of flex in the finger joints.

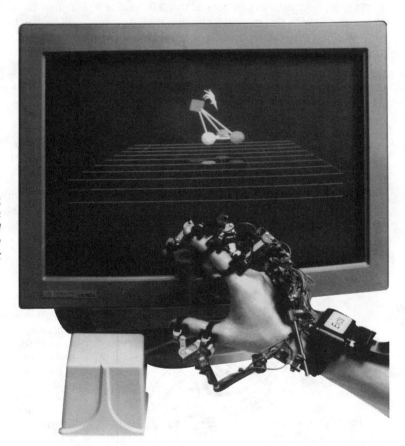

These different types of wired gloves can be used in different ways with a VR system. They can help establish a sense of presence (seeing your hand in the virtual world helps you believe you're really there), help you navigate around, and make it easy for you to manipulate objects.

One important consideration is minimizing the amount of lag between a person wiggling a gloved finger and seeing his virtual finger wiggle in the display. If this lag becomes too great, the glove becomes more difficult to use. Hygienic concerns can also be an issue if a single glove is to be used by dozens of people.

Wired gloves and devices like them offer an intriguing method of interacting in virtual worlds. It will be interesting to see how future applications make use of them.

Wands are the simplest VR device available. As you can see from the illustration in Fig. 8-23, they're nothing more than a 6 DOF sensor with a couple of switches attached. Because of this simplicity, they're very easy to use in public demonstrations of VR.

Wands

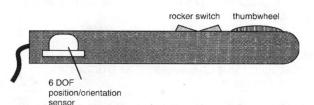

8-23
This diagram shows the simple structure of a wand device. The rocker switch provides discrete actions, while the thumbwheel allows scalable values to be entered.

One of the strengths of virtual environments is that the appearance of an object can be whatever the designer chooses—it need bear no resemblance to the object's physical appearance. At the click of a button, a device like a wand can look like a drill, paintbrush, spray gun, or sculpting tool.

Many computer paint-programs allow you to do the same thing with a mouse. If you select the icon with a spray gun on it, the cursor will change into the shape of a tiny spray gun. Techniques like this allow plenty of freedom in creating a large virtual toolchest with just a single simple device like a wand.

Here are some other ways of using a wand. To select objects, the user points the wand at an object and presses a button. This causes a laser beam to shoot out, and the closest object intersecting the beam is selected. To navigate, he just points the wand in the appropriate direction and presses another button. Wands, like gloves, lose effectiveness if too much of a delay exists between physically moving the wand and seeing it move in the display.

Objects, unless constrained, normally have six different directions or rotations they can move in. This is shown in the illustration in Fig. 8-24.

6 DOF devices

Objects can move forward or backward (X axis), up or down (Y axis), and left or right (Z axis)—these are known as translations. In addition, objects can rotate about any of these principal axes. Borrowing from flight terminology, these rotations are called *roll* (X axis), *yaw* (Y axis), and *pitch* (Z axis). All together, they add up to six different degrees of freedom in which the object can move.

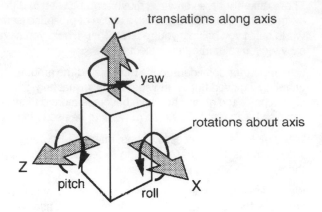

8-24
This illustrates the six different directions a 3-D object can move in. Three translations and three rotations are possible.

In virtual environments, you typically want to be able to move in any direction without being constrained. This might mean combining several translations and rotations all at once. 6 DOF devices support this by simultaneously measuring the three translations and rotations directly.

Even though it's possible to take a 2 DOF device, like a standard mouse, and use its buttons to move virtual objects in all six directions, this doesn't make it a 6 DOF device. Only by concurrently measuring all six parameters does a device warrant this label.

Two very different approaches provide this capability. Force balls use mechanical strain gauges to measure forces and torques applied to a stationary ball. 6 DOF mice, on the other hand, use 6 DOF sensors to keep track of their position and orientation as they're moved around.

Force balls Although they look like someone stuck a baseball on a joystick, force balls differ from joysticks in one crucial respect—they don't move. Instead, they measure the amount of force applied to them. To fly upwards using a force ball, you simply pick up the ball as if you were picking it off a table.

The ball is attached to a base that's secured to a rigid surface, so you can't actually pick the ball up. Instead, the force you exert is measured by several small strain gauges located at the center of the ball.

As they deform, their electrical properties change and this is detected by a small microcontroller located inside the base. It translates this into a set of six values (three translations and three orientations) that are then communicated to the reality engine. These values are relative to the at-rest state of the force ball. In other words, if no one is touching the ball, all the values should be zero.

A force as small as 0.1 lb. can cause the values to change. The simulation manager running on the reality engine receives these values and decides what to do with them. In this case, it moves the viewpoint by the relative amount specified by the transmitted record. The result is that you fly upwards. The illustration in Fig. 8-25 depicts the six forces measured by a force ball.

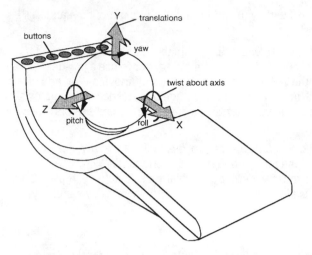

8-25
Force balls can be manipulated in up to 6 different directions simultaneously.

Although this method of navigating might seem a little unnatural at first, after 15 or 20 minutes it will become very comfortable. To fly faster, you just push harder on the ball. To help novice pilots, any multiple of translations or rotations can be ignored or constrained under software control. By turning off pitch and roll motions, novices will find it much easier controlling just the three translations and yaw.

In addition to this feature, some force balls have up to nine software-programmable buttons for developers to configure. Typically, one of them is used as a "panic button"—which resets your viewpoint if you get completely lost.

Force balls work well for navigating or moving objects around. Just as the ball can control your viewpoint, it can also be attached to virtual objects so that moving the ball moves the virtual object in similar like manner. They're durable and simple to use, and they're designed for stationary environments instead of ones where a participant might be physically walking about.

6 DOF mice

Several companies have taken a basic mouse design and modified it by adding some form of 6 DOF or 3 DOF tracking sensor. Either ultrasonic, electromagnetic, or gyroscopic tracking is used. Some designs include the concept of a clutch that allows you to remain within a set physical volume of space, while moving beyond it in the virtual world.

You do the same thing when you pick up your mouse, it reaches the edge of your mouse pad, and you set it back down in the center. 6 DOF mice usually have two or three buttons, like a regular mouse, for user input.

These devices have many of the same capabilities and limitations as wand devices. Their effective use is primarily dependent on the qualities of their 6 DOF tracking system. These factors, more than anything else, determine how the 6 DOF mice are actually used.

2 DOF devices

Interaction in virtual environments doesn't require complicated and expensive devices. Many tasks can be accomplished with simple 2 DOF devices like mice and joysticks. Joysticks are particularly easy to work with. By limiting the degrees of freedom a new user has to deal with, you can reduce the amount of time and frustration in achieving a task.

For example, if the goal is to move a wall from one place to another—changing its position without affecting its orientation—it might be better to use a joystick because it can easily move the wall in one direction without moving it up and down or left and right at the same time. The other advantage of a joystick is that many people quickly adapt to them—an important issue if the participant has only a few minutes to use the system.

Biologic input sensors

Biologic input sensors, also called *biosensors*, process indirect activity, such as muscle electrical signals and the recognition of voice commands. They use correctly placed dermal electrodes to detect particular muscle activity. If placed near the eyes, they can be used to navigate through virtual worlds by simple eye movement (see Fig. 8-26).

8-26
Dermal electrodes contained in the eyeglass frame, track eye movements by measuring muscle electrical activity.

Squinting or blinking an eye could cause the color of an object to change or some other action. Placed on the forearms, you could use them to navigate by clenching either the left or right fist.

Someday they might be sophisticated enough to eliminate the need to wear a wired glove. Instead of a glove, a simple tight-fitting bracelet might be able to distinguish individual finger movements. This kind of technology might also offer people with certain physical disabilities an opportunity to join the rest of us in virtual environments.

Voice recognition has been in development for over 20 years and has recently begun showing up on more and more desktops. Simple voice recognition, using trained voices and discrete commands, has been available for many years. This is a far easier problem than understanding continuous speech and untrained voices.

For virtual environments, the ability to give discrete voice commands, like "open door" or "reset view," is a powerful adjunct to controlling the environment. Voice recognition is useful when keyboard entry is difficult, or the person's hands are involved in some other task. Though this technology isn't part of any commercial VR system as of 1992, it stands a good chance of becoming a standard feature because it's well suited to providing hands-free control of the simulation.

Other interaction devices

On the far fringe of interaction devices are a couple of interesting approaches that don't really fall into any of the other categories. Earlier, we discussed how MIDI sequencers can be programmed to generate sounds. In an interesting twist, MIDI devices like keyboards or other electronic instruments can send signals to the VR system.

This means that you could create a virtual world where every note on a keyboard has a virtual representation. Not only could you hear the music, you could see it. This is an avenue that has yet to be fully explored, but as musicians and artists become familiar with the territory, you can expect some interesting applications.

Another device, recently introduced, solves the problem of bringing your keyboard with you into a virtual world. Based on keyboard-alternative technology (KAT), the single-handed KAT keyboard looks like a handgrip with five keyboard buttons (see Fig. 8-27). Each button has seven different positions, allowing all possible keyboard characters, including upper- and lowercase letters.

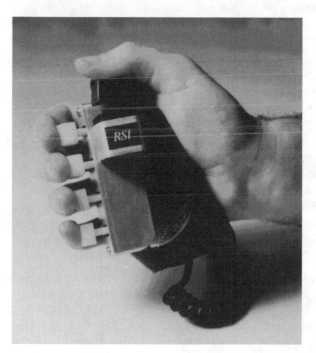

8-27
Prototype of a new device that will allow keyboards to travel with you into a virtual world. Up to 144 characters can be generated with this one device.

And it doesn't have to be used as a keyboard either. You could create a very versatile device for general interaction by attaching it to a 6 DOF sensor. It would be much like a 6 DOF mouse or wand but with more capabilities.

For every device we've talked about in this section, there are probably several other brand-new ones being worked on in garages and labs all over the world. You can already see that there are many different solutions to the problems of interaction in a virtual world. The fun part is picking the right one!

Position/orientation sensors

Many of the devices and capabilities previously mentioned, such as head-tracking, wands, and wired gloves, rely on the basic ability to detect an object's position and orientation at any instant. Whether you're moving your head or raising your hand, the computer needs to track these movements in real time so that the virtual world remains synchronized to your actions.

In the previous section, we mentioned how tracking quality to a large degree determines the effectiveness of interaction. With better tracking, the wand, wired glove, and other devices will become easier to use. Several key parameters determine this effectiveness:

Lag or latency Lag is the delay between sensor movement and the resulting signal being processed for final use. This is one of the most important parameters, as lags above 50 milliseconds (msec) will affect human performance. Unfortunately, not all products specify this crucial parameter. Sensors vary from between four and five msec to over 100 msec.

Update rate The update rate is the speed at which measurements are made. You can have a lag of 100 msec, but still send 100 measurements per second. Update rate and lag are mostly independent of each other. Most sensors support at least 60 updates per second.

Interference Interference is defined as sensitivity to environmental factors. Sensors can be sensitive to various conditions, like large metal objects, radiation from display monitors, extraneous sounds, and objects coming between the source and the sensor. Problems can also occur when more than a single sensor is used in close proximity.

Accuracy Accuracy in tracking effectiveness is the accuracy of position and orientation information. This usually varies with distance from the source, or drifts over time. Translational values vary from about 0.01 to 0.25 inch, while rotational values vary from 0.1 to 1.0 degree.

Range The range is the maximum distance between the source and sensor while retaining specified accuracy. This varies greatly with different sensor types. It ranges from a three- to eight-foot cube surrounding the source to an entire room.

All trackers work by measuring changes in position or orientation relative to some reference point or state. Typically, there's a *source*, which generates a signal, a *sensor*, which receives the signal, and a *control box*, which processes the signal and communicates with the computer. Their relationship is illustrated in Fig. 8-28.

After the sensor is attached to an object and both the source and sensor are correctly oriented, the control box is sent an initialization signal from the reality engine. This establishes the current orientation and position as the reference point.

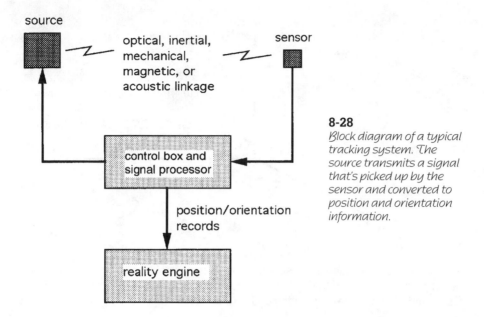

source

optical, inertial,
mechanical,
magnetic, or
acoustic linkage

sensor

control box and
signal processor

position/orientation
records

reality engine

8-28
*Block diagram of a typical
tracking system. The
source transmits a signal
that's picked up by the
sensor and converted to
position and orientation
information.*

If the source and sensor aren't correctly aligned at this stage, you might not know which way is up—up might be down and left might be right.

This is why care has to be taken in holding the HMD or wand in a particular position at startup, though it can be easily reset later on. After this initialization, or calibration, the tracker is ready to start sending values to the simulation manager.

Relative versus absolute tracking   Earlier, we discussed how force balls return relative values based on how hard they're pushed or pulled. If no forces are applied, they return zero values. 6 DOF trackers, on the other hand, return absolute values, which define exactly where objects are in space. This difference is important to understand if you plan on using them.

Let's use the book you're currently reading as an example. If you pick a corner of the room as the origin of a coordinate system and lie the book flat in the corner, you can describe its location using Cartesian coordinates (X, Y, and Z) and its orientation by using Euler angles (roll, pitch, and yaw). If the book is lying flat at the origin, these values are all zero.

Now pick up the book and sit in a chair without changing the orientation of the book. Assume you have translated the book to a new position, which, for example, is ten feet from both walls and four feet up, or (10,4,10). Because you didn't change the orientation of the book, the Euler angles remain (0,0,0). If you now rotate the book 45 degrees around the Z axis, you've changed its *pitch* by 45 degrees and the new Euler angle is (0,0,45). See Fig. 8-29 for an illustration of these orientation values.

By using these six values, you can describe everything you need to know about an object's position and orientation. And, unlike a relative sensor that returns to zero if left alone, an absolute sensor continuously returns its position and orientation if stationary.

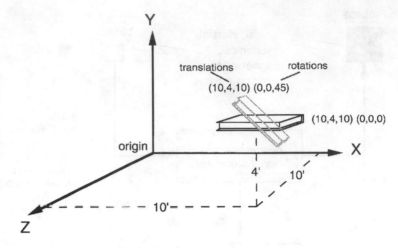

8-29

Any object's position and orientation in space can be defined by using six values —three for its position and three for its orientation.

Once the sensor has made a measurement and the control box has processed it, the *record* must be passed to the reality engine. Most 6 DOF trackers provide two communications modes—streaming and polling—to do this.

In *streaming* mode, records are constantly generated by the tracker as fast as it can send them over the serial line (this is the same serial line that you would use to hook up a modem). In *polling* (or demand) mode, records are sent only when requested by the simulation manager. This is how most sensors are controlled because it reduces the amount of effort required to communicate with the device.

Because most trackers communicate over an RS232, or serial line, the size of the record being transmitted can become a factor in the overall lag or delay of the tracker. Even at 9600 baud, sending six 16-bit words takes at least 13 msec. This is a big chunk of time when you're trying to stay under 50 msec overall.

Tracking technology

Several different approaches have evolved for detecting an object's position and orientation. All of them require a physical sensor attached to the object. This is known as *active* tracking. The alternative, *passive* tracking, doesn't require a special sensor. Instead, it uses several cameras to "watch" an object and determine its position and orientation. Due to the inherent difficulties in this approach, few of these systems have yet made it out of the lab.

Active 6 DOF trackers use either electromagnetic, mechanical, optical, or ultrasonic techniques for making 6 DOF measurements. All these approaches have different strengths and weaknesses.

Electromagnetic   This is the most popular method of tracking because of the sensor's small size and freedom of movement. A low-frequency signal generated by a control box sequentially excites three small coils of wire in the source, creating three magnetic fields.

When a similar set of three coiled wires is positioned in range of the source, a small voltage is induced in each of the coils as the three fields are created. This yields a total of nine measurements that are then processed by the control box to yield six values for position and orientation.

This technique was first developed over ten years ago by a company called Polhemus, for military applications. (The Polhemus Isotrak system is shown in Fig. 8-30.) The same device was used by NASA Ames and by Tom Furness to perform head-tracking for their HMD prototypes.

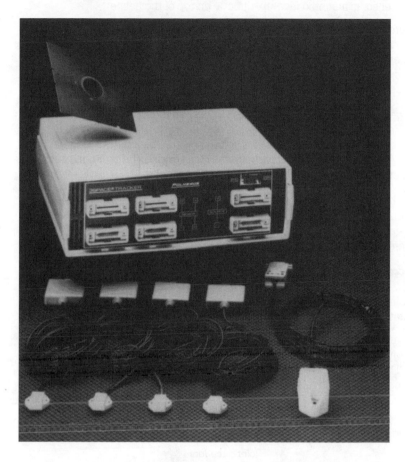

8-30
This electromagnetic tracking device can simultaneously support up to four sensors and two sources. The large cube is the source and the smaller cubes are sensors.

It has since evolved into a reliable and accurate method of tracking. Because the sensor is about the size of a dice cube and doesn't rely on line of sight, it can be buried inside other devices, like the wand or wired glove.

Its chief limitation has been lengthy lag times due to signal processing and filtering each set of nine measurements. However, recent innovations by Polhemus have dramatically reduced this lag to less than 5 msec (unfiltered), greatly improving its usefulness. Its only other problem is a sensitivity to large metal objects or to magnetic fields generated by nearby TVs or workstation monitors.

These problems, however, are usually easy to avoid. From a performance and usability standpoint, this type of tracker is the easiest to work with, though more expensive than other approaches. In addition, a special mode allows multiple sensors to work with a single control box. This allows several objects to be tracked at once within the same control space.

Ultrasonic   This inexpensive approach to tracking uses three ultrasonic transducers and three small microphones. The transducers are mounted in each corner of a triangular frame and set about one foot apart from each other. A much smaller triangle, the sensor, contains the three pin microphones. If used for head-tracking, the sensor is mounted face-up, directly on top of the helmet.

Using the same principle as before, each ultrasonic transducer emits a high-frequency sound pulse that is picked up by all three microphones. A signal processor measures the time delay (and therefore the distance) between each transducer and each set of microphones. Next, the nine distance measurements are easily processed to yield the required values.

An advantage of this approach is that sensor lag is less than 25 msec, allowing rapid head movements with only a small detectable delay. Unfortunately, the tracking system suffers from several other deficiencies. For accurate readings, the transducers must remain in sight of the sensor microphones. If they're obstructed by some other object or are tilted away from the transducers, the signal is lost.

In addition, they're subject to external noise like keys jingling, glasses clinking, or other ultrasonic sensors used for light or security systems. Because someone sitting in a chair wearing an HMD has limited head movement anyway, several of these limitations aren't that important.

Mechanical   Less well known than the previous two techniques is the mechanical tracking system, which uses a direct mechanical connection between a reference point and the object to be tracked. This linkage is typically a mechanical arm with rotating joints, allowing for 6 DOF control.

One version uses a lightweight arm to attach a control box to a simple headband. As the person moves his head, encoders placed at all six joints measure the change in position. This has the advantage of being a very fast (lag time of less than 5 msecs), accurate, and relatively inexpensive method of tracking. However, it suffers from a fairly restricted range of motion and, as of mid-1992, it hasn't seen much use. One version of this approach is depicted in Fig. 8-31.

8-31
A mechanical arm can be used to provide a simple and inexpensive method of head-tracking.

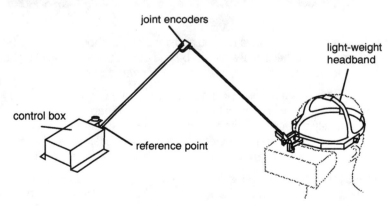

joint encoders

light-weight headband

control box

reference point

Inertial A very different mechanical approach is to use a couple of miniature gyroscopes to measure yaw, pitch, and roll. These aren't true 6 DOF sensors because they can measure only orientation and not translation, but they could be effective as head-tracking sensors where position information is rarely required.

These sensors rely on the principle of the conservation of angular momentum. Using a rapidly spinning wheel suspended in a gimballed housing, any change in orientation is resisted by the wheel. This resistance can be measured several different ways and converted into values of yaw, pitch, and roll. This same principle explains why a bicycle is difficult to keep upright when you first start to pedal it, but takes little or no effort to remain upright once you're up to speed.

For head-tracking purposes, two miniature gyroscopes (no bigger than a film canister) are mounted in the HMD. A tiny motor spins the inertial weight at 10,000 revolutions per minute (rpm). Changes in motion are reflected on a pattern illuminated by an LED. The reflected beam is picked up by an optical sensor and translated into an orientation angle. To get all three values of yaw, pitch, and roll, one gyroscope is mounted vertically and the other horizontally. An exploded view of a miniature gyroscope is illustrated in Fig. 8-32.

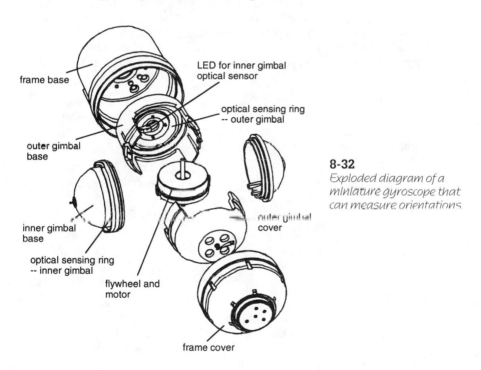

frame base

LED for inner gimbal
optical sensor

optical sensing ring
-- outer gimbal

outer gimbal
base

inner gimbal
base

optical sensing ring
-- inner gimbal

outer gimbal
cover

flywheel and
motor

frame cover

8-32
*Exploded diagram of a
miniature gyroscope that
can measure orientations*

Gyroscopes provide fast, accurate tracking in a compact package. They don't need a separate source, so their range is determined only by the length of their cable. Though initially expensive, in volume they can be manufactured quite cheaply. Their biggest flaw is that they suffer from significant amounts of drift—up to ten degrees per minute. Improved versions will reduce this to two degrees per minute, but this still remains an important drawback to their use as 3 DOF sensors.

Optical   Several infrared trackers, based on principles already covered, are available or are being researched. One system, used in aircraft simulators, has three or four infrared LEDs mounted on top of an HMD. Sensors, mounted on a support above the HMD, perform line-of-sight tracking with imperceptible lag. In fact, in one configuration, the system tracks accurately even at ranges of up to thirty feet. Unfortunately, it uses expensive signal-processing hardware that restricts its use to high-end simulators.

At the University of North Carolina, they've experimented with mounting three cameras on top of an HMD—all pointed up at the ceiling. In addition, they string about 1000 infrared LEDs uniformly across the ceiling. A computer sequentially pulses the LEDs and simultaneously processes the camera's image to detect a flash. Based on this, it calculates the position and orientation.

At other research labs, work has been done on using several cameras pointed at a target wearing a specially marked headset. Again, using image-processing techniques, a computer attempts to correlate the different camera views into a single position and orientation measurement.

Optical tracking is used primarily in cockpit simulators where the range of head motion is fairly limited, but fast update rates are important. The line-of-sight limitation continues to be a thorny problem that needs to be solved in order to build a general-purpose 6 DOF tracker. For now, it can be successfully applied in head-tracking applications where the participant is physically constrained in a cockpit or stationary chair.

Like head-mounted displays, most 6 DOF sensors are a forced compromise between cost and performance. The "perfect" low-cost tracker has yet to be developed. Until a large-volume VR application shows up, bringing low-cost, effective trackers to market, these devices will remain expensive.

Because tracking technology is at the heart of many VR devices, improvements in cost or performance have important repercussions. And like interaction devices, the technology behind tracking devices promises to be constantly evolving and exploring new solutions. More cost-effective solutions are out there; they just need to be found.

Conclusion   The intent of this entire chapter was to communicate the richness of tools and technologies available for interacting with and exploring virtual worlds. We also wanted to show how the first steps are being made to understand the nature of this new man/machine interface.

By exploiting the innate capabilities of our senses, we can achieve insights not possible with other methods. But keeping current with the latest tools and techniques is a constant struggle in such a rapidly evolving field. In this chapter, we hope to have equipped you with a basic understanding of the technology, allowing you to follow the many developments yet to come.

C-1 *Silicon Graphic's Reality Engine, introduced in the fall of 1992, set a new price/performance level for fully-textured, real-time virtual worlds. The art gallery (above) and space station (below) images were rendered at 15-30 frames per second. Within the next five to six years, this level of performance will become possible on powerful desktop systems.*

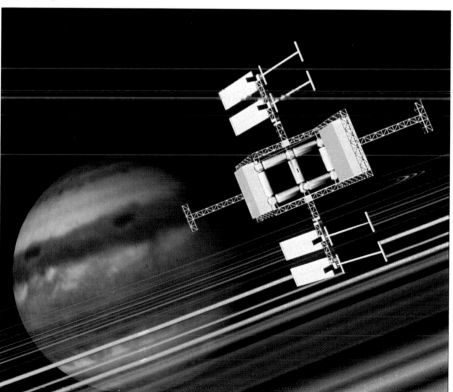

C-2
Exploring the computer of tomorrow, NEC's Advanced Design group built these mock-ups to explore how future PCs could become part of our everyday wear. Note how a couple of the designs sport head-mounted displays.

C-3
Using the most sophisticated head-mounted display available, a pilot prepares to enter a virtual world created by powerful image generators. State-of-the-art equipment like this is capable of blurring the line between reality and the simulation.

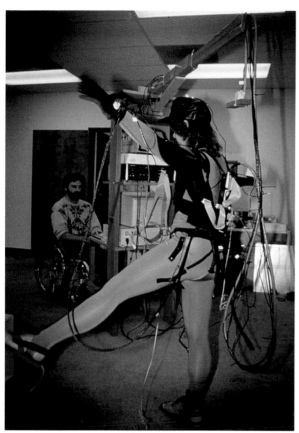

C-4 (left)

A participant tries on a VPL DataSuit for complete immersion in a virtual world. Sensors lining the outside of the suit detect body movements that are then transmitted to a computer. Wearing the suit, the participant can see his virtual body in the simulation.

C-5 (below)

Example of a force-feedback hand and arm system built by the SARCOS Research Corp. The operator "feels" the weight and handle of the hammer, while the robotic arm performs the same action with a real hammer.

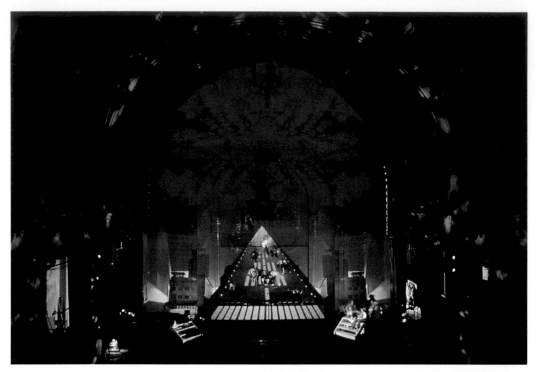

C-6 *In The Architecture of Catastrophic Change, George Coates used powerful projection systems to create dramatic environments that appear to surround the actors.*

C-7 *Jenny Holzer's work on display at the Solomon Guggenheim Museum in New York City, in which provocative messages slowly scroll across the lighted message boards.*

C-8

The first VR movie, or "voomie," is called ANGELS and was created by Nicole Stenger at MIT and Seattle's HIT Lab. These two pictures depict the abstract nature of Stenger's virtual world. By touching an angel's heart (left) at a gateway, you're instantly transported to various settings in Paradise. Angels (below) can also talk and react to your movements.

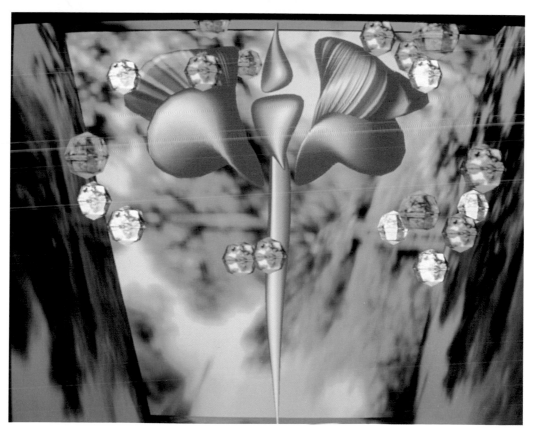

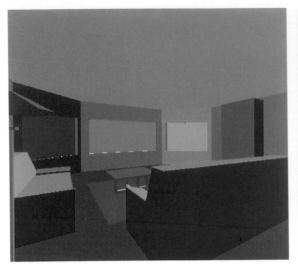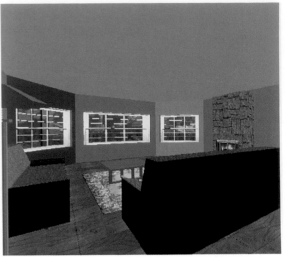

C-9 *The living room (top left) was rendered with flat-shaded polygons. The same room (top right) was rendered with texture-mapped images. Texture-mapping creates a heightened sense of realism in virtual worlds.*

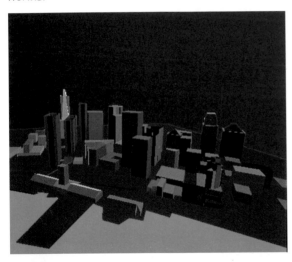

C-10

This scale model of San Francisco represents how city planners can use VR to visualize the effect of new construction.

C-11

To create virtual worlds and objects, modeling tools like Software Systems' Multigen allow not only the construction of 3-D objects, but also fine control over surface attributes such as color and texture-mapping.

C-12

One of the first collaborative virtual environments, in which two users can participate in designing a building. Using a wand, they simply point at an object, press a button, and a laser beam shoots out and selects the object. They can then move it into position or change the surface from wood to brick or even to zebra skin.

C-13

The Artroom, a virtual environment that allows two people to interactively create musical sculptures out of streams of polygons. In the background, a user can be seen drawing with his red wand as a trail of polygons hang in the air.

C-14

Computer-rendered view of Valles Marineris (Mariner Valleys) region of Mars. Researchers use computers to create "movies" of a hypothetical helicopter ride over the Martian surface. Height information, collected by radar, is combined with satellite images to recreate the view from any vantage point.

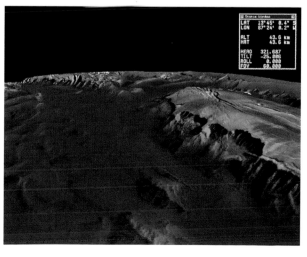

C-15

This model was created at the HIT Lab as part of their collaborative research with Boeing on the VSX vertical take-off and landing (VTOL) aircraft. Using a virtual environment, they studied maintainability and human factors issues.

C-16

Real-time texture mapping is the key to enhanced realism in this ship simulator based on a sophisticated ESIG-2000 image generator. Specialized hardware permits scenes like this to be rendered at 30 frames per second.

C-17

The level of realism achievable in today's top-of-the-line image generators will eventually make it to desktop systems in ten years or so. This image was captured on a Compu-scene V while performing a 60-frames-per-second simulation of an MH-53J helicopter. The visual database was modeled using DMA (Defense Mapping Agency) terrain elevation data and photographs (satellite, aerial, and hand-held camera) of a 60-square mile area in Nevada.

Part three

Brave
new worlds

9 Designing virtual worlds

"To see a World in a Grain of Sand
And a Heaven in a Wild Flower,
Hold Infinity in the palm of your hand
And Eternity in an hour."
    —William Blake, _Auguries of Innocence_

Creating virtual worlds is a new field full of challenges and rewards. Largely unexplored, it beckons the adventurous, the curious, and the inventive mind with its flexibility and power. In a scientist's hands it becomes a tool as basic as a microscope. To a teacher it suggests new ways of educating children and adults. For many people it's simply a great new form of entertainment. And for artists it inspires new forms of art, ones in which there's no longer a separation between art and audience.

There are a handful of world builders who have already begun exploring some of this new territory where almost anything can be simulated or suggested. They find themselves studying perception and psychology, but also borrowing from the art world with its long traditions of creating virtual worlds inside people's imaginations. Theater, painting, music and story telling have lessons and insights for the world builder.

The first question is, What does the world builder want to achieve? How does he set parameters and limits when the dynamic laws of a virtual environment, the basic rules it runs on, can be as unreal as those in *Alice's Adventures in Wonderland?*

There was more to Wonderland than a white rabbit and a cheshire cat; Alice explored a world where distortions of space and time and the human-like response of objects were integral parts of the story. In the playful way that Lewis Carroll structured the reality of Wonderland, he inadvertently foreshadowed some of the scientific insights of quantum mechanics and Einstein's special theory of relativity (40 years before Einstein published his theories and overhauled the paradigm of reality).

At the subatomic level and the speed of light, reality begins to behave in strange ways analogous to Lewis Carroll's Wonderland. For example, if you could travel fast enough you would find that, at the speed of light, there's no duration or movement—everything is stuck in one place, one moment.

Alice learned the same to be true in Wonderland when she was unable to move forward no matter how fast she ran. "Now, here, you see," said the Red Queen to Alice, "it takes all the running you can do, to keep in the same place."

Such a playful virtual world might be helpful today to teach Einstein's nonintuitive discoveries in grammar school or college. But how can you be sure the users will come away with the knowledge you want them to gain and won't just become lost and confused?

More so than engineers and scientists, painters, musicians, playwrights, and storytellers have specialized in developing ways to enchant and engage the mind. They have used abstraction, perspective, plot, memory, ambiguity, mystery, suspense, and symbolism to communicate, educate, and inspire. These techniques are available to the world builder to create more useful and engaging virtual worlds.

Every element of a virtual world is a design decision. What colors, shapes, and sounds should you use? What effects will your choices have on the user? How do you make something appear realistic, and does that really serve your purposes? How do you structure an application when you can make it do anything you want? How do you guide a user when he can do anything he wants—or anything might happen?

None of these problems are definitely answered yet; the field is just too new. In the chapters ahead you'll read about the brave new worlds already being created and see how the creators of virtual worlds have tried to answer some of these questions. But first, let's look into how the mind works and plays and discover some of the insights the early virtual world builders have uncovered.

"The virtual world is to the cognitive map as the ecosystem is to the biostructure."
  —Bob Jacobson, VR consultant

Software of the mind

Building virtual environments requires some understanding of the patterns and behaviors of the mind. Working together, our senses and central nervous system create our own personal virtual reality—sensing *is* believing. Marshall McLuhan pointed out that an enhancement of any one sense alters the information reaching the brain, thereby changing the way we think, act, and perceive the world.

For example, the invention of the microscope and telescope extended our ability to see; they made us aware that our world contained forms of life smaller than we could see, and planets floating far out in space.

The invention of the telephone and the radio extended our ears and gave us the ability to instantly communicate around the world, thereby changing our notions of time, distance, and community. Anyone who wears glasses or a hearing aid can testify how even these simple tools can change one's sense of reality.

Computers designed for virtual reality are the first tools that can act as an extension of the entire mind because they enhance all the senses to create environments. Just like the mind, these computers can create new realities.

As humans, we experience the world through the sensory portals of sight, hearing, kinesthesis, smell, and taste. These sensors impose limits on what we know and bias our understanding of the world. Many animals have seeing, hearing, or a sense of smell far more acute than our own, giving them a very different experience of their surroundings.

The brain takes in data from the senses and analyzes, filters, and abstracts it, thereby imposing limits on what we know. Consider the researcher who wore special glasses that made the world appear upside down—initially he couldn't make sense of the world or walk around, but after a few days his brain adapted and the inverted view became "normal" to him. He was able to walk around without any assistance. In fact, without the glasses the world now appeared inverted. Without conscious effort the brain abstracted the sensory information and imposed its own interpretation.

Representational systems

One of the most important facts about how the brain creates individual experience is that each of us processes our experiences differently, in terms of *representational systems*. Representational systems are those internal sense media that we use to experience the world around us. These internal media channels mimic the brain's input sensors. Just as our eyes bring in outside images, our brains use internal pictures and movies to represent ideas and memories.

We have ears, and we can talk to ourselves and create or remember sounds and music. And we rely on internal sensations such as emotions and "gut feel" for guiding our decisions. While the "hardware" of the brain is chemically based, the "software" operates by using these internal representations of the five senses. Representational systems are the internal media that convey thoughts—the software of the mind.

Dr. John Grinder, a linguist and co-founder of the Neuro Linguistic Programming field, has done extensive research into how people's representational thinking is reflected in their language, habits, beliefs, and behaviors. He found that, while everyone's representational systems are operating all the time, we each have a favorite—a learning bias. This favorite mode shapes our sense of reality by twisting and filtering our point of view.

Mathematicians, architects, and engineers tend to be visually-oriented people who think in terms of images. Musicians obviously tend to favor the auditory mode, while physical therapists, sculptors, and athletes are usually examples of kinesthetically-oriented thinkers.

This isn't to say that their other modes aren't operating. Thinking is a combination of all the modes working together. But when visually-oriented people are trying to understand something, they tend to focus on the visual portion of their experience—it's the mode they've specialized in to comprehend the world.

For example, decision-making is an imaginative trial-and-error process where many people compare images to other images while experiencing certain reactions to the options. However, for a more auditory-oriented person, images are accompanied by an internal conversation that's judged as equal to or more significant than the imagery.

The critical interactivity of all these thinking modes and the way they vary from person to person is why multisensory world building is vital for creating convincing, engaging environments.

When developing a virtual world, a developer's own biases can inadvertently cause him to favor one sensory mode over others. Much of the early world building has been done by engineers and scientists who have concentrated on visual experiences. Teachers will tell you that, while the visual mode is the strongest sense among humans, there are many people and cultures who pay more attention to the other channels.

The first lesson virtual world builders need to learn is to fully exploit all the sensory software channels available. Reality is a multisensory experience.

Submodalities

"There are children playing in the street who could solve some of my top problems in physics, because they have modes of sensory perception that I lost long ago."
—**J. Robert Oppenheimer, father of the atom bomb**

Unlike the randomness of everyday reality, a virtual experience is a planned experience in which every sensory detail is a design decision. The usefulness of virtual environments is not that it duplicates all the details of reality (a feat technically impossible), but because it functions like our consciousness as a filter and focus, presenting only those details essential for enhancing a specific experience or solving a given problem.

Storytelling is an auditory method of creating virtual worlds. Words evoke images, experiences, meaning, and when properly used, they can vicariously give us powerful experiences. In his 1978 book, *Therapeutic Metaphors*, the research therapist David Gordon laid out a process for intentionally structuring stories he told to people to help them understand and resolve problems—personal or intellectual.

David Gordon went beyond the abstract study of story structure and delved into the individual's personal experience of the story. He approached his task as a developer of virtual worlds and explored how the brain makes meaning, how it handles internal representations to create engagement with the listener. He discovered that the smallest elements of experience actually hold the most significance.

People divide sensory information into small, discrete units. These units are called submodalities. The submodalities of vision include color, brightness, form, movement, saturation, and patterns (among others). Auditory submodalities include pitch, intensity, pattern, location, and timbre.

Each type of submodality is responsible for encoding information along a particular dimension of an experience. Normally, as information is processed at increasingly complex levels, generalization is gained at the expense of detail. Submodalities are the way in which humans compress meaning and significance into the smallest details our minds can represent to us consciously.

When you ask people to describe their experience, they'll usually use words that stand for the whole experience: they feel upset, they smell flowers, they hear music. These kinds of words describe the entire category of the experience. But if you ask them to specify what they're seeing, hearing, feeling, and smelling, they'll answer with submodalities: there's a pressure in my chest, it smells light and kind of sweet, the music is strong and quick.

What this suggests is that the smallest details of experience are understood at the submodal level. They are the quantum mechanics of experience, the smallest building blocks of thought in which people assign specific intellectual and emotional meaning.

Understanding submodalities can aid in the design of any virtual world, such as the design and testing of a jet wing created on a computer. Steve Bryson and Creon Levit at NASA Ames have developed a virtual wind tunnel to test computer-designed jets. The application runs on supercomputers and displays its output on a high-resolution Fake Space Boom.

As the computer calculates the effects of wind passing over the virtual wing, Bryson and Levit have imitated the classic wind-tunnel techniques of smoke injection by creating streamers of color that pass over the wing, curling and rippling to reveal the shape of the wind's turbulence.

A designer who's conscious of submodalities could explore additional ways of adding meaningful feedback to the simulation. The smoke stream could be programmed to change color depending on variables like shifts in wind speed or reactions of the wing. Sounds could be added as a separate channel of information with various tones, notes, locations in space, words, and pitches to signify different data.

If we had the haptic technology, even the texture of the wind might be given various levels of meaning. In this way a designer could walk the wing of the virtual jet and each of his sensory channels would bring him specific data revealing a variety of insights about his wing design.

Stretching this paradigm even further, it's possible to imagine a time in the next century when each sensory channel will acquire its own alphabet. The blind already have a touch-sensitive alphabet, braille. Musicians have their musical scales and notes. Individual professions might develop their own multisense languages for providing information at our ears, eyes, noses, and fingertips.

There's already an extensive array of medical and psychological research on how people categorize experience. Table 9-1 lists the relationships between various submodalities. Some of these equivalences have been established experimentally (particularly the relationships between color and pitch, color and temperature, and brightness and loudness). Others arise from David Gordon's work in creating auditory virtual realities for clients.

Table 9-1
Equivalences between submodalities

Vision	Audition	Kinesthesis	Olfaction
color	pitch	temperature	fragrance
brightness	loudness	pressure	concentration
saturation	timbre	texture	essence
shape	patterning	form	– – – – –

The interplay of sensory submodalities affects our experience. For example, auditory stimulation affects color perception. "Low tones make colors darker, warmer, unclear, and dirty. With high tones colors usually become brighter, colder, sharply contoured, and more solid or surfacy." (Rayan, 1940 and London, 1954).

And seeing influences hearing; in a green-illuminated room auditory sensitivity is increased, and in a red-illuminated room sensitivity is reduced. When we're locked up in a dark room sensitivity decreases, but if we're bathed in a white light it increases. The length of a tone will be judged as lasting longer than that of a light stimulus even though they're presented for the same duration.

Blocks appear to be larger or smaller, depending upon the color they've been painted. Going from largest apparent size to smallest apparent size, the subject ranking of colors is yellow, white, red, green, blue, and black.

Color exerts a similar and stronger effect on judgments of object weight (Payne, 1958 and 1961). Objects that are black, blue, or red tend to be judged heavier than identical objects that are green, yellow, or white. McCain and Karr (1970) found that an object's color affects distance discrimination, so that red objects appear to be closer and blue objects farther away than they really are.

One researcher, Birren (1950) speculated that different colors actually evoke or correspond to different geometric shapes. For example, orange supposedly evokes the image of a rectangle; yellow, a pyramid or inverted triangle; blue, a circle; and red, sharp angles, squares, or cubes. Designing a virtual world to test this idea wouldn't be too hard to do and could produce some interesting results.

There are also subtle physical limits to the senses. The eye can perceive blue and yellow farther out on the periphery of vision than red or green because of the distribution of retinal sensors. At its outer limits, only white light is recognizable. The optimal viewing area is a cone of perception stretching straight out in front of the eyes and arching 15 degrees to either side.

Developers of advanced fighter-pilot helmets have used auditory submodalities to improve the human-jet interface. They've learned that a woman's voice, preferably that of a relative or girlfriend, whispering right behind the pilot's ear that he is about to run out of fuel has more effect than any bells and whistles. The close location—inside the pilot's personal space, the low volume, and the use of a woman's voice are all submodalities they've exploited.

Representational systems and their submodalities are the building blocks of experience to which meaning is applied. They give us a language for categorizing the most basic elements of experience and talking about them in terms of a virtual environment. In a virtual world, nothing is taken for granted because everything is under the control of the developer. And every decision will affect the user who steps into the world.

Creating reality with illusion

Mark Bolas has dark hair and eyes and like many small business owners he has a hurried, intense nature. He is the President of Fake Space Labs and one of the earliest developers of virtual worlds. He moves, talks, and gestures with quick, deliberate movements, giving you the feeling that somehow he's made the time to think out everything he wants to say and do.

Like the Soviet space station astronauts who hold records for time spent in space, he's a member of a select club of people who have spent the most time in virtual reality. He became hooked on virtual reality before it had a name, when it was still a scientist's toy at NASA Ames. At that time he was working on a degree in design at Stanford University, a special program between the Art and Computer Science departments (he now teaches in this same program).

After convincing the Stanford faculty to let him do his thesis on this strange new thing, he made an important decision. He froze the system hardware where it was. He decided to focus on developing the experience—building and creating virtual worlds. Along the way he learned a lesson about creating realism by using illusion.

"When someone is in a virtual world and they tell me that they're afraid to look down because they're up too high, or they come out and act disoriented, I know I've succeeded. They've accepted the virtual world as if it is real," Bolas says, sitting on a park bench near his offices in Palo Alto, California. "But when I started out there was nothing to go by, I just experimented at building worlds."

No matter what improvements to the frame rate or resolution came along, he decided that his job was to push the technology as a medium as far as he could without improving it. He stuck to this religiously. Even if it meant taking twenty minutes to make a change in the software code, he left the machine alone. The temptation would be too great to go on tinkering with the equipment instead of with the worlds.

"The first thing I decided to do was to spend an hour a night for a week using the equipment. But after twenty minutes the first night I decided it was a big mistake—there was nothing to do after flying around but stare at my virtual hand. It was boring. So my goal became over the course of the year to create worlds that people would want to spend time in."

It was 1988 and Mark's previous experience had been studying computer music at the University of California, San Diego. He knew how captivating good music could be (and it didn't need goggles), and it seemed to him virtual worlds could be equally captivating.

But he found that most people using the early virtual reality systems never lost a sense of the other people around them, the room, the line of people waiting to use the system. They rarely got caught up and taken away by the experience, something that music lovers are familiar with.

At that time, even with sophisticated workstations, all he could animate was simple wireframe outlines of shapes. So he designed a suite of offices from real blueprints. At first he constructed the world without coloring in the polygons so the walls were only outlined and transparent. You could get a sense of size but also see how each room affected the other rooms if you started moving walls around.

When he colored in the walls to make the rooms more realistic all he could see was the room he was in—and viewers enjoyed the experience less! This started him wondering about the usefulness of abstraction versus realism. The colored wall might be more realistic, but the see-through boundary lines were more useful and enjoyable for certain tasks. And by leaving the world more abstract, versus building in more realism, Mark could draw users deeper in.

Abstraction isn't a reason to reject VR worlds as being unrealistic. Apple Computer's desktop metaphor for interface software between the person and the computer was quickly rejected as a childish toy by many when it first appeared. Yet the use of icons and windows provides a better way of simplifying and focusing on a computer for many users. The graph in Fig. 9-1 describes Mark's results of trying to get people involved in virtual environments.

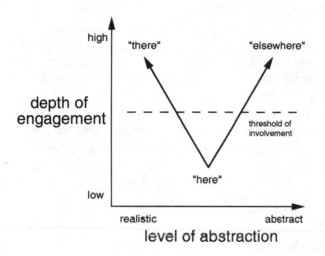

9-1
Illustration that depicts two different approaches to immersion. Both realistic and abstract environments can result in the same sense of being somewhere else.

At first people start off *here*, in a room putting on a helmet, loading software, etc.

The person's orientation is to the room. As they enter the virtual world, their depth of engagement gradually meanders away from *here* until they cross the threshold of involvement. Now they've become absorbed in the virtual world, similar to becoming engrossed in a good book.

The model or paradigm that most people use to construct virtual environments is based on flight simulators. Their goal is to bring the person to the building, to the wind tunnel, to the office. Flight simulators offer a very powerful illusion of being *there*, on the plane.

But most VR systems don't come with all the motion control chairs and environmentally accurate plane cabins like flight simulators. Yet designers keep trying to build the software as if everything else was real. Mark Bolas found that by being more abstract he could pull people up further into the environment.

"I don't know what to call it to differentiate it but *there* and *elsewhere*. I found that no matter how good the world, you could only get so far to *there*. The more abstract, the more *elsewhere* the world, the more people felt "in there" than anything else. I feel that *elsewhere* represents the true nature of the VR medium."

Humans are spatial creatures; we're always aware of and scanning our environment. The most important and single most common piece of information all our senses provide us with is a sense of location. So Mark started experimenting by building an entry world to quickly orientate people to the new environment.

He devised movements and events for the front end of the application that forced users to become involved "in there." Mark had people quickly fly around in a figure eight racecourse pattern before they entered the rest of the world. As they did this they saw themselves passing through a chain of open boxes.

Part Ferris wheel, part rollercoaster, the image cognitively engaged people, forcing them to orient themselves to the new environment. It also effectively spun them around before they entered the intended world.

He didn't just design worlds and let people try them; he spent time watching them as they went through the experience. What sections did they spend a lot of time in? What maneuvers were the most attractive? Where did people like to go? He'd watch on a side monitor as people moved around with the goggles on so he could see what they were seeing as they moved about.

By trial and error he discovered visual and spatial guides to draw people into and through virtual environments. Discoveries were accidental, hit and miss. One time he created a world that used a stairway and found that people loved to go up the stairway.

"You have to ask yourself why?" Mark says. "There was a white light at the top of the stairs and people are attracted to bright lights. But there's more to it than that—people love to go up in virtual worlds. I don't understand why. They also love to go down. If you tilt your head down you wind up flying down. People seem to love to do off-sets, things they can't do in normal everyday modes."

By the end of the year he was able to build a couple of worlds that people would spend 40 minutes in, but 75 percent of the worlds he tried failed. He had no guides to go by, no one had ever created worlds before. By experimenting he began to learn what the real power of the medium could be and the power of illusion in designing worlds.

He learned to use grid patterns on floors to create a railroad-track effect to enhance the sense of depth in the rooms (a lesson from the Renaissance). He began drawing white lines around the outside edges of polygon boundaries to make them punch out. It's a standard artist's trick to give shapes a border, because whenever there's a change in contrast the brain actually enhances the contrast.

One of his most successful worlds was based on a 1920s musical instrument called a Theremin (see Fig. 9-2). The project allowed him to mix his background in music with his desire for abstraction. Working with another engineer, Phil Stone, he created a world in which you could modify pitch and change the character of sound by using a wired glove to make sweeping gestures with your hands. It allowed them to compose soaring organ-like music.

9-2
A virtual Theremin, developed by Marc Bolas and Phil Stone while at NASA Ames.

There are many more sophisticated techniques for pictorial communications, depending on what the world builder is trying to design. Besides perspective, there's the use of shadows to aid in the illusion of depth, suggest a single light source, and also imply a time of day.

Cartoon animators have developed a visual language for characters that engages the viewer while replacing the subtle clues that real body language provides. Anticipation, for example, has its own motion characteristic in cartoons, which provides information and produces dramatic effects. By pulling backwards slightly just before they move, cartoon characters telegraph their intentions. Their movement adds visual continuity and a sense of realism that keep audiences involved with the character.

Sound can represent position, direction, and speed of motion in a character. Sound can be similarly applied to virtual worlds to establish continuity and provide information for the user. All these submodal elements are dynamic functions that can be built into objects or environments within virtual worlds.

One area awaiting experimentation is the use of standard film techniques. Film shots like fade-ins, fade-outs, close-ups, and continuity cuts are pictorial communication techniques we've already been trained to unconsciously understand. Some might work well in virtual realities; others will only be disruptive.

Just as D.W. Griffith imported literary storytelling techniques into his visual style, world builders must experiment to see what other fields have skills they can use. Movie editing and the camera's point of view make up a very effective language of the eye for influencing our emotions. If you doubt their effectiveness, just try recalling the face of someone very important to you and notice how you feel as you zoom in on their image or change it from color to black and white.

Full sensory stimulation isn't always useful or effective. In the 1920s, the theatrical producer David Belasco introduced aromas and fragrances into the production of his realistic plays. He wanted to increase the sense of realism.

He stopped the experiments when he noticed how the smell of bacon frying distracted his audience from the action on the stage. Perhaps it threw the audience into confusion because it blurred the lines between the designed experience and random everyday life. They were unprepared to deal with the information, to categorize it as part of the show. If frying bacon could unexpectedly appear, what other "real" events might threaten the audience?

There's a subtle agreement, a kind of social contract, between the audience and the experience designer. For a simulation to be believable and engaging, there needs to be roles and boundaries assigned to both sides of the curtain. Neither the designer nor the user actually believe the actions on the stage or in the computer are real, but they agree to pretend as if they are real. There's safety in the knowledge that they can escape at any time by leaving the theater or turning off the computer.

This contract between the designer and the user is even more crucial in a virtual world because they need each other to complete the work. Sudden shifts in the boundaries and roles, and mistakes in continuity of design aren't just bothersome, they destroy the entire illusion of being "elsewhere."

When a world builder decides to construct an environment, before he decides on what objects to include or colors to use, he needs to determine the goals of the application. What is the user of the experience supposed to learn or experience? What benefit is someone going to get out of this simulation?

The next step is determining the associated tasks required to deliver the benefit. What tools, activities, and perceptions will allow the user to acquire the knowledge or produce the product he wants? Once these activities are identified, it's important to decide how to represent them in a world and how to interact with that world.

Just as an icon designer for a Microsoft Windows' application must be sure the iconic symbol communicates its function clearly, the world builder must think about what his tools look like in the world and how well they work together with other tools to communicate function. Too much creativity and imagination can result in worlds that are annoying and unnecessarily difficult to use.

Many VR world designers are beginning to design wands into their worlds as multifunctional hand tools, instead of using wired gloves. The wand can be programmed to function in a manner analogous to the use of a mouse—you zap and click instead of point and click to activate objects and processes.

Always focus on ease of use. At the core of all virtual realities is the activity—the performance is the difference that sets VR apart from other computer applications. Most of today's world builders have focused on solving a particular problem. In the future, most virtual worlds will be designed in and of themselves to generate new discoveries, new insights, and new delights.

VR as theater

Virtual world travelers find themselves in environments with limitations and freedoms that aren't immediately apparent. Touch an object and it might tell you its name, crack open to reveal more detailed information, fall to the floor, or fly through the wall to fetch yesterday's mail. Each application will have its own images, metaphors, structure and its own dynamic laws of interaction.

Virtual worlds operate in a more demanding realm than traditional computer applications; unlimited freedom is the ultimate responsibility. If the application is clumsy or confusing to use or if it doesn't engage the user, he'll simply abandon it. The world will fail and the market will decide its fate.

A virtual world must not merely be functional or user friendly. It has an absolute test to pass, not a relative one—it should be user delightful. This isn't to say it must be a game (though computer games have valuable lessons to offer). Few people think of a spreadsheet program as fun to use, but the power it gives the user over previous methods is decisive.

"Focus on designing the action. What do you want the user to do? The design of objects, environments, and characters are all subsidiary to this central goal," advises Brenda Laurel, author of *Computers as Theater* and editor of *The Art of Human-Computer Interface Design*.

Brenda Laurel has been inside the personal computer industry since it began, first as a programmer and later as a software designer, marketeer, producer, and researcher. Her academic background in theater aided her in developing interactive fantasy architectures at Atari Research Lab in the early 1980s.

Since then she has worked as a consultant in interactive entertainment and human-computer interface design for Apple, LucasArts Entertainment, and the School of Computer Science at Carnegie Mellon University. In 1990, she joined Scott Fisher (fresh from his virtual reality work at NASA Ames) in founding Telepresence Research, but left in 1992 to resume her independent consulting career.

"A piece of computer software is a collaborative exercise between the imaginations of the program's creator and the people who use it," Laurel said while talking on the phone from her home in California. "It's never finished because it only comes alive when someone uses it and each use is slightly different. Designing human-computer experiences isn't about building a better electronic office. It's about creating imaginary worlds that have a special relationship to reality—worlds in which we can extend, amplify, and enrich our own capacities to think, feel, and act."

Virtual reality allows the user unique capabilities, such as the ability to fly, to occupy any object as a virtual body, to observe the world from multiple perspectives, and to be in places too small or far away for humans. It's a powerful setting in which you can control time, scale, and physics through the dynamic laws of the environment.

"I used to imagine that to design really great interactive software we'd require Artificial Intelligence (AI) behind the action," Laurel says. "We would script out these elaborate plots and the AI would shuffle events around, so as the users made choices they would still be invisibly guided toward the climax of the story. What I've come to realize is that my traditional ideas of authoring are heading toward a train crash.

"In interactive media, the author can't make the entire experience and give the user any choices! Our notions of traditional media can't come with us. We've limited the choices for users and all that is broken now. We are in a region where the authorship of the experience is about collaborating with the user in real time. You don't want to force them to meekly go through the plot you've authored; you want to give them enough constraints and resources so the plot they invent by taking action in the world is an interesting one.

"To find precedents for what I'm talking about we have to go outside traditional Western ideas of authoring and art. The ideas we need aren't where we expect to find them. An architect authors a building, but he doesn't author what people will do inside the building. He knows how to design a space that provides materials for people doing certain things in that space.

"We need to ask different questions, such as, How do people relate to landscapes? When gardeners in Japan create landscapes designed for specific contemplative experiences, they are engineering experience (see Fig. 9-3). We are stuck with a top-down Western model of authoring. The use of VR is a new frontier closer to imaginative play than anything else, closer to playing cowboys and Indians as a child. The one traditional area we can look to is the stage."

9-3

A traditional Japanese garden is designed to encourage a contemplative environment. This one is part of the Imperial Palace in Kyoto, Japan.

Brenda Laurel suggests that the theater presents us with a powerful metaphor for creating virtual worlds. At the theater we relax our psychic boundaries to become engaged with the action, feel empathy with the characters, and struggle with the problems enacted on the stage. The action and the performance is what matters.

Theater allows us a safe place to experiment and explore various emotions, ideas, and situations. One of the great themes of Classical Greek theater was the debate over honor and revenge. In a society that prized both, how much revenge was enough when it required an endless cycle of murders? It was both a public and a personal debate, simultaneously carried on in the virtual world of the Greek theater.

At the theater, we agree to ignore that there's a backstage with ropes, risers, stage hands, costume makers, and a director making last-minute changes. With a computerized virtual world, the user enters into the same conspiracy and agrees to forget about the computer, the software, the head tracker, the glove and goggles. They're all "out of sight"—the performance is the thing.

"Now there's a rule to theater set design, whatever is on the stage is there for a reason—you don't put random stuff around," Laurel says. "If there is a candelabra, it's there for light, to hit someone with, maybe it's connected to one character's past, but it has a purpose, everything has a purpose.

"The set is the visible aspect of a designed world all focused on aiding the action. If you don't have a script, the elements that guide the actor come from the lighting, the stage, the props, the clothing. Even on a bare stage with improvisational theater, the first thing the actors do is start to define the space. They begin describing where they are standing, what furniture is there, what food; they create boundaries for each other to work and create in.

"The well-designed world is, in a sense, the antithesis of realism—the antithesis of the chaos of everyday life. We get to play 'what if' in an organic world where everything is there for a purpose. This is what virtual world designers need to be investigating, this is what's new about this new media. We will have to design in cues, clues, and overviews to serve as advance organizers for travelers new to the territory. The key to a great experience is going to mean a well-designed setting."

Coyote World

Brenda is testing her ideas by turning them into reality—that is, virtual realities. She and her partner Rachel Strickland are working with the Banff Center for the Arts on the Coyote World project. It's a virtual world for two people in which the environment is animistic and endowed with multisensory objects. In it, materials like trees, rocks, hills, and grass are conscious beings with the capacity for action.

The characters will be derived from Native American fables: The Great Spirit, Coyote, Bear, Antelope, Quail and Fox. Her goal is to create a world full of potential causes and potential effects that will act as catalysts for creative possibilities. Simply moving through this virtual environment will invite reactions.

"You need to give people enough constraints so the plot they create is an interesting one, but enough ambiguity so they have a variety of directions to go in. Ambiguity is not the absence of meaning, but the presence of more than one. If you give too much realism you cauterize imagination, it hasn't room to work.

"The theory behind the Coyote World project is that if you put people in a virtual world with enough enticing possibilities and things to play with and things that play with them, then the technology bumps us up into a new kind of media experience. It bumps us into a new place where our imaginations are heightened and emboldened, where we have confidence that we can take action in the world without falling off the edge," Laurel says.

Instead of Native American folk tales, the characters and objects of the Coyote World project could be replaced by molecules and atoms with their own particular dynamic properties and capabilities. A chemist let loose in such a world could bring to it a vast personal library of information, a personal history of what these elements were supposed to do, could do, and might do if combined. Most discoveries are the result of many failed attempts and experiments.

But, for the first time, he would be able to mix and match in real time as if assembling molecular building blocks on a workbench. What new life-saving drugs or chemical reagents might be created if molecular chemistry became a hands-on design process, a new kind of high-tech craftsmanship?

Questions that Laurel is currently exploring include: How do you develop guides and techniques that will help people develop and conjure up the details of situations? How can someone develop and keep track of (and maintain some control over) their ideas in a world that's constantly changing in response to ideas? What methods might an artist employ, either in real time or through program design, to introduce new situations for moving the action along?

Laurel and Strickland have spent the past two years working with children in schools to research this approach. The children were told Native American folk tales by their teachers for several months. The themes were used in drawing exercises and games. After several months, when the children had clearly absorbed the mythos and its characters, they were given paints, paper, bits of walnuts, and wool and encouraged to work up their own versions of the stories.

As the groups of children created their own stories and stepped into the roles of various characters or created new ones, Laurel and Strickland changed the collection of tools the children were using to see which ones contributed the most as creative catalysts, and to understand how the narrative process changed. Then they were ready to use what they learned to create worlds for grown-ups, a new kind of narrative and a foundation for other virtual world builders.

"It's a chance to enter into a fully formulated world of the imagination, but one which will truly be new to most people," Laurel says. "You discover all this stuff about yourself you didn't know. And you are free to try things you might not feel comfortable doing in public.

"Nobody hasn't had the fantasy of being an actor, of thinking what it would be like to be that character, what it would be like to be in that world. What we have with VR is the possibility to walk into the world of Hamlet or Wiley E. Coyote. But you don't have the problem of being watched, you are not performing, you are stepping into the world."

Laurel's plan is ambitious. The use of structured plots has been refined over hundreds of years by playwrights and authors to guide us through experiences in a set amount of time. They play on our emotions, values, and assumptions about life to create catharsis.

The characters and parameters of a Coyote World, or any other dynamic mythic world, will need to be familiar to the users—whether from Shakespeare or Road Runner cartoons—so they can relax and participate, not stand around and puzzle out what they're supposed to do. Then users can bring to the world a sense of what their roles could be and more readily grasp what the connections between the various pieces suggest.

The schoolchildren Laurel worked with had several months to absorb the new characters, myths, and magic. If the parameters aren't understood by the user, entering such a world could be like visiting an interactive house of mirrors. Users would wander around amazed and delighted at the strange effects, altering mirrors as they went, playing in the maze, chasing each other into strange new experiences, but never achieving more than a great thrill.

The challenge Laurel has set for herself is to create a new kind of storytelling. She might be ahead of her time. It might be that the children of today's baby boomers, the schoolchildren she worked with who are growing up with computers, are the ones who will one day fully appreciate virtual worlds.

In the multimedia theatrical drama, *Invisible Site*, George Coates and his company of actors explore a host of ideas by imagining what could happen during a visit to a future virtual-reality store. Because computers as powerful as the show supposes don't exist yet and because they couldn't afford to give everyone a pair of VR goggles anyway, the company turns the entire theater into a single, giant VR helmet. They immerse the audience in the performance by using 3-D slide projectors and 3-D glasses, film, trick lighting, sounds, and images projected throughout the theater, while actors float in mid-air—and much more.

"The job of artists, whatever the medium, is to direct attention. But when the user is directing his own attention, the user becomes the artist," George Coates said while sitting in the middle of his theater in San Francisco, a stylishly decayed cathedral, abandoned for over 30 years until his company took it over. Packed with computers, projectors, lights, cables, wireless mikes, hidden speakers, and other high-tech equipment, the place has a post-apocalyptic *Blade Runner* feel perfectly matching the show.

"Developing *Invisible Site* made me realize how wide a range of creative possibilities the designers of virtual worlds will have," Coates says. "It's different from a film or theatric experience, or even an author writing a novel. The designer will have to take into account all the options a participant might want to avail himself of in a given world.

"The designers of virtual worlds create complete sensory environments which the participant will be navigating through and interacting with. And not just strange or magical or peculiar or ordinary environments, but different eras, different times, different cultural places. They will be able to create situations where characters from different time frames can meet. Elizabethan England can collide with 18th-century China."

The characters in *Invisible Site* come to the store to change identities, take on the image of their heroes, switch their sex, visit exotic locations, and have adventures in cyberspace. They shift from city to city with the speed of film, reverse time, repeat time, fly, crawl, and meet their double when a software hacker breaks into the network and takes on the same identities they have (see Fig. 9-4).

"Like talking on the phone, but disguising your voice, users of virtual worlds will eventually create digital identities—digidentities," Coates suggests. "Someday in the future, instead of watching a film of Shakespeare's *Tempest*, you'll go to an island in a virtual world and become Prospero. And if the network is big enough you are bound to find someone who wants to be your Caliband. You'll enter into the Tempest as a performer instead of a spectator."

The play explores the dynamic possibilities of a future virtual-reality era. It also mirrors VR's structure within its own theatrical model of hidden backstage tricks used to create on-stage magic.

Whether discussing design techniques or the resulting virtual experience, creating virtual worlds leads into a discussion of art because they both share many of the

9-4
In this scene from Invisible Site, an actor becomes trapped in a projection of a broken TV set while a large eye looks on.

same concerns. Dr. William Bricken of Washington State University's HIT Lab (and a former co-founder of Autodesk's VR program) has addressed these issues by summing up his years of VR design experience in a short manifesto:

Psychology is the physics of VR.
Our body is our interface.
Knowledge is in experience.
Data is in the environment.
Scale and time are explorable dimensions.
One experience is worth a trillion bits.
Realism is not necessary.

VR designers borrow from every field and discipline of thought. Along the way they're creating a new tool more flexible than anything mankind has previously invented. Historically, tools have been good for some single purpose. Computers and virtual reality are flexible tools that can serve a wide range of applications.

The remainder of this book will show how people are already taking this new tool and putting it to a wide range of uses. Along the way they're also redefining what it means to be a tool builder.

"It's a new creative form which we don't have a language for yet," Coates concluded. "The designer will need to be conversant in a vocabulary that treats all the languages of experience equally: verbal language, visual language, musical language, textural languages, languages of graphics and animation. A virtual designer is going to become a kind of theater impresario, someone who is going to be able to develop the art of the mix."

Business enters the cyberage

10

"...unlike a lot of people who think the computer industry's maturing, I think it's in its infancy. I think there are technological breakthroughs that happen once every ten years, maybe. Sometimes a little more frequently, but not too much. And that those technological breakthroughs have the force to reshape the tools that we build, and to reshape the industry along with them, as certain companies pay attention to them earlier and certain companies wake up fairly late."

—Steve Jobs, *MicroTimes*, 1992

Few technologists understand better than Steve Jobs the dynamics of turning a new technology into a successful industry. It not only requires good workers and good products with customer solutions, it requires that trends be nurtured when customers find a feature or solution that works especially well for them. Sometimes a single trend can become the key feature that allows a product to stand out. Is there such an application for virtual reality?

The visual emphasis of the Apple Macintosh computer's design made it ideal for automating the typesetter's job of page layout and text integration. For the first time, what users saw on the screen was what came out of the printer. The job of activating commands was simplified with the innovation of the mouse; on-screen windows and graphical icons made accessing and organizing information much easier.

But it wasn't typesetters or graphic artists who first jumped to the Mac; they were already comfortable with the tools they had. It was their customers. Hundreds of small businesses and private individuals saw a way of reducing their costs, increasing control, and becoming more directly involved in the creative effort of communicating with others.

As the word spread, these users were joined by more and more small desktop publishers. Brochures, fliers, and newsletters by the thousands sprang forth as people found a new way of communicating. No one forecasted desktop publishing, but it became the key application that drew many people's attention to the Macintosh, allowing them to discover all the other great things a computer could do.

There are a wide range of applications under development for virtual reality, tools like virtual prototyping, air-traffic control, molecular modeling, spreadsheets you can walk inside of, and trips into space without leaving earth or into the chambers of a beating heart.

Hollywood is working on virtual movies where the audience participates in their own entertainment. And artists are building experiences in which the user becomes both co-artist and a part of the art itself. No one knows which one of these ideas could be the "killer application" that pulls the VR industry forward. Perhaps virtual reality has such broad applications that its widespread use will eventually pull the computer industry forward into the next century.

It isn't enough to just do a job better; a new technology needs to provide distinctive benefits. A rule of thumb is that it must deliver a ten-to-one improvement over existing methods of solving the same problem before people will adopt it. Can it help us learn faster, more easily, and more accurately? Will it reveal insights we wouldn't discover otherwise? Can we use it to improve or speed up the invention and production of new products? Can it make our jobs easier and more enjoyable? How can it help us enjoy the time we have with our families in new ways?

There are two major benefits to using virtual reality applications. First, it gives us a new way to explore reality. Like the microscope and telescope, it can extend our senses so we can learn or do something with reality we couldn't do before.

For example, chemists have traditionally built stick figures to visualize the molecular structure of the chemicals they design. With VR they can perceive the molecule from any size, distance, and color, as shown in Fig. 10-1. They can animate it to study how it moves and affects other molecules.

Today, you can't touch and hold a virtual molecule with the same physical satisfaction that a stick figure provides. Both the stick-figure model and the VR model communicate certain aspects of the same idea equally well.

However, simulating reality is something the computer does especially well. While you can hold a stick figure in your hands, you can't fly inside it or watch it vibrate as it interacts with other molecules. Virtual reality allows you to experience and manipulate reality in new and productive ways.

The second thing virtual reality allows us to do is perceive abstract ideas and processes for which there's no physical model or representation. VR acts as a translator, converting concepts into experiences our senses and mind can appreciate and analyze.

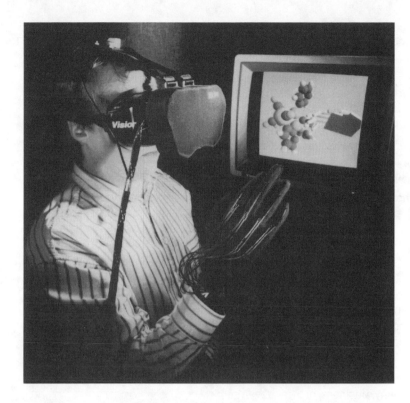

10-1
Using a wired glove, humans can "shrink" themselves and enter a world where virtual molecules can be manipulated. The picture on the monitor shows the image the participant sees in the VR goggles.

For example, telephone companies use massive software programs to coordinate and maintain communication networks across cities, states, and nations. Such programs are incredibly complex, but have no physical substance. They're electronic signals and instructions operating within vast networks of computers and equipment. It's as if they existed in another dimension from our own.

Using virtual reality, a Japanese university is creating living 3-D models of just such a telecommunications hub to monitor and control its activity. With such a visualization tool, problems in a phone system could be quickly located and diagnosed, saving hundreds of thousands of dollars for each hour the system is shut down.

There are many abstract ideas awaiting visualization and virtualization. You could bring the stock market, a database, or the behavior of a company to life. No one single use has emerged yet to dominate developers' attention, and it's possible that none will for some time. But one area that's constantly hungry for new and better ways to understand information is finance.

It's often said in Silicon Valley that the VisiCALC spreadsheet program created Apple Computer and that Lotus 1-2-3 is responsible for the success of the Intel-based personal computer. Neither hardware platform would have enjoyed the early surge of success it did without these killer applications.

The demand for financial software tools, therefore, created a demand for the hardware systems they ran on. Despite the more than 50,000 applications that run on personal computers today, financial applications continue to make up one of the largest and most demanding segments of computer use and are a likely area where VR's first killer applications might emerge.

Spreadsheets   Spreadsheets can be viewed as replacements for accounting ledgers, but their real value is in allowing business people to simulate the behavior of their markets, products, and companies. A spreadsheet program is a simulator—a symbolic metaphor for the behavior of a business.

The fundamental characteristic of this metaphor is that the events (represented as monetary figures or measurements) entered into the spreadsheet are equivalent, or *isomorphic*, to the real events and transactions within the situation.

As a metaphor, the spreadsheet simplifies and condenses a lot of complex data without losing the essential structure of the activities. It allows a businessperson to track the health of a product (or his own lifestyle) and explore "what if" scenarios such as the costs of offering a discount to spur sales or the personal impact of buying a new house.

Virtual reality and other graphical computer simulations work the same way. The designers of computer chips use sophisticated computer animation to graphically simulate the behavior of microprocessor circuits they're designing. The microprocessor doesn't yet exist, but an isomorphic simulation mimics the flow and storage of electrons in the circuits.

This kind of data visualization can model the flow of energy through a living creature or ecological system—or the accumulation, distribution, and use of dollars within a company, business, or local government.

In many large-scale companies, spreadsheets reside on mainframes or personal computer networks. They automatically monitor and store financial data from various locations around a company. Using this software as a foundation, it's possible to monitor the health of a company: parts in storage, shipments and deliveries, outstanding debt, utility costs, overtime paid, orders coming in, new product design schedules, etc. The entire life of the company is stored here. What's lacking is an easy way for anyone to represent and present this information.

"The power of the computer is locked behind a door without a doorknob," says Brenda Laurel.

One use for virtual reality is to take this abstract financial information and give it life by creating large-scale virtual flowsheets. It's a kind of second-generation spreadsheet that can encompass dozens of variables for the interactive illustration and animation of large sets of data.

Bradford Smith, Director of Research for the Institute for Nonprofit Organization Management, has been working on the design of just such a flowsheet program to monitor the health of a company.

"On the nightly news we see complex weather patterns moving over the earth's surface," says Smith. "Like slow-motion photography, the display compresses 12 to 24 hours of data into a period of a few seconds, allowing the viewer to gain an understanding of the weather that no numerical presentation of the data could possibly convey—even to an expert. The same kind of information compression can be done for a business with a flowsheet."

A company is a living thing made up of dozens, hundreds, even thousands of people. And a single day in the life of a company can be expressed in the hundreds of complex variables contained or derived from its profit and loss ledgers, balance sheets, and cash flow statements.

If these transactions can be meaningfully packaged into a visual metaphor, a viewer could watch several days in the life of a company go by in a few seconds. He could "see" a business as an evolving, living entity and make predictions about its behavior, just as many people do with the weather.

Working out of the College of Professional Studies at the University of San Francisco, Bradford Smith began to develop his ideas for the display of complex data over 15 years ago while researching the criminal justice system. Back then the system was undergoing a period of dramatic growth. At the time, the U.S. per capita incarceration rate was number three in the world, just behind the Soviet Union and South Africa; today it's the highest.

The flow of individuals through the criminal justice system required the simultaneous examination of at least 25 (and up to 150) variables. The results of a "get tough on crime" policy were that more criminals were locked up for longer periods of time, resulting in changes throughout the entire criminal justice system. Prison populations grew, the demographic mix and length of prisoner stays changed, court caseloads backed up, resources were constrained, social pressures were building, and finally more prisons needed to be built. And parole boards were forced to change their release practices.

"The patterns were there to forecast if you had the time and interest to pore over thousands of numbers, something few people and no decision makers have time for," Smith notes. He came to realize that he needed a symbolic representation of the criminal justice "reality" to share with people, a reality he could see by looking at the numbers but which he couldn't quickly share with others.

He created a diagram, visually analogous to the criminal justice system, on a large sheet of paper and modified it many times as new data or analysis became available.

"I remember thinking that I needed Disney's animators to make this display come alive. It was a short step from there to concluding that this was a task for a computer—at the time, a supercomputer," Smith says.

He came to realize that the idea he was pursuing could be applied to many other organizational problems besides the criminal justice system. He began developing a more all-purpose display that could be applied to businesses. The goal was to graphically represent how various tasks and activities contributed to the creation of wealth.

If he could do this, people could easily get a broad overview of a company's health and then debate the consequences of various decisions or the causes of the situation.

He wanted to create a visual metaphor as good as the traditional statistical metaphors. For example, the metaphor of average bushels of corn per acre was originally devised to help farmers and merchants make meaning out of numbers through mental visualization. An acre was a place with size and depth they were intimately familiar with. The harvesting of corn required a certain amount of time and effort per acre.

Smith wanted to create icons and metaphors that were isomorphic to a business' own environment, that condensed data while preserving the structure, and could accurately help people visualize the outcome of their work. Smith's flowsheet has three underlying concepts:

- A boundary between the system to be described (the company) and the environment (market, government, competitors, etc.)
- Flows of value (like rivers) measured over some span of time
- Reservoirs where value accumulates measured at any instant in time

Openings in the boundary around the company represent the flow of value (represented by dollars) in and out of the system. The size of these flows can change depending on the amount of value entering or leaving the system. Icons represent various services, departments, or product groups.

Reservoirs (cash, debt, fixed assets, etc.) are depicted by a stepped icon that easily conveys a range of several orders of magnitude. A general funds reservoir might swell with value from an increase in sales and then decrease as a particular debt is paid off or its funds are diverted into research and development. Research and development is a separate reservoir that feeds value into various product groups as new products are invented and commercialized.

The flow of resources in and out of the organization acts as a framework for the collection and assimilation of other information about the organization, e.g., personnel, the physical plant, and inventories. The display can be run at different rates, stopped, run backwards, and shifted to reflect particular time periods—monthly, quarterly, yearly, etc.

The flows and icons can then be integrated into a display, shown in Fig. 10-2, that fosters contemplation and discussion about the performance of the company and the possible future results of specific decisions.

This flowsheet is flexible in its uses because it can be a very large and complex field in which someone can see and move within an extensive range of flows and reservoirs. And the display can be expressed on a wide screen for a kind of projected reality, so many individuals can view the data together and negotiate the meaning (or consequences) of the display based on their own personal knowledge and experience.

This graphical display runs in a nonVR multitasking environment with data for the animation contained in a spreadsheet. Users can move back and forth between the graphical flowsheet and the numerical spreadsheet. Smith's next goal is to design the system so everything can be done in the display. With a fully implemented projected reality version, he can build a system that can represent very large data sets in three dimensions.

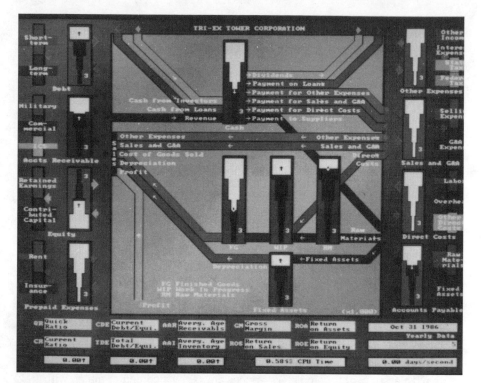

10-2
This 2-D image graphically depicts the "holistic" state of a business or institution at any moment in time. By animating parts of the image based on changing financial conditions, various aspects appear to grow or shrink.

"In the future you'll hear voice commentaries as you examine the details of particular flows. Windows will open with video clips and extra data about assets, equity, liabilities, or assumptions about the future. The same graphical display can be used to represent divisions within the company and then departments within divisions, or other records so a common metaphor is established for easier cross-referencing and analyzing patterns. The viewer will always begin and end with a holistic representation of the entire system," Smith says.

The quality of insight a user can obtain from the flowsheet can be only as good as the data it's based on. The elegance and effectiveness of such metaphors create the need for better methods of gathering the data of a company's transactions. The ability to monitor a wide range of variables gives a businessperson a better insight into the health not only of a company, but of a market—or many markets.

Today's money manager sits with several computer screens in front of him and watches data come in from a wide variety of sources in real time. While mentally juggling the movements of the markets and other influences on his portfolio, he needs to make quick decisions that might result in thousands, even millions of dollars in profits or losses.

On Wall Street, information is wealth, and virtual reality offers a way to increase the effectiveness of money managers by condensing and streamlining the way abstract information reaches them so they can make faster, more effective decisions.

Cyberspace meets the stock market

The world's financial markets are irrevocably speeding toward a one-world, 24-hour-a-day, totally computerized market. The chaotic image of the floor pits of the world's stock and commodities exchanges are fast becoming an old-fashioned anachronism.

The British and French stock markets are completely computerized, and the Toronto exchange plans to shut down its trading floor by the end of 1992. All the trading firms and investment houses already use scientific workstations and personal computers to create graphical maps and charts as metaphors of their portfolio holdings.

Chemical Bank of London has attached more than 50 workstations to a decision-support system that allows traders on the floor to monitor incoming real-time data using complex graphical models. Barclays Bank of London has already installed workstations on the floor of its trading room to do foreign exchange cross-rate and bond analysis.

Meanwhile, Reuters and two major Chicago commodities exchange plans to launch a system called Globex, a 24-hour electronic trading system for futures and options contracts. It's a way for the partners to extend the Chicago market around the globe and across all borders and time zones.

The traditional process of buying and selling futures can take upwards of twenty minutes. A customer calls a broker, who phones the order to the trading desk, which in turn hands it over to floor traders in the pits. They haggle over the best price for the order, which is then tallied and recorded. The new computerized system bypasses all this completely—prices are set by a computer match with incoming orders, and it's all done in just three seconds.

Such speed in transaction processing, however, could lead to volatility of markets in the same way that computer-generated program trading has done. It will require traders to become masters of the instant decision, and that will be possible only if their ability to manage incoming information is as fast and powerful as the trading systems they work with.

"I see VR providing the same kind of advantage I got from the Microsoft Windows interface early on, before it was popular, the benefit of being able to share data live with other programs and keep track of many variables. VR will be very powerful, it will allow me to integrate the abstract information coming from many different programs and sources, pull in data from international boards, back-room databases, and keep track of it all in three dimensions," says Paul Marshall, President of Maxus Systems International.

Maxus creates international portfolio management systems for pension funds and money managers, specializing in global securities and derivative products. Maxus' software already allows a portfolio manager to integrate data from existing external sources, such as Reuters or Knight-Ridder, with in-house and proprietary databases, including links to back office systems.

"With the downsizing of Wall Street all the business is being done by the numbers now," Marshall says. "Today's portfolio manager has more information to swim through; a complex sea of variables involved in trading strategies. And the people making money are the pure arbitrageurs who are dealing with low-risk strategies, working much more quantitatively on risk management.

"There is a lot of hedging of options and managers want to play out a lot of `what-if' scenarios. He is asking himself, `do I buy the stock, the option on the stock, the convertible bond, or can I synthetically create the same security for less?' He wants a more complete risk profile and by dealing in three dimensions he is able to map in all the variables. We can make the data come alive."

Paul Marshall along with his partner Sean Manefield got into the international arbitrage field in the mid-1980s. They developed 3-D surface maps (see Fig. 10-3), and visual metaphors of positions and risks associated with those positions. Both have extensive backgrounds in money management as well as computers. Manefield formerly worked for the Reserve Bank of Australia (the equivalent of the U.S. Federal Reserve).

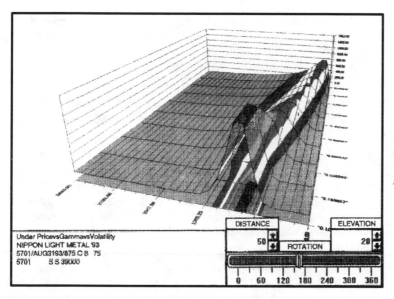

10-3
This 3-D surface map is one way of representing complex stock market data in a more understandable form.

"In doing these kind of trades, the way you beat your competitors is by having better software that signals movements in the market to you," Marshall says. "With virtual reality I can take a quantum leap in representing data. There are so many different variables I can monitor, different attributes of different stocks, abnormal volume or occurrences, fundamental inefficiencies. The output of 45 different reports could be summed up in the behavior of a polygon which changes color, blinks or spins, behaves in a pre-set way to instantly communicate with the manager what has happened to that security."

Using Sense8's WorldToolKit on an Intel486 CPU-based computer, Marshall has created a vast ocean of data on which securities rise and fall on the tides of the market. The area can be interactively divided into any combination of subregions on a grid. You can pick a single industry and look at it across all markets, or look at all industries across a single market.

A grid can be broken out based on the American Stock Exchange: transportation, health care, pharmaceutical, computers, and retail subregions. A segment like automotive could be organized across categories such as trucking, passenger cars, farm machinery, and heavy equipment, or it could be divided by international regions: America, Japan, Germany, England, Sweden, etc.

The viewer can fly down into each subregion and move among the stocks and bonds, each of which is represented by a flat polygon that's rising or falling among an undulating sea of similar panels. The stock's shape, position, behavior, and color are dependent on conditions in the market. Each panel can have a company's logo (which is itself an informational icon) texture mapped onto it for fast recognition.

Like Bradford Smith's flowsheet, Paul Marshall's ocean of securities represents a new way for professionals to "get inside the numbers." The possibilities for representing information is greatly expanded by moving from the flat 2-D world of screen and paper into a dynamic 3-D world.

The advantage that VR provides is the ability to creatively represent vast amounts of abstract data in new and interactive ways. And it can do it in real time. This combination allows users to organize information in new ways and find relationships that previously lay buried in the numbers.

Information management magic

The financial world isn't the only area that will benefit from VR's ability to take people "inside" abstract data. It can also be used to bring information about real events to users in more useful and efficient ways to allow better control of activities as they happen.

A nuclear engineer has up to 30 CRT displays strung out around him in a control room. An air-traffic controller has dozens of planes to monitor on one screen. A fire chief needs to direct and manage dozens of crews at a major blaze with a barrage of information coming at him from many different channels. Managing not just the display of abstract data, but also the influx of real information is another way computers and virtual reality can be of benefit.

With virtual reality, the nuclear engineer can be sitting almost anywhere wearing a set of goggles (on a plane, in a closet) and everywhere he looks can be a display space. If he wants something in particular, he gestures with a wave of his hand, or verbally requests a screen be moved. He can put various display spaces together as the need arises and organize incoming information in the best way to suit his needs, moment to moment.

This kind of customization of information and conservation of space is especially important in confined areas such as submarines, aircraft, and spaceships, where the amount of volume determines the cost and limits flexibility. Every cubic inch you send into space is expensive, and a lot of the space shuttle is taken up with CRTs.

These are multi-function monitors, but sometimes you want to oversee a tremendous amount of things. By being "inside" the data, the VR user is no longer dependent on the location and number of screens for the amount of information he can handle. *Where he looks* determines *what he sees* and what he needs to see will be where he wants it to be.

Add to this that the control panel he's working with can be adjusted as well (like a music synthesizer keyboard that can become a piano, a flute, an organ, or a cello with the flick of a switch).

Reconfigurable virtual control panels like the one in Fig. 10-4 will allow a worker's station to become many stations. The operator will either use a physical control panel whose functions will be changeable, or potentially wear a wired glove for touching completely virtual controls (the glove's functions will be instantly reconfigured depending on the virtual display it's touching).

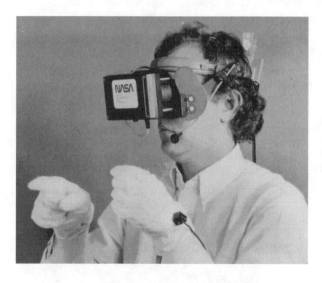

10-4
This NASA researcher appears to be pressing a button on a virtual control panel.

"This is a whole new paradigm shift," suggests Jerry Slambrook of Sandia Labs. "Artificial Intelligence software fell short of people's expectations because we found out how hard it is to duplicate how the human mind analyzes and does pattern recognition. The tack we are taking now is that our job with the computer is to present the data to the senses in the most natural way possible and put the knowledge and skills of the human to work."

Sandia Labs started off in the nuclear weapons business, building safety devices and developing weapons. The labs are a Department of Energy engineering house for doing extensive research in robotics and nuclear waste dump clean up.

Slambrook's specialty is satellite applications. He has over 25 years of work experience for the U.S. Air Force in nuclear test ban treaty verification, finding ways of detecting underground bomb tests by using satellites.

"We put sensor systems on satellites for monitoring nuclear test activity around the globe," Slambrook says. "Today, we can't write filter applications fast enough to sort through the data we get. When something new happens we have to go off and write new applications which takes weeks, months. With virtual reality, we can write one whole new display interface and let the mind's eye discern the data. It allows a macro look at the data instead of reading one measurement at a time and then struggling with clever ways of combining data."

Today, just like the weather photos on the TV news, satellite information is accumulated over many hours and then played back swiftly to reveal overall patterns to the viewer. For example, heavy rains in West Sahara are a forecast of stronger than normal hurricane seasons in the Caribbean. Rather than having to shift through piles of reports and numbers on rainfall, being able to sit above the world and watch weeks or years worth of weather patterns could reveal similar connections elsewhere.

Slambrook is working on several VR application design projects. One is a VR world that allows the operator to sit at the center of the earth. Shock waves from earthquakes and underground bomb explosions naturally travel through the center of the earth because of its molten liquid mass.

As satellite and earth station data come in from a sudden disturbance, the data could be accumulated, analyzed, and displayed so that the viewer sees cross-references, measurement data, and locations of recording stations from inside the earth.

Like watching the time-compressed weather data from satellites, the operator can use his own physical capabilities to see patterns in the shock wave data that the numbers would hide. In this way he can much more quickly judge whether a nuclear bomb has been set off, its strength, and where it has been detonated.

"It is not enough to think about presentation, you have to provide ways for the operator to control and change the representation of data to suit him," Slambrook says.

Another interface project is merging ways of representing reality more usefully and interactively than was previously possible. This long-term project is a satellite command and control system in which the earth and the satellites orbiting it will appear in their natural relationships to each other (see Figs. 10-5 and 10-6).

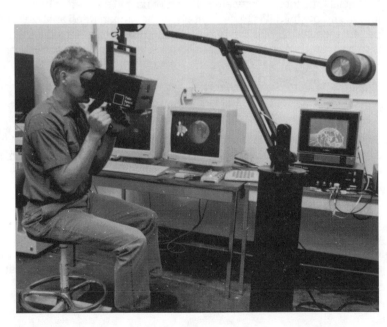

10-5
At Sandia Labs, Jerry Van Slambrook uses the BOOM from Jake Space Labs to research the use of VR to perform satellite tracking visualization.

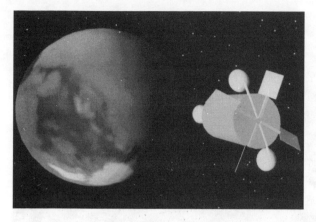

10-6
By using a powerful graphics workstation, this image can be generated in real time, allowing the operator to "fly" up to the satellite or to visualize the section of the Earth that it covers.

Slambrook's first step was to map the earth and several satellites with the dynamics of their orbits. The idea is for the operator to be able to move around in space among the satellites and see how the orbits overlap, what the satellite's footprint on the earth covers (how much it can see or broadcast to), and what happens with adjustments in its position relative to the earth, sun, and magnetic belt.

If satellite designers can actually "sit" in orbit, then they can do a better job in placing solar panels and robotic devices. By simulating the orbit and its view of the earth, weather patterns and solar position information can be added to the orbital simulation to enhance the planning phase for satellite command and control.

A variety of orbit patterns can be quickly evaluated before making emergency changes, such as monitoring a sudden volcanic eruption or a regional war. Eventually, it might be possible that the operator will be able to adjust virtual satellites on the ground and have the vehicles up in space automatically respond.

In a similar fashion, the Air Force is investigating the possibility of using VR to ease the job of air-traffic controllers. From movies and TV, many people are familiar with the image of air-traffic controllers hunched over their screens, monitoring the movement of commercial jets through the sky. At Brooks Air Force base, they're exploring how virtual reality can put air-traffic controllers up in the air with the planes.

Imagine you're an air-traffic controller. Instead of watching a screen while sitting at your desk, you're above the entire airport with everything important within your view, as shown in Fig. 10-7. You can monitor and communicate with planes in the sky based on their positions in 3-D space.

Below, you see a model of the airfield and the planes that are your responsibility are clearly marked, but you can also see other activities around the airfield. You can quickly evaluate an object's distance and altitude just by looking at it, and additional information is just a command word away.

Imagine you're sitting at your station when suddenly you realize that there's a danger situation; a plane is moving onto a runway for take-off just as another jet is beginning its landing run towards the same runway.

10-7
Simulated airports like this can be used to train air-traffic controllers and pilots in order to avoid costly and dangerous mistakes. This image was rendered at greater than 30 fps on an Evans and Sutherland image generator.

Wouldn't it be nice to have everything not essential to the situation disappear? The computer cannot only display what's important, but it can also remove things that are in your way; everything potentially distracting disappears from the air and the airport visualization. Escape routes both on the ground and in the air become highlighted, any trucks or planes in the vicinity remain visible.

All of this would be possible if the airfield was represented by a graphical computer model. It's what sets VR apart from other communications channels; you can decide what to display, where to display it, and what not to display. This same ability to customize information in command and control situations can extend to communicating through partially overlapping or partially shared VR displays.

For example, imagine a fire chief who's fighting a large forest fire with several other crews. Someday he might use a portable virtual display to see a computer model of the events as they're unfolding (see Fig. 10-8). Satellite weather data, field reports on the fire's condition, buildings in flames or in danger of burning are highlighted, the location of a gasoline storage tank is flashing, and the shape of the terrain and the positions of the other crews are all represented. He has a total overview of the entire situation that's constantly updated as new information comes in. Planning out what he'll do, he looks around and can see highlighted areas of danger as well as fire-fighting resources directly under his control and responsibility. Some of what he sees is marked off as an area of shared responsibility with another fire chief; all he has to do is touch the area and he can communicate with the other crew chief to decide together what they want to do.

10-8
A fireman could use a portable virtual display like this one from Reflection Technology to gain instant access to vital information concerning the contents of a burning building, or even its physical layout.

This form of customizable reality got its start with the design of cockpits for modern jet fighters. Tom Furness, currently with the HIT Lab in Seattle, Washington, conceived of the supercockpit during his years working for the military. He knew that pilots performed better if distractions were removed. Sometimes pilots need to know what's really out there, but other times they need to know only the dangers.

Sometimes, just seeing a checkerboard field and little icons of dangers, like a kind of video game, is more helpful in maintaining the concentration they need to survive than seeing burning buildings or low-level surface detail.

In addition, more useful information to pilots can be compressed into these icons. An enemy's position, the type of aircraft and weapons, the speed of approach, along with the condition of their own aircrafts, can be displayed in front of their eyes. Also, data coming in from radar, computers, and even over-the-horizon Advance Warning Aircraft (AWAC) monitoring is at their disposal.

In a unique twist on this idea of customizable reality, NASA is investigating using display management to provide a sense of openness when someone is confined to a very small space for long space flights.

There are certain psychological guidelines for the amount of space and freedom of movement needed by people, depending on the duration of their trip. As the time of the trip lengthens, the bigger the volume should be; however, the longer the trip, the tighter the restraints on size and volume because of the economics of construction.

A trip to Mars will be very expensive, and space will be a priority. So one idea is to let people sit in their chair during the trip, put on virtual reality goggles, and travel around the earth to get a sense of freedom.

Satellites and airplanes aren't the only activities that virtual reality interfaces can help to control. Just as the Maxus Systems' virtual stock market display reveals the behavior of abstract data, Tokyo Electric Power (TEPCO) is developing a VR application to visualize large abstract software programs that control their systems.

Companies like TEPCO need to control huge power grids in which electricity generated by power plants is distributed to industries and homes as needed. These systems rely on software programs that have become very large and complex. The TEPCO program is aimed at creating visualizations of the total structure of the program (and therefore the power grid) to manage problems of data flow and message paths on a time axis.

In the application, the software program appears like a huge, transparent, multistoried building, interlaced with rooms representing sections of the program and connected by piping to represent data flows. The visualization will be connected to the actual operating software to provide a real-time, on-line method of managing local problems while still seeing the overall program.

It's not only possible to use the sensory-stimulating equipment of virtual reality to put people inside abstract data or to manage real information to suit them, but the same equipment can be hooked up to other sensory devices instead of a computer. The goggles can be connected to video cameras. The movement of a wired glove can be mirrored by a robot arm.

Virtual reality can project your presence inside of computer-generated worlds, and it can also project you around the world to places you can't reach, or into environments too dangerous to visit.

Telepresence

"Our astrodynamics people want to actually see what the satellite sees. They want to be able to put on the goggles and feel like they are sitting out in orbit watching the earth below," says Jerry Slambrook, of Sandia Labs.

There are a whole host of sensors on a satellite. If the computer could collect the data and then overlay it on what the viewer was seeing, it would make for a very informationally rich experience.

There are cases where a researcher might want to "sit" above the equator or over the polar regions and watch events unfold, e.g., during a fast-moving crisis situation, such as the eruption of the Mount Saint Helen's volcano in Oregon. The researcher might want to study the formation of the ash cloud and the direction of its movement as it arises, relaying important information to communities downwind of the eruption.

Dr. Stephen Ellis at NASA Ames is investigating the interface between man and machine in which virtual-reality equipment is used to extend a man's body into a robot. Camera eyes on a lunar-roving robot could display data back to earth (with a considerable time lag), allowing a researcher to plot its course and see what the robot sees of the terrain. Figure 10-9 shows a remote-control video setup.

Ellis has a working demonstration of a robot arm hooked up to a DataGlove. It takes some practice to get the hang of commanding the robot because it has two elbows for bending. Using it, Ellis can pick up objects in a room across the building; some day it might allow him to pick up samples on the moon or the bottom of the ocean.

Fujita, a Japanese construction company, is using VPL equipment to develop remote control of robots for inspection and spray painting of construction projects. With a worldwide portfolio of construction projects and limited human resources, Fujita is trying to see if robot-mounted cameras can be used to allow an inspector in Japan to review work in progress in Saudi Arabia. The system would also be useful for inspecting underground work such as tunnels and storage tanks that might be difficult to reach.

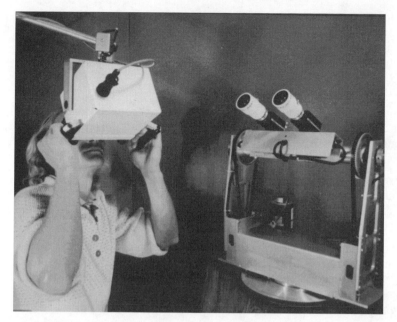

10-9
Early version of the BOOM used with a slaved, remote-camera platform. As the operator moves the BOOM, he can see through the eyes of the two cameras. This is an example of a telepresence application.

At Sandia Labs, a different team of robotic specialists is exploring the use of VR to help clean up toxic waste dumps. They already have a robot developed that can enter and clean storage tanks at nuclear waste dumps. Using VR, they plan to overlay video from the robot with computer-generated graphics to outline what the robot can't see.

The operator can guide the robot through the tank with the computer overlay representing hidden problems that are there but out of sight, while revealing additional information to the controller, such as fluctuating radiation levels. Rather than trying to make the robot smart enough to think like a person, the human controller stays a safe distance away and continues to work as if right inside the tank.

Not only does VR allow you to extend the reach of your eyes and hands into dangerous situations, it allows designers and dreamers to put their hands on their ideas before a single item has been built. Designers are already able to draw and simulate their ideas on 2-D computer screens. The next step is to "put their hands through the screen" and take hold of their ideas in a virtual design space.

Virtual design

We live in a designed world. Not just houses and space shuttles, but doorknobs, toothbrushes, floor mats, clothing, ball bearings, hammers, jewelry, food, pots and pans, egg beaters, saws, carburetors, clocks—the list goes on and on because everything we use has been designed. Design is the first step in the process of building a product. It's the blueprint of a house, the schematic of an electronic toy, and the 3-D computer visualization of a jet engine.

Computer-aided design (CAD) is an area where computers have already contributed tremendous leaps in productivity. Products like Autodesk's AutoCAD allow designers to quickly create and edit complex designs on personal computers for all kinds of products.

Photo-realistic images of products can be created from these computer blueprints with the aid of additional software programs. Computers can animate and simulate how the product will perform when actually built, how light will reflect off a surface, and how sound will bounce around a room. Simultaneously, the computer can automatically check through parts inventories to see if the components a designer has selected for assembly are available.

Already, many companies have teams of designers working together over networks of computers, sharing files, working on common projects, and collaborating together. Combining these systems with a virtual reality interface is the next leap forward in computer-aided design.

"Boeing has made a major commitment to entirely design its next generation of commercial aircraft, the 777, on computers. We can see a big pay-off if we can learn how to integrate virtual reality throughout the process," Chris Esposito, the head of Boeing Computer Services, Advanced Technology Center, says.

Boeing has a company-wide steering council with people from each division to evaluate what applications will benefit most from applying VR. After looking into what Boeing needs to develop in-house, and what it can go outside for (like wired gloves and knowledge from the external VR market), they have set a mission agenda for what in-house research to do first.

Boeing's virtual reality work is divided into three major programs. One group is researching the application of 3-D sound for pilots and AWAC operators who need to have multiple radio channels coming into their headsets at once. Right now the sounds are all right in their ears, mixed together. But if each input could be made to sound like it was coming from a separate and distinct point in space, it would be possible to separately attend to them.

It's the same skill we all use at cocktail parties to pay attention to more than one conversation at a time, except for the pilot each location would have its own designated meaning. For example, priority levels could be set by how far away a sound seems to be from the listener. The more urgent the information, the closer it would be.

Tom Furness, of the HIT Lab, championed this research while he was with the Air Force. The submodalities of auditory experience have boundaries as well as location. There's a sacred space, a degree of distance we each prefer to keep between ourselves and someone else. If someone is within that space it's very difficult to ignore them.

Furness used this naturally occurring condition to devise a warning system for low fuel. He designed a warning using a woman's voice speaking softly but clearly just behind the pilot's ear. This warning proved far more effective than any bells or whistles.

The second group at Boeing is researching transparent, or augmented reality. This is being developed primarily for manufacturing. The goal is to improve the productivity of workers by getting them the information they need when they need it.

Imagine a machinist with a metal form in front of him and he needs to drill holes in it. By wearing see-through VR glasses, he could see images and data instructing him how and where to drill the holes projected on the lenses. A certain sequence of dots could appear that remain stable to the steel's shape and form no matter how the machinist moves his head. Or the dots might light up in sequence.

The graphic requirements of such a display system are limited, but the head-tracking requirements are extensive. To place the information accurately means monitoring not just the positioning of the VR glasses (which is done today) but of the rest of the environment as well.

The third group is investigating fully immersive VR with the goal of integrating it into the design, test, and mock-up process. Traditionally, when blueprints were drawn-up (by hand or computer) the design wasn't finished until after a series of life-size wooden mock-ups were built and reviewed.

These full-scale models of the 727, the 747, and other aircraft were tremendously expensive, but it was the only way to put together such a large and complex creation. Engineering a plane is different than a lot of other design work—a wrong answer here can kill people. Engineers test their designs over and over because there's no room for error.

The Boeing 747 has hundreds of thousands of parts. Versions of the 777 will be flying for the next fifty to seventy years, well into the middle of the 21st century. It will be upgraded and stretched, the avionics will be replaced, and new replacement parts will be designed.

It's a product whose life will span decades and outlast the life of its original developers. There's no way for a single designer or group of designers to keep the entire design of the 777 in their heads when it's finished, let alone as the design goes through evolution and change.

When NASA designed the space shuttle, it had to create an entire wood and plastic life-size model of the ship to see what it would be like. Any time it was discovered that a doorway was too small, an access space too limited, or a control panel not in the best position, the entire section had to be redesigned and that section of the mock-up rebuilt. This included such hidden costs as negotiating with the labor unions to get the work done and losing the original mock-up as a reference.

When the remodeling is all done you have a new mock-up, but unlike a computer you can't go backwards and compare the new with the old just by reloading a database. That's why NASA is converting the entire space shuttle design into an on-line computer model.

Boeing's Chris Esposito had the first challenge of demonstrating the potential and selling the idea of virtual reality inside the company. In October of 1991, his group began showing off a reconstruction of a V-22 aircraft, a tilt-rotor vertical take-off and landing craft. A 3-D model of the plane was designed with all the functional behaviors built-in. This initial project allowed the team to develop the new processes for engineers to utilize the new VR technology.

"The demo allowed us to work directly with our customers, Boeing's design engineers, and get input from them about what problems they had in the 3-D design of aircraft that the CAD systems didn't help them find. What issues would they like to learn more about in terms of maintainability and human factors?" Esposito says.

For the designers at Boeing, realism means using the real product data. The VR team discovered that there was an acceptable trade-off between design realism and design usefulness in the VR simulation. The computational fluid dynamics that affect the surface of a wing are very complex. In the computer model, they found they could replace the design details by a ratio of twenty to one—that is, reduce the need to draw and animate half-a-million triangles down to 15,000 triangles.

What was important was maintaining the integrity of the design structure and function, keeping the metaphor isomorphic so the simulation would reflect accurate behavior. At this level they were able to animate the design in real time so the designers could step inside the V-22 and give it a test flight.

"We gave that demo until we were sick of it and then we gave it for six more months. As we did we turned the table on the engineers we showed it to. We asked *them* to tell *us* what it would be good for. We ended up with a list of some three dozen things that range across all the various points of the product's life cycle, from early concept design to training, education of maintenance engineers for specific procedures and tasks, and even ways of using it when the aircraft is up in the air," Esposito says. See Fig. 10-10 for this list of possible applications.

10-10
Boeing's analysis of where VR could be effectively applied in their business.

	3-D sound	CATIA compatibility	See-through display headset	Rendering engine	Dynamic interaction	Extended position tracking	Collision detection	Graphics optimizing	Precision movement
Defense & Space **Aerospace & Electronics** AWACS Workstation			Multi radio channel tracking						
Eng. Design & Test			RFP oral presentations		Astronaut operations evaluation				
ASW Battle Management Workstation					3-D display				
Auto. & Robl.							Remote assembly control		
Military Airplane Cockpit					Digital cockpit design evaluation				Exocentric situation awareness display
Mat. & Processes					3-D Materials destruction analysis				
Helicopters Manufacturing		Electronic mockup	Wire harness formboarding; Connector & electrical panel assembly		Digital product definition				Digital component installation testing
Human Factors					Digital cockpit evaluation		Digital crew - chief ops. eval.		
Commercial Airplanes Eng. Computing/Fabrication		Electronic mockup; Pre-assembly			Remote concurrent engineering				Eliminate physical mock-up
Operations			Wire harness formboarding; Connector & electrical panel assembly			Strut assembly; riveting; Kevlar duct layup			
Maintainability Methods									Digital maintenance demo/evaluation
Flight Deck						Human model control			Testing of digital airplane cockpit

A10239.08

For maintenance personnel, see-through VR glasses hold the promise of bringing data to them without requiring them to take their hands off their work. In situations where a mechanic doesn't have as much training as his boss would like, or the plane is an unfamiliar model, VR can make a good mechanic wonderful by putting all the information he needs right at his retina.

Such transparent glasses may one day even provide a kind of x-ray vision. In many jet engine repair steps, the mechanic can't see his hands because they're inside the engine. By tracking the positions of the hands in terms of where the parts are inside the engine, he could effectively "see through" the machinery to where his hands are working, as shown in the illustration in Fig. 10-11.

10-11
Illustration of how an aircraft mechanic could use a VR system to view virtual information panels that overlay the real image of the jet engine. This is known as augmented reality.

It won't replace traditional CAD tools, at least not at first, because many designers (just like the printers and graphic artists who initially avoided desktop publishing) will hang back due to the necessary learning curve and the comfort they have with their current tools. And, for many years to come there will a trade-off between the benefits of virtual design and traditional CAD tools.

Traditional CAD will maintain a big lead in usefulness because of the maturity of its functionality and the fact that it's been around longer with more time to invest in refining its usefulness. There's also the lack of affordable high-resolution display goggles. At least for the foreseeable future, wide screen monitors will continue to lead VR goggles in terms of resolution.

Eventually, VR tools will become a natural part of CAD. The early CAD adopters of virtual-reality design tools are going to be people doing 3-D modeling and 3-D positioning. This is a skill that's useful across many industries, from mechanics to architecture, jewelry to automotive design.

In particular, 3-D positioning and modeling are important in ergonomics, the design of environments in which people have to fit into and function. Designing a space or product for a person to use requires a 3-D perspective and interactivity that traditional 2-D design tools don't deliver.

Human factors

"Anytime you have a human who has to do something with a product you are in the realm of human factors," says Pete Tinker, Research Engineer at Rockwell International. Like Chris Esposito, Pete is exploring how virtual reality can help his company produce better products and increase design efficiency.

"Whether they're jet engines or truck axles, there has to be a 'reach envelope' or a 'viewing cone' built into the design for repair work to be effective," says Tinker. "How far can someone reach from a certain position with certain constraints? Such as, he can't bend forward beyond a certain amount, or move something with just the strength in his fingers.

"If you can be sure something is maintainable up front in the design, then a lot of trouble can be saved. Traditionally, once you've reached a certain point in the design process it is going to cost you more money to redesign than to fix it; even if you know that to repair a truck axle will require you to pull the engine and disassemble it.

"One of the worst examples I know of is a certain aircraft for which it takes eight hours to repair a simple problem. Four hours to get to the area of the engine where the problem occurs, a few minutes to change the parts, and then four more hours to reassemble the engine. The engine works fine, but the human factors for repair were not well designed."

Virtual reality will change the way designers work by placing them inside the design and reducing, even eliminating the need for mock-ups. Alias Research of Canada is exploring how virtual design can shorten the design process and reduce errors and eliminate redundant steps, such as repeated creations of product mock-ups.

Originally developed to serve the needs of computer animators, the company's software products are used by designers at companies like Honda, General Motors, BMW, Sony, as well as Industrial Light and Magic and hundreds of others.

Alias Research's automotive customers already have asked for life-size, real-time ray tracing in virtual worlds (a computer graphics process for creating accurate reflections on surfaces, such as the reflection on a chrome bumper). Even with today's supercomputers, however, this is not possible.

The reflective realism of images in such scenes is so complex to compute that it's in conflict with producing smooth motion. The computer spends so much time recalculating the images, frame by frame, that it's impossible to redraw them fast enough to maintain the illusion of reality.

The first stage in enhancing the automotive design process has been to incorporate a high-resolution boom, made by Fake Space Labs. Using the boom like a periscope, designers can climb inside a proposed design and experience it more fully than on a flat display.

By filling the field of view, Alias' designers find that it gives them a better sense of the scale of large objects and of surrounding space in interior designs such as the front seat of a car. They find that the freedom of the boom, the ease with which they can step up to it or walk away and get in and out of virtual reality is a plus. Future innovations in VR goggles will need to address this ease of use to succeed.

Designers who use CAD software are always looking to work faster, with more complex designs, and to integrate their models into one faithful representation instead of having to work on thirty different subassemblies. Combining sophisticated software with VR goggles and gloves, designers will someday be able to slide their hands inside the moving parts of jet engines before they're ever built. Such advances will require new kinds of software and enormous computing power, beyond even today's supercomputers.

Boeing's designers would like to be able to simulate a working jet-engine design so they could literally stick their hands into the engine and test repair practices along with engine performance before the engine is built. To do this will require software that can create objects (engine parts) that can recognize the boundaries or edges of other parts.

Boeing's designers would like the spinning virtual turbine blades to be able to tell them if they're too close to the side walls of the engine housing. They want more than simulation, they want intelligent objects. But to get what they want could be a ten-year wait, the challenge is that big. Figure 10-12 shows a NASA wind tunnel, where results of a flow simulation can be interacted with in real time.

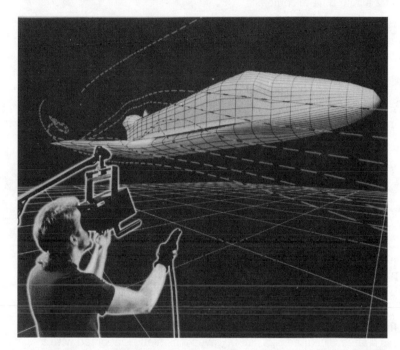

10-12
At NASA Ames, engineers use a BOOM and powerful grapics workstations to experience a virtual wind tunnel, where results of a flow simulation can be interacted with in real time.

To visualize jet engines today takes supercomputers; to interact with tomorrow's designs will require massively paralleled supercomputers and distributed processing. To create a functionally accurate, working jet engine, each part of the engine will require its own piece of software and its own computer to exist. Massively parallel supercomputers do just that because they're made up of hundreds, even thousands of microprocessors.

The software that runs on such supercomputers divides up a task and assigns pieces of it to an individual microprocessor within the system. This means each moving part of the engine would have its own microprocessor to draw its image and compute its relationships to all the other moving parts in the engine. The engine wouldn't have to look real (with shiny chrome and paint) but it would have to function realistically.

These kinds of supercomputers are being built today, but the software to create these simulations has yet to be written. And the software won't be easy to design.

In addition to the problem of creating simulations that can recreate the look and function of a very complex jet engine, there will still be the difficulty of recreating the *feel*. As of today, the wired glove has no way of physically signaling to the user that his hand is stuck. And there are even more subtle issues, such as figuring out how to simulate what is just enough space for a hand to wiggle into a tight opening.

There are software design programs that can calculate, based on real-world examples, how much space is enough for a hand, but just as a stick figure molecule is better at representing the tactile shape of a molecule than a VR simulation, there will continue to be limitations and trade-offs to balance the amazing capabilities of virtual reality for a long time to come.

Virtual prototyping

Once upon a time, people designed a part and then went over to the forge and started hammering it out. There was an intimate, inherent bonding between design and manufacture because the designer really understood how the thing was made.

Virtual prototyping promises to turn the engineer back into an artisan. He will be able to work with the design as if it were a malleable yet solid object, be able to move and handle the product as if he were crafting it in a workshop, and then produce it himself without leaving his office.

When the design is ready, the parts can be "printed out" directly from the computer screen. Designers will eliminate weeks, even months from the process of making prototypes. And eventually they'll be able to fabricate real parts for short production runs with the ease of printing out an engineering diagram. The increase in engagement and personal involvement with the work will go up, along with a sense of realism in the work.

"Virtual prototyping is one area where I think we are going to see good uses of VR," says Pete Tinker of Rockwell. "You can make sweeping changes to a new jet, can change the physical characteristics to something new without having craftspeople tear out everything and destroy the original. It means you'll be able to change the entire design much further along in the process than ever before."

From a wireframe skeleton that the designer can stretch and bend, twist and shape, a rough form is crafted. Then the part can be given a skin and smoothed with a surface modeler, or converted to solids with more traditional 3-D CAD tools. 3-D CAD tools will eventually be available by speech command or whatever interface the designer wants.

Many companies already have advanced 3-D CAD systems coupled to databases of basic parts. As a designer develops a product on the computer, he checks his selection of components against the database. This not only tells him if the parts he needs already exist, but also provides background data on strength, size, amount in stock, etc.

In the future, design analysis and verification will be performed on the computer in real time (it currently can take hours), with interactive finite element modeling so that the stress level in the part will also be modeled as the designer works.

Plastic prototyping is already available on PC-based systems. 3-D Systems, a Valencia, California company (which is 37 percent owned by the pharmaceutical and chemical company Ciba-Geigy) has sold hundreds of systems to produce prototypes with a process known as *stereolithography*.

In this process, the computer takes a set of coordinates from the computer model of the part and uses this to control the movement of an ultraviolet laser. The laser traces cross-sections of the part onto the surface of a liquid polymer solution, causing it to solidify. The pattern builds up the part in layers of plastic a few thousandths of an inch at a time. The process can produce prototypes of engine blocks or diseased hip bones patterned from the data from a medical scanner. Figure 10-13 shows a component that was created using stereolithography.

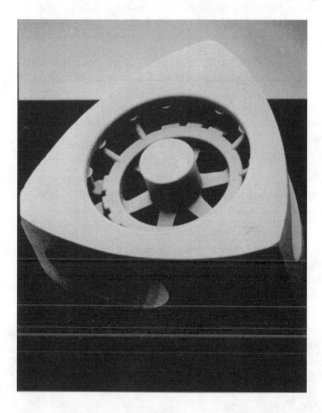

10-13
Using stereolithography, this part was fabricated out of a loose powder with the aid of a laser beam. By using virtual prototyping, objects created in the virtual world can be converted into something you can hold in your hand.

This is fine for prototypes, but a plastic jet-engine block will never stand up to temperature tests. Research is under way at M.I.T. on three-dimensional printing. Researchers take a 3-D computer design and slice it into minute slices. Instead of a laser, a small nozzle (like on some computer printers) squirts a binding chemical onto a bed of powdered ceramic, stainless steel, or another metal. After this process is repeated for hundreds of layers, the semisolidified part is then fired in a furnace.

This method is already being used to develop ceramic molds for metal casting. Called *CAD casting*, it bypasses the task of making metal dies to create wax patterns that are dipped in a ceramic slurry to create such a mold.

There are technical problems yet to be overcome before companies can make metal parts with nearly the same density as those produced through conventional casting and milling. Yet casting and prototyping is already possible for a wide range of products to be produced by "desktop manufacturing."

A new kind of computer network is evolving, one built around "product servers," the manufacturing version of an office automation server. Instead of information on marketing, finance and research, however, it will transmit data on product design from the design department right out to the factory floor.

The entire manufacturing process will be transparent to everyone on the product network. Manufacturing management will be able to monitor the development of products and anticipate retooling needs while having some control over the parts database the designers can draw from. Product marketing input on customer reactions to products in development will be fed directly into the network.

Eric Gullichsen of Sense8 demonstrated the rudiments of virtual prototyping in early 1991. He collaborated with DTM, in Austin, Texas, developers of a selective laser sintering (SLS) process for building up parts out of thin layers of powdered thermoplastic materials by using a laser's thermal energy. Together they produced parts for a new virtual head-mounted display system for NASA using Autodesk's Autosolid CAD software on a Toshiba 386 laptop.

To check for continuity, Gullichsen used Sense8's VR software and stereoscopic glasses to visualize the object in 3-D. He then downloaded the part files to DTM's SLS file server. The main housing was made in polycarbonate, while its support brackets were made in wax for later casting in aluminum.

NEC is already installing their first experimental virtual design network on which engineers can work together to create products, as shown in Fig. 10-14. They've developed several procedures for allowing multiple people to work on the same design while being separated by distance.

10-14
In this picture, a designer uses VPL DataGloves to collaboratively design a new car with the help of another designer located in a building hundreds of miles away. This project is part of NEC's investigation of the uses of VR.

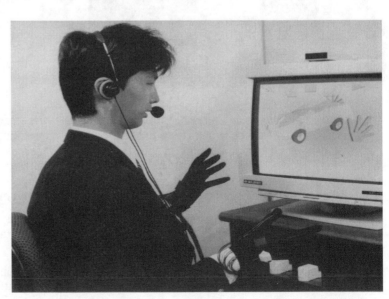

A plain-cursor method speeds up the processing of object cutting operations. A method of approximation-by-polyhedron allows for the quick separation and composition of an object. And a new shape-data-exchange protocol minimizes the amount of object data that needs to be transmitted over the network so that object reconstruction can be made effectively in real time.

NEC is going to study the effectiveness of real-time manipulation of 3-D objects in the design process and how engineers, distributed over many sites, can work together.

This evolving process of computer-aided design and computer-aided manufacturing will contribute to further flattening out organizations and breaking down institutional walls. Nearly all the information product designers will need will reside on the network.

This will make it more likely that a designer could work at home rather than traveling to an office. It also means that a factory might not be a dedicated facility. The product server might be down the hall, across town, or in a vendor's office, a service bureau that specializes in producing quick, short runs of customized parts.

Along the way the designer's role will begin to resemble that of the traditional craftsman or artisan who both designed and built his creations. Large production runs of fixed designs can be replaced by large, medium and small runs of custom designs. Not only will manufacturing and design teams be more closely integrated, the customer will become part of the design process.

In his book, *The Third Wave*, Alvin Toffler prophesied a future production environment where the power of the computer coupled with telecommunications would allow many items, such as clothing, appliances, and furniture, to be produced in a semicustomized manufacturing process.

A businessman could go to buy a suit and, instead of picking one off a rack, his first step would be to select a basic design. His measurements would then be taken with micro-laser exactness; buttons, collar style, and fabric would be selected and all the data sent off to a computer-controlled tailoring factory. A week later the customer would return to pick up his finished tailored suit with its perfect custom fit.

While this tailor shop is still somewhere off in the future, its forerunner already exists for more expensive, large-scale products. Matsushita has installed a Virtual Space Decision Support System (VSDSS) at its Shinjuku showroom in Tokyo. The system has been designed to allow customers to design a kitchen, based on over 30,000 products manufactured by Matsushita for the home.

Imagine you've returned to the Shinjuku showroom after your first visit last week. You're planning to remodel your kitchen. Matsushita will manufacture the entire kitchen, ship it to your door, and install it. But first you have to design it.

Desktop showroom

The Shinjuku staff takes you back into the design room, which is empty except for a table with a few chairs and a computer sitting on it. Last week you sat at that computer with an operator and sketched out the shape, size, and structure of your present kitchen. Then you selected the new appliances, floor tile, shelving and cabinets, colors, and curtains you wanted for your remodeled kitchen. You experimented with dozens of floor plans and countertops.

Today you've returned to visit your future kitchen for a final inspection. The completed computer-simulated kitchen is waiting for you to inspect (see Fig. 10-15).

10-15
A Japanese woman's view of her kitchen as rendered by a graphics workstation in real time. Water "flows" from the faucet that she just turned on.

When you put on the gloves and goggles, the empty display room is suddenly replaced with the simulated animation of your new kitchen. Reaching out with your virtual hands you begin to walk around the room. You study the placement of the new cabinets, the way morning sunlight comes in through the new window. Your virtual hand slips through the wood panel of a drawer, and by curling your fingers you're able to pull it open.

Reaching towards the sink, you turn the cold water handle and bright blue water starts to pour from the faucet. You can hear birds outside and the sound of water pouring down the drain. You decide that the dark granite you selected for the countertop is too dark and there isn't enough room between the counter and the sink to work comfortably. You take off the goggles; it's time to redesign. Figure 10-16 is the finished kitchen design.

10-16
After the design has been approved, in just five days a custom designed kitchen will be installed.

In the case of traditional products, it's been possible for a customer to decide on a purchase only after looking and touching the parts in a showroom. With a virtual showroom, customers can experience their custom-designed product before it's built. How well is a room lit after changing lighting equipment, or how much is the car noise decreased after inserting sound-proofing material in a wall?

Reading specifications off a brochure can never replace experience. No one except a specialist can appreciate a brochure that states, "outside noise is reduced by 10 decibels when upgrading to new insulation."

The showroom now takes on an entirely new function. It's not simply a display center; it has become a design center where the customer comes into direct contact with the manufacturing process. Using the telepresence aspects of VR, it's possible to present many more products than a showroom could possibly hold.

Matsushita has over 30,000 different products. It could never display all of them, nor could they easily be combined with a large-scale product such as the system kitchen, for customer inspection. The virtual showroom is a display without a display space or geographic limitations that allows for an unlimited combination of ideas and products.

The Matsushita Kitchen is the first test case of a new approach to Japanese manufacturing being developed through the New Industrialization House Production Technology and System Development Project, sponsored by the Ministry of International Trade and Industry.

The goal is to make the production of living environments more responsive to customers' wishes. Simultaneously, the project is creating a new kind of just-in-time, customer-driven production process.

With the development of such hands-on design systems for customers to interface with, it's possible to envision a total production system that translates a customer's experience directly into a manufactured product. Architects already use computers to provide limited 3-D walkthroughs inside new building designs. But peering through the window of a computer screen is a very different experience than actually walking around inside the proposed room and making changes as you go.

In presenting a virtual-building walkthrough, the architect can be sure to add features and colors the customer is fond of, emphasize the customer's most important design ideas in the simulation, and give the customer a feel for what the real building will be like. Working together with the customer, the architect can design a floor plan and move walls around, change the landscaping, and even complete the interior design of a house.

The customer then gets to visit, step into, and walk around inside the home before a dime has been spent physically building it. Intel and Sense8 have developed a prototype of this very application, a networked architectural design demonstration, and tried it out on several hundred people at The Computer Museum in Boston.

The application uses a wand device to select and move objects about in the virtual world. Instead of the point-and-click action of a mouse, you point and zap with a wand to select and activate objects and functions. The wand can select from architectural building blocks (walls, walls with doors, windows, bushes, etc.) to construct a multistory house.

While it isn't possible to interactively add Victorian gingerbread touches to the shape of the walls, the basic look of rooms can be changed with texture mapping. Each piece of wall can be individually selected and its color changed. Users can tour the house and alter rooms from wood to brick; paint rooms green, blue, pink; and wallpaper them with zebra stripes or a floor-to-ceiling Dutch painting.

In the future, this kind of decision support will help eliminate the chance of errors or misunderstanding in the production of a new kitchen or home. It draws the customer into the development cycle, making him a partner in the process and helping to close the sale.

There's less of a chance for "buyer's remorse" because the customer has been intimately involved every step of the way. If and when complaints arise with a finished product, both parties will have fully detailed simulations, along with a parts list and blueprints, to use in resolving misunderstandings.

Virtual reality also gives retail stores a new way of testing out a variety of store layouts and aisle-display strategies before committing to remodeling a store. The ways in which products are displayed within a supermarket or a department store are critical to the success of the store. A typical cross-section of customers can be invited in to see their reactions to new designs.

Warehousing duplicate sample products at each showroom can also be cut back. Products displayed in Shinjuku, Tokyo can be seen by a customer using the desktop showroom at Takamatsu as if he were walking through the remote showroom. This reduces the need for redundant display space, and the expense of maintaining multiple showrooms can be kept at a minimum.

Of course, these savings need to be balanced against the cost of the computer equipment, its upkeep, and the training of the operators. The trade-off is only cost-effective with large purchases today, such as the designer kitchen described above, but once the system is in place adding additional products and services is easy.

Matsushita claims that researching customers' experiences relate that they feel a sense of increased control and satisfaction over their purchases by "visiting" their kitchen before purchasing it. Meanwhile, factories await producing certain products until specified customer orders arrive. Just-in-time manufacturing becomes only-when-ordered manufacturing.

In Berlin recently, virtual reality displays were used to build public support for the reconstruction of a major subway station that had been lost since the second world war. The German company, Art + Com, designed several virtual layouts of what the remodeled and restored subway station could look like.

The station had been hidden, walled off directly under the infamous Berlin Wall for 40 years; everyone had forgotten it was there. The city government set up several virtual-reality stations around Berlin for the public to come and view the various proposals for restoring the station in conjunction with plans to restore subway traffic between east and west Berlin. The use of the VR displays helped raise public support for the reconstruction project and provided the public with a limited form of design input in the process.

Not only can customer involvement help with current products, it can help design products that are years, even decades away. Mercedes Benz is using a simulation to test and evaluate new car designs. Unlike Matsushita, Mercedes' manufacturing depends on large-scale production runs of essentially the same car. However, customer input on the ergonomics and the handling of the product are being incorporated into the design process.

They're bringing potential customers and designers to a driving simulator that contains the finished car (see Fig. 10-17). The car is set inside a dome and is wired with an extensive array of sensors. Somewhat like a flight simulator, a driver gets inside the car and goes for a virtual ride. The designers can then simulate all sorts of weather and road conditions. Sound effects add rain, and a motion-control platform supporting the car accurately recreates road conditions.

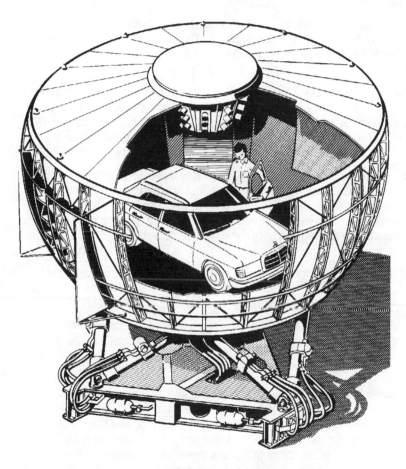

10-17
Illustration of sophisticated driving simulator built by Mercedes Benz.

With this simulator, designers can evaluate the effect on drivers of altering the dashboard, or learn how the driver's experience changes as they change shock absorbers and other equipment. Test-driving a new car will never be replaced by a simulator, but it does provide designers of these mass-produced vehicles the same kind of intimate customer input to the design process that the VSDSS does for Matsushita's kitchens.

In research centers around the world there's a program underway called the Intelligent Vehicle Highway System (IVHS). The goal is to design an intelligent highway system for handling the increasing traffic loads expected in the future. Cities like Los Angeles and New York already suffer from periodic gridlock conditions. Researchers want future highways to incorporate some sort of sensors on the road and on the car itself.

The plan is to produce a computerized highway, analogous to the way trains are controlled by a central switching station that relays traffic speed and congestion data to engineers. The system will take certain kinds of actions out of the driver's control. For example, the sensor will slow the car because it can judge problems faster than the driver.

More futuristic versions of this kind of highway might also involve having vehicles traveling very close together at very high speeds. The faster you're traveling, the safer you are with closer distances between cars. This reduces the stress of impacts, keeping all traffic traveling at similar speeds.

Virtual reality can be used today to find out how close the public can stand to be traveling next to another car at various speeds. What is acceptable? How close can you drive to another car while going 90 miles an hour? You can put people into a mock highway of the future and see what distances are comfortable at which speeds. Situations can be simulated that couldn't be reproduced in the real world.

Is it too good to be true?

Virtual reality is already beginning to change the way business works. It provides new ways to represent and communicate reality and abstract data by customizing it for our senses. It can allow people to use their natural human talents for analysis and pattern recognition in areas from finance to information management, product design, manufacturing, and sales. There's the danger, however, that it will become too good to be true.

Literacy is important in a modern society because language shapes the way we think and also determines what we can think about. This is equally true if you switch the word *visualization* for *language*.

There's no such thing as the last word in data representation in virtual reality. Lotus-style spreadsheets have been the financial simulator of choice for over ten years. Something like Bradford Smith's flowsheet might be the equivalent for the 1990s.

The danger with this new medium is our own unfamiliarity with it. Solutions might arise too swiftly with too much success. A stale set of visual metaphors creates a more subtle and profound problem than wrong data. By restricting the set of available images, we limit the ways we can think about computer-generated models and thereby limit potential insights. In a recent article entitled, "Computer Graphics as Allegorical Knowledge: Electronic Imagery in the Sciences," R. Wright noted:

"There is a danger that once programming solutions to visualization problems have been satisfactorily implemented, they might become entrenched in methodological frameworks difficult to escape from, static interpretations restricting the innovations necessary for the unbounded growth of knowledge."
—Leonardo, 1992

The long-term problem with virtual reality might not be the question of "what can we do with it?" but rather that we can do too much with it and become seduced by the engaging dynamics of interactive reality. It's important to never forget that these are computer-generated models.

Building and managing computer-generated realities for accuracy and honesty is important. The output is only as good as the data fed into the system. Constantly questioning the usefulness of the metaphors that are developed will keep VR applications fresh and productive.

This is important in business, but it's vital in medical research and practice. The American practice of medicine is already big business, infused with high-technology products like CAT scans, MRI, x-rays, endoscopic surgery that puts tiny fiberoptic cameras inside patients, laser surgery, genetic engineering, and much more.

Just as virtual reality is changing the nature of research and work in business, it will provide doctors with new tools for education, investigation, and healing of the human body.

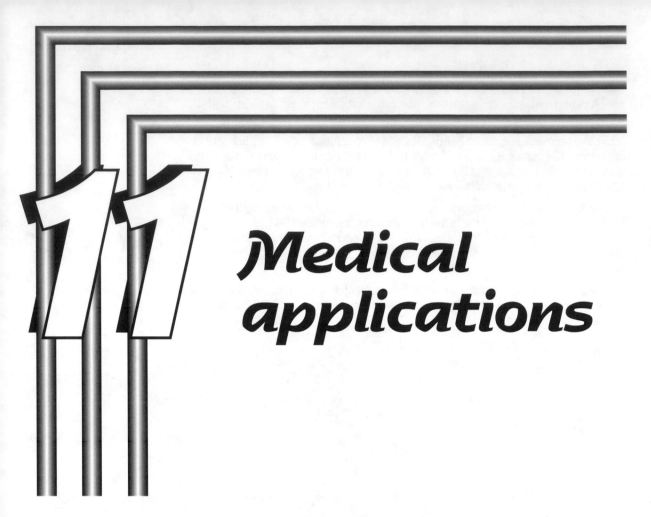

11

Medical applications

Medicine in America has become a high-tech industry. The image of the family practitioner has been replaced by specialists with strange new tools and technologies. Twenty-five years ago the first heart operations made headlines around the world. Today, not only are organ transplants common, but doctors are attempting to transplant baboon hearts and livers into people to find a way to alleviate the short supply of organs.

The grandfather of high-tech medical sensors, the x-ray machine, is joined today by ultrasound, computer-aided tomography (CAT), and magnetic resonance imaging (MRI) machines. These devices are used to create volumetric images of internal organs, or cross-sectional images of the body's interior.

They have revolutionized neurosurgery by providing a window into the structure of the brain, revealing tumors, malformations, hemorrhages, lesions, and a variety of pathologies without the need for a surgeon to go in. The science of medicine seems almost science fiction today.

The medical community and its institutions are careful about adopting new technologies, and with good reason. History shows that many new wonder drugs, techniques, and methods reveal unexpected complications over time.

For every new technique that succeeds many others fail. Because of this, the U.S. Food and Drug Administration (FDA) can take up to ten years to approve a new medical technology as it's studied for side effects and usefulness in long-term clinical trials.

This conservatism has its own side effects as well. Over fifteen years ago, CAT-scan manufacturers offered doctors color monitors for improving the way they studied the interior of the body. Most doctors, familiar with the shades of gray found in x-ray images and the early CAT scanners, turned down the enhancement.

One of the few doctors who bought a color monitor placed it where his patients could see it, set the controls so that the brain would appear purple and the surrounding flesh green, and continued to use his black-and-white monitor for diagnostic work.

But times are changing in the medical community. A generation of doctors are emerging who have been raised on computers and trained on high-tech equipment. Computer technology has dramatically improved over the last few years. Medical schools are beginning to incorporate multimedia training programs, and coursework is being distributed over local-area networks for access by individual dorm room computers.

Pressure from the public, insurance companies, shareholders, the government, and the marketplace is forcing hospitals and doctors to look for ways to increase profits while cutting costs. The tools of virtual reality are poised to contribute to saving lives in several ways.

In research, virtual reality is helping to design new drugs. Biochemists are using it to better understand the structure and properties of large organic molecules while working with these molecules as if they were physically on a workbench in front of them.

Virtual methods are also being tested as an aid in diagnostics. At the University of North Carolina, Chapel Hill, they're developing a set of VR goggles that will hook up to an ultrasound scanner. The ultrasound image will be overlaid on transparent goggles (the same way Boeing hopes to provide jet mechanics with information).

When these methods are implemented, an obstetrician will be able to use see-through VR goggles while examining a pregnant woman, as shown in the illustration in Fig. 11-1. He will be able to see the woman and talk with her while watching her fetus as if with x-ray eyes. Even the individual components of VR are proving useful in medicine. Wired gloves are being used to aid in the rehabilitation of injuries and as a new kind of prosthesis.

The medical community is curious but will wait until serious proof of these products' effectiveness is shown. Unlike buyers of office-automation systems, there's little room for error here; doctors won't buy promises of upgrade features and predictions of future system performance when people's lives are concerned.

Developing medical VR applications is going to take longer than industrial ones because the need for accuracy is higher and harder to produce. It's much easier to test an engine design than an artificial heart. And even once the applications do appear, there has historically not been the competitive pressure found in the industrial economy to drive adoption of innovation. But that too might be changing.

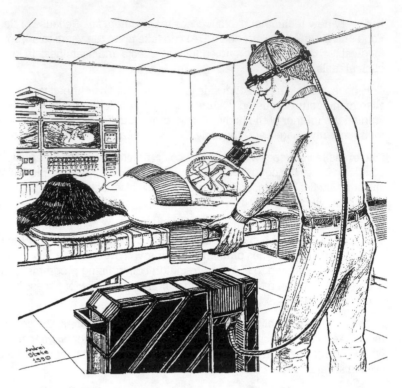

11-1
This illustration is one way future physicians might use virtual reality technology to provide an augmented view of an unborn child using ultrasonic imaging.

The largest and most immediate potential benefit from virtual reality systems might be in improving teaching and training procedures for doctors. Medicine is changing and advancing as fast as computer technology, maybe even faster. New procedures and techniques appear every year.

At the same time, patients are becoming more informed and aggressive as they learn to shop for medical treatment just as they would for other services. Established doctors are being pressured to pick up new procedures faster than ever. Virtual reality's biggest contribution to medicine might be in improving the doctor's learning curve.

The learning curve

There are two kinds of learning curves in surgery. One is when an experienced surgeon first performs a new operation. The other is when a young doctor first performs an established operation. The new doctor gets his or her chance only after much study, and after assisting a doctor who already knows the procedure. Usually his initial practice is done on animals and cadavers, but eventually the new doctor makes the jump to real patients.

Surgeons have long accepted the inevitability that some patients will be injured from the learning curve. But New York health officials have recently stepped in and established ground rules for a new laparoscopic gallbladder procedure, insisting that surgeons not be allowed to perform it until they've shown adequate skill in at least fifteen supervised cases.

Laparoscopic and endoscopic methods are part of a family of new surgical procedures that avoid cutting open major portions of the patient in favor of cutting several small holes. Instead of opening up the patient to reach the work site, a laparoscope, a device with a fiberoptic light and a tiny camera on the end of a thin cable, is inserted and carefully maneuvered through the body for a close-up view of organs and tissues. The images from the camera are displayed on a video monitor in the operating room and instruments are inserted through the other holes and manipulated from outside the body.

The surgeon, then, is actually performing a kind of telepresence, watching on the television the work he's doing while pivoting long-handled instruments through a hole. This method cuts down on the chances for infection and the amount of damage done to the body to simply reach the work site.

For the first time a doctor doesn't have his hands inside his patient where he can touch and see all the organs. Doctors familiar with traditional surgical methods have had to relearn the feel for the tissues and instruments. How much pressure is enough as they find pathways and cut through the body?

Over 500,000 gallbladder operations are performed each year in the U.S. The new laparoscopic method of doing gallbladder surgery promises patients less pain and a shorter stay in the hospital.

The demand for this new procedure has been so dramatic that it has forced doctors familiar with the older method to quickly learn the new technique rather than risk losing patients to competitors who offer the new method. The unprecedented demand for the new procedure highlights an old concern in medical circles surrounding the learning curve.

Most medical complications in surgery occur with doctors who are new or who are performing a new procedure. While doctors are put through lengthy apprenticeships, their chances to observe and assist on actual patients is limited.

In a typical college situation, six or seven young doctors will walk through a ward with an older teaching doctor. Surrounding a bed in a ward (or in a surgical theater) there will only be room for one or two doctors to actually be at the teacher's side. The other students will be listening, taking notes, scanning through textbooks for back-up information on the disease or procedure.

Unlike airline pilots who are trained on flight simulators, there hasn't been a way until now to even consider developing a surgical simulator to help bridge the gap between practicing on cadavers and working with a real patient.

"Endoscopic-type operations are the biggest growing market in surgery," says Charles Lawson, of Intraoperative Imaging Systems. "The most immediate need endoscopic surgeons have is to improve the resolution of the monitors. We are developing a high-definition system for use in operations. Our second phase is going to be to port the tools over into some form of virtual-reality training simulation."

Doctors working with laparoscopic and endoscopic tools have already made the difficult break from hands-on surgery to video-assisted, indirect surgery. The technique is being used in more and more ways. It's applicable any time there's an opening where you can enter without opening up a wound, or have to make only a small incision to insert the camera.

"Endoscopy is already a form of VR," Lawson says. "Once computers are brought into the system to capture and display video we will be able to instantly play back from a disc instead of rewinding tape. In the near future, a doctor will be able to use his voice to request a playback of the last 30 seconds of his work. Then he'll order a printout of it to be made and move on."

As of today only a single camera is used. To see a true 3-D representation would require dual cameras, which the FDA won't allow as yet. Using a camera sporting a larger lens for a wider angle of vision is also under debate.

Every new intrusion into the body raises concerns about side effects and damage. However, the process of getting FDA approval is faster and easier with enhancements to existing procedures than in the cases of entirely new ones. Endoscopes and video in the operating room have become accepted as a standard procedure.

Even if doctors could have 3-D vision, however, it's unclear if they would benefit from the current type of VR-style goggles. A doctor wants to see the arena and the team of people he's working with: the person holding the camera and two or three nurse-assistants who are in the cavity working with tools and positioning fiberoptic light. This would be hampered by wearing goggles.

In many medical situations, from surgery to training, the medical use of virtual-reality technology might benefit less from head-mounted displays and more from wide-screen monitors and projected reality. Surgeons are familiar with working in open settings with a natural 3-D view of what they're doing. Even microsurgery allows natural viewing with stereoscopic microscopes.

Some experiments have been made with using flicker glasses that allow a single-channel image to be split into stereo. Older systems like these, however, can be a health problem for the doctors due to the flickering of the image on the screen. Many operations last three, five, eight hours, or more and no one could wear flicker glasses that long without getting headaches. The latest monitors, operating at 120 hertz, are less prone to this problem.

Lawson wants to develop a way that young doctors and established surgeons can better learn the laparoscopic technique. Actual operating-room video footage can be captured and integrated with computer graphics for the training simulations.

But he feels it might take eight to ten years before a training tool can be developed for abdominal work. The problem is less the graphics than it is developing the right kind of force-feedback tools for the surgeon to work with. Even for surgeons who are working on real patients, knowing how much pressure is enough and where the tools are going is challenging.

David Hon, president of IXON, has been a pioneer in the development of simulated bodies and training programs. He sees medicine at a crossroad. Patients are asking for specific doctors based on the number of times they've previously performed a given procedure. Simultaneously, the emergence of minimally invasive procedures such as laparoscopy is requiring a skill that few doctors have performed a number of times.

Hon developed a CPR simulator and went on to develop a gastrointestinal endoscopy simulator that uses a custom-built endoscope/position-sensor device coupled with an Intel386 CPU-based computer and laser-disc player. This system allows for the display of endoscopic pictures at ⅛₀ of a second to simulate the performance of the procedure in examinations.

The sensor is used with a special mannequin to create a realistic force-feedback "tactile" experience, with sensors relaying the position of the endoscope and catheters within the anatomy. In this way the system reacts in real time to the students' movements and decisions. Developing such a simulation of an abdominal laparoscopic operation, however, would be much more complicated.

Lawson is talking to NASA, which is developing a probe that provides feedback to surgeons. Part of the problem in sliding cameras and tools down small ducts in the body is lacerations. It takes experience and training to know when you're putting the probe or grabber into the wrong area.

NASA has developed a device to give feedback on the pressure being exerted at the end of a probe. This will allow the development of a pressure-sensitive scalpel that could also give feedback during training.

The advent of telepresence interfaces such as the endoscope and intelligent tools like a force-sensitive scalpel is leading some researchers to envision a form of telesurgery in the next ten to twenty years.

Computer-aided surgery

Early in the next century, surgeons might have the choice to work from surgical workstations for some procedures. These stations will sit in a special room or right inside the operating theater. The doctor and his assistants will prepare the patient, correctly placing the endoscope and tools into the operation site and hooking them up to a bilateral robotic system that can control their movement in any direction the doctor requires.

Retreating to the surgical workstation, the doctor will see a 3-D view from the endoscope on his monitor that will let him know exactly where it is in the patient's body. A separate monitor (or a window within a larger screen) will provide a view from a different angle, a computer-generated image of the body for guided positioning of the endoscope's placement.

Assured of the instrument's location, he will take up the interface tools that provide feedback to his hands. These special joysticks (or some other new devices) will provide position scaling and force scaling so that the movements of his hands are carefully transferred down to micron-level movements of the tools at the operating site.

Important medical information will be overlaid on the monitor for easy access or conveyed by speech synthesis, depending on the doctor's choice (foot pedals might offer another form of physical interface).

Such a surgical workstation would also provide a collection point for the integration of other medical information. For example, previously processed MRI or CAT-scan data on the patient, along with his medical record, could be downloaded to the workstation from the hospital's computer network. Or the data might come from an out-sourced MRI clinic's image-processing databank.

The surgical workstation would also allow the surgeon to plan several moves and simulate them on the monitor before actually doing them. By rehearsing his efforts on the computer before instructing the system to automatically carry them out, the doctor could find the best solution before making his move. The uses for a surgical workstation aren't limited to human bodies. When used with an electron microscope, it will allow microbiologists and genetic engineers to work directly inside cells.

Under the direction of Faina Shtern, MD, the National Cancer Institute has been researching image-guided stereotactic diagnosis and treatment of tumors. MRI scans that have isolated a tumor within the brain could be used as a positioning template overlaid on an endoscopic video image coming in from the operation site. A surgeon's biopsy needle, or other treatment delivery device, would be able to plot a precise way of reaching the isolated tissues in question.

Eventually, imaging technology might make the body transparent and allow 3-D viewing in real time of various organs and biological systems. Capturing the real-time events of an operation from a computer system would allow for the training of new surgeons via simulation. Data from various operations could be combined by an instructor as a lesson for a class. The computer would recreate the operation and be able to realistically simulate complications stemming from mistakes or unexpected complications.

In addition, the entire lesson could be captured on disc for the student or instructor to reexamine later. The ability of the computer to incorporate MRI and CAT-scan data, and to simulate biological processes and structures will eventually lead to completely virtual bodies.

Virtual bodies

Joseph Rosen of Dartmouth Medical School in Hanover, New Hampshire, has a team working on a computer graphics-based patient model of skeletal muscle. The team's goal is that this virtual patient will accurately reflect the geometry of the body and the biomechanical behavior of the physiological systems under study.

The generic design will eventually be able to accept MRI, CAT-scan, and other data for customization to a particular patient's physical condition. It will allow for preoperative planning, training, and perhaps even surgical assistance during the actual operation. This is an incredibly challenging task, one that will require years of work. Today, workstations and supercomputers are just beginning to simulate pieces of the body.

Parts or all of this virtual body could be viewed on a surgical workstation. A more useful simulation could involve the use of high-resolution goggles. Putting on the goggles, the doctor would see a virtual body on the table in front of him. It would be transparent in order to reveal the important organs or biological systems he wants to study. Around him would be a virtual display of information, visible wherever he wants it, containing a wide variety of patient data.

For teaching purposes, a group of students could all be wearing similar goggles or viewing on-line simulations from their dorm room computers. Because this would be entirely generated out of a computer model, the students could choose to have a point of view from anywhere in the operating room, even mimicking the doctor's point of view, directly over the patient.

Information screens and the ability to zoom in on various details would be user-specific. The doctor could demonstrate procedures, such as administering a particular drug, and the effects of the drug on various organs and systems could be illuminated as it spreads through the body.

A fully authentic software reproduction of the human skeletal muscle system will require a clear understanding of the structure and function of muscle cells. Rosen's team is investigating how best to represent and recreate them in a computer graphics model. Once they can faithfully represent the muscles and their performance and interaction, the simulation could help plan operations.

For example, large wounds require surgical reconstruction. The best option is often a muscle transfer, in which an insertion point is shifted so that a healthy muscle covers the affected area. Surgeons typically rely on experience to judge which muscle is appropriate in terms of shape and to save as much overall body functionality as possible.

Think of the body's systems of muscles as an interdependent series of springs and pulleys. The repositioning of a muscle will reduce the strength available for coordinating certain body functions. One muscle's gain is another's loss; there's always a trade-off. An accurate computer model of the body could assist in understanding the biomechanical results of reconstructive surgery and help the surgeon make the best choice.

Rosen's group has developed the software models they believe will allow them to construct a complete body. They've developed computational models of several parts of the body (skeletal muscle, skin, and an articulated skeleton) that need to be integrated into a more complete model.

Computer simulations aren't new to the medical field, but the ability of computer graphics to create virtual organs and bodies is. For many years there have been computer-based text-only simulations for new procedures and medications. Pharmaceutical companies often support the production of these programs so that doctors can keep up on new products.

A text-based simulation describes a series of symptoms and then offers a choice of options for the doctor to select from. Depending on his selection, the reaction, side effects, or necessary intervention appears on the computer screen.

Many universities are already developing their own multimedia simulations and databases for eventual sale to other colleges. The medical school at Washington State University has spent over ten years gradually developing a digitized catalog of the human body.

They've already released a laser disc containing 54,000 microscopic photographs of the human heart. And they're mapping the entire human body with the goal that, by the time they're done in the late 1990s, there will be computer technology capable of taking their images and creating an animated virtual body for medical simulations.

Working with a team of medical illustrators, ADAM Software Inc. of Marietta, Georgia has built an interactive multimedia reference guide to the human body, Animated Dissection of Anatomy for Medicine (ADAM). It offers an anatomical database with high-resolution illustrations coupled with detailed medical information.

ADAM lets the user peel away the skin and dig into the body one tissue layer at a time, to as many as 40 layers, revealing every bone, muscle, and nerve. Each area of the body can be viewed from the front, side, back, or cross-section. In side windows, users can consult x-rays, CAT-scans, and tissue studies, and even view typical pathology progression on the displayed section.

The software has authoring tools so that instructors can organize material for training by attaching notes in side screens, animation, and video. Students can be guided through simulated surgery and doctors can use it to brush up on procedures.

ADAM (soon to be followed by a female version, EVE) can provide a more realistic experience of studying the body. For example, a professor at the University of Arkansas School of Medicine is developing course material that will reinforce understanding of the relationship between layers of the body by taking students on a journey through the skin and asking them to identify vessels and muscles and note the nerve supply for each muscle. It can be used to construct animation to illustrate the consequences of injuries, such as a knee's reduced range of motion because of ligament damage.

One professor is even embedding video footage in the program to show a physician diagnosing the same type of injury as displayed in the program. This kind of interactive learning increases student involvement with problem-based learning. It's also a platform for simulating surgical procedures.

James Black, Ph.D., uses ADAM to train and test residents at the James A. Haley Veterans Hospital in Tampa, Florida. He rehearses surgical procedures with his students and then tests them on the system before they actually step into the surgical arena.

Computers have already invaded the medical world. Students coming out of the training colleges will be ready to accept the new virtual methods now under development. Even medical researchers are getting involved. They're taking the same techniques used in virtual design and prototyping and making them available to doctors.

Fantastic Voyage

In the classic science-fiction movie, *Fantastic Voyage*, a team of scientists and their medical submarine are shrunk down to cell size and injected into the body of a political leader to do emergency repair work deep inside his brain. Along the way they travel through the swirling currents of his blood system.

In the real world of the 1990s, researchers are using computers today not only to teach and heal, but to go on fantastic voyages to study biological processes. They're studying the composition of the body in a similar way as NASA engineers study the flow of wind across the wing.

A team in Germany is using a supercomputer to realistically simulate the functioning of the heart. They want to download the results of their computations to a system using VPL equipment so they can tour the interior of the heart as it pumps.

Like the NASA Ames team who's developing a virtual wind tunnel, these German researchers want to take the computational skills developed by material researchers to study fluid dynamics and apply it to the interior of the heart.

How does blood flow through the heart? What happens to the swirl of blood during a heart attack? Virtual reality will allow the German team to stand inside the ventricles of the heart and watch the blood swirl around them.

The fantastic voyage takes on even smaller dimensions as another group of medical researchers are shrinking down to the size of atoms. In a dimly lit room in Chapel Hill, North Carolina, a pair of molecules float in space. DHFR (dihydrofolate reductase) is a protein molecule; its partner is methotrexate, a drug molecule used in cancer treatment. Both appear as collections of different colored spheres, where the colors represent the drug's individual atoms.

A research chemist sitting in this room watches a large molecule, his hand holding the pistol grip of a GROPE-III. Developed by Frederick Brooks over many years, it's a mechanical navigation device that transfers the chemist's hand movements into the behavior of the atoms.

He's been trying to dock the two molecules and find the right spot that will allow them to link up. Molecules not only have shape, they have regions of varying electronic force depending on the placement of their atoms. From every position they're shaking, attracting and repelling from different points at the same time. The researcher has been unable to get the two molecules to link up simply by using visual cues.

Stepping on a floor pedal, the researcher activates the force feedback in the maneuvering arm. The bar he's holding begins to shudder and pull as a motor hooked up to the grip translates the electric behavior of the atoms into his hands. Now he can judge the structure of the atoms and their physical and atomic forces.

This system gives chemists the ability to physically experience how drug molecules dock. Chemists report that they have a new understanding of the details of the receptor site and its force fields, and of why a particular drug docks well or poorly. The chemists who've used the system can quickly reproduce the true docking positions for drugs whose positions are known. They also can find very good docking spots for drugs whose true dockings are unknown.

These haptic displays provide an important design bridge between the stick-figure models chemists have traditionally used to help them visualize molecules and computer graphics. Scientists can acquire a feel for the forces that link and bond atoms into molecules, both the kinds of fields and the distribution of forces within a single molecule. It helps them understand why each particular candidate docks poorly or well, leading to ideas for new candidate drugs.

The molecules are modeled using several feature sets. CPK models are spheres representing individual atoms colored according to type. Sticks represent the bonds between the atoms and a ribbon is the amino acid chain backbone of the molecule. Depending on the power of the supercomputer that does the initial computations for the simulation, very complex molecules can be created.

The National Supercomputing Center is working on very complex simulations of molecules with thousands of atoms. The researchers want to simulate them in real time with the correct representations of their bonding force fields so that they can reach in with a wired glove, tug on the atom, and study how it retains its integrity.

Being able to watch this behavior will give chemists a more intuitive understanding about the nature and construction of molecules.

It's not only atoms that researchers want to position. Treatment procedures can be simulated and ran with the same kind of control as a research chemist juggling molecules. Radiation planning is one of the most difficult parts of cancer treatment.

Doctors try to position the gamma-ray beams to irradiate a tumor with a high enough dosage to kill the malignant cells without damaging the tissues around it. 2-D x-ray films of the body are studied to try and plot the 3-D trajectories of the energy beams.

By incorporating actual 3-D data of the patient's body, doctors could run trials of various beam therapies by hand and see immediately how well they'll work. A handheld wand or other pointing device would be used to angle and control the beam.

Putting on a set of goggles, the doctor could see the patient's body in 3-D as he worked on a tumor. He could position beams, lock in their positions, and then move around to review his own work from a different position. Several beams could be lined up and their configuration adjusted for the best possible effect. A low-frequency hum could be used to give real-time feedback on how far off target the beam is from the tumor. The color of the beam could shift as the doctor moved off target or when his approach touched too much healthy tissue.

Rehabilitation

Most of the attention in virtual reality goes to the immersive experience of putting on the goggles and glove and going into another world. In the medical field, however, there's as much interest in using the separate elements of VR equipment as there is for the total experience.

Walter Greenleaf, co-founder and chief executive officer of Greenleaf Medical Systems (GMS) has licensed exclusive medical rights to VPL's DataGlove and DataSuit technology. He sees a range of applications where the pieces of VR can be as useful as the 3-D worlds.

The GloveTalker is GMS's first VR-based product. It uses the hand-gesture recognition capability of the glove to translate gestures into spoken words (or text on a screen) so patients who can't talk can communicate. Using a Macintosh computer and proprietary software, specific phrases and words can be assigned to individual hand positions.

The product is designed primarily for use in hospital settings and has been tested at Loma Linda University Medical Center in San Diego, California and Cal State Northridge. Stroke victims, someone whose larynx has been removed, or people with cerebral palsy who have both motion and vocal impairment but can still use their hands can use it to communicate with their caregivers. The glove can be programmed with several hundred phrases.

This kind of gesture recognition offers the possibility not only of aiding hospital patients, but also of serving as a new kind of prosthesis in the outside world. Because the DataGlove can translate gestures into computer commands and spoken words, it's possible for someone with very restrictive limitations to control preprogrammed equipment.

For example, there's an application where a DataGlove and a Macintosh II computer are hooked up to a receptionist's PBX telephone workstation. Using hand gestures, the receptionist can instruct the computer to answer and route telephone calls, or to activate prerecorded messages for callers.

Because only two degrees of freedom are necessary to reproduce the position of a cursor on the screen, a user of the glove can control the positioning of a mouse with just his fingers or by the movement of his wrist. In this way he can select icons off a screen to control the equipment.

With a change of software and the addition of an analog-to-digital converter card in the computer, the same glove can be used to measure the freedom of movement for the wrist and hand. In real time, a computer is able to calibrate the glove's position and range of motion at fourteen different joints: finger and thumb, wrist extension, flexion, and radial/ulnar deviation.

This information can be useful for worksite ergonomic analysis for computer operators, assembly-line workers, and other people with Repetitive Strain Injury (RSI). RSI occurs from performing tasks that require limited and repetitive hand movements and is one of the more crippling and prevalent injuries of the modern workplace. The glove can also be used to assist and track patient rehabilitation and therapy.

The interactive ability of the computer to manage and display information and control devices to suit an individual's needs opens up new ways for handicapped workers to participate in society. Already, computers are being used to help severely handicapped individuals to function in society.

The great physicist, Dr. Stephen Hawking, most widely known for his best seller, *A Brief History of Time*, is a victim of ALS (amyotrophic lateral sclerosis), or Lou Gehrig's disease. Often referred to as a successor to Einstein, his body has gradually deteriorated over 30 years while his mind has remained unaffected. He has almost no control over his body and must be propped up in a wheelchair. He is unable to feed himself and needs nursing 24 hours a day.

Dr. Hawking communicates with the world by selecting words on a computer with one finger, which are then converted by a speech synthesizer. In this difficult and limited way he has managed to convey the solutions to some of the great physics problems of our times and write several books. Not only could a VR system with goggles provide him with a sense of openness and escape from the limitations of his body, it could revolutionize his ability to work and communicate his ideas.

Besides the GloveTalker, there are already sensitive-control mechanisms for tracking eye movement that could be coupled with button or joystick controls to serve as an interface to a custom VR information-management system.

In this way, people who are physically impaired could use their minds to the fullest extent possible. Instead of having to conform to their handicap, the handicap could, in a sense, conform to fit them. And very weak physical movements could be augmented by equipment that amplifies the user's body.

Another way that VR equipment can aid in healing is by tracking and recording very small improvements in a patient's physical condition. The DataGlove and the DataSuit can collect data about a body's position and freedom of movement dynamically in three-dimensional space. This allows a level of accurate motion analysis that was unavailable before.

For example, the progress of stroke patients is made up of small improvements; the biggest problem can be keeping their spirits up when they have no way of judging their own progress. As a patient gradually recovers control over his body, accurate tracking of small but increasing freedom of movement and control will provide a way for patients, care providers, insurers, and family members to monitor progress.

Extending their work, Greenleaf Medical Systems has developed an entire computer workstation for doctors who specialize in treating hands. Based on the Macintosh, the EVAL Examination System links new precision-measurement tools with accurate computer evaluations of impairment to the hand and extremities.

The Greenleaf Medical Systems' software can be incorporated with the VPL DataSuit for a motion-analysis system. Instead of just hand movement, the patient's entire body is tracked. This will be useful in rehabilitation programs for stroke victims who are relearning how to use their bodies.

Body movement can be recorded, select areas can be isolated, and the information can be played back at a slower rate to give the patient immediate feedback. It will make relearning tasks much easier and help give the patient a sense of accomplishment so he sticks with the program.

Besides assisting people with disabilities directly, virtual reality is being used to help redesign the buildings they have to move around in. In Chicago, at the Hines Rehabilitation and R&D Center, Dr. John Trimble and Ted Morris have developed a wheelchair simulator using Sense8 software to test the accessibility of building designs to be sure they meet government standards.

The recently passed Americans with Disabilities Act includes legislation designed to ensure that public buildings and spaces accommodate the needs of the physically disabled. Until now it was difficult to test designs, and involve either building large cardboard models of the space in order to simulate what it would be like to navigate through it in a wheelchair or asking a wheelchair user to provide input based on written documents and blueprints.

Now architects can download the computer-designed floorplans of their buildings into the system and then test out the building. The system uses a real wheelchair installed on a platform that transfers the movements of the wheels into navigation information for the Intel486 CPU-based personal computer.

Putting on Virtual Research goggles and a VPL DataGlove, anyone can travel around the building, reach out to shelves, drawers and doors, and tour virtual buildings from the perspective of someone in a wheelchair. Corresponding views of someone using the system and his virtual-reality viewpoint are shown in Figs. 11-2 and 11-3.

The system is set with width parameters so that if a doorway is too small the software won't allow the virtual wheelchair to get through. Not only is the simulation a powerful way to test new buildings for accessibility, it simultaneously educates architects on what life is like when you can't stand up and walk through their buildings.

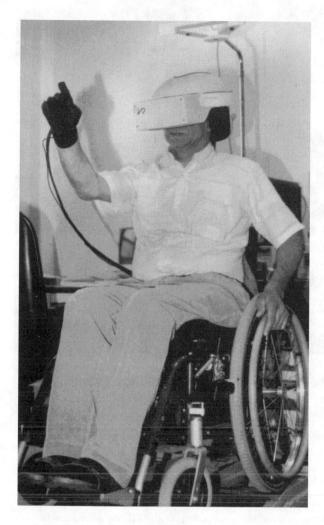

11-2
By hooking up a wheelchair to a VR system, architects can design buildings to be more accessible to the physically disabled. Rollers underneath the wheelchair feed information to the computer controlling the simulation.

By the turn of the century, the "graying of America" will be a major social trend. We're going to see a restructuring of health care in the U.S. as new technologies enter the field and public pressure to reduce costs increases. Computer networks will allow many hospitals to out-source services they once brought in-house.

Hospitals often acquired MRI scanning equipment as a way to attract high-quality doctors who would refer patients to them and as a way of generating extra revenue. These services are going to either be localized at a few hospitals in a region or spun-off into small independent business units as a way to lower costs and increase efficiency.

Research laboratories are going to go on-line as advanced electronic microscopes and scanning tunnel microscopes become accessible by distant medical researchers via telepresence. The results will be greater access to technology for researchers, and lower cost of use as equipment costs are spread out and shared by many more people.

Medical wonders

11-3
An example of the kinds of images seen by the wheelchair VR user. Access to cupboards can be measured with a wired-glove.

Computer-aided imaging technologies will be an on-line resource to every doctor. Doctors will share services over networks of workstations within hospitals or from their private clinics.

More and more computer-aided imagery will be used to explain and educate patients about what is happening to them. In the next century we'll very likely see the emergence of home imaging systems in which patients can monitor and keep track of developments inside their own bodies (much as diabetics already track their own blood pressure and blood sugar levels).

Administrative costs will go down as duplication of records at every hospital is reduced. This will happen through the use of centralized multimedia databases within hospitals and HMOs, or perhaps a national computerized registry of personal health data might be created.

Many of the real rewards from the integration of virtual reality technology with medical technology, however, won't begin to appear until the late 1990s. Just as with computer-aided design, the biggest breakthroughs are going to require a lot of work to be successful.

Luckily, the underlying technology is common across many different fields and industries. As Boeing, Rockwell, NASA, and other companies figure out what it takes to create industrial simulations as rich as a fully functioning virtual jet engine, the same information will become available to medical software developers working on living virtual bodies.

Entertainment 12

"The filmmaker says, 'Look, I'll show you.' The spacemaker says, 'Here, I'll help you discover.' "

—Randall Walser, *Elements of a Cyberspace Playhouse*

It's easy to imagine VR ushering in a new age of very hypnotic computer simulations. Instead of going down to the health club to ride a bike in front of a TV, you'll slip on some goggles and tour the south of France. Instead of looking through the window of a computer screen, you can go inside a video game to play with dinosaurs and Super Mario Brothers.

In *The Psychology of Optimal Experience*, by Mihalyi Czikszentmihalyi, six criteria are described that most often characterize experiences individuals consider optimal, those that:

- Require the learning of skills
- Have concrete goals
- Provide feedback
- Let the person feel in control
- Facilitate concentration and involvement
- Are distinct from the everyday world

Virtual-reality entertainment clearly meets these criteria. The difficulty can be increased with usage in order to challenge the improving user's skill. The goals are concrete whether it's dodging hockey pucks, making music, or blowing up tanks. Virtual reality stands out with its potential for extensive feedback in real time and its unique ability to give the players a sense of being in worlds very different from the one they live in.

Movies already allow us to vicariously step into other worlds. Amusement parks use giant IMAX movie theaters and simulation rides like Disney's Star Tours to thrill visitors. Super Mario Brothers playing on Nintendo home computers have become a permanent fixture in homes around the world. Entertainment and virtual reality seem made for each other.

While other industries study virtual-reality solutions, the technology is already good enough for the storytelling merchants of Hollywood to start developing products. Sega of America, Universal/MCA, LucasArts, and many others are all hard at work to bring a new era in interactive entertainment to global consumers. They're all betting that virtual reality is the television or computer-game innovation of the 1990s. Even the chairman of Sony has been heard to say that, ". . . after the camcorder, the next big thing is going to be virtual reality."

Many entertainment companies (with the exception of LucasArts) sat out the emergence of the computer-game industry. Like the old railroad companies that didn't initially perceive airplane transportation as competition, the Hollywood studios initially disdained the computer-game craze.

While regular software applications are considered successful if they achieve sales in the tens of thousands, computer-game titles regularly sell in the hundreds of thousands. Characters like the Super Mario Brothers have become cultural icons to millions of young boys. The BattleTech computer game has given birth to clubs, books, and now even a virtual-reality arcade business. And Hollywood has finally taken notice.

Amusement parks have already proven the attractiveness of simulation rides. Disney's Star Tours is perhaps the best-known example. It's one of a growing number of fantasy rides that have been married to the motion-controlled platforms of the flight-simulator industry.

Small groups of people are taken inside a cabin decorated to look like some kind of spaceship. The cabin has video screens for windows. The people are strapped into cushioned chairs and essentially taken on a rollercoaster ride with special effects.

Lucasfilm's Industrial Light & Magic has created several of these rides. In one, SpaceRace, the riders are loaded into a long room for a ride up to NASA's orbiting space station. There are rows of airplane seats all facing a big screen at the end of the room. The roar of the rockets fills the riders' ears and the cabin shakes with the lift-off, and clouds fly by, thinning out into darkness, until the stars of space fill the windows.

Over the intercom their friendly space-shuttle pilot narrates the trip with a John Wayne drawl. As the shuttle nears the space station it passes by a black-hole generator. The device inadvertently turns on and sucks the shuttle down a swirling wormhole and ejects it in a distant section of the galaxy.

In the far reaches of space, the riders find themselves caught up in a Star Wars-type stockcar race. The captain aggressively pilots the craft around a racecourse littered with traps and obstacles, all the while dodging competitors who try and crash each other's spaceship.

The ride's most powerful effect is the invisible motion-control platform beneath the ride that tilts and tosses the whole room. It's very effectively timed to work with the visual cues happening on the view screen to manipulate riders' sense of gravity. Relatively limited, yet sharp motions are all that's required to create vertigo and draw screams from the riders as they see themselves crashing into walls and swerving around obstacles.

Virtual reality is coming to a shopping mall, amusement park, and eventually a home computer near you. Similar arcade simulation rides with limited interactivity, single- and dual-person cabs, and free-standing units are the first virtual-reality systems to reach the public. They come with names like BattleTech and Virtuality, and they're showing up around the country, in Europe and Japan.

"It's more than a car race or a flight simulator, these systems are the first to truly take people 'inside' a video game," says Scott Crandall, a VR entrepreneur. Scott Crandall and his partners are building California's first BattleTech Center in San Jose, next door to Silicon Valley.

Developed by Virtual World Entertainments, BattleTech Centers are based on the idea of networked military-tank simulators, but the games go far beyond tanks. BattleTech is configured for two teams of four people who play against each other. Each player sits inside a ten-foot-long cab called a BattleMech (see Fig. 12-1); they're made of metal and plastic and are supposed to be the command cockpits of giant robot warriors.

Driving a BattleMech

12-1
View of BattleTech control pods. Groups of players battle one another in a simulated future war zone.

Each cockpit holds one player who watches the action unfold over two monitors. One is a 25-inch color monitor showing the "outside" virtual world. A smaller secondary screen below the main monitor shows radar and other detection systems to let you know if there are any other Mechs around and whether they're friend or foe (see Fig. 12-2).

12-2
BattleTech control console. The top monitor displays the view outside the vehicle and the bottom screen shows current operating status.

Microphones let team members communicate with each other. The second screen also shows real-time information about the BattleMech's condition: sustained damage, heat buildup, etc. The cockpit's console contains over 100 controls, but beginning players need to use only a few of them, adding more as their expertise increases.

"In the beginning there was Pong," says Scott Crandall, a VR entrepreneur attempting to open a BattleTech franchise. "It was the first video game experience but it was not an interactive game, it was you against the computer. You could beat it once you learned the pattern, if you could learn the pattern. Around 1976 I saw my first truly interactive game. A group of engineering students at Stanford had built a networked computer game they called Galaxy. It was big, each unit was the size of a phone booth. You sat in front of a monochrome screen, in which you flew about hunting your partner while avoiding crashing into planets and flying asteroids. What really made them unique was that you could adjust the laws of reality and change the shape of space and time."

The Galaxy game had a series of dynamic laws users could preset. There were three main world choices: a sea of asteroids, an open space with a central sun around which random asteroids flew, or just space. The users could adjust the gravity so that ships had to avoid getting sucked off screen or drawn into the sun at the center of the screen. Or they might choose to have no gravity at all.

They could set the boundary of the screen to reflect ships, wrap around so the ships could slip off and come back on the other side of the screen, or blow up a ship if it hit the edge. You could also go into hyperdrive and become invisible, but you used up your limited fuel twice as fast. There were lines of people waiting to use it, yet after a year it disappeared, probably to be cannibalized for some other student project.

The first BattleTech Center opened August 1, 1990 at Chicago's North Pier. After signing in at the front desk, visitors are matched up with other people to create teams. The teams are taken to a room decorated as the war room of a giant starship. TV monitors fill up a wall. Some show newscasts explaining the politics of the 31st century. Most monitors are repeaters of the player's cockpit screens, each labeled with the player's name so observers can watch the game from all eight players' points of view.

A uniformed officer instructs the players on their mission, the enemy, and what weather and terrain conditions to expect. There are hundreds of different mission situations available, and the center staff matches the simulation to the expertise of the teams. The officer also gets each player's choice of BattleTech to fight in so his cabin can be programmed accordingly.

The BattleTech is steered like a battle tank with two floor pedals for turning left and right and a forward/reverse throttle. Players are surrounded by speakers, which heighten the sense of realism by supplying the sounds of machinery and battle. There's a joystick with triggers and buttons for controlling different weapons systems. There are panels of switches for configuring which weapons are fired by which buttons.

The graphics, sound, and control system of each pod is based on 26 proprietary PC boards. The four-speaker sound system incorporates three different sound generators, giving it the ability to create 3-D spatially oriented effects from sampled sounds. There's also a subwoofer in the seat, and though it doesn't sit on a motion-control platform the entire pod seems to shake when the BattleTech is hit.

"Nobody gets killed in BattleTech," Crandall says. "This is not a grab a machine gun game where dead bodies litter the ground. If you are injured in combat or your BattleTech breaks down you are ejected. You as the pilot escape safely so getting blown out of the BattleTech doesn't end the game. You just go back to GO and start over."

To avoid the expensive computing power normally required for battle simulations where hundreds of thousands of polygons need to be constantly redrawn, the designers prepared a system that uses 19,000 predrawn images. These are stored in the pod's 32Mb RAM memory and are then called to the screen as needed. This system limits the range of movements and possibilities somewhat, but is cost-effective for public installation and quick enough to provide a sense of realism.

"With BattleTech, the human-to-human competition is the focus, not you against the computer," Crandall says. "Players are not going up against a preprogrammed chip or Artificial Intelligence, they are part of a team. You might be complete strangers when the game starts, but by the time you all go through your first battle together, you're a team.

"It is this connection with other people that has attracted me to the BattleTech product. There is an exciting kind of bonding with virtual reality that goes on even with members of the opposing team. You admire quick moves and get excited by a competitor who challenges you, who gives you a good experience."

A research team from Michigan State University spent four weekdays and one Saturday in September 1991 asking BattleTech players to complete questionnaires after their games. They collected 312 completed forms from 223 novices, 42 veterans, and 47 masters who had completed fifty or more games. The average player was a 23-year-old single male, but the largest group (16 percent) were computer programmers.

Of the frequent players, the veterans had completed an average of 23 games while the masters had an average of 228 games under their belts. Despite the assumption that video-game players never look at a book, the frequent players read newspapers four times a week along with four to five books, and read seven to eight magazines a month. Not surprisingly, they spend an average of five hours a month using on-line computer services.

While the veterans thought it took three to six games to master BattleTech, the die-hard masters estimated it took much longer: nine games to master driving the BattleTech, up to 42 games to become good at using terrain, and 56 games to master cooperating with others. The masters are a close-knit group who get together for social functions away from the center. On average, they've made 15 new friends through BattleTech.

Like the movie industry, the cost of introducing the first generation of virtual-reality arcade centers will depend on amortizing the installation costs over time, using new titles and updated releases of old games to bring in new customers and sustain repeat business.

"What fantasies have you wanted to discover? When I was young and was watching the moon landing, I desperately wanted to be an astronaut. I could never do it because of my eyesight, but in VR I could. We can take all that tremendous film footage from our own NASA missions and go flying around the universe," Crandall says.

Already there are plans for a new BattleTech Center game based on the idea of a treasure hunt. Instead of robots, the BattleTech cabs become individual submersibles with the goal to reach the Titanic on the bottom of the Atlantic ocean. Your team is in competition with another team of divers to bring back a treasure chest buried within the maze of hallways and rooms within the sunken luxury liner.

The game will be designed on a Dungeons and Dragons type of structure in that there are traps, dangers, and sea monsters along the way. There will also be special tools you can find or win that are required to overcome obstacles deeper within the ship. Some of the challenges will be impossible to get through without teamwork, and in a few cases you will even need people from the other team to overcome challenges.

It's a contest requiring not just gaming skill or the ability to figure out a puzzle, but the ability to convince others to work with you. While you're playing, your air tanks are running out, which is the timer on the game. The final twist is that to win, only one person can reach the surface. You aren't just competing against the other team, you're eventually competing against the members of your own team.

"When I went to see the movie *Star Wars*, it was as a passive spectator," Crandall says. "It was a scripted experience I enjoyed, but over which I had no control or interaction. Virtual reality is the next step, it's like the Woody Allen movie, *The Purple Rose of Cairo*. A woman goes to a movie theater and sees a film with friends. She starts commenting about a character in the movie and the character responds to her from up on the screen. Suddenly all the characters start responding and she is drawn into the film, into influencing the course of the film.

"Someday, and it may take fifty years, but virtual reality is going to make that kind of scenario possible. Today, it allows you to play with people in a computer-generated fantasy world; the computer supports you, it doesn't compete with you."

Other companies looking to introduce simulation rides or games include Hughes Aircraft, and they're doing so through their Rediffusion Simulation division. They're working to take all the resources they've developed creating high-quality flight simulators for the military and develop a consumer product.

Realizing that they had the hardware know-how but not the software, they've teamed up with LucasArts Entertainment company to bring the Commander pod to the market. The shiny red, vaguely egg-shaped pod has a black-tinted front window that most closely resembles the long sloped design of the Chevy Lumina van.

Just big enough for two people, it's essentially a flight simulator that will make SpaceRace-style rides modeled after real F-18 jet-flight simulations possible. The front window is actually a high-resolution TV screen. While looking through it, users will be able to change their view as they experience a very realistic ride.

Users don't have to be contained inside a cabin riding on a motion-control platform for a simulation to work. Researchers at the University of California at Davis developed an open bobsled-training simulator for the 1992 American Winter Olympics team. Because of the costs of travel for a five-man team and the number of countries preparing for the games, access to the actual bobsled run in La Plagne, France was limited.

Four weeks before the opening of the 1992 Winter Olympics, the American bobsled team met at the headquarters of Silicon Graphics Computer in Cupertino, California. They used SGI's advanced graphics workstations and a large-screen TV projection system to practice for their competition.

University of California Davis had created a computer graphic simulation of the track, a silvery-white trough with a thin green center line for steering (an addition not found on the real track). They rigged a real bobsled's steering mechanism to the computer and positioned it in front of the giant TV screen. The computer drew the track out in front of the riders as they flew down the chute. It gave the illusion that the riders would never reach the end of the track; it just continued to get longer.

The image on the wide screen violently shook whenever the sled "hit" the side of the track. The computer kept time, adding calculated fractions of a second for each crash against the wall, letting the team strive to beat their best time. "We were only able to get four good runs on the actual track in France," said the team's coach. "At Silicon Graphics we did more like 400 runs."

Free-standing projected reality

The Vivid Group, inventors of the Mandala System, has been developing the idea of free-standing wide-screen projected reality. The Mandala System captures your image in real time and projects it on a wide screen so you can step inside a virtual world without having to put on any equipment or sit inside a cab. They've also created musical simulations where you can play virtual instruments by watching yourself in the virtual world and guiding your own movements.

They've developed a hockey goal-tending simulation for the National Hockey League's new Hockey Hall of Fame in Toronto, shown in Fig. 12-3. In it you get to tend the goal, guarding the net and deflecting pucks as they come shooting at you. The sport gets very engaging as the computer increases the skill level until you're jumping and diving about to block the pucks, which luckily don't hurt even if you do get hit.

12-3
Vincent John Vincent demonstrates his Mandala hockey game simulator.

This idea can be easily modified for soccer or volleyball and, with the addition of other input devices, a golf or baseball simulation would be possible.

For many people, however, this kind of simulation isn't enough. They want to go into worlds they've never been to before. They want to be immersed in that world and not watch a screen and see themselves projected into the world. They expect to step through the screen and be free to move about in another world.

As far back as 1985, when NASA Ames started assembling their VR system, researchers in England were also investigating how to create virtual environments. One of these men, John Waldern, came across Sutherland's 1968 paper describing the head-mounted display system built at the University of Utah. Working on his Ph.D. in Computer Science at the Human Computer Research Center (HCIRU) at Loughborough, England, Waldern realized that such a system could be used for entertainment as well as business. Figure 12-4 shows a spatial workstation he created.

12-4
John Waldern's initial explorations with VR resulted in a spatial workstation as early as 1984. It used rapidly rotating mechanical shutters and a stereoscopic display to see 3-D images. The entire system was wheeled around while ultrasonic sensors tracked the system's position and orientation.

Before NASA or VPL revealed the results of their work to the public, Waldern was busy creating virtual entertainment systems. Along with three partners, he founded W Industries in 1986, and by 1988 had created the first operational system, nicknamed the Giraffe (see Fig. 12-5).

Waldern's system used several Amiga home computers and was limited in resolution and image complexity, but it incorporated stereophonic sound and used the Doppler effect to provide velocity cues. This is the same effect used to judge whether a train is approaching or receding based on the pitch of the sound (rapidly approaching sounds compress, increasing their frequency, while receding sounds stretch out, reducing their frequency).

In addition to the audio effects, a mechanical head-angle sensor tracked the orientation of the participant's head, while a hand-trigger allowed games to be played against the computer.

The system wasn't rugged enough to withstand the abusive environment of an arcade parlor. But it was good enough to attract investment by one of England's biggest sports and entertainment conglomerates, Wembley PLC. With new funding, W Industries was able to go back into the research lab and develop Virtuality, the world's first virtual-reality system using head-mounted displays and exclusively designed games.

For $60,000, you can purchase either a sit-down or stand-up game. In the sit-down game, players use joysticks to fly a simulated Harrier jump jet on various missions and dogfight with other networked game players.

Accelerated Amiga computers generate the real-time stereoscopic images and quadraphonic sound, and interface with the various sensors and trackers. A six-pound custom head-mounted display called a Visette (based on LCDs and an electromagnetic tracker) is clamped to the participant's head.

In the stand-up game, shown in Fig. 12-6, you move about on a platform that houses the equipment and are surrounded by a circular railing that keeps you from having an inadvertent collision with a reality called the floor. Putting on the helmet, you see a fairly simple world called Dactyl Nightmare, where one or more players are represented by a humanoid, cartoon form.

You stalk and pursue each other around a multilayered set of chess boards, like the 3-D chess set on Star Trek. The idea is kill or be killed in this shoot'em-up game. And if battling other people isn't thrilling enough, there's a giant green pterodactyl swooping about the world looking to turn you into its lunch. Newsweek called it a video game on steroids.

During a 1991 tour across the U.S., people waited in line for three hours to play the new games. Being the first on the scene gives W Industries a lead on other companies expected to enter the market. They've signed an agreement with

12-6
The Virtuality VR game system from W-Industries Ltd. Participants use pistol-gripped devices to shoot each other in the game Dactyl Nightmare.

Spectrum Holobyte, maker of the popular PC game Falcon, to provide a steady supply of new experiences.

Fantasy experiences aren't the only ones possible with head-mounted displays. The Department of Computer Science, University of North Carolina at Chapel Hill, has developed a mountain-bike virtual-world simulation for the health and sports minded.

Using VPL EyePhones and a real mountain bike, the user sees a textured terrain with several hills and valleys to explore. There's a road that designates a path through the world and, as you ride along it, you can see most of the signs, buildings, and other objects in the world.

You don't even have to stay on the road; you can explore the countryside. The bicycle has sensors mounted on its back wheel and front fork to measure the user's distance and direction changes. The number of rear-wheel revolutions are used to measure distance and speed, while turning the handle bars determines the bicycle's direction. The designers have even thought to equip the pedal with force feedback so that going uphill is more difficult than pedaling downhill, just as in the real world.

And if mountain biking or hockey playing isn't your thing, there's a group of engineering students in Finland who want to do bungie jumping (a sport where you're strapped into a harness attached to a giant rubber band and then jump off a bridge) in virtual reality. How these students plan to simulate the gravitational effects of free-falling off a bridge is anyone's guess.

VPL's DataGlove device was the inspiration for the first VR product to ever achieve mass-market commercialization. Mattel offered a very simplified version of the glove for use with Nintendo computer games called the PowerGlove, shown in Fig. 12-7. While it was available for only about a year, tens of thousands of the gloves were bought for home systems.

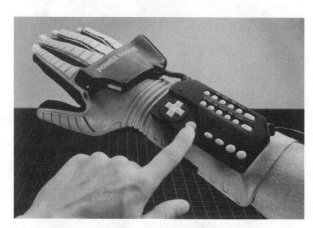

12-7
VPL's DataGlove recreated as the Mattel PowerGlove for use with Nintendo video game systems.

The glove might be staging a comeback in the future as several researchers around the world are studying how to use it. Professor Ooteru of Waseda University in Japan is studying how the glove could be used by musicians to create music without physical instruments. More complex than the drum beating of the Mandala system, Professor Ooteru is experimenting with piano keyboard and violin simulations.

Home systems

Where are the home systems? What are Sega and Nintendo up to? They both have research projects underway, but with virtual reality hardware still costing thousands of dollars it will be a couple of years before they can bring affordable virtual reality into the home. However, the gradual trend towards home VR is already apparent as companies lay the foundation for the kind of high-performance systems needed for home VR.

As computing power gets better and cheaper, we'll see a dramatic change in the entertainment industry as Hollywood "software" is married to Silicon Valley hardware. It has already started to happen on a sound stage in Redwood City, California.

Inside a converted office building next to Highway 101, Sega engineers Spencer Nilsen and David Javelosa are translating the actual movie footage from *Jurassic Park*, a new techno-thriller by director Steven Spielberg based on the book by

Michael Crichton, into a computer game that will put users face to face with a rampaging Tyrannosaurus Rex.

For *Jurassic Park*, Sega has a team of writers, artists, and composers combining actual film footage with animation and sound to produce the game. The movie is due to reach the theaters in the summer of 1993. In it, genetically engineered dinosaurs created by a fictional Palo Alto research firm run amok on an island off the coast of Costa Rica, terrorizing a half-dozen hapless humans (sort of an updated Lost World).

Sega of America has built its own multimedia production studio so they're able to release the game at the same time the movie debuts. To bring film-quality images and sounds to a video game, Sega (as well as Nintendo) have both developed CD-ROM drives to attach to their systems.

CD-ROM, short for compact disc, read-only memory, is exactly the same size and design as the audio CDs that now dominate the music industry. And they can hold 100 times more information—including video and sound—than the traditional game cartridges used by Sega's Genesis system and the Super NES from Nintendo.

This kind of storage capacity will give the game makers a foothold in the home for the emerging world of multimedia computing. And it's the same kind of data storage device that will help bring VR into the home. Sega's plans, however, don't stop with *Jurassic Park*; they're also planning games based on the Looney Toons characters, including Bugs Bunny and Daffy Duck.

The D. W. Griffiths, Orson Wellses, and Alfred Hitchcocks of VR haven't appeared yet. However, the people with the most experience in creating simulated experiences haven't been sitting idly by as this new entertainment form emerges. The major dream factories of Hollywood have their own VR projects underway. With the time and money to develop their ideas before revealing them to the public, they're heading from the video-game paradigm in directions closer to the "computer as theater" vision of Brenda Laurel.

Virtual movies

"There hasn't been a change in the basic [movie] technology since *The Jazz Singer* in 1930."

—Roy Aaron, president of Showscan Corporation

Over the past decade, the percentage of the U.S. population going to movies has been declining. Gross-attendance levels have remained flat and the only reason box-office totals have continued to go up is because of increased ticket prices. Meanwhile, other forms of movie delivery improve on almost a monthly basis: laser discs, cable, and home video, with high-definition TV and CD-ROM just around the corner.

The basic process of movie making and the quality of the technology seen on the screen hasn't changed because the industry's perception is that it won't bring in more people. Like books, movies are a stabilized form of media; it's the content, the story, that sells a book or a movie.

How can the producers use technology to attract more people to movie houses when most of the audience is generally satisfied with the image quality? MCA is trying to answer this question by experimenting with an entirely new kind of movie-going experience. They're turning virtual reality into a shared group experience.

"There are no words in our language for what we're doing, this new kind of game/entertainment. It's neither one nor the other, yet it draws from both and from other sources as well," says Alex Singer, the creative director of MCA's project. "A very rough analogy I resort to requires you to think of Nintendo's Super Mario Brothers as being at the same level of sophistication as tic-tac-toe. Then I can compare the kind of group experiences we're striving to build as being like 3-D chess.

"Our plans call for two VR adventurers who have input on their own experience in the virtual world. Then there's an audience who has input on the experience and a show manager who has great control over the entire adventure to see that the show is interesting. All this gets combined into a huge number of variations for each experience because the game itself introduces all sorts of characters and forces which are variables."

TV was invented in the 1920s and yet took 30 years to catch on. All the technical components already exist to create a shared VR experience. Will it take as long as TV to achieve public acceptance? MCA is betting that the success of TV and computer games has prepared a generation of consumers for virtual movie experiences. They're relying on VPL Research to develop the actual technology that will be used in these new theaters, which Jaron Lanier calls *voomies*.

Their plans call for a room about the size of the small theaters now common in multiplex cinemas around the country. The recreational division of MCA has prepared several different floorplans to study the flow of people and the space allotments needed for such a creation.

One idea calls for an area in the center of the theater where two people would be fully equipped to enter a VR world. They would have very sophisticated data gloves and goggles and the freedom to move about in the virtual world. Seated around them would be 36 spectators/participants.

The actual virtual experience would last about 15 minutes in itself, but the entire group experience would tie up people for the better part of an hour. Because of its experimental nature—with an unskilled group enjoying and interacting in unfamiliar ways—it's important that there be someone monitoring the show to be sure it is interesting.

The entire system will be under the management of a single host, visible to everyone, an actor who will be a kind of master of ceremonies. The actor will manage the experience to be sure it doesn't get dull or out of hand.

"To create this new kind of movie experience with multiple levels of participation requires the possibility of interaction between the group, the host, and the two who are fully in the virtual world. The two adventurers will have a richer, more textured experience being fully immersed in the world.

"It's not cost-effective or technically possible yet for everyone to be fully immersed in the virtual world. So whatever level of experience the group shares with the two central players has to be vital enough that these 36 people are willing to pay a movie fee and are willing to return. So we've created a way for these people to have a supportive role," says Singer.

Instead of goggles, the 36 viewers will peer into the virtual world from large screens mounted above the two central players. This view will be separate from the view the two players have through their goggles. It will be an overview of all the action and it won't have the same level of resolution or create the same sense of immersion that goggles provide. Each of the 36 will have their own data glove with which they can have limited influence in the virtual world. This will create a kind of three-way play among the two players and the audience.

"For the two people in the world it will be a very intense and exciting experience," says Singer. "They will need to be prepared to compete with their colleague as well as with the audience. And they may be compelled to be cooperative with each other to move from one challenge to another. For the audience, each person's particular experience will vary depending on the location of their seat and the decisions they make. As a result, everyone can attend the same virtual experience many times and yet have a different experience each time."

Singer describes himself as one of the "old guard" in terms of background and practice. He has directed feature films and episodes of the television shows *Hill Street Blues*, *Cagney & Lacey*, and *Lou Grant*. Like the theater director George Coates, Singer's traditional role has been to control all aspects of the viewers' experience. He had a passive audience to whom he delivered the words, images, and experiences.

With VR, the contract between the audience and the dramatist has changed. Instead of a passive audience, the interaction is dynamic and unfamiliar, and there are a tremendous number of possible combinations to consider. (To give up the past has been hard, but Singer finds voomies challenging.)

"In the first scenario we have found a way to touch on a number of values beyond gaming and competitive ones, such as social human values. It is not necessary to be a murderous arcade game to amuse people, even young people. We are shooting for a PG audience, but still trying to create an intense experience. The brutality of most arcade games results from a lack of imagination of what can entertain people. If not hazards, there will be choices that vary, a little of the `Lady or the Tiger' type story, but even that is too simple to suggest what we are creating," says Singer.

It's unclear yet whether the first voomie theater will be in Japan or Los Angeles, or if both sites will get a theater. Singer has found that the Japanese are more enthusiastic and aware of the exciting possibilities for voomie theaters.

The first units will be the focus of experimentation as MCA struggles to fine-tune the experience and understand what audiences want. Virtual reality and computer-gaming enthusiasts will be the first wave of consumers the experience will attract, but for long-term success Singer and his team must create a format that will have something for everyone.

Because the debut of this virtual theater is still many months away, no one at MCA was willing to discuss details of the first version. As a suggestion of where this new entertainment form is heading, Singer pointed to the popular experimental play *Tony & Tina's Wedding*. Audience members are given the role of guests at a make-believe, but realistic, blue-collar Italian wedding in the Bronx, complete with food and fights.

In the 1960s there were attempts at audience-participation theater. Most of it failed because the people randomly selected from the audience didn't have the skills to participate, were unprepared, and didn't have a defined role to play. In addition, they suddenly found themselves up on stage with a room full of people watching them, an unexpected and uncomfortable experience for most people.

Tony & Tina's Wedding takes place in a cheap hotel instead of a theater. You don't get a theater ticket, you get a wedding invitation. You aren't the audience, you're a guest at a wedding. In this format, the audience is assigned a fixed role they're familiar with before they even arrive.

Instead of being required to contribute to the drama or propel the plot along, the entire experience has been designed to amuse you, the guest. And there's no separate audience watching you; in fact, it's often impossible to tell who are the guests and who are the actors, because everyone is an actor.

Each time Alex Singer has gone to see the show (bringing the entire MCA virtual reality team with him) he has had a different experience. He would do different things, sit in different places, talk with different members of the cast and guests. The show is closer to free-form jazz than the linear scripted format of traditional theater, and it's very much an inspiration for what MCA is developing.

To make the show work is very challenging; it has to be vital, exciting, and subject to endless revisions while maintaining its energy. The show needs to be very carefully planned and programmed so that the routines flow from the actors. The actors and actresses are constantly acting out variations on themes, and improvising on ideas and routines.

"I feel I'm compelled, whether I want to or not, to move closer to my audience and give up control," Singer says. "In exchange for giving up control I get new kinds of creative possibilities I never had before. Instead of an audience, I get a cast of actors. There is going to be this intense feedback loop whereby the audience influences what happens in real time. As a creator, I set the ground rules, and if I've done my job right, those rules will color the experience in an important way."

If they take off, voomies won't replace, but will instead complement movies, providing an alternative form of entertainment. It's easy to imagine a future where movie studios develop two versions of a movie simultaneously, like the work Sega and Steven Spielberg are doing with *Jurassic Park*.

Perhaps by the late 1990s, when the fifth sequel to *Batman* comes out, not only will there be comic books and clothing spinoffs, but a voomie and a home CD-ROM VR version. You'll be able to roam Gotham City with the caped crusader in search of cartoonish criminals, in a virtual world constructed out of actual film footage, computer animation, and sound effects.

While game and entertainment experiences—from BattleTech to voomies—will be the initial offerings to the public, creators are already looking beyond these forms of enhanced video games. Just as radio incorporated vaudeville before finding its own entertainment forms, and TV incorporated radio variety shows before finding its own way, virtual reality entertainment will use video games and movies as a stepping stone to something new and original.

Alex Singer is trying to understand what that might be and so is a small team inside LucasArts. They call themselves Rebel Arts & Technology and their goal is to use today's best technology to leapfrog entertainment into the 21st century.

"Whether it's film, simulator rides, sound tracks, or special effects, LucasArts is primarily a software company. We are not a hardware, technology, or a film company, everything we do is software—it's the experience that concerns us. There aren't too many companies out there with the creative base we have," says Adam Grosser, director of Rebel Arts & Technology.

They are a part of LucasArts, a company spun-off from parent Lucasfilm, George Lucas' dream factory. LucasArts is made up of many divisions, including computer games, toys, sound effects, and the famous special effects shop Industrial Light & Magic.

The birth of Lucasfilm and Industrial Light & Magic (ILM) goes back to *Star Wars*. To create the right kind of "space opera" look and feel George Lucas wanted for his film, he had to create his own special-effects team. He needed special matte painting artists and he needed to invent computer-controlled cameras to realistically portray spaceships spinning though dog-fight battles inside asteroid belts. And he hired mask makers who could create strange new creatures.

When the movie was done he had the best special-effects team in the business, with all the traditional studios calling for their services. The team named itself Industrial Light & Magic and opened its doors to service Hollywood's endless hunger for new special effects.

With the money from *Star Wars*, Lucas built up his own studio away from Hollywood in the Marin county countryside. Over the years, ILM has consistently set the standards by which all other movie special effects are measured: *Close Encounters*, the Indiana Jones series, the sets for *Hook*, the transforming *morphing* technique in *Willow*, and most recently the liquid metal man for *Terminator 2*.

ILM has a full-time team of over 75 computer-graphics artists, and souped-up Macintoshes, PCs, and SGI workstations fill the studio. One of the directors at ILM is the coauthor of the Photoshop software from Adobe Systems Inc., the leading computer application program for manipulating images. Now the LucasArts division is hoping to set the standard for virtual-reality experiences.

Rebel Arts & Technology is a small group formed within the company to discover new ideas and technologies that can either be turned into products or passed on to other departments. David Fox, a veteran of Lucasfilm's video game division, heads up the creative team. Together with Grosser he has put a team together to create a virtual-reality experience that will be second to none.

"We will never develop technology for technology's sake," Grosser explains. "It is a necessary evil only when we feel it is required to deliver the quality of experience we are aiming for. Working within LucasArts has given us a tremendous leg-up.

"For example, Skywalker Sound, which just won the Academy Award for sound, is doing the sound effects for the real-time sound system we are developing. ILM did the explosions. Everyone in the company is excited about contributing to this new medium. They are looking at it like a new computer paint-box; but instead of just manipulating images, they will be able to create entire experiences."

Leveraging the company's experience with amusement park rides like SpaceRace and cinematic special effects, Grosser is using the Commander pod project for Hughes Aerospace as a training experience for his team.

Simultaneously he has a much bigger project under secret development. Like BattleTech and voomies, Grosser envisions a string of virtual-reality centers around the country and overseas showcasing LucasArts experiences. They will use the best technology available. There will be a computer controlling the interactive experiences of many different players. The centers will be networked to allow players to compete with one another and to compete with other centers internationally.

"Our ultimate goal is to deliver experiences to the home," Grosser says. "The reason we are starting with a large-scale public experience is that we feel there is going to be a learning curve for the public. There are a lot of people who don't understand the power of this experience. They don't know they want it yet. So we are choosing to open a public forum that will expose as many people as possible. Eventually, someone will be able to dial into the network from their home and have the same kind of high-quality experience they would at a center. But that is years away."

The quality of experience LucasArts is designing will be as unique and accessible as possible. They have joined up with a technology partner to build networked, multiplayer systems that will be installed in amusement parks and special shopping mall centers. Grosser promises that the systems will provide cinematic-quality stories that are very, very interactive.

"After much thought we decided not to use head-mounted displays or wired gloves. We don't want to have to teach people how to use a system or intimidate them. Like a movie experience, you should be able to sit down and immediately participate. Instead, there will be small rooms with surround sound and wide-angie screens. Joysticks and touch screens are the first interfaces we are going to provide because they are intuitive and easy to use," says Grosser.

LucasArts was concerned that some of the gestural requirements of a wired glove were not intuitive even though most people are fine after ten minutes of playing around. Only die-hard enthusiasts are going to pay money to play around for ten minutes before they can have some fun.

There was also the question of survivability in an arcade setting. The base technology they're designing will be flexible enough to support a wide variety of input devices—touch screens, joysticks, steering wheels, 6D force balls—so that the centers can provide a wide range of experiences and customizable cabins to meet the needs of new experiences or a user's selection.

They're hoping to have their system out by 1994. While Grosser wants the experiences to be easy for people to slip into, David Fox wants the content of the experience to be meaningful, exciting, and available to all ages and genders.

A simple example of the kind of experience they're thinking of providing would be that of working in space like the shuttle astronauts who retrieve communications satellites. The players would find themselves out in space trying to assemble a space station.

But the pieces are so massive that it requires two or three other players to get the job done. If you can't get the other people to work with you to build the station then you can't go inside to discover what new experiences are awaiting you there. Group cooperation and a way of teaching values, along with providing entertainment, is a concern of the team.

"First of all we are in the business of providing entertainment, but we can do much more," says David Fox. In the early 1970s he was a counselor. When personal computers came along he and his wife started the first public-access microcomputer center. He was the second person to join Lucasfilm Games and created Rescue on Fractalus. Distributed by Atari, it was the first computer game to use fractals to create mountains and backgrounds.

"There's a couple of science-fiction books which can give you a sense of our philosophy of experience development. *Dream Park* is one, but *Ender's Game* is closer. It's by Orson Scott Card and the lead character, named Ender, is living on a space station in some distant future where he is training to be a warrior. He's learning to grow up with a powerful simulation computer as a teacher and mentor.

The computer is powerful enough and knows him well enough that it can design problems for him that he will have a hard time solving because of his own mind-set. The problems the computer develops for him are linked to his personal blind spots. The way he solves them is that he has to alter his way of thinking, his point of view, or his personality in some way to see the world differently."

The idea that someone can grow and learn by solving computer games is Fox's hope for LucasArts virtual realities. He's just not sure how to do it yet. There are classes of experiences and problems that people go through at certain ages around which experiences could be designed.

It might take a hundred years before there are computers as powerful as the one in *Ender's Game*. However, it's not too soon to think about how to design games in which people learn about themselves while they're having fun.

The designers of virtual world experiences are beginning to cross an invisible boundary between the known and the unknown. It's a new field for which there aren't a lot of precedents. The tools of virtual reality seem to be leading designers further away from controlled experiences and into creating environments and landscapes filled with possibilities for the user to discover.

Adam Grosser sees the potential for responsive environments in which the journey is its own reward. He's inspired by outdoor clubs for a sport called *orienteering*. Primarily a European phenomenon, people are given a destination, a map, and a compass and not told how to get there or what problems there will be along the way. The idea is to challenge the players' ingenuity and resourcefulness while providing excitement and surprises without direct competition.

The optimal experimental experiences

In the Michigan State University BattleTech survey, players rated the game nearly off the scale as challenging, fun, exciting, and unique, and very high as creative, competitive, intense and absorbing. Rather than being a system of alienation, where people are drawn away from social activities, virtual reality can be a very social technology.

The Michigan State study consistently identified strong desires for interaction with real people in addition to virtual beings and environments. Just two percent would prefer to play only against the computer, while 71 percent preferred to play on teams, and the remainder wanted to play individually against everyone else. With such a positive reaction, is there more to be gained from the experience than friendship and fun? What about entertainment that teaches?

The very nature of virtual reality forces us to ask questions about perception, learning, and ethics. What kind of experiences do we want to have? David Fox of LucasArts sees a possible future where virtual worlds are designed out of movie magic, animation, sound effects, and psychology to provide modern-day "rites of passage." Alex Singer is already seeking to design voomies that touch on social and human values.

Henry James wrote, "Learning is the development of experience into experience." As the entertainment industry begins to provide total experiences that we couldn't have before, it begins to cross over into the deeper questions of virtual reality's impact.

How will the frequent use of designed virtual experiences alter our perception of the world? How will meeting and playing with people in virtual worlds change our relationship to the world and each other? These are the kinds of questions that artists have been asking for hundreds of years. At what point does virtual entertainment cross over into art, and is there a boundary?

In the hands of the first virtual artists, we can begin to catch an idea of where virtual reality will take us, and what kind of experiences it will bring us. And perhaps, the same way the works of Van Gogh, Picasso, and Matisse changed the world, we can learn how VR might alter our way of thinking, our point of view, and perhaps even our personalities by changing the way we see the world.

Art in VR

13

"If men were able to be convinced that art is precise advance knowledge of how to cope with the psychic and social consequences of the next technology, would they all become artists? Or would they begin a careful translation of new art forms into social navigation charts?"

—Marshall McLuhan, *Understanding Media*

In ancient Greece the patron goddess of both science and art was Techne. From her comes the Greek word *techne*, which means "to create." And from her name the words *technique* and *technology* were derived. Over the last 2000 years science and art have gradually gone their separate ways, but once they both looked to the same source for inspiration—the will to create and understand the world. Today, art and science are coming back together again.

In his recent book, *Art & Physics*, Leonard Shlain builds a compelling case for the idea that the effect of artists' work in changing the attitudes and perceptual filters of a culture makes way for the insights and discoveries of its scientists.

Shlain suggests that a way to understand Einstein's revolution in physics is to juxtapose it with radical breakthroughs in modern art. Each strive to perceive and interpret the world, yet seem completely opposed to each other in spirit. Shlain builds his case by tracing insights and discoveries in both fields over the last 2000 years.

"In the case of the visual arts, in addition to illuminating, imitating, and interpreting reality, a few artists create a language of symbols for things which there are yet to be words . . . the radical innovations of art embody the pre-verbal stages of new concepts that will eventually change civilization . . . . This collation leads to abstract ideas that only later give rise to descriptive language."

—Leonard Shlain, *Art & Physics*

Computers and virtual reality are seminal inventions whose future impact we can barely guess at. How many people watching the first steam engines 300 years ago could foresee the Industrial Revolution and the changes to the world that would come?

Only as artists explore the new electronic media will we get clues to the long-range potential for the changes it will bring to our lives. We're entering an age in which everything can be digitized and expressed in a computer as an object or environment with which we can interact.

By the last half of the 19th century, the techniques of representational painting had all been pioneered. Not only had traditional still life and portrait painting been done to death, but a new technology had appeared that was quickly displacing them—photography. Not only was it faster and easier to do, but reproductions of the original work could be done quickly, in large quantities with little or no degradation in quality.

Mirror of the mind

Beginning with the Impressionists (and followed by the Surrealists, Fauvists, Futurists, etc.), artists turned their attention from the outer world to their own inner world of thought and perception to find new artistic challenges. They used art as a mirror of the mind.

This modern art of concepts and ideas frequently rejected Giotto's 3-D perspective techniques and was so different from the representational art that came before it that the general public still has not acclimated to the shift one hundred years later.

Marcel Duchamp was one of the first to create this art of the mind. But even as he tried to suggest and express concepts, he felt confined using the same material media that artists had always used (paint, canvas, and stone). He knew he needed to break free, so he shattered forms to create mobiles, used glass instead of canvas, and used found objects and motors instead of stone for sculptures. He did all he could to suggest unseeable ideas.

This century has seen a creative explosion of styles and methods for representing and expressing concepts, and exploring perception with nontraditional and unusual materials. Now it appears that almost all methods of artistic expression have been pioneered.

Virtual reality represents an entirely new and unexplored universe for creation. It's an art form in which shape, space, and time can be bent, and in which viewers can participate. Take, for example, the unusual series of virtual compositions shown in Fig. 13-1. The first expressions of virtual art worlds evoke the emotional wizardry of the surrealists such as Dali, with barren lonely landscapes where anything can happen. Here at last is an art medium as fluid as the mind itself.

Throughout the fall and winter of 1991, there was a unique gathering of artists and technologists at the Banff Center for the Arts in Calgary, Canada. As part of a special program run by Doug MacCloud, for the first time ever artists were given

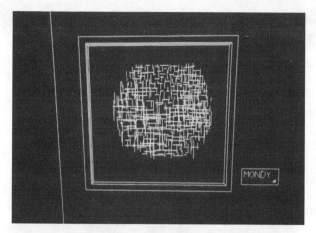

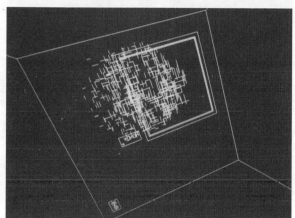

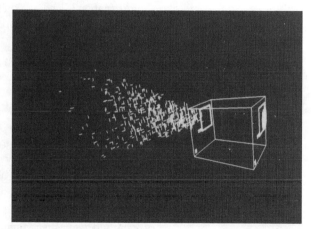

13-1

The first picture (left) in this sequence shows a virtual art gallery with a painting that appears identical to one by Piet Mondrian, entitled Composition with Line. As the user flies around the painting, it falls apart into a 3-D sculpture (below left to right).

the opportunity to work with Sense8 VR tools to explore the power of this new medium. Several fascinating virtual experiences combining sound and images resulted from this collaboration.

The Ottawa-based artist, Robert McFadden, created a piece called *Picture Yourself In Fiction*. In a vast, empty void, a box without top or bottom floats. The inner and outer panels of the cube are covered with scanned photographs of the artist's body. As you pass near panels, digitized samples of his poetry are triggered and audibly played. The very nature of space itself distorts and loops back on itself as you move about.

Virtual art is a technology, media, and concept. It's not three different things, but three different aspects of the same idea—the ability to control and create experiences:

- It's a magic cauldron for integrating the techniques of painting, film, sculpture, and literature with the dynamic structures of music, theater, and even dreaming.
- It's a meta-medium that can encompass all art styles simultaneously: cubist, religious, realistic, abstract, primitive, postmodern, etc.
- By its very nature, it's an experience in which art viewers are transformed from vicarious voyeurs into co-creators of their own experiences.

By drawing us into art worlds, the computer's ability to store and retrieve events becomes a way for us to explore our notions of time, space, and memory. After spending a certain period in a world, the virtual traveler could be confronted by virtual memories of his own virtual experiences. Key incidents and phrases seen and heard could come tumbling back. Some day he might even be able to reexperience episodes from his own life.

Places can be constructed that don't physically exist in real life. For example, the worlds of M.C. Escher and Magritte, Mobius strips and convoluted stairways, the geometry of mysterious spaces where people and creatures blend back and forth into each other, or a train floats out of a fireplace.

A virtual traveler might find that, depending on the direction he moves in an Escher art world, he could have the form and capabilities of either a fish or bird, but not both. A virtual traveler returning again and again to a virtual world, trying to achieve a goal so he can get into another world—isn't this a metaphor for reincarnation? Is he working through his virtual karma, unable to advance into another reality before completing certain tasks in the current one?

Art isn't just a way of observing, a way of doing; it's fundamentally a way of knowing. Virtual art can be used as a new kind of mirror to explore and challenge ideas, experiences, and states of mind in the real world. Visits to virtual worlds will undoubtably change the way we think about ourselves and the world, and will ultimately alter our understanding of reality.

Becoming the art

Two women dance in front of a screen. A camcorder above the screen picks up their image and feeds it into a computer that projects them into a graphical 3-D world. As they dance, they see themselves weightless on the screen: moving mirror reflections, puppet-selves playing amid planets and space—musical refrains triggered as their hands brush against the stars.

On separate screens, people interact with poems such as *Risk My Shadow Kissing Yours* and *The Geisha Snail and The Phosphorescent Samurai*, which offer eight possible endings, depending on the choices you, as the viewer, make.

All great works of art have one thing in common, the German philosopher Arthur Schopenhauer maintained: they have the power to pull the viewer out of himself and into the work of art. They suspend the division between inner and outer, self and other, and usher you—if only for a moment—into the realm of the timeless. You momentarily become the art.

This description captures the essence of what makes virtual reality such a special medium. The viewer is no longer a passive observer, but becomes an active insider "doing" the art.

The immersive/interactive quality of VR removes the traditional chasm between art viewer and art object, pointing the way to a new kind of awareness as the viewer becomes a participant "inside" the art. Virtual travelers who experience several points of view or reside inside several different personalities will become confronted by questions of identity and the social masks they wear.

As VR concepts and technology develop, VR art creations will be able not only to suggest insights and altered states of consciousness, but to actually simulate them the way the artist experiences them. The inner experience of an artist will become as portrayable as a still life in the material world. Virtual art spectators won't look through windows that contain static or moving objects (as in paintings or film); they will step through into the various points of view the artist creates.

Will virtual realities eventually replace reality? No. The feel and taste of a carrot, the look and smell of a rose, the robust richness of the world we live in will never be completely representable (unless in some far-off future we can only dream about).

And we don't need virtual reality to be a substitute for reality—we have the fresh, vivid reality of our everyday experiences already. Instead, VR offers a way to experience life in a way that adds to our everyday experiences.

For example, when we see a play or movie, read a book, or stand before a great painting, we give ourselves up to its special reality for a purpose. Our surrender to these guided intentional experiences allows us to feel and learn more than we normally would from the capricious occurrences of everyday reality.

When the creation is effective it produces a very special reaction. Aristotle called this experience *catharsis*, the pleasurable release of emotion, specifically those emotions evoked by the art. He didn't mean that the emotions were necessarily pleasurable, but that the release of the emotions was pleasurable (the popularity of slasher, horror, and thriller movies attests to the variety of pleasure people find in the release of unpleasant emotions).

The multisensory symphony of virtual-reality worlds offers a new and very powerful way of delivering catharsis; the freedom of the medium is a challenge to both the linear tradition of storytelling and the structured methods and media traditionally used to deliver tales.

Will the VR artist's role be subverted by the VR audience in this new media? Will the audience get into the art and make a mess of it? If the world isn't carefully constructed, most certainly. But the rewards available to an artist can be greater, too.

As Alex Singer, the director at Universal who's creating voomies has found, the VR relationship between artist and audience is much closer, more intimate and involved than with traditional art. The connection between them is more like mind to mind without intermediary.

The virtual artist will need to use *all* of the skills and lessons artists have struggled to amass over the last two thousand years. This new art media combines the power of the eye and ear, and the lessons of the musician, painter, film maker, sculptor, and playwright.

Our great-grandchildren will lack our generation's close attachment to the Impressionists because their appreciation of art will have evolved far beyond them. They themselves will want to be creators and doers, not simply the viewers of art. They might look to Jackson Pollack's abstracts and intense form of creation as their foundation for appreciating art:

"My painting does not come from the easel . . . . On the floor I am more at ease. I feel nearer, more a part of the painting, since this way I can walk around it, work from the four sides and literally be in the painting . . ."

—Jackson Pollack, in Jose Arguelles's *The Transformative Vision*

Future artists will know of Pollack not from copying him but from being immersed in his simulations. Artists will step into Pollack's point of view, he will whisper his ideas in their ears, his insights will be synchronized to the fling and swing of virtual paint on virtual canvas. They will learn from his spirit as they learn from the canvas. In the process, tomorrow's artists will leave Duchamp and Matisse behind.

The material techniques of conceptual art have all been well developed. New generations will pioneer nonmaterial, audience-inclusive creations, where the dynamic laws of reality depend on their own creative, intellectual, and spiritual maturity. As these creations appear, they will blaze a way to a new kind of conceptual and spiritual art.

Spiritual art   The crescent moon is high in the Canadian night sky. You cross the green forest floor to the red walls of a spirit lodge. As you draw closer, you begin to hear the drum beat coming from within the lodge. A coyote howls in the distance.

Passing through the open door, the drumming grows louder. There's a fire burning in the center of the lodge. Smoke escapes through the hole in the roof. You can hear soft, hypnotic chanting in time to the drum, but no one is here, just the totem obelisks, great blocks standing tall along the red walls, traditional spirit paintings sketched in vibrant Van Gogh colors.

You move down the long room under the watchful eyes of the totems. The music stays by the door. You pass the fire and the moon peeks in through the hole in the roof. You come up to the great eagle totem. It reaches over your head up to the roof, beak pointed at the moon. Suddenly the lodge shakes with the cry of an eagle. The drumming and chanting continue by the door.

Lawrence Paul, a native Canadian of the Salish tribe, created this virtual environment using the WorldToolKit software and calls it *Inherent Vision, Inherent Rights*. It's the first virtual-art world to be selected for exhibition at the National Gallery of Canada in Ottawa. As the only modern art piece of its kind, and a very high-tech one at that, it will have a unique place among the traditional Native American arts in an exhibition entitled, *Land, Spirit, and Power*.

Lawrence Paul is the first artist to use VR for the purpose of crossing cultural and religious divides to immerse other Canadians in the spiritual world in which he was raised. This is the great artistic and social potential of virtual reality—to take us into the artist's mind, into another culture, and into realms of the spirit.

The philosopher Ken Wilber notes, ". . . men and women possess at least three different modes of knowing: the eye of the Flesh which discloses the material, concrete, and sensual world; the eye of Mind which discloses the symbolic, conceptual, and linguistic world; and the eye of Contemplation which discloses the spiritual, transcendental, and transpersonal world. These are not three different worlds, but three different aspects of our one world, disclosed by different modes of knowing and perceiving."

From the Renaissance until the Impressionist period, art was mainly concerned with the eye of the Flesh, representing the real world. Modern art has focused on the eye of the Mind, using physical materials to convey nonmaterial ideas and concepts to teach people new ways to think about the world. Virtual reality provides the artist with the first purely conceptual medium for exploring not only the eye of the Mind, but evoking the spirit world as well.

The traditional painter's canvas is a two-dimensional medium: length and width. To suggest a third dimension of depth using traditional painting methods you must use Giotto's tricks of perspective, yet the result is still only two-dimensional lines on a flat page. Modern art has been limited by a constraints on expression.

Four-, five-, and six-dimensional ideas have had to suggest, hint, and inspire within the limits of two- and three-dimensional art media to create full experiences. Some have succeeded very well. Duchamp's *Nude Descending The Staircase* is both a cubist view of form, a Futurist commentary on time, a study in shattered perspective, and a statement on the use of the nude in art.

To understand the great works of conceptual art requires the viewer to expand beyond his accustomed habits of perceiving the world. You have to struggle to see what isn't there, to make a mental leap with a limited number of physical clues.

Dali's painting, *Abraham Lincoln*, reveals one image from far away—the dead president's outline appears in the picture's blurred colors. From ten feet away, details emerge and it's clear that the painting is about a nude woman with her back to the viewer looking out a window at the sea. As you step closer, still more details emerge until finally with your nose to the canvas you can see that Dali has embossed religious and spiritual symbols and figures into the fabric of the painting.

The more dimensions there are in art, the harder it is for people to make an essential initial connection to change their mind's eye so they can step into the art and let it carry them away. In its multisensory and therefore multichannel modes of communication, VR allows for art environments such as *Inherent Vision, Inherent Rights*, which asks us to see the world through a new pair of eyes; it provides multiple ways to actively discover the many possible meanings of both virtual worlds and the real world.

Environmental art

Jenny Holzer is one of the few internationally recognized artists who have made the leap from traditional art to digital art. She is now at work developing VR art worlds.

Holzer has found an accessible way to stack multiple meanings into her work by creating total environments. In 1990, she represented the United States at the Venice Biennale, one of the most prestigious international art events, where she was awarded one of the three grand prizes, the Leone d'Oro (golden lion). She was the first woman to ever receive this award. Holzer communicates ideas through phrases delivered in unconventional environments, such as:

Abuse Of Power Comes As No Surprise

Protect Me From What I Want

Murder Has Its Sexual Side

In A Dream You Saw A Way To Survive, And You Were Full Of Joy

These statements catch viewers by surprise as they flash across the baseball scoreboard at San Francisco's Candlestick Park, loom from a roadside billboard (see Fig. 13-2), peek out from a bus stand, or show up on the back of a cash register

13-2
Jenny Holzer uses provacative messages to break through the perceptual filters of passers-by, as seen by this spectra-color board in Times Square, NY (The Survival Series, 1985–1986).

receipt. Her work uses surprising and startling environments to break through viewers' informational filters.

One of the installations she created for the Venice Biennale was *The Child Room*. Biancone marble tiles cover the floor in a diamond pattern, a red marble tablet is inscribed with text, and twelve vertical, three-color LED signs hang from the wall. Her words flow up the signs like a colored fountain of ideas, reflecting against the marble and immersing the viewer in the moment.

Another time, in an installation she called *Laments*, she filled a quiet room in the Dia Art Foundation with thirteen colored LED signs and thirteen stone sarcophagi inscribed with her text. The mood was both startling and somber as the room created its own special environment.

One of her most famous installations resided inside the spiral rotunda of New York's Guggenheim Museum. Designed by Frank Lloyd Wright, the central stairway of the museum spirals up several floors to the skylight like the interior of a seashell. She lined the sides of the well with LED signs and programmed them so that the text silently swirled from the bottom, up to the skylight at the top.

Previously, other artists had hung giant mobiles in the rotunda, but no one had ever incorporated the entire rotunda in an installation before; she incorporated the building's architecture into her work of art.

In Holzer's current effort to create a virtual art world, she sees virtual reality as a way to create environments finely tuned to the emotions of her words. The virtual world she's developing will be both responsive and spontaneous, like the Coyote World project Brenda Laurel is developing.

Depending on where you go and what you do, words will reach your ears and new events will occur. Her plans are to both maximize the virtual experience and challenge it. Nearly all virtual realities create a subtle sense of control and therefore power. Events unfold depending on the VR user's directions and actions. In her work, the visual experience begins to acquire almost musical qualities of immersion, rythm, and tone.

But what happens when the virtual world takes over? What happens when the virtual world becomes as spontaneous and capricious as the real world? Or as threatening? In such unexpected moments there are breakthroughs when people's mental filters and guards drop, emotion takes over, and involvement is heightened. This is the method Holzer will use to maximize and challenge the virtual art experience.

The designers of Disneyland, the builders of cathedrals, and even the humble gardeners of Kyoto Zen gardens understand the power of the environment to influence our inner world. Using virtual reality, artists will be able to take us into their inner environments of mind and spirit. And the way is open for artists like Lawrence Paul and Jenny Holzer to pioneer the art techniques for virtual reality's full flowering.

Two people sit down in different locations and enter a room. They see each other as cubes floating in a great art gallery, along with paintings floating in space. A single eye on the side of each cube identifies the other person's point of view. In one hand they each hold a wand whose counterpart floats in the virtual art gallery.

On-line museums

Together, the two people begin a dance of creation. Touching a button on the wand, they release rippling streamers of 3-D color, tiny triangles linked in a ribbon of light like the long tail of a dragon kite. The streamers float in the air and new colors ripple down the length of the ribbons to their ends, where triangles disappear one at a time like soap bubbles popping in the wind.

3-D, spatial music moves along with the rippling color. The two people shape and paint designs together, bathing each other in color and music. They fly into and through their temporary creations, working together to create art that lasts only moments.

This simulation, called the *Artroom*, was created by Sense8. It teases the viewer with the potential of this new media. Instead of music, the wands can release words or the cry of birds; whatever the artist wants.

The technology of computers will allow artists to express visual experience in terms of music, and to give any medium the function and properties of another: sound can have saturation and color can have duration and rhythm.

VR artists will involve us in journeys by linking images, places, and events; layering words; painting with music; and singing with pictures in a rhythmic stream of consciousness to carry us to the epiphany of their insights.

And to see these works of art won't require a trip to a distant country; art created on computer will be available on-line. Virtual art galleries will be open to anyone with access to the network. New wings of the museum will mean additional memory instead of new buildings.

A glimpse of this future is underway at Carnegie Mellon University (CMU). A research team is developing long-distance networked virtual art spaces. The first project is an art museum that's accessible over 9600-baud modem lines from two sites, one on the CMU campus in Pittsburgh, and the other in Japan. The first public test of the system was successfully staged in September 1992, between CMU and a VR conference in Germany.

The first wing of the museum will be a Renaissance-perspective exhibition. It's being designed on Sense8 WorldToolKit software by a team led by Atsu Shiga, president of Interactive Management Associates in Tokyo. From Intel486 CPU-based PCs at CMU, users will be able to dial in over a modem, tour the galleries, and dive into 3-D representations of each painting.

In another wing of the on-line museum, multiple users can enter together and take on the personas of characters (such as Batman and Frankenstein) to wander through a funhouse. In a hall of mirrors, their images are warped, twisted, and scaled in real time as they move in front of the twisted mirrors. In another room, they can pick up a ball with their VR gloves, toss it, and watch as it bounces. There's a merry-go-round that they can grab onto as it's moving, climb onboard, and be swung around the room.

CMU has a number of large research programs devoted to networking, multimedia, and virtual reality. Carl Loeffler, the VR project director, has been able to borrow resources from various teams as a result of the open atmosphere of CMU.

Several programmers from Bellcore, who are on campus researching broadband telecommunications, donated some of their time to solving the long-distance telecommunications problems of virtual reality. CMU's multimedia group has created another idea for a VR project.

"There is an Egyptologist working here on a multimedia application, cataloging thousands of Egyptian artifacts," Carl Loeffler says. "He is cross-referencing pictures and text and artwork to provide a new kind of art history database. He also has AutoCAD files detailing the structure and layout of all the great temples of ancient Egypt."

"Using artists' recreations of what the temples looked like when in full flower, we are going to recreate them in virtual reality so that groups of people can tour the temples and study the art in a way that approximates what it really was like thousands of years ago."

Another pioneer is Nicole "Natalie" Stenger. She has created the first VR art movie, *Angels*. It was originally commissioned by the Paris Museum of Science for its show, Machines a Communiquer (June 1992). To view the movie you need to wear goggles and a VPL DataGlove.

Each visitor begins his journey to paradise by standing in front of a surreal merry-go-round that looks like a temple. Instead of horses on this merry-go-round, however, the symbolic hearts of angels spin around. Touch one and you're transported into a world. In each world a different story evolves between you and an angel, using a simple form of communications between the angel's voice and your hand gestures.

Everything in these worlds invites the user to touch. For example, touching one angel's heart causes him to spin colors and new environments out of crystals that float around him. Two angels ask to be united because they are in love and their union causes a dual-flame, dual-heart angel.

In Stenger's virtual world, she purposely eliminated any effectiveness from grabbing gestures; to communicate with angels you have to softly touch their hearts. The angels were modeled using Wavefront software on an SGI Iris workstation and will be making their debut on a VPL system with high-resolution HRX goggles.

These first virtual art works are only the beginning of what's possible. They are a series of suggestions. How far can this theater of experience go? In San Francisco, Bryan Hughes and the Renaissance Foundation are designing a virtual children's opera based on Alice in Wonderland.

Each participating child will become one of the characters: Alice, The Mad Hatter, the Red Queen, Humpty Dumpty, etc. They'll find a world that's alive and responsive, much like Brenda Laurel's Coyote World project. Enter a room and a caterpillar will talk to you, walking through a garden might trigger music, pick up a bottle and it will say, "Drink Me." The familiarity of the Wonderland myth will help children become quickly comfortable with the situation and create new ways of using what they find there.

Because everyone will be a character, Hughes believes that the experience will teach children to look beyond someone's face to find out who they really are inside. It will teach them not to depend on stereotypes and differences based on race. Shy children will be more likely to express themselves and participate because they feel safe.

He also wants to set up VR workshops for children from all walks of life. Someday a white businessman will be able to spend time in the art world of a black child and "walk in his shoes" to experience how the child sees the world.

Perhaps the most immediate way to get a taste, a hint of where virtual art worlds will take us in the next century is by watching Akira Kurosawa's film, *Dreams*. In one section of the film, an art patron is walking through a museum gallery. He stops to admire a series of Van Gogh paintings. Suddenly he notices that a fellow patron has disappeared. Then he sees her wandering around inside the paintings. Intrigued, he too manages to step inside the paintings and journey through all of Van Gogh's brilliant art. He becomes disoriented and lost until he meets the artist working in the middle of a cadmium yellow field.

For a moment, step into this dream yourself. Close your eyes and go inside and imagine the brilliant yellow of a Van Gogh field. Walk around in the field; move your feet amid the luminous colors and see trees churning in the distance. Can you recall the thin black line of a crow flying overhead in a cobalt blue sky?

Does being *in* the field bring back some of the special feelings that seeing the real art creates? Imagine how much more intense those feelings would be if you could put on a pair of VR goggles and actually go for a walk through a Van Gogh countryside and meet the artist—possibly even become the artist!

This is the emotional and spiritual potential of virtual reality when it's used for art. It represents a fundamental shift in art, a new kind of 3-D environment through which any content can be expressed, and space and time can be bent. It's a medium for which every expression has multiple perspectives, where media is content, content is media, and viewing becomes doing.

A new art form

The variety of virtual art projects suggests many new ways of thinking about the world. By taking on various characters and socializing in art worlds, people might become more tolerant of the differences between themselves and others. The ability to simulate and quickly change the worlds we play in should make us more aware of the transient nature, the illusion of the permanence in the real world.

Einstein taught us that our experience of reality was relative, that what we know depends on our point of view, our position in time. All our experiences are designed and shaped first by the circumstances of the moment, secondly by our senses, and thirdly by the filters and attitudes of our minds.

Virtual reality drives this point home again and again. Each world is a designed experience and each experience is a learning situation. VR will change the way we think as it turns our thoughts into commodities and artifacts we can share or sell to others.

Just as the alphabet and printing press changed the way people thought, virtual reality will shape our notions of community, self, space, and time. The future is arriving; it's happening at computer arcade shopping malls, inside software and hardware companies, and in artist's lofts.

By using a full spectrum of artistic techniques, including painting, theater, film, and music, VR artists will merge together all art forms. They'll simulate as well as stimulate mental and emotional states and experiences and make possible the emergence of a new holistic art experience of the mind.

The term *virtual reality* doesn't do justice to what this art form can accomplish. Perhaps a new word, like *visualmusic*, is a more appropriate, creative name for virtual art experiences. It suggests the blending of the senses, fluidness of forms, and mixing of all the arts.

The next generation 14

Just like the Wright Brothers' airplanes, today's VR technology is crude compared to what can be envisioned, but it's good enough to get us off the ground and into the air for an exciting experience. To try and predict what the future trends of virtual reality are going to be, you must put it in context: we're in the barnstorming days of VR when it's possible for almost anyone to jump in and make a contribution.

The next few years are going to see rapid growth and development in virtual-reality applications and hardware. Eventually, in the next century internationally networked VR, or cyberspace, might become a reality. But as VR becomes a part of our culture, there are serious questions that need to be asked about the consequences of turning experience into a commodity. We need a new literacy for this new age of experiential information.

VR is being championed by a small group of inventors, artists, and software programmers who enjoy using their inventions and enjoy improving them. Unlike Artificial Intelligence (AI), which also received a lot of public attention early in its life, VR's limitations are bound more by computing power than by a lack of understanding.

This is the key difference between AI and VR. Early AI developers assumed that what was easy for a human to do would also be easy for a computer. But it turned out to be the opposite. A computer can do things that are very hard for people, such as complex mathematics. But skills a two year old has mastered, such as recognizing a face or an object on a plate, has been a 40-year struggle for AI-based systems.

VR doesn't require a major breakthrough in software or in our understanding of how the brain works. Like the dynamics of the Wright Brother's plane—the wings, motor, and steering—all the major components of VR already work. Continuing the industry's growth is mostly an issue of delivering graphics at higher resolution for less money. Where we go with VR is more important than how we build it.

The experience industry

The invention of the phonograph and its mass distribution created a means of reproducing music that had never existed before. Previously, each community had its own bands and orchestras that reproduced the music of the leading composers of the day.

Phonographs allowed the band, composer, or singer to create copies of their own work for sale. They could now sell their talents directly to their mass audience. This allowed lovers of music to create and control their own private worlds of music in the same fashion that books allow readers to create their own private world of ideas.

Today, the music industry is one of the biggest forms of entertainment in the world, providing a common link among diverse people through the shared experience of music. This same type of commoditization occurred with the visual experience as photography evolved into movies, which were followed by TV and VCRs. Sales of cameras, camcorders, video tapes, and VCRs have led to personal libraries of movies and still images.

Over 100 million personal computers have been built and distributed in just over a decade of their existence. More than 20 million are built each year now. And the technology trends of the computer and telecommunications industries are converging. In the course of the 1990s, all forms of media are going to become available on personal-computer-based knowledge stations: video, digital photography, text, and audio.

Think of the personal computer as the phonograph of the 21st century. By combining it with telecommunications and compact-disc digital technology, the stage is set for the creation of a new kind of home theater—a personal library of experience.

In the near future, artists will create virtual art and entertainment worlds for public consumption. These experiences will range from very linear, passive experiences (movies delivered like a Disney Star Tours ride), to nonlinear worlds alive with interactive insights and delights.

These will be worlds you can return to again and again for new surprises and discoveries. They might be delivered over fiber-optic phone lines or conveyed on compact disc. Artwork will be replayed in a digital format that faithfully recreates it as it was intended. This will provide artists with a level of public acceptance and financial reward historically unavailable.

There are implications in this idea of an industry of experience that suggest a gradual but major shift in our culture. Five hundred years ago Giotto changed the way we look at the world by creating a 3-D point of view in static paintings. Five hundred years ago books began to make ideas a widely available commodity.

VR will make experience a commodity and an artifact we can buy and sell, preserve and share. Rather than leading to a homogenized culture, we might be heading for an even more fragmented and individualist society, as people go beyond championing their own particular point of view to emphasizing their particular experience.

Within one hundred years virtual reality could become a semi-invisible service in society, like telephones, light switches, books, and television—a tool for communication, work, and pleasure that we use without hardly thinking about it. We need to know what we're reaching for before it becomes so commonplace that we relate to it unconsciously.

The VR industry is set to experience a period of rapid growth and innovation over the next thirty to forty years. But in the near term, VR firms struggle to exist in a small but growing market. As of mid-1992, we estimate that only 300 head-tracked, fully immersive VR systems exist in the entire world, as shown in Fig. 14-1.

Near-term growth

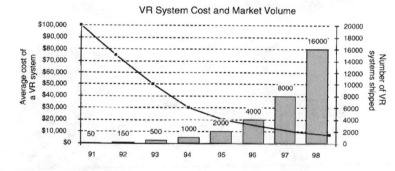

14-1
Estimated growth in number of VR systems sold each year and the declining cost of the sytems.

This estimate is based on data from other industry watchers, including data from VPL Research, Sense8, and other VR companies. Even if you assume that the market will double every year, it probably won't be very large for quite some time. And it's anybody's guess what the VR market will look like by 1995. This growth curve could be seriously altered upward by the emergence of a major computer maker into the market. Today, all the firms are small pioneer developers.

The growth in VR systems will be driven by steadily increasing graphics performance at lower and lower prices. As this technology becomes more affordable and useful, the market will begin to expand and drive costs down even further.

Long before the workplace accepts VR, the entertainment industry will become the driving force behind VR's introduction to the public. The limitation of today's low-end technology isn't a factor for VR game systems. They're selling the excitement of the experience.

On the other hand, acceptance of VR in the workplace will require at least a magnitude increase in both graphics performance and HMD resolution. This should occur by 1995 as color VGA-quality goggles become available for around $1,000 and PCs with ten times the performance of today's systems become affordable.

An affordable PC-based VR system, with the power of today's more expensive systems, should be available for less than $7500. Along with a powerful set of software tools, VR can begin solving problems for architects, scientists, and professionals from many different businesses.

What we can't foresee is what the Japanese are going to do; they're the wildcard in the forecast. The large Japanese corporations (Sharp, NEC, Toshiba, etc.) are driving screen technology towards higher resolution and improved color. Palmtops or the new PDAs (personal data assistants) might provide a volume market for LCD screens of the appropriate size and resolution to make personal data goggles affordable (see Fig. 14-2).

Work by Reflection Technology and Sun Microsystems on a portable workstation/resolution-display screen that clips onto a pair of glasses might also challenge the dominance of LCD displays. Any number of technologies could lead to the introduction of goggles with acceptable resolution that would cost only a few hundred dollars by 1996. We don't expect this to be an isolated offering, but rather part of a packaged introduction of a home entertainment system.

14-2
From NEC's Advanced Design group comes this futuristic version of a wearable VR system that could be used as a portable data terminal.

The first company to market a system that offers compelling, interactive experiences will potentially reap big rewards. Virtual reality systems might provide the consumer pull to create a new computer platform. The first systems that sell will create the critical mass volume to drive prices down and make the goggles and hardware widely affordable. The late 1990s will see a battle for the home VR market similar to the VCR battles of the early 1980s.

At that point, composers of virtual experiences and applications will begin to work out of their homes developing applications, just like the early software program developers did for the Apple I.

The big news by 1995 will be in entertainment arcades. The computer revolution first reached the public with the introduction of Pong. By the late 1970s the video arcade revolution was in full swing. The pattern is repeating itself. Already the computer-game manufacturers are rushing out 3-D games they claim are virtual reality.

VR arcades are going to come in and blow away the 2-D computer-arcade game business in much the same way Pong and Pac-man displaced pinball machines. This process will familiarize many people with virtual reality so that, as home systems appear in the second half of the 1990s, there will be consumers eagerly awaiting them.

Virtual reality is a power-hungry proposition. Today, it runs on systems that cost from $20,000 to $200,000 and beyond. At a minimum, powerful desktop computers are required for even low-end VR systems. For example, using an Intel486 CPU-based PC and a special graphics board, textured worlds of 300–400 polygons can be displayed at 10–15 frames per second. Even with this power, the world appears cartoonish with a hint of visual lag as you move your head about.

Computer power

At the high end of the VR business, Silicon Graphics Inc. (SGi) announced a $100,000 RealityEngine in July of 1992, which was advertised as a solution for sophisticated VR applications. In doing so, SGi became the first computer company to market a product emphasizing its use for virtual environments.

The RealityEngine is designed to create fully textured worlds at 30 frames per second. The fully configured system is capable of 600,000 textured polygons per second. This impressive performance requires eight Intel i860 RISC CPUs, four raster, and 20 low-level graphics processors. To achieve the utmost sophistication in representing colors, 36 bits per pixel are used instead of the 24 normally associated with high-quality "true-color" displays (a standard PC rarely has more than 8 bits per pixel, allowing it to display 256 different colors).

It also includes other features, like a staggering 160 megabytes of video RAM, compared with one to two megabytes on many desktop PCs. With technology like this, the distinction between what's real and what's virtual begins to blur just slightly.

One of the first applications of the RealityEngine was creating a virtual model of the riot-torn neighborhoods of South Central Los Angeles. Bill Jepson, director of computing at the Graduate School of Architecture and Urban Planning at UCLA, along with several students, created an 80-square-block representation of the area, showing how it looked before the riots.

They combined aerial photos with scores of personally collected photographs to accurately depict how each building looked. Next, the pictures were scanned into the computer and mapped onto the appropriate surface of each 3-D cube that represented a building. This detailed model was then linked with information on zoning, traffic flow, and population data.

As you flew over this virtual neighborhood, you could highlight all the liquor stores in red, or find out who owned which building and what its assessed value was. Applications like this, currently running on powerful graphics workstations, will eventually be possible on your desktop computer in five or six years.

What will home VR be able to do in 2001? That will depend on what kind of microprocessors are at the heart of affordable computers. Intel's plans are driven by an internal vision of what the microprocessor of the year 2000 can be (see Fig. 14-3).

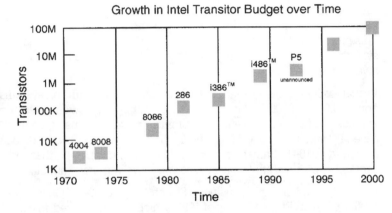

14-3

Moore's law states that the technology that microprocessors are developed on doubles in complexity (as measured in transistors) every couple of years. Intel's series of microprocessors demonstrate this trend.

Called the Micro 2000 project, it envisions a microprocessor with 80–100 million transistors on a single piece of silicon. It will have four processing units on the same chip running like a parallel supercomputer. The speed of this chip will be 250MHz and, with complex circuitry and four processors on board, it will execute over two billion instructions per second!

Besides processing units, the chip will very likely have special circuitry for graphics and digital video, based on the DVI technology already in use in IBM's Ultimedia machines and Sense8's virtual-reality systems.

Virtual reality simulations that run on this kind of chip will be unlike anything in today's applications. Photo-realistic imagery in VR worlds will be possible. Speech recognition will be widely used to input and receive information and commands. New devices and modes of interaction will be available. It's even possible that your gestures will be monitored by a pair of small TV cameras and converted into meaningful signals to the computer and to the VR system.

The display system of choice in the 21st century might not be a pair of lightweight VR "sunglasses." Instead, homes might have their own media room. The first media-room prototype has been developed at the Electronic Visualization Lab of the University of Illinois in Chicago. In research papers it's known as the Audio-Visual Experience Automatic Virtual Environment, but the team calls it the CAVE.

The CAVE is a cube with display screens on all six sides. Stereo images are displayed by six Silicon Graphics VGX workstations that drive individual rear-projection displays. Everything is controlled over an Ethernet network with an SGI Personal Iris system acting as a master controller.

The user of this system wears liquid-crystal glasses that shutter at a rapid rate to trick the eyes into seeing the 3-D stereo worlds. The user's head position is tracked by a Polhemus ISOTRAK sensor mounted on the glasses.

There are already several worlds you can literally walk into with the CAVE and explore. The Cosmic Explorer is a combination of stored database images and real-time CRAY computations allowing a viewer to fly through and explore the Great Wall (a supercluster of galaxies over 500 million light years in length). Like Carl Sagan in his PBS series *Cosmos*, the viewer is able to walk the length of the Great Wall and zoom in on individual galaxies.

Another application allows a user to create a weather system over part of North America and be inside the storm to study it. Yet another application developed by the University's Biomedical Visualization Lab is a trip through a human fetus via simulation.

The quality of simulation available on systems twenty years from now will allow the quality of the animation in Terminator 2 to be a reality on desktop computers. Today, Hollywood stars like Elizabeth Taylor license their name and photographic image to clothing and perfume merchandisers. In the next century, they'll license their face, body, voice—their digitized persona.

Artists like Michael Jackson, Madonna, and the Grateful Dead might continue to perform in VR simulations. New music, new movies, new simulations will be created that incorporate their digital images. Fifty to one hundred years from now virtual realty users worldwide might be communicating over vast networks. At that point William Gibson's cyberspace will stop being science fiction and will become reality.

"Cyberspace: The tablet become a page become a screen become a world, a virtual world . . . . A new universe, a parallel universe created and sustained by the world's computers and communications lines. A world in which global traffic of knowledge, secrets, measurements, indicators, entertainments, and alter-human agency takes on form: sights, sounds, presences never seen on the surface of the earth . . ."

—Michael Benedikt, *Cyberspace: First Steps,* **1992**

Cyberspace

Cyberspace. A term coined in the novel *Neuromancer*, by William Gibson. It's an imaginary computer world and a word that stands for a kind of computer network that doesn't yet exist. Cyberspace has been envisioned as the fully accessible sum total of all the interconnected computer networks spanning the globe.

It's a word with mythic power. A global computer network with the completeness and openness of the telephone system, but instead of just an auditory experience it's multisensory. Instead of listening on the phone you fly into the network. In

Gibson's vision, it's an alternate universe, a computer dimension of reality you can enter via special virtual-reality machines.

At the University of Central Florida in Orlando, the Institute of Simulation and Training is working on the problems of large-scale networked simulations. Started in 1988 by Director Michael Moshell, it carries out research and development projects in computer simulations, as well as training a new generation of virtual world builders.

They've taken on projects for a wide range of clients, but their most impressive customer is SIMNET, the U.S. military's giant battle simulator. More than anywhere else, SIMNET is where the first steps into cyberspace are being taken.

In two huge warehouses, one in Kentucky and the other in Germany, over 250 tank simulators train personnel. The job here isn't to learn how to drive, but how to fight, win, and survive. The two centers can be networked over satellite so different numbers of tanks can fight with or against each other. Not only can the computers be networked together, but they can simulate fake Russian tanks (and helicopters) so well that the drivers are never certain whether they're engaged against the computer or other people.

This giant network is the testing ground that will result in software tools and solutions for wide-area networked VR. How do you keep all the stations updated in real time? If one tank fires a missile, how do the other tanks get an accurate perspective of the missile's trajectory and speed reflective of their position and proximity to the launch? How do you design very realistic, networked worlds with lots of variety in the terrain?

"A big challenge we're working on is figuring out how to do dynamic terrain," says Brian Blau, a software researcher at the Institute. "If a tank fires a shot in SIMNET there is no crater left when it hits the ground. If I have a bulldozer and it puts its blade down, I want it to leave a trench as it pushes dirt in front of it."

"For more useful and realistic simulations a car should leave tracks when it drives through the mud. This is a feature no one ever thought about adding before to a computer simulation. You can easily imagine some day a construction company will use such a feature to train bulldozer drivers. Or, Caterpillar may want to test new farm equipment designs by putting several farmers in simulators and having them plant a virtual field together."

Many companies are still in the experimental mode with networked virtual reality. Boeing wants to make it another design tool for engineers working on the in-house network so they can tour their work as it grows. NEC is installing a virtual-reality network to see how designers can collaborate together in a virtual design environment.

In Nottingham, England, anyone can take their first step into cyberspace by visiting *Legend Quest* (see Fig. 14-4). Based on W-Industries virtuality stations, it's a very elaborate Dungeon and Dragons world for four players. What raises this game above being a simple extension of computer gaming and into the fringes of cyberspace is the new identities the players assume (or *digidentities*, as George Coates would say).

14-4
Legend Quest, based on the W Industries Virtuality machine, is the first role-playing VR game that has been developed. Each person in the game assumes a character.

Each player selects an identity from eighteen different characters: an elf, human, or dwarf of either gender whose profession is wizard, thief, or warrior. You can personalize characters by adjusting them to match your real height and hair color. According to the choice of persona, the player's voice is modified as well by passing it through an electronic filter.

A database behind the scenes keeps track of players' progress and attributes, and when they return to the game they resume playing right where they left off. In the game, the team of four meet monsters who are based on simple AI learning techniques, so they behave differently on different occasions and the game is never played the same way twice.

Just like the characters in Gibson's *Neuromancer*, Legend Quest players leave their bodies behind and assume new personalities in virtual reality. They go questing for wealth and knowledge across the network and into software worlds. To be free in such a virtual world is very exciting. There's sense of control over new powers and a new body, whether flying or casting a magical spell.

Yet it's also intimate and safe. People's responses resemble how they behave on the telephone. You share a sense of presence with the characters even though they appear as living cartoons before your eyes. Like being at a play or reading a good book, you become absorbed, but you know you can leave if it gets too uncomfortable.

Young people, those who have grown up with computer arcades and home Nintendo systems, readily figure out how to interact with these systems—they expect to interact. Older people, baby boomers, and the TV generation sit and wait to be told—they seem used to getting their data passively.

The day when people will hook up to and enter a globally networked virtual-reality universe is at least 50 to 100 years away. William Gibson's vision of people directly plugging their central nervous systems into a computer might always remain a fantasy. It's just too complex. And our five senses already provide a natural connection into our brains.

Although there are hundreds of VR enthusiasts who look forward to the day they can enter cyberspace, it's questionable if the rest of the public will feel the same way. The technology for delivering videophone service to the home has existed for thirty years, yet even now it has yet to be adopted.

There are other cultures that judge social changes not in terms of years, but in terms of generations. Just as television and video games have raised a generation of children ready to adopt computer technology, a generation that seems to feel instantly at home with virtual reality, it might take several generations before the public is ready for cyberspace.

A new literacy

The alphabet was created as a coding system to allow people to share their internal thoughts and realities without having to meet. Reading and writing created a form of external, nonperishable memory, one that retained its original information despite additional events. It became much easier to go back and compare new ideas to previous ones, to shape and refine an idea over time. Ideas could be quickly communicated, and copies could be made and distributed across boundaries, time zones, and cultures.

What we don't have from the early days of writing is a good record of the resistance or the social upheaval caused by the appearance of this new technology. How did Homer and the other Greek bards feel about having their stories written down? They depended on memory to store their sagas, and interaction with the audience to influence the telling. Did they argue that writing was destroying their culture?

What about the average merchant—did he change the way he did business? It took many generations for the use of writing to spread, and even in modern times there are vast numbers of people who never learn to read or write. But it has changed the world by changing the way people think even without everyone using it. What will VR's impact be?

Literacy means more than the ability to read and write, though these are its most basic requirements. Reading allows for reflection and contemplation about the ideas on a page. What does the writer mean? What is he trying to convince me of? What are the implications of these ideas to other ideas, institutions, and people—to me and my life? Do I agree or disagree?

Meredith Bricken, a research scientist with the HIT lab in Seattle Washington, points out that reading and writing are basically cognitive functions, but virtual reality is both cognitive and behavioral. The act of participating in a simulated world involves us physically, visually, emotionally, magically, and rationally in organized and spontaneous events.

Learning and understanding in a virtual environment involves you very differently than in an alphabet-based curriculum. The educational theorist, S. Papert, expressed the value of visual mental experience to learning in his 1980 book, *Mindstorms*:

"If you can *be* a gear, you can understand how it turns by projecting yourself into its place and turning with it . . . . As well as connecting with the formal knowledge of mathematics, it also connects with the body knowledge, the sensory-motor schemata of a child. It is this double relationship—both abstract and sensory—that gives a transitional object the power to carry mathematics into the mind."

Every virtual environment is an educational environment. VR was originally nurtured and developed by the military as an evolution of flight simulators, to train pilots and help them manage the information required to fly today's complex aircraft. Every simulation steps the user through a series of activities with rewards and penalties of various degrees—we learn by doing.

Someday teachers will be able to take students to the bottom of the ocean without leaving their classroom. Students will play with atoms and make their own molecules in VR to experience chemistry, instead of just reading about it. The development and widespread use of VR raises valid concerns about what we will teach ourselves and our children in these simulations. Optimistically, it will lead to a revolution in teaching and learning. Students will acquire a sense of control over knowledge.

But what about the violence of video games? Will home VR systems teach children to all be Mutant Ninja Turtles? There's a striking difference between the passive viewing of violence on television and being invited to spend hours hunting and shooting opponents in a virtual game.

When the context is a simulation it might be that adults are able to make the moral distinction between reality and fantasy, but what about children? How old is old enough to appreciate the difference when you're immersed in a world of 3-D sound and color and the enemy is attacking? Ray Bradbury asked this question allegorically over 30 years ago in his horror tale of a future virtual reality-like media room, *The Veldt*.

Will the military's use of VR lead to desensitized soldiers who fight video game wars, never seeing the enemy? The use of VR, computers, and telepresence in war could shield people from the disturbing consequences of their actions. It could also save lives by removing people from the battlefield.

It's dangerous, of course, to jump to conclusions too quickly, to look at the individual isolated from home, family, society and work, as if he is devoid of free will and easily influenced by every media message. More study and debate is needed in this area.

Some critics are ready to denounce virtual reality as a mind-numbing, brainwashing technology that will homogenize culture. The same fears were raised forty years ago with the emergence of television. These are valid concerns—even after 40 years the public debate continues over the numbing and conditioning effects of violence on television—but this is a debate over content, not technology.

As the debate on TV focuses on the negative, the global impact of television is often overlooked. TV has also lived up to its early promise of linking and communicating with vast areas of the world formerly isolated from each other.

Rather than homogenization, televised international communication seems to have lead to an increase in democratic institutions and individuality as demonstrated by the upheaval in Eastern Europe and the recent events in China.

Just as reading and writing can be used for propaganda, pleasure, or critical analysis, so too can VR. VR can be used to educate, train, and make us more aware of our own behavior. The alphabet allows writers and readers to carefully study thoughts and ideas, and virtual reality will allow the same critical analysis of behavior.

Virtual reality, however, will bring about the need for a new kind of literacy, one that is behaviorally based as well as cognitively based. When a designer constructs a world, he'll be forced to consider the actions he's taking a user through.

The implications are that it might force society and culture as a whole to become aware of the messages and meanings in someone's behavior as well as his words. Worlds will be designed (probably first by artists) that attack the potential in virtual reality for abuse and make us aware of our own unconscious habits and behaviors.

Like the Holodeck on *Star Trek: The Next Generation*, future VR might become vast libraries of experience that will be as accessible as opening a door. We'll shift through different points of view, considering ideas and events from several vantage points and personalities.

The founding fathers of the United States had very different points of view about what course the country's development should take. How would it be to study American history first from John Adams' point of view, then Thomas Jefferson and George Washington, before switching to King George for the English side of story? Then the insights of Native Americans, indentured servants, merchants, and slaves.

In the distant future, computers might become powerful enough that spoken ideas can be fully virtualized for sharing with other people on vast networks of computers. The computer will convert our words into simulations as we talk over a network, bringing our visions to life before our eyes.

Twenty years ago, Alan Kay, considered by many to be the conceptual father of the personal computer, developed a singular vision of what computers could contribute. He was inspired by the insights of Marshal McLuhan. It was the sum total of McLuhan's writings that changed the way Kay looked at computers from a tool into a medium. Out of this came his inspiration for the *dynabook*:

"The intensely interactive and involving nature of the personal computer seemed an antiparticle that could annihilate the passive boredom invoked by television. What kind of thinker would you become if you grew up with an active simulator connected, not just to one point of view, but to all the points of view of the ages represented so they could be dynamically tried out and compared? I named the note-book sized computer idea the Dynabook to capture McLuhan's metaphor in the silicon to come."

—Alan Kay, *User Interface: A Personal View*, 1991

Virtual reality-based computers are laying the foundation to finally deliver on Kay's vision. They're part of a paradigm shift as our civilization comes to terms with the powerful new information tools it has developed. As we learn to harness the power of virtual reality, we'll be moving from an information-based age to a knowledge age, in which the information serves us.

Like a child with a new toy on Christmas, who runs excitedly around the house imagining all the different things the toy can do, we too are trying to figure out what to do with our bright, shiny toy. Though virtual reality has many potential uses, it will take innovation, dedication, and a little bit of imagination to change the toy into a variety of tools.

VR is off the ground and flying at last, but the journey has just begun.

Appendices

Product resource guide

There are many different methods and devices for building virtual environments. In chapter 5, *Reality engines*, you learned about the basic components of a VR system and how, working in concert, they create simulated 3-D worlds. In chapter 8, *Gloves, goggles, & wands*, you learned how dozens of different devices and sensors function and are used in these same simulations.

In this appendix, pictures and specifications will provide interesting detail on many of the products and prototypes developed for virtual reality. By looking through this information, you might be amazed at the variety of methods that have already evolved. If you're interested in applying virtual environment technology, then this guide will become an invaluable resource in learning about the state of the current technology.

In several cases, we've estimated specifications due to lack of information from the manufacturer. Because there's no standard on how any of this information is measured, we'll caution you not to take any of these values too literally. Hopefully, this will change as several research labs begin reporting independent results—but for now, be aware of the problem. For up-to-date information, including the latest pricing, you can contact the manufacturers, listed in appendix B.

This guide is organized into similar sections as presented in previous chapters. The first part is a summary of available VR systems, or software packages. The second part covers most of the output and input sensors currently available.

Instead of a list of all products that claim to be virtual reality, we'll once again impose the description of VR used at the beginning of chapter 5, *Reality engines*. We'll stick to describing products that support head-tracked, head-mounted displays, and stereo views, and are commercially available as of mid-1992. In addition, we'll limit the list to products that are based on real-time 3-D renderers.

This narrows the field to the major VR companies that produce 95% of the systems installed in labs and businesses all across the world. There are many other companies, such as Autodesk, that intend to enter the VR business but haven't released a product at the time this book was written.

You can expect the list to grow quite a bit longer in the next couple of years. Also, keep in mind that many of the manufacturers listed here offer many more products and features than there is space to describe, so please contact them for up-to-date prices and information.

Division
Product: PROvision
HW platform: Custom, Intel i860, and INMOS Transputer
Graphics: 35,000 Gouraud-shaded, Z-buffered polygons/sec
Cost: $50,000-$200,000
Comments: Options include VPL DataGlove, stereo HMD, and stereo audio imaging of the virtual world. Provides a C-language toolkit (dVS) for creating custom virtual worlds.

Sense8 Corp.
Product: WorldToolKit
HW platform: PC, Sun, and SGi
Graphics: Varies with hardware
Cost: $3,500-$12,500
Comments: A C library of over 250 functions that support interfacing to many of the common VR devices, such as HMDs, 3-D and MIDI sound, force balls, networking, etc. Reads DXF and other model files and generates stereo, real-time, texture-mapped 3-D images.

W Industries
Model: Virtuality
HW platform: Amiga and TI 34020 graphics accelerators
Graphics: 15,000 flat-shaded, transformed polygons/sec
Cost: $60,000 (varies)
Comments: This includes a Visette HMD, wired-glove, Polhemus ISOTRAK, and the necessary hardware and software for developing virtual worlds.

VPL Research Inc.
Model: RB2 Professional (Reality Built for 2)
HW platform: SGi (also requires a Macintosh)
Graphics: Varies with hardware
Cost: $65,000
Comments: Includes DataGlove, EyePhone LX, 6 DOF sensor, and the necessary software (Swivel 3D, Body Electric, and Isaac) to build and animate virtual worlds. SGi and Macintosh hardware is not included.

VPL Research

Model: Microcosm
HW platform: Macintosh with Division graphics boards
Graphics: 35,000 Gouraud-shaded, Z-buffered polygons/sec
Cost: $75,000
Comments: Includes DataGlove XVR, EyePhone XVR, 6 DOF sensor, and the necessary software (Swivel 3D, Body Electric, and Isaac) to build and animate virtual worlds. Includes a Macintosh Quadra 900 and graphics accelerator boards from Division. Planned for shipment in mid-1992.

Output

These sensors provide either sight, sound, or haptic sensory output. They are intended to provide participants with particular sensory cues regarding the virtual world. We first review head-mounted displays, then some other related display technologies, then 3-D sound systems and various methods of generating tactile or force feedback.

Head-mounted displays

The following products and prototypes are designed to be worn on the head and work with various head-tracking sensors. This list represents the more well-known HMD developers in the VR community. HMD resolution, expense, and usability remains the greatest barrier to the rapid acceptance of VR technology in business and home applications.

Advanced Technology Systems/V.R.G.

Model: VRG HMD (see Fig. A-1)
Resolution: Monochrome CRT, 1280×1024
Weight: 2.5 lbs
Field of view: 50 H, custom optics
Video in: NTSC or RGB
Cost: $60,000
Comments: Working on a 1280×1024 color CRT version, due late 1992. This same helmet is sold by both ATS and VRG as it was jointly developed.

A-1
ATS head-mounted display.

CAE-Electronics Ltd.

Model: FOHMD (see Fig. A-2)
Imaging: Fiber optics, color light valves, color CRT
Resolution: 1,000×1,000
Weight: 5.0-6.0 lbs

Field of view: Up to 127H×66V, Pancake Window optics
Video in: NTSC or RGB
Cost: $250,000-$1,000,000
Comments: Top-of-the-line HMD. High resolution and wide field of view with higher resolution inserted at center of view. Designed for simulator use only. Uses 4,000,000-element fiber-optic bundles. Four overhead sensors are directed at 6 helmet-mounted LEDs to determine head position and orientation.

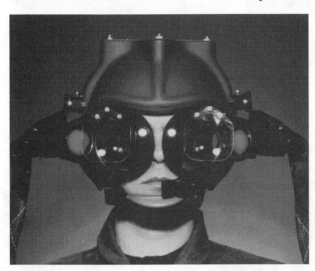

A-2
FOHMD.

Kaiser Aerospace
Model: Wide Eye (see Fig. A-3)
Resolution: Monochrome CRT, 525/875/1024 lines of vertical resolution
Weight: 3.8 lbs
Field of view: 40V×60H, custom optics
Video in: RGB
Cost: $50,000
Comments: Primarily used as a HUD targeting system in helicopters and fighter jets. Working on a lower-cost commercial version that will be based on the Tektronix color CRT. Due in early 1993.

A-3
Wide Eye head-mounted display.

LEEP Systems Inc.
Model: Cyberface 2 (see Fig. 8-5, pg. 110 for an example)
Resolution: Color LCD, 479×234 elements
Weight: 4.25 lbs
Field of view: 140H, LEEP optics
Video in: NTSC, PAL, or RGB
Cost: $8,100

Comments: Counterbalance is worn on front of person like a bib. Largest field of view of any HMD. Requires image correction to use properly.

NASA/John Hopkins Medical Institutions

Model: LVES (see Fig. A-4)
Resolution: Monochrome CRT, 500×500 (est.)
Weight: 1 lb
Field of view: 80 H (est.), custom optics
Video in: NTSC
Cost: Prototype, (estimated $3,000 by 1995)
Comments: Designed for those with serious visual impairment, but not blind. The design includes a single monochrome camera integrated into the front of the housing and a battery pack for portability.

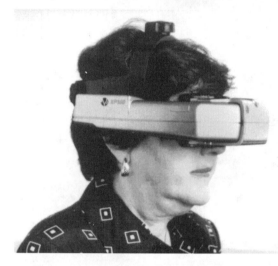

A-4
NASA/Johns Hopkins head-mounted display.

Polhemus Labs

Model: Looking Glass, prototype (see Fig. 8-9, pg. 113 for an example)
Resolution: 4- to 8-foot fiber-optic cables, 500×500 TV line pairs
Weight: 0.88 lbs
Field of view: 40H, custom optics
Video in: NTSC or RGB
Cost: $35,000-50,000
Comments: Requires interface to 200-300 foot-lamberts image sources (very bright). Lowest-weight HMD yet built. Polhemus Labs is not related to Polhemus Inc. (though they were started by the same person).

Virtual Research

Model: VR Flight Helmet (see Fig. A-5)
Resolution: Color LCD, 360×240 elements
Weight: 3.7 lbs
Field of view: 90-100H, LEEP optics
Video in: NTSC
Cost: $6,000
Comments: A custom molded shell contains the drive electronics and the optics. Eyeglasses can be worn with HMD.

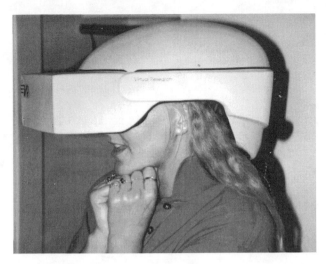

A-5
*Flight Helmet
head-mounted
display.*

VPL Research Inc.
Model: EP-01
Resolution: Color LCD, 360×240 elements
Weight: 2.6 lbs plus 3 lbs counterbalance
Field of view: 90-100H, LEEP optics
Video in: NTSC
Cost: Discontinued
Comments: The original EyePhones. Design based on original NASA-Ames
version.

VPL Research Inc.
Model: LX (see Fig. 1-6, pg. 12 for an example)
Resolution: Color LCD, 442×238 elements
Weight: 2.5 lbs
Field of view: 100 H×70 V, custom optics
Video in: NTSC
Cost: $9,150
Comments: Uses fresnel lens to minimize weight.
Includes Polhemus Isotrak head-tracking system.

VPL Research Inc.
Model: XVR (see Fig. A-6)
Resolution: Color LCD, 442×238 elements
Weight: 2.5 lbs (est.)
Field of view: 108H×76V, custom optics
Video in: NTSC
Cost: (not available as of mid-1992)
Comments: Complete redesign of HMD.
Part of VPL's Microcosm system.

A-6 *XVR head-mounted display*

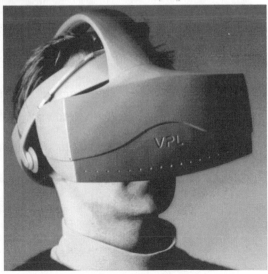

VPL Research Inc.

Model: HRX
Resolution: Color LCD, 720×400 elements
Weight: 2.5 lbs
Field of view: 106H×75V, custom optics
Video in: NTSC or RGB
Cost: $49,000
Comments: Highest resolution LCD product available. Can be set up for either NTSC or RGB signals (factory programmed). Adjustable brightness and contrast controls.

W Industries

Model: Visette (see Fig. A-7)
Resolution: Color LCD, 372×276 elements
Weight: 6.4 lbs
Field of view: 90-120H, custom optics
Video in: NTSC
Cost: Not sold separately
Comments: Designed for arcade use. Clamp design for ease of entry and removal. Weight is a potential issue.

A-7
Visette head-mounted display.

Related display technologies

These products and prototypes reflect slightly different approaches to generating virtual images. Some make use of head-tracking and others take a more unique approach. Each of these represent different solutions to problems with using and viewing virtual worlds.

flogiston corp.

Model: Cyberhood (see Fig. A-8)
Resolution: Monitor-dependent
Weight: NA
Field of view: 30-40H, custom optics
Cost: $250
Comments: The hood is custom-designed for each type of monitor. The software needs to draw the left eye image on the left-hand side of the screen, and the right image on the right side. Similar to a computerized Viewmaster. Flogiston also makes a custom recumbent chair for exploring virtual worlds while relaxing.

A-8 *flogiston cyberhood.*

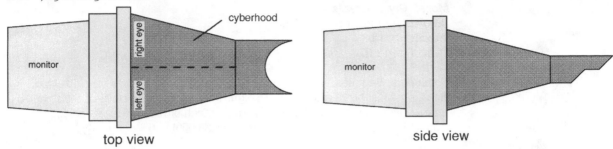

top view

side view

Fake Space Labs

Model: BOOM-2C (see Fig. 5-9, pg. 76 for an example)
Resolution: 2 color CRTs, 1280×1024 pixels
Weight: NA
Field of view: 90-100H, LEEP optics
Cost: $74,000
Comments: Provides simplified access to the virtual world. Uses CRT monitors for high resolution. Limited color space due to the use of only two primary colors instead of three. Other versions exist, starting at $15,000. Counterbalanced design eliminates the weight of the displays. Control buttons on the handles allow control of movement along the view direction.

LEEP Systems Inc.

Model: Freedom Boom
Resolution: Color LCD, 720×240 pixels
Weight: NA
Field of view: 80H, LEEP optics
Video in: NTSC, PAL, or RGB
Cost: $10,000
Comments: In the fall of 1992, LEEP began showing a boom system using a single high-resolution (720×240) color LCD. Though not capable of stereo, this display is designed to be attached to a desktop and is intended for uses where color and resolution are important.

Reflection Technology

Model: Private Eye (see Fig. A-9)
Resolution: Monochrome red LED, 720×280 pixels
Weight: 0.12 lbs
Field of view: 22H×14V, custom optics
Cost: $500
Comments: *Specs* are for a single-eye setup. Company is working on a 1,000×1,000 monochrome display with Sun Microsystems.

A-9
Private Eye display.

StereoGraphics

Model: CrystalEyes (see Fig. A-10)
Resolution: Monitor-dependent
Weight: 0.19 lbs
Field of view: NA
Cost: $1,300
Comments: Requires a monitor capable of scanning at 120hz in order to avoid flickering. Must be viewed within an eight-foot radius of the monitor. Another version called CrystalEyes/VR includes a Logitech ultrasonic head-tracking sensor mounted on the frame of the shutter glasses ($3,900).

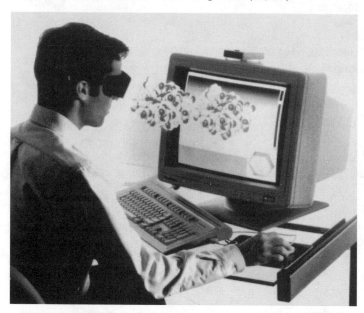

A-10
CrystalEyes LCD flicker glasses.

The Computer Museum (Boston)

Item: Custom design for VR exhibit (see Fig. A-11)
Resolution: Monitor-dependent
Weight: NA
Field of view: About 20-30H
Cost: Not commercially available
Comments: The chair rotates around like a barber chair. Sensors at the base of the chair detect the motion and communicate it to the PC. Users steer themselves with their feet, and push buttons to move up/down and forwards/backwards. Elimination of HMD allows VR exhibit to be left unattended

A-11
Virtual Reality Swivel Chair, designed by William Tremblay, Eban Gay, and Dave Greschler.

Only special digital signal processors (DSPs) have the processing power to perform the necessary calculations to filter or convolve sounds in real time.

Crystal River Engineering
Model: Convolvotron
Input: 4 channels
A/D: 16-bit samples at 50kHz
Cost: $15,000
Comments: Two-board set designed for the IBM PC. Up to four independent sound sources can be convolved at once. A second set of boards can be cascaded to create a simple reflective model of an environment. Requires a separate sound source or MIDI sequencer.

Model: Beachtron
Input: 2 channels
A/D: 16-bit samples at 44.1kHz
Cost: $1,900
Comments: Based on Turtle Beach's digital signal-processing board, up to two audio sources can be convolved. Also has on-board programmable sound synthesizer and sequencer.

Focal Point 3D Audio
Model: Focal Point
Input: 2 channels
A/D: 16-bit samples at 44.1kHz
Cost: $1,800
Comments: Single board for a Macintosh or the PC. Has on-board synthesizer capabilities.

Visual Synthesis Inc.
Model: Audio Image Sound Cube
Input: 1 channel
A/D: Selectable
Cost: $8,000
Comments: A library of C functions for SGi workstations. Provides for control and generation of MIDI-based sounds and 3-D positioning based on volume, panning, filtering, and pitch changes. Package includes the software, MIDI device, and VME board for the SGi.

Research in this field has resulted in a limited number of commercial devices. The ones that do exist have seen only limited use in some labs. Much work still needs to be done from both the software and hardware standpoint before these devices become widely accepted.

ARRC/Airmuscle Ltd.
Model: Teletact II (see Fig. A-12)
Input: 30 air pockets
Output Force: 12 psi
Cost: $4,900
Comments: Improved version has 30 pockets instead of the original 20. In addition, it has a large palm pocket that can be inflated up to 30 psi. Teletact II control system is an additional $13,400. Product is distributed by Division in Europe.

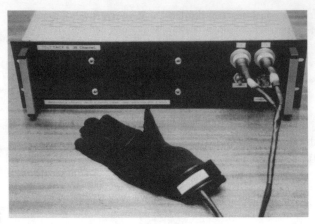

A-12 *Teletact II force-feedback glove.*

A-13 *Teletact Commander force-feedback hand grip.*

ARRC/Airmuscle Ltd.
Model: Teletact Commander (see Fig. A-13)
Input: 3-5 air pockets
Output force: 12 psi
Cost: Prototype
Comments: Simple hand-held device has 5 control buttons. Polhemus or Ascension 6D sensor is mounted internally. Uses a low-cost airbrush.

ARRC/Airmuscle Ltd.
Model: Datacq II
Input: 29 force-sensitive resistors
Cost: $7,400
Comments: This is used as an input device to the Teletact II force-feedback glove. The forces generated by holding an object are first sampled with the Datacq glove, and then duplicated using the Teletact glove. When combined with a wired glove, forces can be measured at particular bend angles.

Xtensory Inc.
Model: Tactools XTT1 (see Fig. 8-18, pg. 125 for an example)
Input: 1 channel
Output force: 30 grams
Cost: $1,500 (with 1 tactor)
Comments: Uses a controller that can support up to 10 tactors. Communicates over serial or MIDI ports.

CM Research
Model: DTSS X/10
Channels: 8 (input or output)
Cost: $10,000
Comments: This device provides temperature feedback by using thermodes. A solid-state heat pump moves heat into or out of a heat sink based on signals from a controller. Each thermode can be used to either generate hot and cold sensations or to measure them. Their small size allows them to be placed directly on the fingertip.

Due to the difficulties in simulating forces reliably and accurately, few devices exist to generate force feedback. This is an area where only a few companies are researching the possibilities.

Sarcos and the Center for Engineering Design
Model: Exoskeletal Master
DOF: 10
Cost: $100,000 (prototype)
Comments: Can also be used with the Sarcos Dexterous Arm for teleoperation. This was developed at the University of Utah and is the leading system of its type in the world. High-pressure hydraulic lines precisely control the forces being applied to the operator's arms and hands

These are the various devices that are worn or manipulated in order to interact within a virtual world. Together, they represent many different approaches to establishing a dialogue between man and machine.

This covers all the various fiber-optic, electronic, and mechanical methods of measuring various body-joint movements. Though originally designed for just hand movements, wired clothing can monitor almost any part of the body now.

EXOS Inc.
Model: Dexterous Hand Master (see Fig. 8-22, pg. 130 for an example)
Type: Mechanical Hall-Effect sensors
Sensors: 20
Cost: $15,000
Comments: Mechanical design allows for accurate (0.5 degree) and repeatable measurements. Bulkiness limits its use for some applications.

Mattel, Inc.
Model: PowerGlove (see Fig. 12-7, pg. 220 for an example)
Type: Resistive sensors
Cost: Discontinued (originally $89)
Comments: Developed in cooperation with VPL, Abrams-Gentile Entertainment, and Mattel. Based on conductive ink deposited on a strip of plastic inside each gloved finger. Low-cost ultrasonic sensors were used to detect glove position and orientation. First available late 1989. Discontinued in late 1991.

Sarcos and the Center for Engineering Design
Model: Exoskeletal Hand Master (see Fig. A-14)
Type: Mechanical sensors
Sensors: 16
Cost: Prototype
Comments: Mechanical design allows for accurate and repeatable measurements. Bulkiness limits its use for some applications.

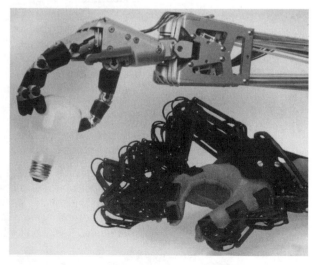

A-14
*Utah/MIT
Dextrous Hand with
Sarcos Exoskeletal
Hand Master.*

Virtual Technologies (Virtex)

Model: CyberGlove CG1801 (see Fig. A-15)
Type: Fiber-optic sensors
Sensors: 18 (up to 22)
Cost: $6,500
Comments: Designed to fit all-sized hands and to be less sensitive to joint positioning. Virtex also supplies CyberForce, a force-feedback system, and various CyberWear, such as a CyberSuit for measuring other body motions. Comes with software for visualizing motions on a computer screen.

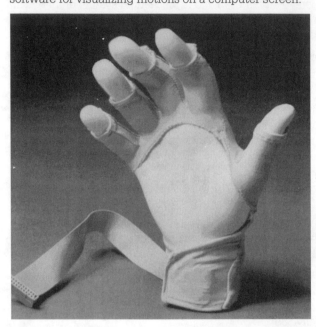

A-15
CyberGlove.

VPL Research

Model: DataGlove 2+
(see Fig. A-16)
Type: Fiber-optic sensors
Sensors: 10 (more available as an option)
Cost: $8,800
Comments: Includes Polhemus ISOTRAK position/orientation tracking system. Gloves come in different sizes for different hands.

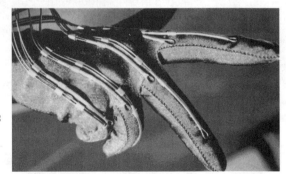

A-16 *DataGlove.*

Model: DataSuit
Type: Fiber-optic sensors
Sensors: 20 (est.)
Cost: Prototype
Comments: Designed for full-body immersion. Sensors are attached to major body joints.

These devices have only recently become available, so little is known of their performance. They're very similar to 6 DOF mice in operation, but physically different enough to deserve a separate classification.

Wands

Virtual Research
Model: Wand
DOF: 6
Specs: (see Polhemus ISOTRAK)
Cost: Prototype
Comments: A cylindrical tube containing a Polhemus sensor. A rocker switch provides for two user-defined actions. Performance specifications are the same as the ISOTRAK described in the section on 6 DOFs.

Both of these force balls share a common heritage from a research lab in Germany. The two different companies each licensed the technology and have created separate versions of the device.

Force balls

Polhemus Inc.
Model: 3Ball (see Fig. A-17)
DOF: 6
Specs: (see Polhemus ISOTRAK)
Cost: Prototype
Comments: A single switch and a Polhemus sensor are mounted inside a real billiard ball. Performance specifications are the same as the ISOTRAK described in the section on 6 DOFs.

A-17 *3DBall.*

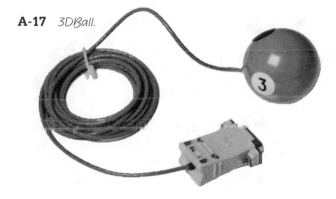

CiS
Model: Geometry Ball (see Fig. A-18)
DOF: 6
Detectable force: 4.5 lbs maximum, 0.1 lbs minimum (est.)
Cost: $1,400-3,000
Comments: The ball doesn't actually move; instead, sensors measure the forces and torques applied to the ball. Nine user-definable buttons are also available. Four different models of the ball are available.

A-18
Geometry Ball.

Spaceball Technologies Inc.
Model: Spaceball 2003 (see Fig.5-7, pg. 75 for an example)
DOF: 6
Detectable force: 4.5 lbs maximum, 0.1 lbs minimum.
Cost: $1,600
Comments: Based on the same technology as the Geometry Ball. Nine user-definable buttons are provided.

6 DOF mice Several companies have tried to create the 3-D equivalent of the 2-D mouse. Though all the products are similar in approach, methods of position and orientation tracking differ widely.

Ascension Technology Corp.
Model: The Ascension Bird
DOF: 6
Accuracy: 0.1" position/0.5-degree orientation
Range: Up to 3' (8' optional)
Lag: 15 msecs (unfiltered), 30-90 msecs (filtered)
Update rate: 100Hz
Cost: $3,100
Comments: An electromagnetic 6 DOF sensor buried inside a mouse-like device. Three user-programmable buttons are available. Angular range for elevation is less than 360 degrees. Uses pulsed DC method, which is intended to be less sensitive to interference.

Gyration Inc.
Model: GyroPoint (see Fig. A-19)
Type: Gyroscopic
DOF: 3
Accuracy: 0.1-degree orientation
Lag: 4 msecs (unfiltered)
Update rate: 100Hz or better
Cost: $700
Comments: Mouse device with 2 micro gyroscopes mounted inside. Mouse also has 5 programmable button controls. Completely integrated sensor, doesn't require a source transmitter. Biggest problem is accuracy drift of up to 10 degrees per minute. Design change will reduce to 2 degrees per minute by end of 1992.

A-19
GyroPoint
3 DOF mouse.

Logitech Inc.

Model: 3-D Mouse (see Fig. 5-8, pg. 75 for an example)
DOF: 2/6
Accuracy: 2% of distance from source/0.1-degree orientation
Range: Up to 2' and 8" for the fringe area
Lag: < 20 msecs (filtered)
Update rate: 50Hz
Cost: $1,000
Comments: Uses ultrasonic tracking. Mouse can operate in normal 2-D desktop mode, and automatically switches to 3-D when picked up from the desk. Five user-programmable switches are available.

MULTIPOINT Technology Corp.

Model: Z Mouse
DOF: 5
Accuracy: 300 dpi (est.)
Range: NA
Lag: < 10ms (est.)
Update Rate: > 60Hz (est.)
Cost: $250
Comments: This device is the result of combining a 2-D mouse with a 2-D trackball. A thumbwheel on the side provides an additional degree of freedom. No external form of position or orientation tracking is used.

SimGraphics

Model: Flying Mouse (see Fig. A-20)
DOF: 2/6
Specs: (see Polhemus ISOTRAK)
Cost: $4,000
Comments: Uses electromagnetic tracking. Mouse can operate in normal 2-D desktop mode, and automatically switches to 3-D when picked up from the desk.

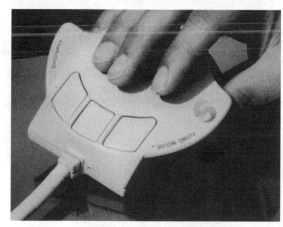

A-20
Flying Mouse.

This is an interesting group of products that's just beginning to be explored. Many unique applications will be based on the technologies present in this section.

Biologic

BioControl Systems, Inc.
Model: Bio-signal Processing Unit (see Fig. 8-26, pg. 134 for an example)
Channels: 8 (independent)
Cost: $10,000
Comments: Multiple dermal electrodes can track muscle activity or brainwaves. Electrical signals can be processed to control other devices such as MIDI sound hardware or video games. Each channel can support multiple sensors and can run an independent processing algorithm.

Dragon Systems Inc.
Model: DragonWriter and DragonDictate
Cost: $1,500 and up
Comments: PC-based voice recognition software. Doesn't require specialized hardware. Capable of discrete or continuous voice recognition

AICOM Corp.
Model: Accent SA
Cost: $500 and up
Comments: PC-based text-to-speech synthesis board.

Voice Connexion
Model: Micro IntroVoice
Cost: $1,200
Comments: Provides voice recognition of up to 1,000 words, and text-to-speech synthesis. PC-based.

Covox Inc.
Model: SoundMaster II
Cost: $230
Comments: Supports audio, music, and voice recognition. PC-based.

Keyboard

Robicon Systems Inc.
Model: Single-hand KAT keyboard (see Fig. 8-27, pg. 135 for an example)
Lag: 2 msecs
Update rate: 100Hz
Cost: $1,500 (est.)
Comments: This is the only product of its type, and deserves special mention because it could solve the problem of losing your keyboard when entering a virtual world. A molded hand-grip contains 5 special switches (one per finger). Each finger switch can produce seven unique values and the thumb key is used to choose 1 of 5 character sets. Up to 141 characters can be generated this way.

6 DOF sensors

These are all the devices used to track either various body parts or other physical objects. Many of these devices are found integrated into other VR tools.

Electromagnetic

Ascension Technology Corp.
Model: A Flock of Birds (see Fig. A-21)
DOF: 6
Accuracy: 0.1" position/0.5-degree orientation
Range: Up to 3' (8' optional)
Lag: 15 msecs (unfiltered), 30-90 msecs (filtered)
Update rate: 100Hz
Cost: $5,200 (with two sensors)

Comments: Up to six sensors can be controlled by a single box. Effective for head-tracking. Angular range for elevation is less than 360 degrees. Uses pulsed DC method, which is intended to be less sensitive to interference. Sensor lag can be noticeable.

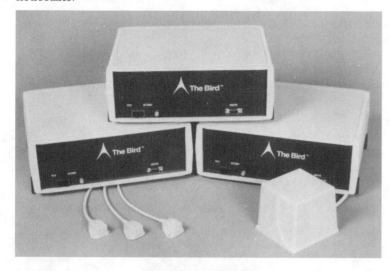

A-21
A Flock of Birds tracker.

Polhemus
Model: ISOTRAK II
DOF: 6
Accuracy: 0.25" position/0.85-degree orientation
Range: Accurate up to 3', tracks up to 5'
Lag: < 25 msec (unfiltered), 50-150 msec (filtered)
Update rate: 58Hz
Cost: $3,200
Comments: Supports unrestricted angular motion. Sensor cube is about 0.5 cubic inches. Subject to interference from large metal objects or nearby TVs or monitors. Sensor lag can be noticeable.

Model: FASTRAK (see Fig. A-22)
DOF: 6
Accuracy: 0.03" position/0.15-degree orientation
Range: Up to 10'
Lag: 4 msecs (unfiltered)
Update rate: 120Hz
Cost: $5,700
Comments: Improved model over original ISOTRAK. Reduction in lag is significant, but some uses would require filtering of the signal which will increase the lag. Supports up to 4 sensors with one source.

A-22 *FASTRAK tracker.*

Logitech Inc.
Model: Head-tracker
DOF: 6
Accuracy: 2% of distance from source/0.1-degree orientation
Range: Up to 7'
Lag: 20 msecs (filtered)
Update rate: 50Hz
Cost: $1,000
Comments: Low-cost method of head-tracking. Limited to line-of-sight tracking, and therefore has reduced angular range. Subject to interference from other high-frequency sounds.

Mechanical

Gyration Inc.
Model: GyroEngine (see Fig. A-23)
Type: Gyroscopic
DOF: 3
Accuracy: 0.1-degree orientation
Range: Limited by cable length
Lag: 4 msecs
Update rate: 1,000Hz (depends on interface)
Cost: $1,500 (prototype)
Comments: Single miniature gyroscope. Suffers from same drift problem as GyroPoint. Available as a directional or vertical gyro. Each one has some limitations on the range of angular motion.

A-23
GyroEngine's size, compared to a film canister.

Shooting Star Technology
Model: ADL-1 (see Fig. 8-31,pg. 140 for an example)
Type: Mechanical linkage
DOF: 6
Accuracy: 0.2" position/0.3-degree orientation
Range: 18" high and 30" diameter half-cylinder
Lag: 2 msecs
Update Rate: 300Hz
Cost: $1,500
Comments: Uses shaft encoders and lightweight mechanical arms to measure positions and orientations. Not subject to interference, but also limited by mechanical arm.

GEC Ferranti (Gaertner Research Division)
Model: GRD-1010
Type: Infrared LEDs and optical sensing
DOF: 6
Accuracy: 0.1" position/0.6-degree orientation
Range: About 2'
Lag: 4 msecs (filtered)
Update rate: 240Hz (RS-422)
Cost: $50,000

Comments: Based on three infrared LEDs that must be mounted on an HMD or glove. An optical sensor, pointing at the glove or HMD tracks its movements. Requires that a line of sight be maintained between LEDs and optical sensor.

Spatial Positioning Systems, Inc.

Model: RtPM (see Fig. A-24)
Type: Laser transmitters and optical sensing
DOF: 3 or 6 DOF
Accuracy: 1 part in 100,000 (0.01 inches at 100-foot range)
Range: 3-800 feet
Lag: Unknown
Update rate: 100Hz
Cost: $50,000-70,000
Comments: System is based on the use of several lasers to accurately detect the location of either a passive sensor or an active optical sensor. It operates in either a passive mode using retroreflectors, or in an active mode using an optical sensor connected to a portable Macintosh computer. In active mode, multiple sensors can be tracked without additional laser transceivers. Three laser transceivers are required to measure both object position and orientation. This system is based on line-of-sight tracking and therefore has some inherent limitations.

A-24
Laser-based optical tracking system.

Company & institution guide

This lists in alphabetical order, the many companies who produce various types of products for constructing virtual environments. Included also are a few of the university research groups mentioned in the book. This is by no means a complete list of all companies and institutions working with VR. It is only intended to help you gain additional information about technologies mentioned in this book.

Advanced Robotics Research Centre
University Rd.
Salford, England M5 4PP
ph: (4461) 745-7384
fx: (4461) 745-8264

Advanced Technology Systems
800 Follin Lane
Suite 270
Vienna, VA 22180
ph: (703) 242-0030
fx: (703) 242-5220

Advanced Gravis
7033 Antrim Ave.
Burnaby, BC, Canada V5J 4M5

AICOM Corp.
1590 Oakland Rd.
Suite B112
San Jose, CA 95131
ph: (408) 453-8251
fx: (408) 453-8255

Artificial Reality Corp.
Box 786
Vernon, CT 06066
ph: (203) 871-1375

Ascension Technology Corp.
P.O. Box 527
Burlingtion, VT 05402
ph: (802) 655-7879
fx: (802) 655-5904

Autodesk Inc.
Advanced Technology Dept.
2320 Marinship Way
Sausalito, CA 94965
ph: (415) 332-2344

Battletech Centers Inc.
1100 W. Cermak
Suite B404
Chicago, IL, 60608
ph: (312) 243-6515
fx: (312) 243-7818

BioControl Systems, Inc.
430 Cowper St.
Palo Alto, CA 94301
ph: (415) 329-8494
fx: (415) 329-8498

CAE-Electronics Ltd.
8585 Cote De Liesse
Saint-Laurent, Quebec
Canada H4L 4X4
ph: (514) 341-6780
fx: (514) 341-7699

CIS Graphics Inc.
1 Stiles Rd.
Suite 305
Salem, NH 03079
ph: (603) 894-5999

CM Research
2815 Forest Hill
League City, TX 77573
ph: (713) 334-4661
fx: (713) 334-4860

Covox Inc.
675 Conger St.
Eugene, OR 97402
ph: (503) 342-1271
fx: (503) 342-1283

Crystal River Engineering
12350 Wards Ferry Rd.
Groveland, CA 95321
ph: (209) 962-6382
fx: (209) 962-4873

CyberEdge Journal
928 Greenhill Rd.
Mill Valley, CA 94911

ph: (415) 383-2458
fx: (415) 389-0251

Dimension International
Zephyr One, Calleva Park
Aldermaston, Berkshire
England RG7 4QW
ph: (44) 734-810077
fx: (44) 734-816940

Division Ltd.
Quarry Rd.
Chipping, Sodbury
Bristol, England BS17 6AX
ph: (44) 454 324527
fx:(44) 454 323059

Dragon Systems Inc.
320 Nevada St.
Newton, MA 02158
ph: (617) 965-5200
fx: (617) 527-0372

DTM Corp.
1611 Headway Circle
Building 2
P.O. Box 141069
Austin, TX 78754
ph: (512) 339-2922

Evans & Sutherland
Simulation Division
600 Komas Dr.
Salt Lake City, UT 84108
ph: (801) 582-5847
fx: (801) 582-5848

EXOS Inc.
8 Blanchard Rd.
Burlington, MA 01803
ph: (617) 229-2075
fx: (617) 270-5901

Fake Space Labs
935 Hamilton Ave.
Menlo Park, CA 94025
ph: (415) 688-1940
fx: (415) 688-1949

flogiston corp.
462 Cape Hill
Webster, TX 77598
ph: (713) 280-8554

Focal Point 3D Audio
1402 Pine Ave.
Suite 127
Niagara Falls, NY 14301
ph/fx: (416) 963-9188

GEC Ferranti
Gaertner Research Division
140 Water St.
Norwalk, CT 06854
ph: (203) 866-3200
fx: (203) 838-5026

General Electric
Simulation & Control Systems Dept.
P.O. Box 2825
Daytona Beach, FL 32115
ph: (904) 239-2906

Gyration Inc.
12930 Saratoga Ave., Building C
Saratoga, CA 95070
ph: (408) 255-3016
fx: (408) 255-9075

Human Interface Technology Lab
FU-20
University of Washington
Seattle, WA 98195
ph: (206) 543-5075

Institute for Simulation & Training
University of Central Florida
12424 Research Parkway
Suite 300
Orlando, FL, 32826
ph: (407) 658-5074
fx: (407) 658-5059

International Telepresence Corp.
655 West 7th Ave.
Vancouver, B.C.
Canada, V5Z 186
ph: (604) 873-3300
fx: (604) 275-2233

Kaiser Aerospace & Electronics Corp.
2701 Orchard Park Way
San Jose, CA 95134
ph: (408) 432-3000 x1435
fx: (408) 432-8440

LEEP Systems Inc.
241 Crescent St.
Waltham, MA 02154
ph: (617) 647-1395
fx: (617) 899-9602

Logitech Inc.
6505 Kaiser Dr.
Fremont, CA 94555
ph: (510) 795-8500
fx: (510) 792-8901

MULTIPOINT Technology Corp.
319 Littleton Rd., Suite 201
Westford, MA 01886
ph: (508) 692-0689
fx: (508) 692-2653

NASA Ames Research Center
Moffett Field, CA 94035
ph: (415) 604-3937
fx: (415) 604-3953

Polhemus Labs
P.O. Box 5
Cambridge, VT 05444
ph: (802) 644-5569
fax: (802) 644-2943

Polhemus Inc.
P.O. Box 560
Colchester, VT 05446
ph: (802) 655-3159
fx: (802) 655-1439

Reflection Technology
230 Second Ave.
Waltham, MA 02154
ph: (617) 890-5905
fx: (617) 890-5918

SARCOS
261 East 300 South, Suite 150
Salt Lake City, UT 84111
ph: (801) 531-0559
fx: (801) 531-0315

Sense8 Corp.
4000 Bridgeway
Suite 101
Sausalito, CA, 94965
ph: (415) 331-6318
fx: (415) 331-9148

Shooting Star Technology
1921 Holdom Ave.
Burnaby, BC
Canada
V5B 3W4
ph: (604) 298-8574
fx: (604) 298-8580

SimGraphics Engineering Corp.
1137 Huntington Dr.
South Pasadena, CA 91030-4563
ph: (213) 255-0900
fx: (213) 255-0987

Software Systems
1884 The Alameda
San Jose, CA 95126
ph: (408) 247-4326

Spaceball Technologies, Inc.
600 Suffolk St.
Lowell, MA 01854
ph: (508) 970-0330

Spatial Positioning Systems, Inc.
Innovation Center
1800 Kraft Dr.
Blacksburg, VA 24060
ph: (703) 231-3145
fx: (703) 231-3568

StereoGraphics Corp.
2171-H East Francisco Blvd.
San Rafael, CA 94901
ph: (415) 459-4500
fx: (415) 459-3020

StrayLight
150 Mount Bethel Rd.
Warren, NJ 07059
ph: (908) 580-0086
fx: (908) 580-0092

Telepresence Research
635 High St.
Palo Alto, CA 94301
ph: (415) 325 8951
fx: (415) 325-8952

Textronix
Display Products
P.O. Box 500, M/S 46-943
Beaverton, OR 97077-0001
ph: (503) 627-6499

The Computer Museum
300 Congress St.
Boston, MA 02210
ph: (617) 426-2800

The Vivid Group
317 Adelaide St. W. Studio 302
Toronto, Ontario
Canada M5V 1P9
ph: (416) 340-9290
fx: (416) 348-9809

University of North Carolina
Dept. of Computer Science
Chapel Hill, NC 27599
ph: (919) 962-1700

**Virtual Technologies
(Virtex)**
P.O. Box 5984
Stanford, CA 94309
ph: (415) 599-2331

Virtual Research
1313 Socorro
Sunnyvale, CA 94089
ph: (408) 739-7114
fx: (408) 739-8586

Virtual Reality Group
800 Follin Lane
Suite 270
Vienna, VA 22180
ph: (703) 242-0030
fx: (703) 242-5220

Visual Synthesis, Inc.
4126 Addison Rd.
Fairfax, VA 22030
ph: (703) 352-0258

Voice Connexion
17835 Skypark Circle
Suite C
Irvine, CA 92714
ph: (714) 261-2366
fx: (714) 261-8563

VPL Research Inc.
950 Tower Lane
14th Floor
Foster City, CA 94004
ph: (415) 312-0200
fx: (415) 312-9356

VR News
Cydata Limited
P.O. Box 2515
London, England N4 4JW
ph/fx: 44(0) 81-292-1498

VREAM
2568 N. Clark St. #250
Chicago, IL 60614
ph: (312) 477-0425
fx: (312) 477-9702

W Industries Ltd.
Virtuality House
3 Oswin Rd.
Brailsford Industrial Pk.
Leicester, England LE3 1HR
ph: (0533) 542127
fx: (0533) 542127

Xtensory
140 Sunridge Dr.
Scotts Valley, CA 95066
ph: (408) 439-0600
fx: (408) 439-9709

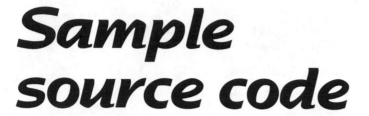

Sample
source code

This is an example of a program written using Sense8's WorldToolKit C libraries. This program reads in a 3-D model called HOUSE.DXF, which was previously built using Autodesk's AutoCAD or some other 3-D modeller. Once the file is loaded, you can fly around and inspect the model from any angle.

Attached to the PC's COM1 serial port is a special device called a Geoball. This is a type of force ball that simplifies navigating in the virtual world. WorldToolKit supports many different types of device drivers.

The two buttons on the Geoball are programmed to either end the simulation or to reset your viewpoint back to your original view if you get lost.

```
/*   This program loads in a model stored in the file
     HOUSE.DXF, and lets you navigate your viewpoint using a
     Geometry Ball device.
*/

#include <stdio.h>
#include "wt.h"

static Sensor *sensor;        /* the Geometry ball */
static Posn6d initial_p;      /* stores initial viewpoint */

/*   The user's action function is called once each time
     through the simulation loop. This particular action
```

```
             function looks for and acts upon Geometry Ball button
             presses. A left button press ends the program by calling
             universe_stop(). A right button press resets the
             viewpoint to its original position and orientation by
             calling viewpoint_moveto().
     */
     static void user_actionfn();

     main()
     {
             /*      Initialize the universe. (This must be the 1st
                     WorldToolKit call.)
             */
             /*      This loads the graphical information from the 3-D
                     model called HOUSE.DXF. The house is loaded as a
                     "stationary backdrop."
             */
             universe_load("house.dxf", &initial_p, 1.0);

             /*      Move the viewpoint to the position read from the
                     model.
                     This provides the initial view upon entering the
                     world.
             */
             viewpoint_moveto(universe_getviewpoint(), &initial_p);

             /*      Initialize a Geometry Ball sensor on serial port
                     COM1. This "wakes up" the Geoball device and
                     establishes communication with it.
             */
             sensor = geoball_new(COM1);

             /*      Attach the sensor to the viewpoint. By doing this,
                     the Geoball will now control where you're looking
                     and the direction you travel in.
             */
             viewpoint_addsensor(universe_getviewpoint(), sensor);

             /*      Prepare the universe for start of the simulation.
             */
             universe_ready();

             /*      Scale sensor sensitivity with the size of the
                     universe.
             */
             sensor_setsensitivity(sensor, 0.01 *
             universe_getradius());

             /*      Set the action function so that button presses will
                     be acted on. This tells the simulation manager that
                     a particuler user-supplied function needs to be
                     executed once per "tick."
             */
             universe_setactions(user_actionfn);

             /*      Enter the main simulation loop. Once this is
                     called, the program will begin rendering the world,
                     and will not return from here until it is told to
                     stop.
```

```
    */
    universe_go();

    /*    all done; clean everything up. (This must be the
          last WorldToolKit call.)
    */
    universe_delete();
    return 0;
}

/*    This is the user's action function. The user can define
      whatever he wants to occur, and WorldToolKit will
      execute this function once per simulation loop. In the
      case of this example, the user wants the following to
      occur:
            Check for button presses on the Geometry Ball.
            Exit the simulation loop if the left button is
            pressed. Restore the original viewpoint if the
            right button is pressed.
*/
static void user_actionfn()
{
    short buttons;

    /* get button press data from ball */
    buttons = sensor_getmiscdata(sensor);
    if ( buttons & GEOBALL_LEFTBUTTON ) {
        /* quit the simulation */
        universe_stop();
    }
    else if ( buttons & GEOBALL_RIGHTBUTTON ) {
        /* reset the view to the original viewpoint */
        viewpoint_move(universe_getviewpoint(),
        &initial_p);
    }
}
```

Glossary

3-D   Three-dimensional; refers to the visual display that exhibits breadth, height, and thickness or depth (standard 2-D computer images and television displays create a flat image with only height and breadth).

3-D sound   Filtered sound that appears to be emanating from locations in front of, below, above, behind, and to either side of the listener. Any sound, such as a jet plane taking off, can be convolved or filtered so that it's spatially located. The listener can seem to hear the plane approach from the front, pass over, and then continue on behind them.

6 DOF   Six degrees of freedom; refers to the number of simultaneous directions or inputs a sensor can measure. Typically used to describe the combination of spatial position (X,Y,Z) and orientation (roll, pitch, yaw) measured by many tracking sensors.

application   The software that describes the context of the simulation, its dynamics, structure, and the rules of interaction between objects and the user. For example, how doors open, where sunlight falls, and which way gravity works.

artificial intelligence   The effort to build computers that mimic and automate human cognitive skills (e.g., understanding visual images, recognize speech and written text, can solve problems, make medical diagnoses, etc.).

artificial reality   Introduced by arts and computer visualization scholar Myron Krueger in the mid-1970s to describe his computer-generated responsive environments. As realized in his VIDEOPLACE and the Vivid Group's Mandala system, it's a computer display system that perceives and captures "a participant's action in terms of the body's relationship to a graphic world and generates responses [usually imagery] that maintain the illusion that his actions are taking place within that world." (M. Krueger, *Artificial Reality*).

augmented reality   This is the use of transparent glasses on which data can be projected. This allows the user to work on a car, for example, and have the data he needs displayed on the glasses while still seeing the car.

backdrop   In a virtual world, this is the stationary background, analogous to the backdrop in a stage show—the boundary of the world. It cannot be moved or broken into smaller elements.

biosensors   Special glasses or bracelets containing electrodes to monitor muscle electrical activity. Potentially capable of tracking eye movements by measuring muscle movements.

BOOM   A 3-D display device suspended from a weighted boom that can swivel freely about so the viewer doesn't have to wear an HMD; instead, it steps up to the viewer like a pair of binoculars. The boom's position communicates the user's point of view to the computer.

bus   A means of distributing a set of electronic signals so that the microprocessor at the heart of a computer can be connected with memory, external devices, and the display screen.

CAT scans   Computer-aided tomography; the use of x-ray scanning devices to map cross-sections of the human body without damaging it or having to surgically enter it.

CD/CD-ROM   The abbreviation for compact disk, read-only memory. Familiar to most people as the new standard for storing digital music. ROM means that the information stored on the disk cannot be rewritten or rerecorded over during use. Seen as the next standard for storage of music, text, and video for reproduction by computers.

cathode ray tube (CRT)   A vacuum tube like the one in a television set, a computer monitor, or an oscilloscope.

central processing unit (CPU)   The part of the computer that controls the fetching of instructions from memory, the interpretation of those instructions, and their execution. The "computer inside the computer," the CPU is responsible for initiating and coordinating all activities of the computer.

Cinematographe   The first true motion-picture system, and the one today's technology is descended from. Developed in Paris in 1895 by the brothers Auguste and Louis Lumiere.

Cinerama   A motion-picture technique for delivering a highly realistic visual image. It used a screen four times larger than traditional screens to provide an enhanced field of view.

compiler   A software program that translates a program written in a human-readable programming language into a binary form (ones and zeros) that can be read by the computer.

conceptual art   A recent movement in art where a work is intended to be appreciated for its ideas and its conceptual qualities as well as, or in lieu of, its perceptual ones.

convergence   In stereoscopic viewing, this is when the left and right eye images become fused into a single image.

convolve   The process of filtering sounds so that they can be spatially placed. *See also* 3-D sound.

CAD   The abbreviation for computer-aided design. A CAD software package is a precision drawing tool that speeds up the design process by automating the work of the architect and engineer (editing, printing, plotting, and data import and export functions).

CPU   *See* central processing unit.

CRT   *See* cathode ray tube.

cyberspace   Coined by science-fiction author William Gibson in his book *Neuromancer* to describe a shared virtual universe operating within the sum total of all the world's computer networks. A global computer network allegorical to the current phone system, but providing a multisensory experience of "being there," not just an auditory experience.

DataGlove   A glove wired with sensors and connected to a computer system for gesture recognition. Also known generically as a wired glove. It enables navigation through a virtual environment and interaction with 3-D objects within it. DataGlove is a trademark of VPL Research.

DataSuit   Same as a DataGlove, but designed for the entire body. DataSuit is a trademark of VPL Research.

digital   Having discrete, as opposed to continuously varying values. The difference can be illustrated by comparing the surfaces of an analog record and a compact disk. The record's grooves are long-playing wavy lines, while the much smaller tracks on a compact disk are a series of very distinct pits. With compact disk, digital information is broken up into small packets and then reassembled into a whole.

driver   A low-level routine of software instructions for controlling the interaction between the computer and a hardware device.

dynamics   The dynamics of a virtual world are the laws that govern all actions and behaviors within the environment. A real-world example of such a dynamic is gravity. However, in a virtual world many nontraditional dynamics are possible, such as the dynamics of the interior of the human body or laws of reality that governed Alice's Wonderland.

effectors   The input and output sensors that either communicate a user's movements or commands to the computer or provide sensory stimulation from the computer to the user (HMD).

endoscopic   Part of a family of new surgical procedures that avoid cutting open major portions of the patient in favor of making small holes through which tools and a tiny camera are inserted and the surgery performed. The surgeon manipulates the tools by observing the surgery site on a monitor via the tiny video camera.

environment   In VR terms, this is a computer-generated model that can be experienced from the "`inside" as if it were a place.

event loop   The sequence of events the computer loops through to maintain a simulation. Each pass of the event loop checks all the input devices for viewpoint positioning and command changes before instructing the computer to recreate the environment. This needs to happen at least sixteen to twenty times a second to create a sense of realism.

force balls   Mechanical strain gauges used to measure 6 DOF forces or torques applied to a ball-shaped device. Used as a navigational device for many VR systems.

force feedback   An output device that transmits pressure, force, or vibration to provide the VR participant with the sense of touch. Tactile feedback simulates sensation applied to the skin. Force feedback simulates weight or resistance to motion.

fractal   A self-similar pattern generated by using the same rules at various levels of detail.

geometry Information stored and processed by the software application describing the physical attributes of objects or worlds.

gesture A hand or body movement that conveys information.

haptic Refers to all the physical sensors that provide us with a sense of touch at the skin level and force feedback information from our muscles and joints.

HMD (head-mounted display) A set of goggles or a helmet with tiny monitors in front of each eye that generate images, seen by the wearer as being three-dimensional. VPL Research refers to the HMDs they sell as EyePhones.

immersion As applied to virtual reality, this is when one or more of a user's sensors (eyes and ears generally) are isolated from the surrounding environment and fed only information coming from the computer.

impressionists A group of a painters of the late nineteenth century who sought to capture the dynamic art of perception, as opposed to the static photographic recording of a scene.

interface The interconnection between two pieces of equipment, hardware or software, in which information or energy is transferred. By this definition, the transmission in a car is the energy interface between the wheels and the engine. And the wheel, clutch, and brake are the information interface with the engine.

Kinetoscope Invented by Thomas Edison, it was the first personal viewer for motion pictures. It consisted of a three- to five-minute long loop of film, powered by a hand crank and viewed through a small window on the top of the device.

LCD Liquid crystal display, used in products like portable computers and wristwatches.

LED Light-emitting diode.

MRI Magnetic resonance imaging, a nonintrusive method for mapping the interior of the body through the use of magnetic energy.

megabyte (Mb) A million bytes.

microprocessor Invented in 1971 by Ted Hoff of the Intel Corporation, a computer implemented as a tiny integrated circuit, smaller than a fingernail semiconductor technology. The small size, low-power requirement, and low cost of microprocessors have revolutionized computer applications. Microprocessors are being used to put intelligence in everyday appliances, power virtual reality systems, and (when hundreds are strung together) build the world's most powerful supercomputers.

model Construction of the physical representation of a computer-generated world and all its objects.

monitor A video display that has no tuner and can't receive broadcast signals on its own. It can receive signals that are generated locally by a camera, computer, or videotape recorder.

MIDI Musical instrument digital interface, a standard that many electronic musical instruments support. Provides a simple method of controlling various devices through a single computer.

motion parallax The way the eyes can judge distance by noticing how closer objects move more than distant ones when you move your head about.

motion platforms These are mechanical platforms originally developed for flight simulation to provide a pilot trainee with the correct physical sensations when he turns the plane or enters rough weather. These platforms are now commonly found in amusement park rides such as Disney's Star Tours.

NASA National Aeronautic & Space Administration.

network A way of connecting computers so that software and information can be transmitted among them as if on a highway. A local area network (LAN) might link up a couple of hundred of computers within a building. The Internet is a global network that encompasses thousands of smaller computer networks.

NTSC National Television Standards Convention, the television standard used in the United States and other parts of the world. An interlaced signal displays two fields of information in 1/30th of a second. A total of 525 horizontal lines of resolution is possible. There are several other standards in use around the world.

objects Discrete 3-D shapes within the virtual world that you can interact with.

occlusion You can judge how close objects are to you because the closer ones overlap and occlude objects in the background.

operating system A master software control program that allows other programs to run by acting as a translator and interface between them and the microprocessor. It also provides them with utility services as they're running.

parallax Refers to the difference in viewing angle created by having two eyes looking at the same scene from slightly different positions. The combined input to your brain helps create a sense of depth.

pixel A contraction of *picture element*, it refers to one point in a graphics image on a computer display. A standard VGA display might have 640×480 pixels. The number of bits per pixel determines how many colors can be represented on the image. VGA displays typically have eight bits per pixel. True-color displays typically use 24 bits per pixel.

polygon A flat plane figure with multiple sides, the basic building block of virtual-reality worlds. Think of them as sheets of wood that can be cut in any shape and size and linked together, colored, and texture-mapped with additional images. Virtual worlds are constructed from hundreds of thousands of colored polygons displayed on monitors or stereoscopic displays. The more polygons a computer can display and manipulate per second, the more realistic the virtual world will appear. "Alvy Ray Smith of Pixar has estimated that we perceive the equivalent of 80 million polygons at 30+ frames per second when we look at a view of the real world.'' (M. Bricken, 1991).

projected reality The use of a computer with a camcorder attached. The video camera captures your picture and mixes it into a computer-generated graphical world, which is then projected on a wide screen. As you move, your figure on the screen moves with you.

real time The definition varies with use. In computer simulations, it means that the computer responds to inputs in a time frame that a human would perceive as instantaneous. Typically, this means a response less than 50-100 milliseconds.

reality engine Any computer system specifically designed to generate virtual-reality worlds. Silicon Graphics has recently chosen this name for their new line of scene generators.

rendering The computer process of calculating and then drawing images on a screen.

representational systems This is the mind's different ways of representing the outside world and its own internally generated worlds. They are a reflection of the input senses (vision, auditory, kinesthetic).

RS232 *See* serial line.

scan conversion This is the process of taking video signal from one format to another. It's typically used to convert noninterlaced computer video signals to the interlaced video signal needed for many head-mounted displays.

scripted languages A more natural language-styled software programming language that even nonprogrammers are able to pick up in a short amount of time. It translates the user's instructions into the complex code a simulation manager can understand.

Sensorama Invented by Mort Heilig, it was the first completely immersive entertainment experience, consisting of a simulated motorcycle ride that provided visual, kinesthetic, auditory, and even olfactory sensations.

serial line Also known as an RS232 line. Most PCs and workstations have ports or connections that allow serial communications between the computer and another device like a modem. Communication speed is measured in bits per second, which is know as the baud rate. Most modems and devices communicate anywhere between 2400 and 9600 baud.

server A computer dedicated to providing shared resources, such as files and printers, to a computer network. A product server is a special server tailored to support the manufacturing process, such as support for 3-D graphics and product testing simulations.

shutter glasses Wireless, battery-operated, stereo-viewing glasses used to view 3-D computer-generated graphics.

simulation manager This is the core software program that organizes and manages the resources and devices available to a VR application to create its world.

spatial Refers to space (region, area, void) in all directions.

submodalities These are the smallest categories into which your senses can divide experience. For example, visual information can be broken down into brightness, saturation, location, and hue. The ears can differentiate sounds by their frequency, rhythm, tone, and duration.

tactile Refers to your sense of touch, or pressure applied to your skin.

telepresence   The experience of being in another location. Usually accomplished by transmitting the user's view through the eyes of a camera. This can include the operation of remote machinery through the computer translation of human movements into equipment commands.

texture mapping   The process of displaying a single digitized image on a polygon or structure that's made out of polygons. This display technique saves computing power because the image is stored in memory and displayed, as opposed to being recalculated and redrawn.

toolkit   This is a compiled library of software commands and instructions for developing applications. While it provides the most flexibility and control, a world developer generally has to be a programmer to use it.

universe   This refers to the active environment of a simulation: all the objects, sensors, viewpoints, etc., being operated on. Only those elements present in the simulation's universe are drawn by the computer.

viewpoint   This represents the point of view of an observer in a virtual world.

virtual   Refers to the essence or effect of something, not the fact. IBM started using the word in the late 1960s to refer to any nonphysical link between processes or machines, such as virtual memory (random-access memory being simulated using disk drives).

virtual reality   At a minimum, it's the use of VR goggles and a computer to create a 3-D artificial world in which the wearer of the goggles has the impression he's in that world. He can look around, move around, and really be in the world.

visualization   Formation of an image that can't be seen. The ability to represent abstract data that would normally appear as text and numbers graphically on a computer.

wired glove   *See* DataGlove.

workstation   Traditionally, this has referred to a specialized stand-alone computer with enough computational and graphical human-interface power to serve design engineers. With the increased power of personal computers, this distinction has now become very fuzzy.

References

Carroll, Lewis, 1865. *Through the Looking-glass*. New York, NY: Exeter Books.

Gibson, William. 1984. *Neuromancer*. New York, NY: ACE Books.

Electronic Frontier Interview with Barlow and Kapor. 1991. *Mondo 2000.*

Bricklin, William, 1991. Definitions. *Virtual Reality Report*. September, 1991. Westport, CT: Meckler Corp.

Ellis, S.R. 1991. Nature and Origins of Virtual Environments: A Bibliographical Essay. *Computer Systems in Engineering*. Great Britain: Pergamon Press.

Ellis, S.R. (editor) 1991. *Pictorial communication in virtual and real environments*. NY: Taylor & Francis.

Ellis, Stephen R. 1990. Pictorial Communication: Pictures and the Synthetic Universe. *Leonardo*. Great Britain: Pergamon Press. 81-86.

Kay, Alan. 1990. User Interface: A Personal View. *The Art of Human-Computer Interface Design*. Cupertino, CA: Apple Computer. Menlo Park, CA: Addison-Wesley Publishing Co.

Laurel, Brenda (editor). 1990. *The Art of Human-Computer Interface Design*. Cupertino, CA: Apple Computer. Menlo Park: Addison-Wesley Publishing Co.

McLuhan, Marshall. *Quentin Fiore*. 1967. *The Medium Is the Massage*. Bantam Books.

Ofeisch, Gabriel. 1991. *Virtual Reality Report*. Westport, CT: Meckler.

Rheingold, Howard. 1991. *Virtual Reality*. New York, NY: Summit Books.

Walker, John. 1988. *Through the Looking Glass: Beyond "User Interface"* Autodesk whitepaper.

Cook, David A. 1981. *A History Of Narrative Film*. New York, NY: W.W. Norton.

Griffith, Linda A. 1969. *When the Movies Were Young*. New York, NY: Dover Books.

Laurel, Brenda. 1991.*Computers as Theater*. Menlo Park, CA: Addison-Wesley Publishing Co.

Rheingold, Howard. 1991.*Virtual Reality*. New York, NY: Summit Books

Shlain, Leonard. 1991.*Art & Physics: Parallel Visions in Space, Time & Light*. NY: Morrow Williams and Co.

Brooks, Frederick P., Jr., Ming Ouh-Young, Michael Pique, John Hughes, Neela Srinivasan. 1988. Using a Manipulator for Force Display in Molecular Docking. *IEEE pub*, CH2555-1. 1824-1829.

Epigraph

Introduction

Chapter 1

Chapter 2

Chapter 3

Brooks, Frederick P. 1986. Walkthrough—A Dynamic Graphics System for Simulating Virtual Buildings. *ACM Workshop on Interactive 3D Graphics*. Chapel Hill, NC. Oct. 23-24.

Fisher, Scott S. 1991. Virtual Interface Environments. *The Art of Human-Computer Interface Design*. Menlo Park, CA: Addison-Wesley Publishing Co. 423-438.

Fisher, Scott S. Michael McGreevy, James Humphries, Warren Robinett. 1986. Virtual Environment Display System. *ACM Workshop on Interactive 3D Graphics*. Chapel Hill, NC. Oct. 23-24.

Foley, James D. 1987. Interfaces for Advanced Computing. *Scientific American*. October, Vol. 257(4). 126-135.

Krueger, Myron W. 1991. VIDEOPLACE and the Interface of the Future. *The Art of Human-Computer Interface Design*, ed. Brenda Laurel. Menlo Park, CA: Addison-Wesley Publishing Co. 417-422.

Palfreman, Jon, Doron Swade. 1991. *The Dream Machine: Exploring the Computer Age*. London, UK: BBC Books. 99.

Schmandt, Christover. 1982. Interactive three-dimensional computer space. Processing and Display of Three-Dimensional Data. SPIE Vol. 367. 155-159.

Sutherland, Ivan E. 1965. *The Ultimate Display.Proceedings of the IFIP Congress*. 506-508.

Sutherland, Ivan E. 1968. Head-Mounted Three-Dimensional Display. *Proceedings of the Fall Joint Computer Conference*. Vol. 33. 757-64.

Thompson, Steven L. 1987. The Big Picture. *Air & Space*. April/May. 75-83.

Chapter 4 Barlow, John P. 1990. Being in Nothingness. *Mondo 2000*. Summer. 44-51.

Brand, Stewart. 1988.*The Media Lab*. New York NY: Penguin Books.

Rheingold, Howard. 1991.*Virtual Reality*. New York, NY: Summit Books

Walker, John. 1988. *Through the Looking Glass*. Internal Autodesk memo. Sausalito, CA: Autodesk.

Chapter 5 Huxley, Aldous. 1931. *Music at Night*. 17.

Chapter 7 Luther, A. 1989. *Digital Video in the PC Environment*. NY: McGraw Hill.

Chapter 8 Begault, D.R. 1987. *Control of Auditory Distance*. Dissertation, University of California, San Diego, CA.

Gyration. 1992. *Gyration Overview*. Company handout.

Howlett, Eric. 1991. *Product Information - Doc #11540*. LEEP Systems/Pop-Optix Labs.

Foster, S.H., Wenzel, E.M., Taylor, R.M. 1991.*Real Time Synthesis of Complex Acoustic Environments*. Crystal River Engineering literature.

Friedhoff, R. M. 1989.*The second computer revolution Visualization*. NY: W.T. Freeman and Co.

Greuel, Christian. 1991.*Simulation of Three-Dimensional Audio.* Internal document. May.

Rebo, Robert K., Phil Amburn. 1989. A Helmet-Mounted Virtual Environment Display System. *SPIE.* Vol. 1116. 80-83

Stone, Robert. 1992. *Virtual Reality: A Tool for Telepresence & Human Factors Research.* UK Advanced Robotics Research Center.

Wenzel, E. M., Wightman, F.L., Foster, S.H. 1988. A virtual display system for conveying three-dimensional acoustic information.*Proc. Human Factors Society.* Vol. 32. 86-90.

Birren, F. 1950.*Color Psychology and Color Therapy.* NY: McGraw-Hill.

Bryson, Steve. Creon Levit. 1992. *The Virtual Windtunnel: An environment for the Exploration of Three-Dimensional Unsteady Flows.* NASA Ames Research Center, Mountain View, CA: CA Applied Research Office, Numerical Aerodynamics Simulation Division.

Gordon, David. 1978. *Therapeutic Metaphors.* Cupertino, CA: META Publications.

Grinder, John. Robert Dilts, Richard Bandler, Leslie C. Bandler, Judith DeLozier. 1980. *Neuro-Linguistic Programming: The Study of the Structure of Subjective Experience.* Cupertino CA: Meta Publications.

Laurel, Brenda (editor). 1990.*The Art of Human-Computer Interface Design.* Cupertino, CA: Apple Computer. Menlo Park, CA: Addison-Wesley Publishing Co.

Laurel, Brenda. 1991. *Computers as Theater.* Menlo Park: Addison-Wesley Publishing Co.

London, I.D. 1954. *Research on sensory interaction in the Soviet Union.* Psychological bulletin. 531-568.

McLuhan, Marshall and Quentin Fiore. 1967. *The Medium is the Massage.* Bantam Books.

McLuhan, Marshall. *Understanding Media. The Extensions of Man.* NY: McGraw-Hill. 1967-70.

Payne, M. 1958. Apparent weight as a function of color. *American Journal of Psychology.* Vol. 74. 724-730.

Payne, M. 1961. Apparent weight as a function of hue. *American Journal of Psychology.* Vol. 74. 104-105.

Ryan, T.A. 1940. *Interrelations of sensory systems in perception.* Psychological Bulletin. 659-698.

Wallis, W.A. 1935. The influence of color on apparent size. *Journal of General Psychology.* Vol. 13. 193-199.

Esposito, Chris. Meredith Bricken, Keith Butler. 1991. *Building the VSX Demonstration: Operations with Virtual Aircraft in Virtual Space.* Whitepaper. Seattle WA: Boeing.

Chapter 9

Chapter 10

Nomura, Junji. Hikaru Ohata, Kayo Imamura, Robert J. Schultz. 1992. *Virtual Space Decision Support System and Its Application to Consumer Showrooms*. Matsushita whitepaper.

Smith, Bradford. 1992. *The Flowsheet: Animation Used to Analyze and Present Information About Complex Systems*. Presentation at EFDPMA Virtual Reality Conference. Arlington, VA.

Stix, Gary. 1992. Desktop Artisans. *Scientific American*. April 1992. 141-142.

Tuori, Martin. 1991. *Immersive Simulation-Applications in Design*. Presentation to The International Virtual Reality Symposium, Nagoya, Japan. November 1991.

Wright, R. 1991. Computer Graphics as Allegorical Knowledge: Electronic Imagery in the Sciences," *Leonardo*, supplemental issue. Pergamon Press. 65-67.

Chapter 11 Altman, Lawrence K., M.D. 1992. When Patient's Life Is Price of Learning New Kind of Surgery. Medical Science, *The New York Times*. June 23, 1992.

Brooks, Frederick P. James Batter, P. Jerome Kilpatrick, Ming Ouh-Young. 1990. *Project GROPE—Haptic Displays for Scientific Visualization*. Dept. of Computer Science, University of North Carolina at Chapel Hill.

Charles, Steve and Roy Williams. *Dexterity Enhancement in Microsurgery Using Telemicrorobotics*. Presentation at Medicine Meets Virtual Reality Conference. June 1992. San Diego, CA.

Chung, James. Bradley A. Crittenden, Suresh Balu, Terry Yoo. 1991. *Radiation Therapy Treatment Planning*. Siggraph handout. August 1991. Dept. of Computer Science, University of North Carolina at Chapel Hill.

Holloway, Richard and Warren Robinett. 1991. *Molecule Museum*. Siggraph handout. August 1991. Dept. of Computer Science, University of North Carolina at Chapel Hill.

Holloway, Richard. Warren Robinett. 1991. *Flying Through Molecules*. Siggraph handout. August 1991. Dept. of Computer Science, University of North Carolina at Chapel Hill.

Mercurio, Philip J., Philip S. Cohen, Mark H. Ellisman, T. Todd Elvins, Kevin R. Fall, Stephen J. Young. 1992. The Distributed Laboratory. *Communications of the ACM*. June 1992. Volume 35, Number 6. 54-63

Rosen, Joseph. David Chen, David Zeltzer. 1992. *Surgical Simulation Models: From Body Parts to Artificial Person*. Presentation at the Medicine Meets Virtual Reality Conference. San Diego, CA.

Shtern, Faina. *Imaging-guided Stereostactic Tumor Diagnosis and Treatment*. June, 1992. Presentation at the Medicine Meets Virtual Reality Conference. San Diego, CA.

Stewart, Doug. 1991. Through the looking glass into an artificial world—via computer. *Smithsonian*. January 1991. 36-45.

Todd, Daniel. 1992. ADAM Makes Anatomy Come Alive. *New Media*. July 1992 20-21.

Bricken, Meredith. 1991. *Virtual Reality Learning Environments: Potentials and Challenges*. Seattle, WA: Human Interface Technology Laboratory.

Carrie, Heeter. 1992. BattleTech demographics. *IEEE Computer Graphics and Applications*. March 1992. 4-7.

Grimes, Jack. 1992. Virtual reality goes commercial with a blast. *IEEE Computer Graphics and Applications*. March 1992. 4-7.

Helsel, Sandra. 1991. *BattleTech Center*. Virtual Reality Report. Westport, CT: Meckler.

Ohbuchi, Ryutarou. Erik Erikson, Andrei State, Russell Taylor. 1991. Mountain Bike. Siggraph handout. August 1991. Dept. of Computer Science, University of North Carolina at Chapel Hill.

Smith, Dawn. December 1990. The Practical Side of Virtual Reality. *Marketing Communications*. December 1991.

Langberg, Mike. 1992. The Multimedia Game Plan. *Mercury News*, May 25, 1992.

Chapter 12

Arguelles, Jose. *The Transformative Process*. 1975. Berkeley, CA: Shambala.

Haggerty, Michael. 1992. Serious Lunacy: Art in Virtual Worlds. *IEEE Computer Graphics and Applications*. March 1992. 4-7.

McLuhan, Marshall. 1967-70. *Understanding Media: The Extensions of Man*. NY: McGraw-Hill

Shlain, Leonard. 1991. *Art & Physics: Parallel Visions in Space, Time & Light*. NY: Morrow Williams and Co.

Chapter 13

Benedikt, Michael. *1992. Cyberspace: First Steps*. Cambridge, MA: The MIT Press.

Bricken, Meredith. 1991. *Virtual Reality Learning Environments: Potentials and Challenges*. 1991. Siggraph presentation at the Human Interface Technology Laboratory. Seattle, WA.

Crua-Neira, Carolina. Thomas A. Defanti, Robert W. Kenyan, John Hurt, Daniel J. Sandin. 1992. The CAVE: Audio Visual Experience Automatic Virtual Environment. *Communications of the ACM*, June 1992. Volume 35, Number 6. 64-72.

Kay, Alan. 1990. *User Interface: A Personal View. The Art of Human-Computer Interface Design*. Cupertino, CA: Apple Computer. Menlo Park, CA: Addison-Wesley Publishing Co.

Papert, S. 1980. *Mindstorms*. New York: Basic Books.

Smarr, Larry. Charles E. Catiett. 1992. Metacomputing. *Communications of the ACM*, June 1992. Volume 35, Number 6. 44-52.

Chapter 14

M. Bricken. 1991. *Cyberspace: First Steps*. Cambridge, MA: The MIT Press.

Glossary

Photo & illustration credits

12-3 Vincent John Vincent, The Vivid Group

12-4 W Industries Ltd. UK, 1992

12-5 W Industries Ltd. UK, 1992

12-6 W Industries Ltd. UK, 1992

12-7 Mattel, Inc., 1989, used with permission

13-1 Fake Space Labs

13-2 Dia Art Foundation New York, NY, Barbara Gladstone

14-2 Intel Corp.

14-3 W Industries Ltd. UK, 1992

A-1 Advanced Technology Systems, Inc.

A-2 CAE Electronics

A-3 Kaiser Electronics

A-4 Virtual Research

A-6 VPL Research Inc., 1991, photo by Sydney Stein

A-7 W Industries Ltd. UK, 1992

A-8 Reflection Technology

A-10 StereoGraphics Corp.

A-11 The Computer Museum

A-12 Mark Burgin, ARRL

A-13 Mark Burgin, ARRL

A-15 Virtual Technologies, photo by Mitch Heynick

A-16 VPL Research Inc., 1991, photo by Sydney Stein

A-17 Polhemus Inc.

A-18 CIS Graphics, Salem NH

A-19 Gyration

A-20 SimGraphics

A-21 Ascension Technology Corp.

A-22 Polhemus Inc.

A-23 Gyration

A-24 Spatial Positioning Systems, Inc.

Color

C-1 Silicon Graphics, Inc.

C-3 CAE Electronics

C-4 VPL Research Inc., 1991 photo by Sydney Stein

C-5 Sarcos Research Corp.

C-6 George Coates Performance Works, *Invisible Site*, 1991, photo by Jennifer Sauer

C-7 Dia Art Foundation, NewYork, NY, Barbara Gladstone

C-8 Nicole Stenger

C-9 Sense8 Corp., 1992

C-10 Sense8 Corp., 1992

C-11 Software Systems

C-12 Sense8 Corp., 1992

C-13 Sense8 Corp.,1992

C-14 NASA Ames Research Center

C-15 Evans and Sutherland, Inc.

C-16 GE Aerospace

C-17 HIT Lab, 1991; World-Builder: Meredith Bricken

Index

*****Boldface** page numbers refer to art

*Boldface** page numbers refer to art

*****Boldface** page numbers refer to art

Virtual reality videotape ($35)

A compendium presenting an overview of the exciting field of VR. This tape features demonstrations from the pioneering researchers and research laboratories at the forefront of this exciting new technology. Experience what's being created, see how it's done, and learn all the different ways it's being used. Included is work from NASA Ames, University of North Carolina, Sense8, VPL Research, and several others, 60+ minutes.

3-D sound compact disk ($15)

A sampler of three-dimensional recordings, captured with the latest binaural recording equipment and digitally recorded. When listening to it with a set of quality headphones, you might be startled by the vividness of the audio imagery. Separating real sounds from virtual ones suddenly becomes a challenge. Closing your eyes, you'll find yourself in the middle of a thunderstorm or seated at a table in front of an orchestra. Includes selections like Thunderstorm, Percussion, San Francisco Tour, Connie Champagne Orchestra (I Want You), Hesla Robinson Big Band (If I Had a Million Dollars), and many more. Over 30 different samples.

Instructions

1. Make a photocopy of this page.
2. Fill in your name and shipping address.
3. Select the quantity and total the cost.
4. Determine the shipping charges using the simple guidelines below.
5. Mail the form and a check or money order to the address listed below.
6. Allow 4–6 weeks for delivery.

Ordered by:	Ship to (if different):
NAME ————————	NAME ————————
COMPANY ————————	COMPANY ————————
STREET ADR. ————————	STREET ADR. ————————
CITY ————————	CITY ————————
STATE, ZIP————————	STATE, ZIP————————
PHONE (____) ————————	PHONE (____) ————————

Item	Quantity	Item Price	Total Price
Virtual reality video tape (VHS format)		$35	
3D Sound demonstration CD		$15	
Shipping		Subtotal	
PLEASE ALLOW 4-6 WEEKS FOR DELIVERY		Sales Tax 7% (CA Residents Only)	
Continental USA - UPS: $4.00 first item, $1.50 each add'l item		Shipping	
Alaska/Hawaii - US Post: $4.50 first item, $2.50 each add'l item		TOTAL	
International - $15 first item, $5.00 each additional item			

Please make checks or money orders payable to:

Fresh Concepts
PO Box 2517
Sausalito, CA, 94965

This offer is good until 12/94. After this time, please write us about our latest video and audio offerings.

HIGH-PERFORMANCE C GRAPHICS PROGRAMMING FOR WINDOWS®
—Lee Adams

Take advantage of the explosive popularity of Windows with the help of computer graphics ace Lee Adams. He offers you an introduction to a wide range of C graphics programming topics that have interactive and commercial applications. From software prototypes to finished applications, this toolkit not only explores graphics programming, but also gives you many examples of working source code.

■ 528 pages ■ 224 illustrations ■ Includes coupon for supplementary C graphics for Windows programming disk.

Book No. 4103 $24.95 paperback
$34.95 hardcover

SUPERCHARGED BITMAPPED GRAPHICS—Steve Rimmer

Create bitmapped graphics using the latest graphics file formats, display drivers, and printers with this guide. It includes tight, comprehensible C code that lets you read, write, display, print, and manipulate bitmapped image files. Plus, it demonstrates how to work in such popular formats as Windows 3 BMP, Targa, Pictor PIC, IFF/LBM, and CompuServe's revised GIF standard.

■ 664 pages ■ 113 illustrations ■ Includes 5.25" disk.

Book No. 4102 $34.95 paperback only

BUILD YOUR OWN 386/386SX COMPATIBLE AND SAVE A BUNDLE—
2nd Edition—Aubrey Pilgrim

Assemble an 80386 microcomputer at home using mail-order parts that cost a lot less today than they did several years ago. Absolutely no special technical know-how is required—only a pair of pliers, a couple of screwdrivers, and this detailed, easy-to-follow guide.

■ 248 pages ■ 79 illustrations.

Book No. 4089 $18.95 paperback
$29.95 hardcover

GRAPHICS FILE FORMATS—
David C. Kay and John R. Levine

This book offers for the first time, detailed specifications and descriptions of all major available graphics file formats in a single source. You'll find practical information on WMF (Windows), PICT (Macintosh), DXF(AutoCAD), PIC (Lotus), TIFF (Tag Image File Format), GEM (GEM Draw and Graph), and many other IBM PC, Macintosh and workstation formats, focusing on uses, versions, system requirements, and applications for each format.

■ 296 pages ■ 105 illustrations.

Book No. 3969 $24.95 paperback
$36.95 hardcover

WRITING AND MARKETING SHAREWARE: Revised and Expanded—
2nd Edition—Steve Hudgik

Profit from the lucrative shareware market with the tips and techniques found in this guide. If you have new software ideas, but are not sure they'll be competitive in today's dynamic PC market, this reference will show you how to evaluate and sell them through shareware distribution. Plus, you get a 5.25" disk—featuring a shareware mailing list management program and a database with over 200 shareware distributors—through a special coupon offer.

■ 336 pages ■ 41 illustrations.

Book No. 3961 $18.95 paperback only

ONLINE INFORMATION HUNTING—
Nahum Goldmann

Cut down dramatically on your time and money spent online, and increase your online productivity with this helpful book. It will give you systematic instruction on developing cost-effective research techniques for large-scale information networks. You'll also get detailed coverage of the latest online services, new hardware and software, and recent advances that have affected online research.

■ 256 pages ■ 125 illustrations.

Book No. 3943 $19.95 paperback
$29.95 hardcover

ORACLE® SQL DEVELOPER'S GUIDE—
Carolyn J. Hursch and Jack L. Hursch

Whether you work in DOS, VAX, mainframe VMS, or any other Oracle operating environment, you'll find tips and techniques in this guide that will streamline your Oracle tasks—through version 6.0. You'll learn how to take advantage of the special program features such as the report writer, forms package, and Oracle SQL server when designing and implementing your databases. Plus, several example programs show you how to embed SQL statements directly into Oracle programs.

■ 256 pages ■ illustrated.

Book No. 3942 $21.95 paperback
$32.95 hardcover

Look for These and Other TAB Books at Your Local Bookstore

To Order Call Toll Free 1-800-822-8158
(24-hour telephone service available.)

or write to TAB Books, Blue Ridge Summit, PA 17294-0840.

Title	Product No.	Quantity	Price

☐ Check or money order made payable to TAB Books

Charge my ☐ VISA ☐ MasterCard ☐ American Express

Acct. No. _____ Exp. _____

Signature: _____

Name: _____

Address: _____

City: _____

State: _____   Zip: _____

Subtotal	$ _____
Postage and Handling ($3.00 in U.S., $5.00 outside U.S.)	$ _____
Add applicable state and local sales tax	$ _____
TOTAL	$ _____

TAB Books catalog free with purchase; otherwise send $1.00 in check or money order and receive $1.00 credit on your next purchase.

Orders outside U.S. must pay with international money in U.S. dollars drawn on a U.S. bank.

TAB Guarantee: If for any reason you are not satisfied with the book(s) you order, simply return it (them) within 15 days and receive a full refund.

BC